Praise for *Fostering Nurse-Led Care*

"The Institute of Medicine's landmark report The Future of Nursing: Leading Change, Advancing Health calls for nurses to be full partners in redesigning health care. Jeanette Ives Erickson and her colleagues offer us a path to this future. They set out a vision for professional nursing practice in an era of change and reform. The text moves easily from philosophy and theory to practical strategies for nursing leaders. Insightful and helpful!"

–Karen Haller, PhD, RN
Vice President for Nursing and Patient Care Services
The Johns Hopkins Hospital

"Nurses, whether at the bedside or in the executive suite, will want to keep handy *Fostering Nurse-Led Care: Professional Practice for the Bedside Leader From Massachusetts General Hospital* as they develop and advance the professional practice environment at their organizations. Ives Erickson, Jones, and Ditomassi have generously shared the MGH experience, including rich examples of how they translated theory into successful practice models and how they continue to evolve their professional practice environment. Their work exemplifies evidence-based leadership at its best."

–Brenda Nevidjon, MSN, RN, FAAN
Professor, Nursing & Healthcare Leadership
President-elect, International Society of Nurses in Cancer Care

"This timely book on the 16-year history of implementing a professional practice model at Massachusetts General Hospital (MGH), one of the premier hospitals in the world, provides ample evidence that the role of the CNO and leadership is to create and sustain a PPM. I can unequivocally say that the leadership and staff at MGH, as collaborators in the creation of dedicated education units and the Clinical Leadership Collaborative for Diversity in Nursing, not only talk the talk, but walk the walk. All of us, whether in academics or practice, can learn from their transformational leadership."

–Greer Glazer, PhD, RN, CNP, FAAN
Dean, University of Cincinnati College of Nursing
Schmidlapp Professor of Nursing

"Professional practice models reflect the philosophical belief systems and support of leadership in organizations. *Fostering Nurse-Led Care: Professional Practice for the Bedside Leader From Massachusetts General Hospital* reflects not only support, but the highest level of expectation for excellence for practice model implementation and institution-wide embeddedness. The book is cogent, influential, and inspiring. This text brings to mind iconic names such as Clifford, McClure, and Jacox—Ives Erickson and her MGH leadership team are visionaries for a new generation of nurses at the cutting edge of what the practice model can and should be. Changes taking place in the national health care arena mandate strong patient- and family-centered practice models that provide continuity and accountability. The centrality and authority of the nursing role are once again brought to the forefront in this important text, which gives us not only examples but mandates for how we must better understand and explicate our work, our environment, and lessons of contemporary professional practice. Reading this text, I felt the elation that comes with confidence that the future is full of promise."

–Terry Fulmer, PhD, RN, FAAN
Dean, Bouvé College of Health Sciences
Northeastern University

"This 'must-read' book tells a compelling story of how nurse leaders drive a vision for the future health care delivery system. The authors address the importance of the professional practice environment as the foundation of care delivery, creating a structure to foster interprofessional clinical practice and developing knowledge through innovation and leadership. Ives Erickson, Jones, and Ditomassi offer a blueprint for how we advance the professional practice of nursing to deliver superior outcomes for patients."

–Kimberly S. Glassman, PhD, RN, NEA-BC
Senior Vice President, Patient Care Services and Chief Nursing Officer
NYU Langone Medical Center

"MGH nursing leaders have a remarkable track record of contributions to the profession. This book is another one. The reflections on building a nurse-led professional practice environment, the innovation, and the subsequent measurement of the outcomes are breathtaking. This is inspirational work."

–Eileen M Sporing, MSN, RN, FAAN
Sr. Vice President, Patient Care Services
Chief of Nursing
Boston Children's Hospital

"This comprehensive and detailed work provides in-depth insights into the importance of professional nursing practice to beneficial outcomes for patients. It provides clear examples of how nurses and patients can be empowered 'dynamic duos,' so that care is the best it can be. The meaningful examples provide tools that all professional nurses can use. Innovation and nursing leadership are key factors that make the difference. A truly inspiring model from MGH nursing leaders."

–Sharon Gale, MSN, RN
Chief Executive Officer
Organization of Nurse Leaders, MA-RI

"What shines through in *Fostering Nurse-Led Care: Professional Practice for the Bedside Leader From Massachusetts General Hospital* is the depth of experience and wisdom of its authors. It is tempting when health care changes are coming fast and furious to look for easy answers. These authors convincingly reveal what it really takes to create and sustain a patient-centered, evidence-based professional practice environment. If nurses are to lead health care reform, here is the guide that shows the way."

–Mary J. Connaughton, MS, RN
Principal/Owner, Connaughton Consulting

"Ives Erickson, Ditomassi, and Jones deeply understand that the foundation of practice and change is the practice environment and how nurses and leaders work together to create an environment where practice flourishes. *Fostering Nurse-Led Care: Professional Practice for the Bedside Leader From Massachusetts General Hospital* provides a comprehensive view of nursing practice spanning the profession's historical roots through today's practice innovations, leading us to a place of remarkable opportunities for the future. This book is a 'must-read' for our profession."

–Margaret M. Calarco, PhD, RN
Senior Associate Director for Patient Care Services & Chief of Nursing Services
University of Michigan Health System

Fostering
Nurse-Led Care

Professional Practice for the Bedside Leader From Massachusetts General Hospital

Jeanette Ives Erickson, DNP, RN, FAAN
Dorothy A. Jones, EdD, RNC, FAAN
Marianne Ditomassi, DNP, RN, MBA

Sigma Theta Tau International
Honor Society of Nursing®

The Honor Society of Nursing, Sigma Theta Tau International (STTI), is a nonprofit organization whose mission is to support the learning, knowledge, and professional development of nurses committed to making a difference in health worldwide. Founded in 1922, STTI has 130,000 members in 90 countries. Members include practicing nurses, instructors, researchers, policymakers, entrepreneurs, and others. STTI's 485 chapters are located throughout Australia, Botswana, Brazil, Canada, Colombia, England, Ghana, Hong Kong, Japan, Kenya, Malawi, Mexico, the Netherlands, Pakistan, Singapore, South Africa, South Korea, Swaziland, Sweden, Taiwan, Tanzania, the United States, and Wales. More information about STTI can be found online at www.nursingsociety.org.

Sigma Theta Tau International
550 West North Street
Indianapolis, IN, USA 46202

To order additional books, buy in bulk, or order for corporate use, contact Nursing Knowledge International at 888.NKI.4YOU (888.654.4968/US and Canada) or +1.317.634.8171 (outside US and Canada).

To request a review copy for course adoption, e-mail solutions@nursingknowledge.org or call 888.NKI.4YOU (888.654.4968/US and Canada) or +1.317.634.8171 (outside US and Canada).

To request author information, or for speaker or other media requests, contact Rachael McLaughlin of the Honor Society of Nursing, Sigma Theta Tau International at 888.634.7575 (US and Canada) or +1.317.634.8171 (outside US and Canada).

ISBN: 9781935476306
EPUB ISBN: 9781935476313
PDF ISBN: 9781935476726
MOBI ISBN: 9781937554187

Library of Congress Cataloging-in-Publication Data
Fostering nurse-led care : professional practice for the bedside leader from Massachusetts General Hospital / [edited by] Jeanette Ives Erickson, Dorothy A. Jones, Marianne Ditomassi.
    p. ; cm.
  Includes bibliographical references and index.
  ISBN 978-1-935476-30-6 (alk. paper) -- ISBN 978-1-935476-31-3 (e-pub) -- ISBN 978-1-935476-72-6 (PDF) -- ISBN 978-1-937554-18-7 (MOBI)
  I. Ives Erickson, Jeanette. II. Jones, Dorothy A. III. Ditomassi, Marianne. IV. Massachusetts General Hospital. V. Sigma Theta Tau International.
  [DNLM: 1. Nursing, Supervisory. 2. Leadership. 3. Nurse Administrators. 4. Nurse's Role. 5. Nursing--organization & administration. WY 105]

  610.73--dc23
                    2012033330

First Printing, 2012

Publisher: Renee Wilmeth   Principal Book Editor: Carla Hall
Acquisitions Editor: Emily Hatch   Development & Project Editor: Jennifer Lynn
Editorial Coordinator: Paula Jeffers   Copy Editor: Kevin Kent
Cover Designer: Michael Tanamachi   Proofreader: Clifford Shubs
Interior Design/Page Layout: Kim Scott   Indexer: Johnna VanHoose Dinse

Dedication

This book is dedicated to our parents, who provided us with the values that guided us to the profession of nursing. These values and this passion for nursing have led to our shared commitment to creating an environment of care that supports the integrity of the nurse-patient relationship.

Acknowledgements

Nursing leaders believe in the profession, keep their focus on the patient, understand the role of caring in the context of a variety of human emotions... and persevere.

(Fulmer, 2007, p. 161)

Preparing this book has required the support of many people. The editors are extremely grateful to nurses from around the world who partner with patients and families to deliver high-quality care in the many settings where nursing care is delivered. Thank you for your dedication and inspiration, which reminds us all why we chose to become professional nurses.

To the many leaders who have inspired each of us to do our best: Your generosity of spirit, knowledge, and time guides us to continuously advance our practice and our careers, dedicating ourselves to the growth of the discipline and the ultimate good of patient care.

Jeanette Ives Erickson is especially thankful to her family, who has always guided and supported her. To Sr. Consuela White, Eloise Paulin, Barbara Sheehan, Muriel Poulin, and Yvonne Munn, I will be forever in your debt, as you shared your love of nursing and were always there when I needed you. The influence of the incredible nurses, health professionals, and support staff that I have had the pleasure of working with will always be a part of who I am. You give me great joy and make me proud to be your colleague. Being a leader at Massachusetts General Hospital, guided by 200 years of history, has provided me a strong foundation for future innovations that will benefit those we serve.

Dorothy A. Jones is forever grateful for her family, who gives her the freedom "to be." In addition, I am thankful for the presence of Margaret Newman, Dorothy DeMaio, Catherine Murphy, Marjory Gordon—the leaders advancing the use of standardized language worldwide; the inspirational nurses who have led the development of nursing knowledge and health as expanding consciousness; and the current and past colleagues and students at Boston

University and Boston College, William F. Connell School of Nursing. You have transformed my life.

Marianne Ditomassi is appreciative for the support and mentorship she has received from her family, from teachers, and from nursing colleagues throughout her career, including Jeanette Ives Erickson, Dorothy Jones, Ann Minnick, and Marilyn Neuman. Your belief and trust in me have enabled me to have a nursing career and life full of creativity, influence, and learning.

We also acknowledge Massachusetts General Hospital and its leadership, past and present, including MGH presidents Dr. Samuel Thier, Dr. James Mongan, Dr. Peter Slavin, and Dr. David Torchiana, who have helped design a distinguished work environment, recognized worldwide for excellence—the embodiment of a professional practice environment—allowing all disciplines to excel. It is within this environment that all nurses, especially those influencing care at the bedside, set the direction and lead initiatives advancing the delivery of care that supports the integrity of the nurse-patient relationship.

Reference

Fulmer, T. (2007). Three principles of leadership: Willingness to communicate, negotiate, and compromise. In T. Hansen-Turton, S. Sherman, & V. Ferguson (Eds.), *Conversations with leaders* (p. 161). Indianapolis, IN: Sigma Theta Tau International.

About the Authors

Jeanette Ives Erickson, DNP, RN, FAAN

Jeanette Ives Erickson is chief nurse and senior vice president for patient care services at Massachusetts General Hospital, instructor at Harvard Medical School, assistant professor at Massachusetts General Hospital Institute of Health Professions, and chairperson of the Board of the Lunder-Dineen Health Education Alliance of Maine. As chief nurse and senior VP, she is responsible for clinical practice, research, education, and community service, serving 4,800 nurses, health professionals, and support staff.

While fostering nursing research within an interdisciplinary, professional practice model, Ives Erickson has developed new measures to evaluate innovations that influence professional nursing practice. Her tool, the Staff Perceptions of the Professional Practice Environment Survey, is used to evaluate nurses' and other clinicians' perceptions of, and overall satisfaction with, the professional practice environment. Currently, this instrument has been requested by 96 individuals or organizations in 15 countries and has been translated into Spanish and Chinese. She has presented globally and consults on multiple issues affecting nurse autonomy, leadership development, collaborative decision-making, and Magnet hospital designation.

Dorothy A. Jones, EdD, RNC, FAAN

Dorothy A. Jones is director of the Yvonne L. Munn Center for Nursing Research at Massachusetts General Hospital (MGH) and a professor of nursing in the Boston College William F. Connell School of Nursing. As director of the Munn Center, she has the opportunity to promote a research agenda across the MGH community and create opportunities for nurse researchers to advance their own programs of research. Between these two roles, Jones has developed several areas of teaching excellence and research concentration, including nursing theory development and evaluation; language development and classification; instrument development and testing; workforce evaluation and intervention research, especially around coaching; and recovery at home after surgery. Jones earned her

BSN from the Brooklyn Hospital School of Nursing and Long Island University, her MSN from Indiana University, and her doctorate from Boston University. She is a fellow in the American Academy of Nursing and a past president of the Eastern Nursing Research Society and NANDA-International. She has been the recipient of external funding from the National Institute of Nursing Research of the National Institutes of Health, the United States Department of Health and Human Services' Division of Nursing, specialty organizations (e.g., AORN), and foundations. Currently, she is project advisor to the newly funded Connell Nursing Research Scholars program at MGH.

Jones has numerous publications in leading journals, has published or co-authored 12 books, and has received two *American Journal of Nursing* Book of the Year awards. Her books have been translated into many languages, including Spanish, Italian, and Japanese. Jones has presented globally and consults on multiple issues affecting nursing education, clinical practice, and research. She currently holds a position as a visiting professor at the University of Navarra in Pamplona, Spain. Her scholarship continues to support the advancement of nursing knowledge through research and discovery and the growth of professional practice environments to improve care for patients, their families, and communities.

Marianne Ditomassi, DNP, RN, MBA

Marianne Ditomassi is executive director of patient care services operations at Massachusetts General Hospital (MGH), which supports the work of the senior vice president of patient care, and the chief nurse, who oversees the operations of nursing, the therapy departments, and social services. Her key areas of accountability include strategic planning, recruitment and retention initiatives, business planning, fundraising, and communications. In addition, she is the Magnet program director for MGH and successfully coordinated MGH's initial Magnet designation journey in 2003 and subsequent Magnet redesignation in 2008.

Prior to her current roles, Ditomassi served as founding director of the Center for Clinical and Professional Development at Massachusetts General Hospital. Under her leadership in this position, she launched a department that focuses on translating the professional practice model for nursing and other health professions into reality. She is a graduate of Georgetown University and Loyola University in Chicago, Illinois, for her undergraduate and graduate degrees in nursing, respectively, and of University of Illinois for her graduate degree in business. She recently received her doctorate of nursing practice degree in executive practice from the MGH Institute of Health Professions.

Contributing Authors

Jeffrey M. Adams, PhD, RN

Jeffrey M. Adams is a nurse scientist with the Yvonne L. Munn Center for Nursing Research and the Center for Innovation in Care Delivery at Massachusetts General Hospital (MGH). His interests stem from his practice and experience as a researcher and consultant working in health care leadership settings in more than 20 states across the United States. His expertise spans executive health care practice, professional practice environments, and clinical informatics. His two published models—1) the Adams Influence Model (AIM), which defines the factors, attributes, and process of influence, and 2) the Model of the Interrelationship of Leadership, Environments and Outcomes for Nurse Executives (MILE ONE)—synthesize existing literature to provide the structure of emphasis for nursing administration education and care delivery roles that guide his work.

Adams's educational credentials include a BSN from the University of Michigan, an MSN in Administration from the University of Pennsylvania, a PhD from Boston College William F. Connell School of Nursing, and postdoctoral fellowship training at Massachusetts General Hospital's Yvonne L. Munn Center for Nursing Research. He was recently appointed a Connell Research Scholar in the Munn Center.

Gaurdia Banister, PhD, RN

Gaurdia Banister is executive director of the Institute for Patient Care at Massachusetts General Hospital. The institute provides a next-generation infrastructure that is designed to serve as a catalyst for promoting interdisciplinary research, education, and clinical practice. She also serves as co-project director of the Clinical Leadership Collaborative for Diversity in Nursing in partnership with the University of Massachusetts College of Nursing and Health Sciences in Boston. The purpose of this program is to develop diverse nursing leaders to influence health care delivery, policy, and administration. Understanding the importance of academic practice partnerships,

Banister has appointments as a clinical assistant professor at MGH Institute for Health Professions, a visiting scholar at William F. Connell School of Nursing at Boston College, and an adjunct associate professor at the University of Massachusetts Boston, College of Nursing and Health Sciences. She is a former Johnson & Johnson Wharton Nurse Fellow and an alumna of the Robert Wood Johnson Foundation Executive Nurse Fellows Program. In 2008, she was selected as the Fay W. Whitney School of Nursing distinguished alumna at the University of Wyoming, where she received her BSN. In 2009, she was selected as the distinguished alumna at the University of Texas at Austin, where she earned both her master's and doctoral degrees. In 2012, Banister received the American Nurses Association's Mary Eliza Mahoney Award for her outstanding achievements in promoting the integration, retention, and advancement of minorities in nursing.

Lynda Brandt, MS, RN-C

Lynda Brandt is clinical project specialist in the Yvonne L. Munn Center for Nursing Research at Massachusetts General Hospital, where she also serves on the Research and Evidence-Based Practice Committee. Her work is focused on teaching, mentoring, and supporting nurses in evidence-based nursing practice (EBP) as well as advancing EBP among several health professions at MGH. She completed a career in the U.S. Air Force, where her clinical expertise in obstetrics was combined with numerous leadership positions across the care spectrum. Brandt served as faculty at the William F. Connell School of Nursing, Boston College. She received her BSN from Mt. Mercy College in Cedar Rapids, Iowa, and her MS from the University of Colorado Health Sciences Center, Denver, Colorado.

Elizabeth J. Brown, MSN, MBA, RN

Elizabeth J. Brown is director of global programs at Partners HealthCare International within the Partners HealthCare System in Boston. She has been working in international health for almost 15 years, with a strong focus on building collaborations in nursing professional development, quality and patient safety, and interprofessional education. She has presented in numerous international forums on nursing leadership development and quality improvement and has programmatic experience in multiple countries, including China, Ecuador, Germany, Greece, India, Qatar, Thailand, Turkey, United Arab Emirates, and Zimbabwe. She received her MSN from Rush University in Chicago, Illinois; her MBA from the J. L. Kellogg Graduate School of Management at Northwestern University in Evanston, Illinois; and her BSN from Boston College in Massachusetts. Brown completed a postgraduate administrative fellowship at Beth Israel Deaconess Medical Center in Boston, Massachusetts.

Debra Burke, MSN, RN, MBA

Debra Burke is an associate chief nurse at Massachusetts General Hospital in Boston, Massachusetts. She graduated from the Malden Hospital School of Nursing with a diploma in nursing; she received her BSN at Northeastern University and her MSN and MBA from Salem State College in Salem, Massachusetts. Burke has held numerous positions at MGH, beginning as a staff nurse. She then served as a clinical educator and nurse director. An associate chief nurse for 10 years, she oversees a wide variety of clinical areas: women's health, obstetric, pediatric, oncology, mental health, and ambulatory practice areas. As a member of the Nursing Executive Leadership team, she participates in the efficient and effective management of the Department of Nursing and the development of its strategic plan. She also plays a leadership role in the creation of the Primary Care and Inpatient Care Redesign teams.

Linda Burnes Bolton, DrPH, RN, FAAN

Linda Burnes Bolton is vice president for nursing, chief nursing officer, and director of nursing research at Cedars-Sinai Medical Center in Los Angeles, California. Her research, teaching, and clinical expertise include nursing and patient care outcomes, improving organization performance, quality care, and cultural diversity within the health professions. She is co-investigator of the regional Collaborative Alliance for Nursing Outcomes research team. Burnes Bolton is a past president of the American Academy of Nursing and the National Black Nurses Association. She has provided leadership for several state and national programs, including service as chair of the National Advisory Committee for Transforming Care at the Bedside and the Veterans Administration Commission on Nursing, and vice chair of the Robert Wood Johnson Foundation Initiative on the Future of Nursing at the Institute of Medicine. She is a trustee at Case Western Reserve University and serves on several nursing school advisory boards. Burnes Bolton serves on multiple national and international editorial boards. In 2010, she was elected as the Region 9 representative on the AONE board of directors. She was named one of the top 25 women in health care in 2011 by *Modern Healthcare* magazine and woman of the year in 2012 by Women in Health Administration. She was appointed to the Robert Wood Johnson Foundation board of directors in 2012. Burnes Bolton is the recipient of numerous awards for her scholarship, leadership, public policy, advocacy, and community service efforts. She received her BSN from Arizona State University and her MSN, MPH, and doctorate in public health from UCLA.

Mary E. Duffy, PhD, RN, FAAN

Mary E. Duffy, currently a senior nurse scientist in the Yvonne L. Munn Center for Nursing Research at Massachusetts General Hospital and professor emerita in the William F. Connell School of Nursing at Boston College, has worked in nursing practice, nursing education, and nursing research for the past 30 years. In addition to serving as principal investigator and co-investigator on numerous NIH-funded projects, Duffy has published extensively throughout her career. The majority of her publications focus on descriptive and experimental clinical research, instrument development, and psychometric evaluation and on methodological issues in various types of research design.

Theresa Gallivan, MS, RN

Theresa Gallivan is associate chief nurse for medicine, emergency, and heart center nursing at Massachusetts General Hospital (MGH). Her primary areas of focus are patient- and family-focused care; leadership development; continuous improvement and process redesign; and the professional practice environment. She oversees and collaborates with nurse directors and their respective clinical nurse specialists and operations managers spanning 22 clinical settings. When asked about programs or outcomes of which she is most proud, Gallivan speaks to the team of nursing leaders she has formed. Building upon the caliber of candidates the MGH is able to attract, she invests considerable thought, time, and resources to the recruitment, selection, orientation, and ongoing support and development of nursing directors and their associated leadership teams. She is the recipient of numerous Partners in Excellence Awards for individual outcomes as well as for team-led initiatives. In 2006, Gallivan and physician colleague Hasan Bazari, MD, director for the MGH Medical Education Program, were co-awarded the prestigious Nathaniel Bowditch Prize for their leadership of a major interdisciplinary process improvement initiative focused on improved care coordination, improved care quality, and reductions in length of stay. In 2010, the Massachusetts Association of Registered Nurses (MARN) named her the recipient of the 2010 Mary A. Manning Nurse Mentoring Award. Gallivan is known for her authentic leadership and role modeling, and nurses she has mentored have established innovative clinical programs, led national studies, and achieved executive-level nursing administrative positions. In 2010, she was awarded the Champions in Health Care Award by the *Boston Business Journal* for her work in developing future nurse leaders in health care.

Susan Gennaro, DSN, RN, FAAN

Susan Gennaro is dean and professor of the William F. Connell School of Nursing at Boston College. Prior appointments include the Florence and William Downs Professor in Nursing Research at New York University and professor at the University of Pennsylvania, where she was director of the doctoral program and co-director of the Center for Health Disparities. Gennaro also served on the faculties of the University of Alabama at Birmingham and the Medical University of South Carolina. Her research focuses on the improvement of perinatal health and has been conducted in the United States, Malawi, and Uganda. She is currently identifying mechanisms underlying preterm birth in minority women in a study being conducted at Jacobi Medical Center, New York, and in Austin, Texas, funded by the National Institute of Nursing Research. Gennaro's long history of funding from the National Institutes of Health (for more than 20 years) has also focused on improving nursing education through innovative programs to increase the number of nurse scientists from a minority background trained to work with vulnerable populations. As founder of the evidence-based practice program at the Association of Women's Health, Obstetric, and Neonatal Nurses, her goal is to translate research into clinical practice internationally. She currently serves as the leading nurse scientist on the Harvard Catalyst, the clinical and translation science initiative of Harvard Medical School. Gennaro is the editor of Sigma Theta Tau International's *Journal of Nursing Scholarship*. She is a fellow of the American Academy of Nursing, a McClure Scholar at New York University Medical Center, a lecturer at Harvard University's Medical School, and a distinguished alumna at the University of Alabama at Birmingham School of Nursing. She has been recognized for her outstanding contributions to maternal and child health by the Distinguished Service Award of the Association of Women's Health, Obstetric, and Neonatal Nurses.

Pamela J. Grace, PhD, APRN, FAAN

Pamela J. Grace is an associate professor of adult health and ethics at the William F. Connell School of Nursing at Boston College. An experienced nurse who originally trained in the United Kingdom, she completed bachelor's and master's degrees in nursing in the United States and completed a PhD in philosophy with a concentration in medical ethics in 1998. She has been actively involved in teaching nursing, nursing and health care philosophy, ethics, and moral reasoning for the past 15 years and has lectured and published extensively on these and related topics. She is a former medical ethics research fellow at Harvard School of Social Medicine, and she received a Fulbright Scholarship to Denmark in 2003, where she provided lectures on medical ethics and researched obstacles to good practice that exist in differently funded health care systems. She is a co-investigator on an HRSA-funded retention and recruitment grant, The Clinical Ethics Residency for Nurses, spearheaded by Ellen Robinson of Massachusetts General Hospital, and is a nurse scientist in the Munn Center for Nursing Research. Her research interests are in issues of professional responsibility, justice, and the tensions existing for professionals at the intersections of individual and societal good. Most recently she authored a textbook, *Nursing Ethics and Professional Responsibility in Advanced Practice*, which received a 2009 national book award in the category of Health Sciences from the Association of Jesuit Colleges and Alpha Sigma Nu honor society.

Ashley L. Grau, MSc

Ashley L. Grau completed her Bachelor in Psychology from the University of Western Ontario in 2007, followed by her Master in Health and Rehabilitation Sciences with a specialization in measurement and methods in 2009. Since 2009, Grau has worked in the Arthur Labatt Family School of Nursing at the University of Western Ontario, coordinating a program of research committed to understanding and addressing critical issues in health human resources and the recruitment and retention of the nursing workforce.

Heather K. Spence Laschinger, PhD, RN, FAAN, FCAHS

Since 1992, Heather K. Spence Laschinger has been principal investigator of a program of research designed to investigate the impact of nursing work environments on nurses' empowerment for professional practice, their health and well-being, and the role of leadership in creating empowering working conditions. A major focus of her research is examining the link between nursing work environments and nurse and client outcomes. The results of this research have been translated into several policy documents, including the Magnet Hospital Accreditation Program in the United States. Laschinger has received four major awards in recognition of her work since 2003. She is a fellow in the American Academy of Nursing and was elected to the prestigious Canadian Academy of Health Sciences, considered one of the highest honors for individuals in the Canadian health sciences community. In 2007, she was awarded the Distinguished University Professor Award at the University of Western Ontario and, in 2003, was the first Canadian researcher to receive the prestigious Sigma Theta Tau International Elizabeth McWilliams Miller Award for Excellence in Research. Laschinger has served on numerous advisory groups at the provincial and federal levels in relation to healthy workplace issues and is currently a healthy workplace champion for the Ontario Ministry of Health and Long-Term Care (MOHLTC). As principal investigator, her current projects include two Canadian Institutes of Health Research studies—(1) a national study of new graduate nurses' transitions to the workforce and (2) a national study of nurses' career aspirations to management positions across the country—and a

MOHLTC-funded longitudinal study of new graduate nurses' work life, with a focus on predictors and outcomes of new graduates' experiences of bullying in Canadian hospital settings within the first two years of practice. In 2009, she was awarded the Arthur Labatt Family Nursing Research Chair in Health Human Resources Optimization and will lead a five-year program of research focusing on factors influencing new graduate nurses' successful transition to practice and workplace violence.

Susan M. Lee, PhD, RN, NP-C

Susan M. Lee is a nurse scientist in the Yvonne L. Munn Center for Nursing Research, where her work has focused on bringing evidence to the bedside. A nurse for 37 years, Lee had dual practices in critical care as a staff nurse and primary care as a nurse practitioner. She is dedicated to building nursing workforce capacity in geropalliative care as the new standard of care for hospitalized older adults. As program director of the national AgeWISE pilot, currently in 12 U.S. hospitals, Lee has disseminated a six-month nurse residency program to practicing nurses whose formal education did not include the latest knowledge from the newer specialties of geriatrics and palliative care. Her interest in implementation science stems from her desire to teach nurses in ways that will meaningfully influence their practices in patient- and family-centered care. She received her doctorate from the William F. Connell School of Nursing at Boston College. She has recently been appointed a Connell Research Fellow in the Yvonne L. Munn Center for Nursing Research.

Ellen M. Robinson, PhD, RN

Ellen M. Robinson is a nurse ethicist at Massachusetts General Hospital (MGH), Boston, Massachusetts. In her role as nurse ethicist, Robinson provides ethics consultation to clinicians, patients, and families at MGH. She serves as co-chair of the MGH Optimum Care Committee that provides end-of-life consultation to patients, families, and clinicians at times of conflict. In addition, she serves on the MGH Hospital for Children Pediatric Ethics Committee, the Partners HealthCare

Ethics Leadership Group, and the Harvard Ethics Leadership Council. In 2010, Robinson received a three-year Health Resources and Services Administration Bureau of Nursing grant to educate and mentor practicing staff and advanced practice nurses to serve on ethics committees, facilitate ethics discussions, and learn the process of ethics consultation. She is director of the MGH Institute for Patient Care Connell Ethics Fellowship and holds faculty appointments in the MGH Institute of Health Professions Program in Nursing and in the William F. Connell School of Nursing at Boston College.

Kathleen B. Scoble, EdD, RN

Kathleen B. Scoble has more than 3 decades of experience in academic, administrative, and consultancy roles. She is director for the Division of Nursing and associate professor at Elms College, Chicopee, Massachusetts, leading the division's development from a traditional baccalaureate nursing program to include several educational pathways for advancing the education of RNs and a Master's of Science in Nursing. Scoble has previously held faculty appointments at Teachers College, Columbia University, and the University of Massachusetts Boston, and several administrative positions in acute care organizations ranging from unit manager to chief executive nurse. Recognized for her leadership in professional nursing nationally and internationally, she has served as senior associate for the Institute for Nursing Healthcare Leadership (INHL). She is president of the Massachusetts Association of Colleges of Nursing and co-chairs the Massachusetts Institute of Medicine Action Coalition. Consulting internationally for the INHL and Partners HealthCare International (formerly Partners Harvard Medical International) since 1999, Scoble has had programmatic experience in multiple countries, including Colombia, Mexico, India, China, Dubai, and Turkey. She received her nursing diploma from St. Vincent's Hospital, Ohio; BSN from Madonna College in Michigan; master's in both nursing administration and education from Columbia University, Teachers College; and doctorate in education from Columbia University, Teachers College, Department of Nursing Administration and Education.

Thomas Smith, DNP, RN, NEA-BC

Thomas Smith is chief nursing officer and senior vice president at Maimonides Medical Center in Brooklyn, New York. Smith's prior positions include chief nursing officer at Cambridge Health Alliance in Cambridge, Massachusetts, and senior vice president for nursing at The Mount Sinai Hospital in New York City, the first full-service hospital in Manhattan to receive the Magnet award for nursing excellence. He currently serves as senior clinical advisor at the Hartford Institute for Geriatric Nursing at New York University College of Nursing. Smith has served on the board of commissioners of the Commission on Collegiate Nursing Education and is an active member of the American Organization of Nurse Executives. His research interests and publications focus on the nurse-patient relationship, care of the older adult, and organization and improvement of patient care delivery and nursing practice.

Dawn Leslie Tenney, MSN, RN

Dawn Leslie Tenney began her career at Massachusetts General Hospital (MGH) as a surgical technologist in the operating room. She then graduated from Boston State College with her BSN and her master's in nursing administration from the University of Massachusetts Amherst. Tenney continued her nursing career in the operating rooms at MGH and at Queens Medical Center, Honolulu, Hawaii; Franklin Medical Center, Greenfield, Massachusetts; and Yale New Haven Hospital, New Haven, Connecticut. She has spent 90% of her career in a variety of nursing leadership positions, including nursing supervisor, nurse manager medical/surgical, nurse manager of the emergency department, director of nursing services, nursing director of perioperative services, and, currently, associate chief nurse at MGH. Her career has been devoted to identifying talented individuals with leadership potential, developing and coaching them into strong managers and directors, and supporting them as they move forward with outstanding careers. She has spoken locally, nationally, and internationally on various clinical and leadership topics and is involved with a variety of professional nursing organizations.

Deborah Washington, PhD, RN

Deborah Washington is director of diversity for patient care services at Massachusetts General Hospital. A 1993 graduate of Boston College School of Nursing with a master's in adult mental health, she completed her doctorate in 2012 with a research focus on ethnic bias in clinical decision-making. Washington is a 2010 graduate of the Robert Wood Johnson Foundation Executive Nurse Fellows Program, where her project was an exploration of grassroots coalitions as social capital in minority communities. Her present work involves assessing medical errors and their impact on communities of color and the elimination of health disparities through community empowerment. Washington is currently national co-chair of the Future of Nursing Campaign for Action Diversity Steering Committee for the State Action Coalitions and a board member of the American Organization of Nurse Executives Foundation. She serves on the diversity advisory board for five schools of nursing and is a nationally recognized content expert on cultural competence, managing multicultural teams, and effective mentoring of minority nursing students.

Kevin Whitney, MA, RN, NEA-BC

Kevin Whitney is an associate chief nurse at Massachusetts General Hospital (MGH) in Boston, Massachusetts. With more than 25 years of clinical and leadership experience as a paramedic and RN, he is responsible for nursing practice and patient care delivery for the Inpatient Orthopedic, Neurosciences, and Surgical units, which include surgical critical care, burns, transplant, the trauma nurse program, and the IV therapy team. Whitney holds a master's in health care administration from Framingham State University, Framingham, Massachusetts; a BSN from the University of Massachusetts Lowell; and an associate's degree in paramedic technology from Northeastern University. He is a board-certified nurse executive, advanced (NEA-BC) through the American Nurses Credentialing Center, and is a member of Sigma Theta Tau International. Whitney has been an active member of the Organization of Nurse Leaders of Massachusetts and Rhode Island and is serving as the organization's immediate past president. He played a key role as leader of the application process that resulted in Massachusetts's acceptance as a State Action Coalition by the Robert Wood Johnson Foundation and AARP's Future of Nursing Campaign.

Table of Contents

Foreword

by Karen Drenkard, PhD, RN, NEA-BC, FAAN
Executive Director, American Nurses Credentialing Center

Transformational Leadership Informing Care at the Bedside

As the pace of health care delivery increases and health care delivery models and systems continue to make fundamental shifts in structures and processes, strong and effective nursing leadership is paramount. Developing a professional practice model to guide the work of leaders and nursing staff fostering care at the bedside can and should enhance satisfaction for patients, families, and clinicians. Understanding the qualities, traits, behaviors, and characteristics of a good leader can help capture those successful behaviors.

Working within professional practice environments that demand responsive and knowledgeable caregivers requires a learning environment that embraces changing models of care delivery. Having resources available to assist executive leaders, administrators, and staff nurses navigate a significant change is critical to ensuring satisfaction and to creating heath care delivery models that provide strategies to achieve desired outcomes.

Fostering Nurse-Led Care was written to provide nurse leaders and care providers with a resource that describes the development, implementation, and evaluation of a professional practice environment that is responsive to staff, patients, and families. This book offers a detailed accounting of the elements identified by the authors through their work at Massachusetts General Hospital (MGH) as critical to a professional practice and discusses strategies used by executive nurse leaders at MGH to accomplish the desired professional practice environment for delivery of safe, efficient, effective, timely, equitable, and patient- and family-centered care (IOM, 2001).

Leadership as the Cornerstone of Patient Care

This book stresses the importance of leadership as a critical link to excellence. Discussions reflect the literature to support the important role leaders play in health care reform and care redesign. The Great Man theory of leadership used as primary concept guiding all leadership was based on the thought that the masses were led by a superior few leaders (Dowd, 1993). These leaders were thought to shape and lead institutions using their individual personal intelligence, energy, and moral force as the intellectual elite that could lead the masses. Later, trait and behavioral theories began to emerge, followed by theorists analyzing situational and environmental factors in leadership (Chan & Drasgow, 2001; Chemers, 2000).

Other theoretical perspectives have supported the belief that the style of leaders, their perception of themselves as leaders in relation to others, and the environment they develop facilitates change and motivates others to do their best. "The genius of leadership lies in the manner in which leaders see and act on their own and their followers' values and motivations" (Burns, 1978, p. 19). Burns and later Bass and Avolio (1994) emerged as seminal theorists around the concept of transformational leadership. *Fostering Nurse-Led Care* uses the concept and principles of transformational leadership to bring professional nurses and others to a place where they can consider a new idea about the role environment plays in stimulating others to do their best. Transformational leadership is seen as a "process whereby leaders and followers raise one another to higher levels of morality and motivation" (Burns, 1978, p. 19).

The evolution of transformational leadership emerged from an understanding of leadership based on transactions, where an exchange of incentives occurs for desired accomplishments (Bass, 1990). Transactional leadership (Burns, 1978) also places emphasis on work standards, assignments, task orientation, and task completion. Bass (1990) and other researchers (Burns, 1978) have identified the characteristics of transformational leadership as "a leadership process that is systematic, consisting of purposeful and organized search for changes, systematic analysis, and the capacity to move resources from areas of lesser to greater productivity to bring about a strategic transformation" (Bass, 1990, p. 34).

This movement from transactional leadership to transformational leadership is based on an exploration of characteristics that move beyond the transactional mode of relationship. Leadership at the bedside supports the important role professional nurses play in knowing the patient and fostering an environment to achieve satisfaction and desired care outcomes

Celebrating leadership is essential to advancing health care. The qualities of transformational leadership are celebrated within this book using exemplars and reflections by nurses. Transformational leadership is linked to the leader's ability to mentor, coach, and treat each person equally (Atwater & Yammarino, 1993). The other characteristics of transformational leadership include:

- Intellectual stimulation, the leader's ability to ask questions, find ways to problem solve, and approach old situations in new ways (Avolio, Waldman, & Yammarino, 1991)

- Inspirational motivation, being able to generate excitement and provide vision and direction, motivating others to do their best and giving work meaning (Howell & Avolio, 1993)

- Idealized influence by serving as a role model and emulating high ethical standards for others

The key distinguishing factor of transformational leadership is discussed in relation to a leader engaging with and in relationship with those they are charged to lead. This book gives multiple examples of the importance of a professional practice environment, the importance of continuously innovating, the role of mentoring to facilitate change, and the obligation to support global opportunities that promote sharing and dissemination of knowledge while working with others with limited exposure to advanced knowledge.

Framework for Personal and Professional Leadership

This book discusses a useful framework for professional leadership as:

- Personal leadership

- Leadership in relation to others

- Leadership in relation to systems

Throughout the text extensive discussion showcases leader's competencies that impact dramatic change within the organization, at the unit level, and, most importantly, in the direct care of patients and families.

Personal Leadership—Leadership of Self

Leadership of self focuses on a leader's awareness of personal leadership traits and behaviors with an understanding of what gaps or complementary skill sets might be needed to create a highly effective leadership style. Recognizing your personal attributes as a leader, knowing your style and influence on others, and having awareness of your leadership strengths can enhance one's potential to lead and mentor others.

Professional Leadership—Leadership in Relation to Others

Leadership in relation to others reflects on the work of Burns (1978) who linked the traits and behaviors of a leader to those of the follower. Each must trust the other while coping with feelings of dependence on the other. This dynamic holds important implications for nurse managers and their effectiveness in improving patient outcomes.

Professional Leadership—Leadership in Relation to Systems

Leadership in relation to systems supports strong personal leadership as the ability of the leader to work within a system to create transformational change. This transformative power is unleashed through the partnership of the leader with the team. Nurse executives must become effective change agents and create a space where innovation can occur.

Magnet Recognition

Fostering Nurse-Led Care discusses multiple strategies and organizational developments that occur through effective leadership. Magnet recognition is discussed not only in relation to leadership but also in relation to evidence-based professional practice, mentoring, research, and use of nursing knowledge to advance care. "Becoming a transformational leader requires thoughtfulness, inclusivity, good listening skills, flexibility, and resiliency. Critical to achieving Magnet recognition are nurse executives who have taken on the transformation of their nursing services through the process of the Magnet recognition journey" (Wolf, Zimmerman & Drenkard, 2010, p. 32). The key areas that are required from leadership in Magnet organizations are discussed as:

- Strategic planning, to include the creation of a nursing vision, mission and values, and plan and outcomes

- Advocacy and influence from the chief nurse, including evidence of an organization-wide change led by the chief nurse and innovation that includes clinicians in the care of patients

- Visibility, accessibility, and communication that result in outcomes being impacted by everyone on the care team

Fostering Nurse-Led Care discusses these elements in detail. The planning used to create a professional practice care model at MGH, the testing and refinement of the model, the revisions and further development guided by evidence and organizational change, the vision of executive leaders and responsiveness of MGH as an organization, and the importance of creating collaboration and communication across disciplines to achieve goals are all discussed and explored.

Research and Leadership

Research related to models and characteristics of leadership are explored in *Fostering Nurse-Led Care*. Traits such as "comfort with ambiguity" and "sense-making" (Ebright, Patterson, Chalko & Render, 2003) are skills that nurse leaders need to meet the demands of future fast-paced changes. Quantum leadership characteristics such as being fluid and flexible serve to further understanding as we move to a quantum world where change is constant.

Linking the characteristics of effective leadership is essential to describing changes in care at the point of delivery at the bedside. *Fostering Nurse-Led Care* explores many of these concepts and incorporates the latest evidence to implement change and redesign needed to respond to a dynamic and evolving health care environment. Recognizing that leadership is a social influence process (LoBiondo-Wood & Haber 2010) can help guide the potential for future research for executive nurse leadership. New knowledge and sources of evidence reflecting the impact of transformational leadership on patient outcomes, quality, and safety emerge as important areas for future investigation.

Summary

Research shows strong nurse leadership is critical to building a positive workplace (Anthony et al., 2005; Spence Laschinger & Leiter, 2006; Tichy & Devanna, 1990; Upenieks, 2003; Ward, 2002). *Fostering Nurse-Led Care* discusses the development of a care culture guided by optimal professional practice, where leadership motivates and inspires the staff at the bedside to do their best; to feel supported in their work; and to feel encouraged to innovate, experiment, and create, and this culture can be the factor that helps health care providers respond most effectively meet future patient demands. This book explores elements that help sustain professional practice environments and motivate clinicians to flourish. Effective professional practice environments create a sense of belonging and develop a culture of care that can use knowledge and expertise to achieve cost-effective outcomes as well as patient and clinician satisfaction.

References

Anthony, M. K., Standing, T. S., Glick, J., Duffy, M., Paschall, F., Sauer, M. R., Sweeney, D. K., Modic, M. B., & Dumpe, M. L. (2005). Leadership and nurse retention: The pivotal role of nurse managers. *Journal of Nursing Administration, 35*(3), 146-155.

Atwater, L. E., & Yammarino, F. J. (1993). Personal attributes as predictors of superiors' and subordinates' perceptions of military academy leadership. *Human Relations, 46*(5), 645-668.

Avolio, B. J., Waldman, D. A., & Yammarino, F. J. (1991). Leading in the 1990's: The four I's of transformational leadership. *Journal of European Industrial Training, 15*(4), 9-16.

Bass, B. M. (1990). *Bass and Stogdill's handbook of leadership: Theory, research, and managerial applications (Third ed.)*. New York: The Free Press, p. 34.

Bass, B. M., & Avolio, B. J. (Eds.) (1994). *Improving organizational effectiveness through transformational leadership*. Thousand Oaks, CA: Sage Publications.

Burns, J. M. (1978). *Leadership*. New York: Harper & Row Publishers, p. 19-20.

Chan, K. Y. & Drasgow, F. (2001). Toward a theory of individual differences and leadership: understanding the motivation to lead. *Journal of Applied Psychology, 86*(3), 481-498.

Chemers, M. M. (2000). Leadership, research and theory: A functional integration. *Group Dynamics: Theory, Research, and Practice, 4*(1), 27-43.

Dowd, J. (1993). *Control in human societies*. New York: Appleton-Century.

Ebright, P. R., Patterson, E. S., Chalko, B. A., & Render, M. L. (2003). Understanding the complexity of registered nurse work in acute care settings. *Journal of Nursing Administration, 33*(12): 630-8.

Howell, J. M., & Avolio, B. (1993). Transformational leadership, transactional leadership, locus of control, and support for innovation: Key predictors of consolidated business-unit performance. *Journal of AppliedPsychology, 78*(6), 891-902.

Institute of Medicine (2001). Crossing the quality chasm: A new health system for the 21st century. Washington, DC: National Academy Press.

LoBiondo-Wood, G. & Haber, J. (2010). Nursing Research: Methods and critical appraisal for evidence-based practice. St. Louis. MO: Mosby Elsevier.

Spence Laschinger, H. K., & Leiter, M. P. (2006). The impact of nursing work environments on patient safety outcomes: The mediating role of burnout engagement. *Journal of Nursing Administration, 36*(5), 259-267.

Tichy, N. M., & Devanna, M. A. (1990). *The transformational leader: The key to global competitiveness*. New York: John Wiley & Sons.

Upenieks, V. V. (2003). The interrelationship of organizational characteristics of magnet hospitals, nursing leadership, and nursing job satisfaction. *Health Care Manager, 22*(2), 83-98.

Ward, K. (2002). A vision for tomorrow: Transformational nursing leaders. *Nursing Outlook, 50*(3), 121-126.

Wolf, G., Zimmermann, D., & Drenkard, K (2010). Transformation leadership in Wolf, G., Drenkard, K., Morgan, S. Magnet: The next generation: Nurses making the difference , Silver Spring, MD: American Nurses Credentialing Center.

Introduction

Nursing is a human discipline that facilitates the wellbeing of individuals, families and communities using a scientific knowledge base within caring relationships.

(Roy & Jones, 2007, p. 2).

Rapid advances in health care and the promotion of care that is timely, cost effective, high-quality, safe, and patient-centric create new challenges and yet-to-be-realized opportunities for all health care providers. Nurses are in a key position to take the lead in redesigning and creating changes in health care delivery and redefining health both in illness and well-being. Nurses at the bedside are leaders in this effort as they work independently and with other disciplines to achieve this goal.

Who This Book Is For and What the Book Covers

This book introduces nurses and other health care providers to one institution's response to the goals realized in the 2010 Institute of Medicine's Report on the Future of Nursing. Innovation within nursing practice reflects the goals of nursing and optimizes the use of the scientific knowledge embedded in professional practice to optimize the patient care experience. Readers are given the opportunity to reflect on a Professional Practice Model (PPM) designed to enhance the professional practice environment created at the Massachusetts General Hospital (MGH) as a model to optimize patient care outcomes. The PPM acknowledges the unique contributions of nurses working within the interdisciplinary health care team to provide care and identifies multiple ways nurses can bring their knowledge to the bedside and lead in advancing care redesign. The supports and resources available to professionals within the practice environment are used to assist nurses and other providers to deliver care that is patient centric, relationship-based, and grounded in evidence and the expert knowledge of caregivers across disciplines.

The goal of this book is to share the development, implementation, and evaluation of a professional practice model while giving voice to strategies that enhance care at the bedside. The professional practice environment attends to human-to-human interaction, and we view it as an essential strategy to promoting patient, family, and staff satisfaction. As you read this book, you will gain new insights into the contributions of nursing, its influence on leading change and innovation at the bedside, and the unique contributions nurses make to the outcomes of care and health promotion.

How This Book Is Organized

The book's Foreword introduces the reader to transformational leadership as critical to the future of care at the bedside. This discussion sets the stage for the chapters to follow and creates a context for change and redesign needed to advance patient care.

Chapter 1, "Influencing Professional Practice at the Bedside," and Chapter 2, "Professional Practice Model: Strategies for Translating Models into Practice," present a discussion on the importance of a professional practice model (PPM) in acute care and other settings. Core to its development is effective nursing leadership. The PPM at the MGH is then discussed along with strategies used to translate the model into clinical practice.

Chapter 3, "Creating Empowering Work Environments to Promote Professional Nursing Practice," provides the context within which care is delivered. The discussion focuses on the practice environment, the Magnet Recognition journey, and evaluation of the work environment.

The scope of work is explored in Chapter 4, "Scope of Work—Care at the Bedside," with an emphasis on nursing leadership, nursing's social policy (ANA, 2004), and the standards of practice as they impact nurse's delivery of patient care.

Chapter 5, "Nurse-Patient Relationship: Knowledge Transforming Practice at the Bedside," explores the importance of the nurse-patient relationship and "knowing the person." Strategies related to addressing immediate patient problems and using a process/dialogue approach to uncover meaning and the patient response to health and the illness experience are discussed with exemplars to enrich application of the content in practice. The use of standardized nursing languages to communicate the patient experiences and responses to illness are incorporated into the presentation.

The moral/ethical responsibility of nursing care and nurse's role as advocate and interventionist are explored in Chapter 6, "Nursing's Moral Imperative," along with the outcomes of a Health Resources and Services Administration (HRSA) Clinical Ethics Residency for Nurses project (CERN).

Introducing innovation within the PPM framework is presented in Chapter 7, "Innovations in Care Delivery," along with a discussion of several strategies and potential patient care outcomes resulting from creative approaches to care.

The importance of diversity in the workplace is explored in Chapter 8, "Promoting Diversity in the Workplace," with inclusion of specific actions and approaches to ensure that the care needs of patients and nurses from diverse backgrounds are addressed.

The value of the mentoring role is presented in Chapter 9, "Mentorship and Best Practices for Mentorship," and research-based best practices are shared, including collaborative governance models, unit-based resources, and programs designed to support the new graduate's transition from academia to practice.

In Chapter 10, "Strengthening a Culture of Evidence-Based Nursing Practice," the value and use of evidence-based practice within a PPM is presented, reflecting the knowledge and strategies developed through an HRSA-funded project to improve patient care.

Administrative leaders in Chapter 11, "Designing the Infrastructure to Foster Nurse-Led Care at the Bedside," offer creative strategies to use in promoting the goals of the PPM, especially at the unit level with staff and patients.

Attention to the value of strong leadership and its influence on nursing practice and patient care is expanded in Chapter 12, "Nurse Leaders: Influencing New Paradigms of Care Delivery."

Evaluation of the PPM is discussed in Chapter 13, "Measuring the Hospital Work Environment: Development, Validation, and Revision of the Professional Practice Environment Scale." The Revised Professional Practice Environment (RPPE) tool as a measure of the practice environment is elaborated on and the components of the RPPE discussed in relation to tool reliability, validity, and international use.

Chapter 14, "International Nursing Leadership: Impact at the Bedside," offers a global perspective of professional nursing's impact on patient, family, and community care and highlights multiple programmatic opportunities worldwide to advance professional nursing practice at the bedside.

Concluding thoughts, as discussed in Chapter 15, "Concluding Thoughts," present a synthesis of the thoughts around developing a PPM to signal change and redirection and provide nurses with an opportunity to actively participate in the redesign of care at the bedside and beyond.

Our Goals for This Book

It is our hope that this book will serve to inspire and motivate all nurses to acknowledge the critical role they play in patient care delivery and to seek ways to voice the contributions to the delivery of quality health care for all. We also hope that this book validates what it means to be a nurse and appreciate and value our unique role as we collaborate with other disciplines to deliver the best care.

References

American Nurses Association (ANA). (2003). *Nursing's social policy statement*. Silver Springs, MD: Nursesbooks.org

Institute of Medicine (IOM). (2010). *The future of nursing: Leading change, advancing health*. Washington, DC: National Academies Press. Retrieved from http://thefutureofnursing.org/IOM-Report.

Roy, C., & Jones, D. (2007). *Nursing knowledge development and clinical practice*. New York, NY: Springer Publishing, p. 2.

Chapter 1
Influencing Professional Practice at the Bedside

Jeanette Ives Erickson, RN, DNP, FAAN

Invisible architecture is to the soul of your organization what physical architecture is to its body. Invisible architecture, not the building, determines whether you are a good hospital, a great hospital, or just another hospital.

–Joe Tye, CEO, Values Coach, Inc.

Florence Nightingale is viewed as the inspiration for modern-day nursing. Nightingale first published "Notes on Nursing" in 1859, educating everyone on the critical importance of the environment of care and nurses' responsibility for ensuring that setting is based on an understanding that healing environments have an impact on patients, families, and the care team. Over one hundred and fifty years later, understanding Nightingale's thinking, her ability to inspire all who knew her, and the key message that data is of critical importance to inform and advance clinical practice is still important. Nightingale worked tirelessly to improve sanitation laws and the physical design of health care institutions. She is said to be the first health care biostatistician (Dossey, 2000).

Today through research and patient satisfaction surveys, we understand that patients perceive health care quality is better when the environment is clean and quiet and when nurses are responsive to their questions and concerns (Studer, Robinson & Cook, 2010). Key to this quality is the chief nurse, whose job it is to improve the environment in which health care delivery is provided. This chapter, which is structured in a step-by-step outline format, discusses the important components of a chief nurse's perspective gained over 40 years of administrative practice.

Developing Environments of Care

Nurse satisfaction runs high when administrative nurses are responsive to nurses' needs and create an environment of care that is built upon mutual respect and is safe. One of the primary responsibilities of the chief nurse is developing healthy, safe work environments to promote the highest standard of care for patients and staff. This responsibility coincides with providing a safe environment for nurses. Aligning this work demonstrates to all that quality, safety, and promoting the integrity of the nurse-patient relationship in a safe environment of care is of paramount importance.

The Professional Practice Environment

In the current care delivery environment and executive nursing practice literature, several competing "names" represent the nursing environment concept. These terms include a) *work environment* (McClure, Poulin, Sovie & Wandelt, 1983), b) *practice environment* (Lake, 2002), c) *professional practice environment* (Ives Erickson, 1997), and d) *healthy work environment* (Sherman & Pross, 2010). Given the rapid pace of today's health care organizations, we must measure, understand, and improve the work environment. This chapter uses the term *professional practice environment (PPE)*, operationally defined as the organizational culture that advances the clinical practice of nurses and other health professionals by ensuring unity of purpose and organizational alignment. The theoretical foundation of the PPE advocates collaborative decision-making to ensure that all stakeholders have the opportunity to knowingly participate in change (Ives Erickson, 2012).

A Call to Action

Today, the environment of care, especially for professional nurses, can be described as not for the faint of heart—the work can be demanding and emotionally draining. Yet nursing, with over three million practicing nurses in the United States (U.S.) alone, remains the most trusted profession (Jones, 2011). Perhaps that is why the Institute of Medicine (IOM) has called together national leaders twice over the past two decades to assess, analyze, debate, and confirm the important role that all nurses play in every aspect of the health care delivery system. The first report, *Keeping Patients Safe: Transforming the Work Environment of Nurses* (IOM, 2004), identified solutions to problems in hospitals, nursing homes, and other health care organization work environments that threaten patient safety through their effect on nursing care. The 2010 Institute of Medicine report *The Future of Nursing: Leading Change, Advancing Health* provides an important blueprint and a call to action to transform nursing to meet the needs of the patients we serve (IOM, 2010).

Like Nightingale's call to action during the Crimean War, the IOM calls upon nurses to improve access to care, to improve nursing education and training, and for all nurses to practice at the top of their profession. The timing of this report coincides with the 2010 Affordable Care Act, commonly referred to as health care reform. This represents the broadest overhaul of health care since the 1965 creation of Medicare and Medicaid. With the nursing profession representing the largest segment of the national health care workforce, nurses are playing a pivotal role and will continue to play a pivotal role in the future of health care in the U.S. and internationally.

What's clear is that as health care reform unfolds, hospitals are going to be called upon to do more with less to reduce the rising expense of U.S. health care. Along with this is the fact that the nation and many countries throughout the world are facing difficult economic times. Care redesign, cost control, and the elimination of waste will be the primary focus of health care organizations for the foreseeable future. The more volatile the economic climate, the more we need to remain true to our values. We must continue to use every resource at our disposal to ensure we deliver the highest quality care to our patients and families. To that end, designing and developing an environment that supports the nurse-patient relationship is key.

Sacrificing quality of care is not an option. Limiting access to care is not an option. If we are to maintain the same high standards of patient care, we must learn how to provide that care differently. We must be innovative in our thinking. True reform cannot be achieved through payment reform alone. Some of the barriers and challenges confronting the profession (and the nation) as we work to improve health care delivery while reducing costs need to be discussed candidly. We know that nurses are going to play a key role in health care reform by being a part of the decision-making and policymaking efforts that will define our future by addressing the PPE (Ives Erickson, 1997).

The Role of the Chief Nurse

At the Massachusetts General Hospital, we believe the PPE is the single most accurate measure of nurse leader success across constituencies and the means by which nurse leaders can best advance the profession, discipline, and science of nursing. Presently, many nurse leaders are evaluated differently depending on institutional-specific competencies and criteria set by subordinates, peers, and superiors (Adams et al., 2008). However, most if not all constituent criteria are included or correlated to measures of the PPE. Nearly every professional nursing organization, including Sigma Theta Tau International, the International Council of Nurses (ICN), the American Nurses Association, the American Organization of Nurse Executives, and the American Nurses Credentialing Center have all emphasized the importance of the PPE. However, it was not until relatively recently in nursing's 200+ year history that the PPE concept has become identified as a viable means by which to explain, value, and advance nursing (Ives Erickson, 2012).

Simply stated, the primary objective of the chief nurse is to improve the environment in which health care delivery is provided. Thus, the chief nurse must influence others to achieve positive patient/organizational outcomes, as research in the area by Adams and Ives Erickson (2011) and Adams, Ives Erickson, Jones, and Paulo (2009) has shown an identified relationship between nursing leadership, practice environments, and patient outcomes. With the chief nurses' emphasis on developing the practice environment, they will in turn be developing staff ambassadors that improve patient and organizational outcomes

(Adams et al., 2008, 2009). In this capacity, chief nurses must effectively lead by empowering others while always monitoring, measuring, and transparently communicating data and outcomes related to the PPE.

The Practice Environment Conceptual Framework

As mentioned, this chapter is structured in a step-by-step outline format, discussing important components of a chief nurse's perspective gained over 40 years of administrative practice. The resulting compilation of ideas is represented as a thorough yet early conceptual model. The Practice Environment Conceptual Framework, as represented in Figure 1.1, provides a frame for leadership thinking when you want to influence professional practice at the bedside.

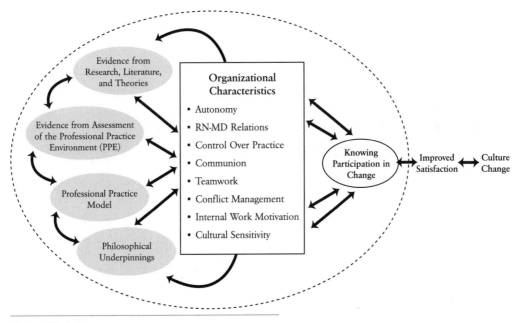

FIGURE 1.1

Representation of dynamic interactions within a professional practice environment.

The representation was developed to demonstrate the dynamic and changing interrelationships between the elements necessary to improve the PPE. The graphic incorporates four areas of influence that result in shared understanding between constituents in the environment of care that have the potential power to improve the environment in which they practice. These areas are described in detail in the following sections.

Philosophical Underpinnings

The Merriam-Webster Dictionary (2011) defines *underpinnings* as something that serves as a foundation: "a basis, a support." Who we are as nurses and leaders is shaped by many influences, including values, family, friends, colleagues, and life experiences. Who I am as a nurse leader was greatly influenced by two of my educators. Sister Mary Consuela White, RN, RSM, head of the Mercy Hospital School of Nursing, exuded professionalism. She was a woman of great stature, who continuously pushed me and all who encountered her to continuously learn. Her early work was an influence on the importance of creating learning environments. Also, Muriel Poulin, EdD, RN, FAAN, who led the graduate program in nursing at Boston University, was an especially influential nursing role model when I was a graduate student at Boston University, especially after she and others published the Magnet Hospital study in 1983.

Their work, values, and teachings became the basis for how I approach clinical practice and leadership. Recently, the text *Magnet Hospitals Revisited* (McClure & Hinshaw, 2002) supported the authors (McClure et al., 1983) of the original text, which described healthy practice environments that impacted nurse and patients, noting that "it is the combination of element (forces of Magnetism) that creates a positive practice environment." They added, "more than a matter of strategy, it is the quality of administration and leadership that distinguishes Magnet hospitals from others."

Professional Practice Model

The Massachusetts General Hospital (MGH) Patient Care Services Professional Practice Model (PPM) provides a framework that guides professional practice across multiple health care disciplines (Ives Erickson, 1997). The PPM was designed to facilitate the interdependent relationships between staff nurses and other health professionals within the context of their own practice (Ives Erickson, Hamilton, Jones & Ditomassi, 2003).

The intent of the original MGH PPM was to provide clinicians a framework to explore, develop, learn, and articulate their contributions to patient care. The MGH PPM is driven by the commitment to provide the highest quality care to patients and their families. Developed and disseminated in 1996 and revised in 2007, the MGH PPM is grounded in values and beliefs that embrace patient-centered care in partnership with the nurse and other providers of care within the patient care environment.

In total, the MGH PPM symbolizes the delivery of seamless, knowledge-based patient care and demonstrates the importance of each component as part of a greater whole. The MGH PPM is predicated on the availability of resources; qualified professionals; and an institutional commitment to safe, timely, efficient, equitable, cost-effective, quality patient care (IOM, 2001).

The importance of a professional practice model has been well documented since the first criteria for Magnet hospitals were identified in 1983 (McClure et al.). Salient elements of a professional practice model were identified as:

- Autonomy

- Control over practice

- Collaborative relationships with physician colleagues

The MGH PPM built upon that foundation and incorporated additional emphasis on the following elements:

- Organizational behavior

- Descriptive theory models

- Importance of clinical narratives as an aspect of culture

Disch, Sochalski, and Seamon (2004) suggested that a strategy for improving the health care system would be to create a database to a) monitor nurses' work environments; b) measure the correlations between staffing and patient outcomes; and c) support policy development. MGH nurse leaders and other researchers viewed developing an instrument to measure the effectiveness of the MGH PPM and the PPE as an essential approach to enhance clinicians' roles and working conditions and to align their relationship to both patient and organizational outcomes (Ives Erickson, 1997; Lake, 2002).

Understanding the organizational concepts supportive of activities to advance clinical practice and improve the environment of care provides us with an opportunity to gain insights into how best to measure the impact of the MGH PPM. The research literature provides evidence that organizational structures are needed to enhance safety, efficiency, and timeliness of care. The MGH PPM is explored in detail in Chapter 2, "Professional Practice Model: Strategies for Translating Models into Practice." This concept is especially important because it advances and gives a foundation for organizational alignment and influencing professional practice at the bedside.

Evidence from Research, Literature, and Theories

Leaders influencing care at the bedside must develop, support, and utilize evidence to inform and influence the delivery of high-quality, safe care. At MGH, what has emerged is based on a commitment to the creation of a culture of inquiry that fosters a healthy exchange of ideas, competition of ideas, and a commitment to optimize care through knowledge. The art and science of nursing are advanced through the utilization and integration of knowledge and the dissemination of evidence into practice. Nurses are not the only developers of knowledge; we have the unique opportunity to integrate new and developing knowledge across the discipline(s) and assimilate that knowledge with our own nursing voice to better patient outcomes, the organization, and discipline. Developing, coordinating, and integrating our own work along with current evidence developed by others is a constant effort to optimize care delivery at the bedside.

Evidence from Assessment of the Professional Practice Environment

Initial efforts to identify a comprehensive measure of the effectiveness of the MGH PPM led to the development of the MGH Staff Perceptions of the Professional Practice Environment (PPE) survey (Ives Erickson et al., 2004). In 2007, the MGH PPM was updated as a direct result from feedback by clinical nursing staff responses to the PPE. This change was a direct result of feedback from nursing staff that the organizational efforts to create a narrative culture and to include patients and families in all levels of decision-making were part of the organizational culture (see the PPM figures in Chapter 2). Whereas the original MGH PPM led to the development of the original version of the PPE survey, the revised MGH PPM led to the Revised Professional Practice Environment (RPPE) survey instrument (Ives Erickson, Duffy, Ditomassi & Jones, 2009).

The PPE/RPPE survey instruments were designed as a multidimensional measure of professional clinical practice in the acute care setting. The results from the survey provide the leadership with a report on the clinician's perception of the PPE from eight organizational characteristics:

- Autonomy
- Clinician-MD relations
- Control over practice
- Cultural sensitivity
- Teamwork
- Communication
- Conflict management
- Internal work motivation

The RPPE survey provides clinical staff with a mechanism for sharing their perceptions of the environment. Those results guide chief nurses with an evidence-based approach towards improvement efforts. Accordingly, they initiate adjustments in the practice environment within the overall institution and at the unit level. Subsequent surveys provide input on the effectiveness of organizational improvement efforts, which can be quantified at the same time that chief nurses identify new insights for further action. Evidence documenting changes are used as measures of effectiveness reported to support the quality of patient care outcomes as well as giving a voice to clinical nursing staff. As an example, at MGH, all clinical nurses and other professional providers who are invited to participate in the survey have a significant response rate (61% on the returns in 2006, 58% in 2008, and 53% in 2010).

Four current publications describe the development, psychometric evaluation, and utilization of the PPE and RPPE survey (Chang, 2009; Halcomb, Davidson, Caldwell, Salamonson & Rolley, 2010; Ives Erickson et al., 2004; and Ives Erickson et al., 2009). The original research conducted at MGH in 2002 demonstrated that the tool produces reliable and construct-valid scores (Ives Erickson et al., 2004). In 2006, MGH leadership conducted a psychometric validation study of the RPPE survey instrument demonstrating parity to those reported in 2002 (Ives Erickson et al., 2009). Additional research conducted in Australia and Taiwan confirmed that, when adjusted for minor cultural differences, the PPE survey instrument and its eight organizational characteristics were an effective method for assessing the professional practice across cultures (Halcomb et al., 2010), Chang, 2009). These studies, validating the PPE and RPPE survey instruments provide chief nurses with an evidence-based mechanism to evaluate the professional practice environment of nurses and other clinicians under their purview.

NOTE

Chapter 13, "Measuring the Hospital Work Environment: Development, Validation, and Revision of the Professional Practice Environment Scale," includes a complete discussion of the PPE.

Providing further support of the necessity of evaluating the professional practice environment is the significant body of literature relating the professional practice environments to both patient care and organizational outcomes such as nurses' turnover behavior, intention to leave the profession (Chiang & Lin, 2008), and the quality of health care (Aiken et al., 2001; IOM, 2004). Adams and colleagues (Adams et al., 2008; Adams et al., 2009) have expanded on these findings and further suggested relationships between the chief nurse, the professional practice environment, and organizational/patient outcomes. These relationships include concerns of the chief nurse, which have been well articulated in the literature, such as:

- A nursing shortage

- Threatened patient safety associated with gaps in knowledge related to nurse staffing

- Ineffective tools to measure nursing workload

- Challenges to developing environments of care healthy for patients and their care providers (Ives Erickson, Bridge, Chisari & Ditomassi, 2010)

Additionally, there is increased interest in public and professional understanding of the PPE for nurses and its effect on the quality of health care globally (ICN, 2010).

Knowing Participation in Change

Elizabeth Barrett's (2010) mid-range theory of power, defined as knowing participation in change offers an expanding understanding of how the professional practice environment can influence the characteristics just described. Barrett's work operationalized further the fundamentals of Martha Rogers's conceptual system or the science of unitary human beings (Rogers, 1990). From the Rogerian perspective, Barrett described the dimensions of power, which included the capacity to participate knowingly in change (Barrett, 1989).

Barrett utilized Rogers's theory of power to assist nurses in understanding people and the culture they worked in. As Barrett's understanding of power developed, she proposed her theory as being power-as-freedom and power-as-control. Within this concept, power is not static nor is it linear but varies based on how the person or the environment change. Barrett (2010) described these changes as:

- Nature of awareness of experiences

- Type of choices made

- Degree to which freedom to act intentionally is operating

- Manner of involvement in creating changes

Power is traditionally thought of as dominance or manipulation (power-as-control). Power-as-freedom might be another way to look at how leadership supports and advances the eight characteristics, especially in the arena of autonomy over practice and decision-making. It may also be a factor associated with leadership influence over the eight characteristics measured in the PPE/RPPE.

The Adams Influence Model (AIM) (Adams, 2009) suggests that power is equal to being influential over multiple issues and across domains. This idea is synergistic with Barrett's definition of power that indicates knowing participation is essential to enact influence or power. The AIM is based on the operational definition, "Influence is the ability of an individual (agent) to sway or affect another person or group (target) about a single issue based on authority, status, knowledge-based competence, communication traits and/or use of time and timing" (Adams, 2009). Influence is a key determinant in motivation, decision-making, and securing support and resources (Yukl & Falbe, 1990). Adams describes influence as an essential part of the nurse leader's role in maximizing professional practice/work environments and patient and organizational outcomes (Adams, Ives Erickson, Jones, & Paulo, 2009).

Improved Satisfaction

In the English vernacular, the word *motivation* was originally derived from the Latin concept *movere* meaning "to move" or something that causes a person "to act" (Merriam-Webster Dictionary, 2011). The study of the phenomenon of motivation to work is extremely complex. As motivation is not directly observable, it can only be inferred from an individual's behavior. This inference has resulted in the formulation of many theories based on multiple foci including human behavior, goal setting/attainment, and rewards.

A Conceptual Model

In their seminal work on motivation, Steers and Porter (1979) developed a conceptual model, assuming that motivation can best be understood within a framework that involves the interrelationship between the following factors:

- **Characteristics of the individual:** At least three major characteristics have been shown to affect the motivational process, including interests, attitudes, and needs.

- **Characteristics of the job:** The focus is what an employee does at work, how much feedback is provided, and whether the work offers intrinsic rewards.

- **Characteristics of the work environment:** The two major categories here include characteristics of the immediate work environment, including the work group and those characteristics associated with organization-wide actions.

Steers and Porter (1979) additionally suggest that when an organization designs jobs, the goals of the organization are paramount, but other factors should be considered, including individual needs and organizational climate. The functions, expectations, and roles of the job itself are a very important factor in the motivation of employees. Feelings of job satisfaction motivate people to go to work and to remain within an organization. The dynamics between these major sets of variables can be expanded to see the influence of needs and interests, which motivate a person to work, and of the job and environment, which might affect the person's effort and performance.

Maslow's Hierarchy of Needs

Another prominent theory that has considerable impact on the study of motivation was developed in the 1942 book *Motivation and Personality* by Abraham H. Maslow (1987). Maslow's theory of human motivation is known as

New Hierarchy Theory (Kast & Rosenzweig, 1985), but is now better known as Maslow's Hierarchy of Needs (Wikipedia, 2010).

Maslow's model is inclusive of the concepts of physiological, safety, love/belonging, esteem and self-actualization needs. It is representative of the tenants of a Professional Practice Environment. These first-level needs—physiological, safety, love/belonging, and esteem—must be achieved to maximize a professional practice environment. The fifth and final need is self-actualization. Self-actualization is the equivalent of a "Magnet-like" professional practice environment where staff are supported and developed to influence positive outcomes. As lower needs are satisfied, the higher needs of esteem and self-realization including achievement, mastery, confidence, independence, recognition, and the realization of all that one is capable of becoming emerge as dominant.

People attach meaning to and derive satisfaction from their experiences (Davis, 1977). Some believe that the needs of employees can be satisfied by providing wages and letting employees then use money to acquire their own satisfaction. However, this economic approach does not hold up when applying Maslow's needs hierarchy because money applies mostly to the first two needs. The needs priority model (Davis, 1977) identifies that gratified needs are not as strongly motivating as unmet needs. That is, people are motivated by what they are seeking more than what they already have. The study of Maslow's needs hierarchy is useful in understanding that people do not work only for money. They have individual differences in the motivation to work.

Motivation

Motivation as discussed within Maslow's theory is linked to self-actualization and does not decrease as lower-level needs become satisfied. As people experience growth and self-actualization, they want more and seek new ways to discover and uncover life experiences (Dale, 1978; Kast & Rosenzweig, 1985). Actualization as a goal of a positive professional practice environment is realized as staff conceptualizes, utilizes evidence, and works to continually inspire and develop knowledge (Adams, 2011). Self-actualization for people includes choosing an occupation that allows them to receive certain satisfaction from accomplishing tasks while at the same time searching for more. To the degree that a PPE promotes the search for personal fulfillment, people will find their work a challenge and will experience an inner satisfaction or self-actualization (Davis, 1977).

Another approach applicable to the study of work motivation within the professional practice environment surrounds motivation theories. Motivation theory grew out of the work of Harvard professor Henry Murray (McClelland, 1975), who developed a system for classifying individuals according to the strength of various needs that have the potential for motivating behavior. Theories centering on this concept articulate that the majority of an individual's performance can be explained by the intensity of the individual's need for achievement. Murray believed that people have the need for achievement, order, affiliation, dominance, and change (Litwin & Stringer, 1968) and this "needs for achievement" concept was further explained by McClelland and Burnham (1976) as the desire to perform to high standards or to excel at the job.

Organizational Influences

In addition to the need for understanding the individual in the motivation to work, the characteristics of an organization also influence the behavior of its members and serve to differentiate one organization from another (Sisk and Williams, 1981). Because chief nurses are well-established, identified leaders of nursing within organizations, they also are essential in setting the organizational climate.

Though several variables such as needs, values, expectations, and leadership style of managers and informal leaders have been identified as influencing the development of the organizational climate, the chief nurse leader's relationships, work standards, and goals also impact the climate (Litwin and Stringer, 1968). Litwin and Stringer (1968) found that the need for achievement, affiliation, and power as defined by McClelland (1975) were affected by organizational climate.

Summary

A critical success factor of the chief nurse is the ability to scan the environment and detect signals to inform the operational and strategic direction. This consistent evaluation of the professional practice environment is core to understanding the impact of changes to the increasingly complex health care delivery system. Identifying approaches for accommodating this complexity is a key step in improving the quality of patient care and in retaining nurses in the workforce. Barrett's work suggests that knowingly participating in change by being aware of what you choose to do, feeling free to do it, and acting intentionally should be guiding principles of chief nurse practice and should be a part of how the chief nurse encourages the interdisciplinary team to sort through clinical problems at the bedside. The use of a theoretical approach with exquisite leadership skills represents an important aspect of how a chief nurse might begin to measure, implement, and enhance an evidence-based approach to improving the professional practice environment.

This framework identifies opportunity for the focus of the chief nurse to influence organizational change when all nurses have the freedom to knowingly participate in change. The representation was developed to demonstrate the interrelationships between the elements needed to improve the professional practice environment and to assist chief nurses in anticipating needed PPM changes that should be consistent with culture change. Figure 1.1, shown earlier in the chapter, incorporates four areas of influence that result in shared understanding between constituents in the environment of care. These constituents have the potential power to improve the environment in which they practice. Consistent with Barrett's theory of power as freedom, access to organizational structures that enable the nurse to work at the top of the profession can affect a nurse's willingness to participate in change. This work begins to identify a relationship between nurses' perceptions of their ability to influence.

Exploring the relationship between employee work motivation and the leadership understanding of employee needs can strengthen motivation and enhance professional practice. In short, work motivation might serve as a proxy for a positive professional practice environment or vice versa. Within this context, chief nurses must respond to the motivation of individuals and design, develop, and refine the professional practice environment to maximize motivation and performance toward improving patient and organizational outcomes.

Future research might further link freedom of control and the ability to change organizational culture. A deeper understanding of culture and freedom to participate in change is needed. Further studies should explore any association between freedom to participate in change and other key characteristics. Increasing nurse autonomy, control over practice, and giving nurses a strong voice in decision-making should be explored as a mechanism to improve the professional practice environment.

References

Adams, J. M. (2009). *The Adams Influence Model (AIM): Understanding the factors, attributes and process of achieving influence.* Saarbrüken, Germany: VDM Verlag.

Adams, J. M. (2011). *Influence and the professional practice/work environment: A guide for nursing leader success* [PowerPoint slides]. Association of California Nurse Leaders – South Bay. Retrieved from jeffadamsllc.com

Adams, J. M., & Ives Erickson, J. (2011). Understanding influence: An exemplar applying the Adams Influence Model (AIM) in nurse executive practice. *Journal of Nursing Administration, 41*(4), 186-192.

Adams, J. M., Ives Erickson, J., Jones, D. A., & Paulo, L. (2009). An evidence-based structure for transformative nurse executive practice: The model of the interrelationship of leadership, environments & outcomes for nurse executives (MILE ONE). *Nursing Administration Quarterly, 33*(4), 280-287.

Adams, J. M., Paulo, L., Meraz-Gottfried, L., Aspell Adams, A., Ives Erickson, J., Jones, D. A., & Clifford, J. (2008). *Success measures for the nurse leader: A survey of participants from the 2007 INHL conference.* Boston, MA: The Institute for Nursing Healthcare Leadership.

Aiken, L. H., Clarke, S. P., Sloane, D. M., Sochalski, J. A., Busse, R., Clarke, H., ... Shamiam, J. (2001). Nurses' reports on hospital care in five countries. *Health Affairs, 20*(3), 43-53.

Barrett, E. A. M. (1989). A nursing theory of power for nursing practice: Derivation from Rogers' paradigm. In J. Riehl (Ed.), *Conceptual models for nursing practice* (3rd ed.), (pp. 207-217). Norwalk, CT: Appleton & Lange.

Barrett, E. A. M. (2010). Power as knowing participation in change: What's new and what's next. *Nursing Science Quarterly, 23*(1), 47-54.

Chang, C. C. (2009). *Development and evaluation of psychometric properties of the Chinese version of the Professional Practice Environment Scale in Taiwan.* (Unpublished doctoral dissertation). Boston College, Chestnut Hill, MA.

Chiang, H. Y., & Lin, S. Y. (2008). Psychometric testing of the Chinese version of nursing practice environment scale. *Journal of Clinical Nursing, 18,* 919-929.

Dale, E. (1978). *Management: Theory and practice.* New York, NY: McGraw-Hill.

Davis, E. (1977). *Human behavior at work.* New York, NY: McGraw-Hill.

Disch, J., Sochalski, J., & Seamon, J. (2004). From Nightingale to the new millennium: Charting the research and policy agenda for the nursing workforse. *Nursing Outlook, 52,* 155-157.

Dossey, B. (2000). *Florence Nightingale: Mystic, visionary, healer.* Springhouse, PA: Springhouse Corporation.

Halcomb, E. J., Davidson, P. M., Caldwell, B., Salamonson, Y., & Rolley, J. X. (2010). Validation of the Professional Practice Environment Scale in Australian general practice. *Journal of Nursing Scholarship, 42,* 207-213.

Institute of Medicine (IOM). (2001). *Crossing the quality chasm: A new health system for the 21st century.* Washington, DC: National Academies Press.

Institute of Medicine (IOM). (2004). *Keeping patients safe: Transforming the work environment of nurses.* Washington, DC: National Academies Press.

Institute of Medicine (IOM). (2010). *The future of nursing: Leading change, advancing health.* Washington, DC: National Academies Press.

International Council of Nurses (ICN). (2010). *Health systems strengthening: Working together to achieve more.* Geneva, Switzerland: Author.

Ives Erickson, J. (1997, March 20). Attracting & retaining professional nurses – Staff nurse perceptions of the professional practice environment: A survey. *Caring Headlines.*

Ives Erickson, J. (2012). 200 years of nursing—A chief nurse's reflections on practice, theory, policy, education and research. *Journal of Nursing Administration, 42*(1), 9-11.

Ives Erickson, J., Bridge, E., Chisari, G., & Ditomassi, M. (2010). *Violence in the workplace in health care.* Unpublished manuscript. MGH Institute of Health Professions, NH 760. Population Health. Boston, MA.

Ives Erickson, J., Duffy, M. E., Ditomassi, M., & Jones, D. (2009). Psychometric evaluation of the revised professional practice environment (RPPE) scale. *Journal of Nursing Administration, 39*(5), 236-243.

Ives Erickson, J., Duffy, M., Gibbons, M., Fitzmaurice, J., Ditomassi, M., & Jones, D. (2004). Development and psychometric evaluation of the professional practice environment (PPE) scale. *Journal of Nursing Scholarship, 36*(3), 279-285.

Ives Erickson, J., Hamilton, G., Jones, D., & Ditomassi, M. (2003). The value of collaborative governance/staff empowerment. *Journal of Nursing Administration, 33*(4), 251-252.

Jones, J. (2011). *Record 64% rate honesty, ethics of members of Congress low: Ratings of nurses, pharmacists, and medical doctors most positive.* Retrieved from http://www.gallup.com/poll/151460/Record-Rate-Honesty-Ethics-Members-Congress-Low.aspx

Kast, F., & Rosenzweig, J. (1985). *Organization and management.* New York, NY: McGraw-Hill.

Lake, E. (2002). Development of the practice environment scale of the nursing work index. *Research in Nursing & Health, 25*, 176-188.

Litwin, G., & Stringer, R. (1968). *Motivation and organizational climate.* Boston, MA: Division of Research, Graduate School of Business Administration, Harvard University.

Maslow, A. H. (1987). *Motivation and personality.* New York, NY: Harper Collins Publications.

McClelland, D. C. (1975). *Power: The inner experience.* New York, NY: Irvington.

McClelland, D. C., & Burnham, D. H. (1976). Power is the great motivator. *Harvard Business Review, 54*(2), 100-110.

McClure, M. L., & Hinshaw, A. (2002). *Magnet hospitals revisited: Attraction and retention of professional nurses.* Washington, DC: American Nurses Publishing.

McClure, M. L., Poulin, M. A., Sovie, M. D., & Wandelt, M. (1983). *Magnet hospitals: Attraction and retention of professional nurses.* Washington, DC: American Nurses Publishing.

Merriam-Webster Dictionary. (2011). New York, NY: Simon and Shuster.

Nightingale, F. (1859). *Notes on nursing: What it is and what it is not.* (1st American edition). New York, NY: Appleton and Company.

Rogers, M. E. (1990). Nursing: Science of unitary, irreducible human beings: Updated 1990. In E. A. M. Barrett (Ed.), *Visions of Rogers' science-based nursing* (pp. 5-11). New York, NY: National League for Nursing.

Sherman, R., & Pross, E. (2010, January 31). Growing future nurse leaders to build and sustain healthy work environments at the unit level. *OJIN: The Online Journal of Issues in Nursing, 15*(1), Manuscript 1.

Sisk, H., & Williams, J. C. (1981). *Management and organization.* Cincinnati, OH: South-Western Publishing Company.

Steers, R., & Porter, L. (1979). *Motivation and work behavior.* New York, NY: McGraw-Hill.

Studer, Q., Robinson, B. C., & Cook, K. (2010). *The HCAHPS handbook: Hardwire your hospital for pay-for-performance success.* Gulf Breeze, FL: Fire Starter Publishing.

Tye, J. (2010, September 29). *The Florence Prescription: Building a culture of ownership on a foundation of values.* Presentation for Managing Today's OR Suite Conference.

Wikipedia.org. (2011). *Maslow's hierarchy of needs.* Retrieved from http://en.wikipedia.org/wiki/Maslow's_hierarchy_of_needs

Yukl, G., & Falbe, C. M. (1990). Influence tactics and objectives in upward, downward, and lateral influence attempts. *Journal of Applied Psychology, 75*, 132-140.

Chapter 2
Professional Practice Model: Strategies for Translating Models into Practice

Jeanette Ives Erickson, RN, DNP, FAAN
Marianne Ditomassi, RN, DNP, MBA

Unless we are making progress in our nursing every year, every month, every week, take my word for it we are going back.

–Florence Nightingale, 1914

In the current health care climate, economic and cultural conditions have created an optimal opportunity to envision a new direction for nursing as a profession. Nurses, who have always led with standards undergirded by excellence, must now set the new description of what the nursing profession can be as well as identify contributions to the care delivery model for the future. Towards that end, nurses find themselves in the formative stages of charting a new direction for the profession, regardless of the care setting. The articulation of a professional practice model provides a framework for setting this new direction and, thus, the achievement of exemplary clinical outcomes. In this chapter, the authors describe the evolution of the professional practice model at the Massachusetts General

Hospital (MGH) and how the model continues to be evaluated and modified over time by the nurses within the system.

The Professional Practice Model

A **professional practice model** is a framework that allows nurses to clearly articulate contributions to practice from the profession. With a well-designed framework, nurses feel connected within the context of their relationships to the patient, to their own practice, to the roles of other providers in contributing to the plan, to other nurses, and to the institution. A framework and structure allows the nurse to better plan, manage, and adapt to change. A framework and the structures that ensue facilitate the identification of goals and strategies in addition to roles. Articulation of a model for the nursing professionals within an organization provides a critical mass of energy to support resources, strength, and visibility within an often-complex structure.

The importance of a professional practice model has been recognized since the initial Magnet hospital study in 1983 (McClure, Poulin, Sovie & Wandelt, 1983), which articulated the salient elements of professional practice as follows:

- Autonomy
- Control over practice
- Collaborative relationships with physicians

The MGH model builds on that foundation and incorporates findings from current research on organizational behavior, descriptive theory models, teamwork, and importance of a narrative culture. Each of these elements is a component of the practice of nursing at the MGH across care settings.

Initial Professional Practice Model (1996): Vision and Values

In 1996, the initial model of professional practice at the MGH was framed by a well-articulated patient- and family-focused vision (see Figure 2.1). The unique contributions of each of the professional disciplines and support staff in collaboration with nursing brought special meaning to the relationships that were defined in the initial model, always keeping the patient at the forefront.

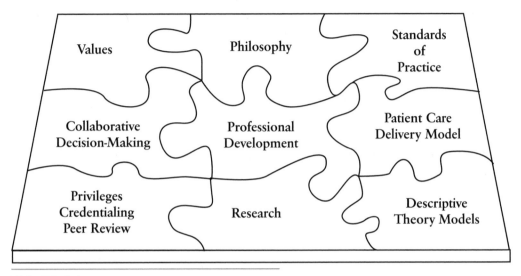

FIGURE 2.1

The MGH Professional Practice Model, 1996.

The vision acknowledging that the primary focus of the model was the patient, however, stressed the importance of preserving the integrity of the relationship between the patient and clinician as a key element for success. The vision clearly demonstrated the need for action in creating a practice environment that did not have insurmountable barriers, was built on a spirit of inquiry, and reflected a culturally competent workforce supportive of the family-focused values of the institution in practice outcomes.

Inspired by this vision, nursing leaders at the MGH launched new committees and initiatives in the late 1990s to publicly describe and exemplify the practice of nursing. This initiative helped to form an initial master plan for nursing focused on practice, organizational effectiveness, and collaborative decision-making.

A clearly articulated set of values supported decision-making and highlighted expressions in policies, practices, and norms of behavior. The development of a professional practice model enhanced and supported the values that leadership and staff followed and was a milestone for the initial journey to Magnet designation.

These values make up the components of the professional practice model:

- Philosophy
- Standards of practice
- Collaborative decision-making
- Professional development
- Patient care delivery model
- Privileging, credentialing, and peer review
- Research
- Theory-based practice

We describe each of these components in detail in the following sections.

Philosophy

A **philosophy statement** is derived from the values, principles, and beliefs that support the individualized contributions of each discipline. Philosophy meant many things within this particular model at the MGH. It was discipline-specific and cited what each discipline believed in and what contributions the professionals wish to contribute to the whole. At the MGH, the philosophy of nursing focused on patient care, education, research, and contributions of nurses to promote the quality and safety agenda.

Standards of Practice

Standards are the practical application of values and philosophy. Standards of practice exist to ensure that the highest quality of care is maintained regardless of the professional providing the care or the experience level of those professionals. In a professional practice model, standards of practice support the "learner" or novice nurse as well as the experienced provider. For a provider lacking clinical mastery skills, standards of practice provide a structure on which to base and build practice and decision-making.

Standards serve as teaching tools by providing guidance in situations in which the provider may not be experienced. By serving as a teaching tool, standards of practice establish a level of expectation about care delivery and patient safety within an organization. Understanding the unique clinical needs of each patient and situation and appreciating the principles of critical thinking in applying standards are imperative to providing individualized, high-quality care. The ability to integrate clinical knowledge and standards of practice within a professional practice model is a competency common to experienced professionals.

Collaborative Decision-Making

Collaborative governance is another component of a professional practice model. **Collaborative governance** is the decision-making process that places the authority, responsibility, and accountability for patient care with the practicing clinician. It is intended to empower professionals to control their own practice and create an opportunity to look at the contributions of each discipline and integrate them into the patient care delivery system. Collaborative governance should be a celebration of each discipline's contribution and is intended to support the staff in the elevation of practice to a more complex level. To ensure that collaborative governance is a success, the practice model framework should address a commitment of dedicated support. Examples of support include learning coaches for staff chairpersons, secretarial support for the teams, and resources within the literature.

Collaborative decision-making is built on the premises of teamwork and team learning. The network of relationships between people who come together under a practice model structure can create strong bonds. Some of the most effective groups and teams at the MGH matured to a point where these groups and teams shared collaborative and interdependent relationships on multiple levels and within diverse practice settings. Members of these teams often described a sense of "feeling like we're making a difference."

Professional Development

As the health care environment evolves and changes, professional development activities take on increasing importance in ensuring that nurses provide quality care as well as in providing a mechanism to attract and retain excellent clinicians. **Professional development** within a professional practice model supports the enhancement of leadership competencies as well as provides avenues for growth and career progression for nurses at all levels.

Outcomes of professional development include mentoring, teaching, generating publications, conducting research and scholarly activities, as well as exemplifying patient care and family support. The context of professional development provides a framework for collaboration with nursing faculty colleagues in designing creative models for teaching, including a dedicated education unit where hospital nursing staff work with students and faculty to trial and monitor interventions supported by evidence-based practice and innovation.

Patient Care Delivery Model

Design and definition of the care delivery model is one aspect of the professional practice model. The best care delivery model included in the optimal design promotes the highest quality while being cost effective and patient-centric. Nurses need to acknowledge that the health care world is changing but that their contributions will always be needed. The model for patient care delivery exemplifies the outcomes of the various components of the professional practice model because they are joined together in a way that can be described and replicated.

Privileging, Credentialing, and Peer Review

Another part of the professional practice model, **privileging** and **credentialing** processes, ensures that patients and their families received quality care from competent nurses in all settings. The public trusts that there is a mechanism in place that ensures that all nurses have the appropriate credentials. In addition to ensuring that the basics of licensure, certification, competency-based orientation, and training are in place, nurses should be encouraged to develop a professional portfolio. Nurses can use this portfolio when they represent their institutions externally or pursue advancement internally. Clinical narratives or exemplars are a key component of these portfolios at the MGH.

Peer review is an important component of privileging as well. This process supports autonomy and accountability for nursing practice within the organization. Through peer review, staff members have the opportunity as well as the responsibility to support each team member in improving both individual and organizational performance. An effective system of peer review and privileging within a professional practice model should ensure that the patient and their family members receive excellent care from competent providers.

Research

At the MGH, the practice model is based on knowledge, experience, tradition, intuition, and research. The implementation and support of evidence-based practice require a setting that promotes the acquisition and application of knowledge, provides access to new scientific knowledge, and fosters the ability of clinicians to use knowledge to affect patient outcomes.

Research is the bridge that translates academic knowledge and theory into clinical practice. Research dictates that evidence is a necessary prerequisite for the establishment of clinical practice, thus building the practice model. The goals of clinical researchers are to identify an issue of significant concern to the discipline of nursing and develop a substantial body of information related to that clinical phenomenon, which is scientifically vigorous and relevant.

Research-based practice within a practice model creates a spirit of inquiry that consistently challenges critical thinking of nurses at all levels. Translating the questions generated at the bedside into formal scientific hypotheses is a part of the continuum of professional development. Research must become an integral aspect of clinical practice as health care professions proceed from novice to expert. These research efforts define a systematic body of knowledge that guides professional clinical practice.

Theory-Based Practice

The challenges of the current practice environment present an opportunity to reflect on our **practice**, to articulate the "whys" of what we do. Understanding the philosophic, structural, and theoretical foundation of practice is an important component of professional development and the overall change processes that need to be taken to ensure that the practice environment is effective. As nurses develop into individual practitioners and collaborative colleagues, they find it exciting to share, explore, and challenge the theoretical perspectives used in the delivery of patient care.

The Revised Professional Practice Model (2006)

Ten years after the articulation and implementation of the initial professional practice model at the MGH, nurse leaders critically reviewed the model of professional practice and identified that updates were indicated to meet the current demands of health care delivery (see Figure 2.2). Updates to the professional practice model framework are described in the following sections.

Narrative Culture

The creation of a narrative culture has been transformational at the MGH. Over time, clinical narratives have become part of the fabric of professional life in the organization. Narratives are part of the application process for the clinical advancement program, awards, and annual performance review.

Clinical narratives have been introduced as an effective vehicle to share and reflect on clinical practice. Benner (1984) cites that, "narrative accounts of practice reveal the clinical reasoning and knowledge that comes from experiential learning. Clinical narratives have been reported to help the practitioner in understanding their practice, including strengths and impediments, and to see and share the clinical knowledge of peers."

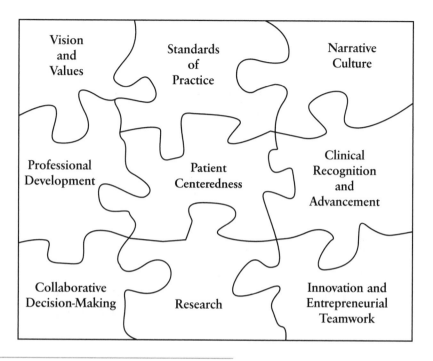

FIGURE 2.2

The MGH Professional Practice Model, 2006.

Although putting pen to paper allows clinicians to see their practice in a different light, it is also a springboard for dialogue with colleagues and clinical experts. Through the very important process of dialogue, and thus communication, clinicians are asking questions that prompt them to delve deeper into their thinking and motivation.

Clinicians might ask themselves the following questions:

- What were my concerns about this patient in this situation?

- How was this situation similar to situations I have experienced in the past?

- How was it different?

- What did I learn?

These questions allow clinicians to enter into the clinical situation from a different perspective, see it in a different way, and, perhaps, identify different interventions and strategies.

Clinical narratives can be difficult to read when they do not describe what is considered to be "perfect practice." At the MGH, it has been found that those are the narratives one needs to write and talk about because they describe the realities of care and the environment in which care is being provided. The practice model has evolved to be open to all stories and the dialogue that follows, thus creating and sustaining the highest quality of care.

Clinical Recognition and Advancement

Clinical recognition and advancement have been found to be effective retention tools within our organization. The Clinical Recognition Program at MGH developed as clinicians reviewed narratives written by other clinicians; they identified themes and criteria, which applied to the following six disciplines:

- Nursing
- Physical therapy
- Occupational therapy
- Respiratory care
- Speech-language pathology
- Social work

Themes including the clinician-patient relationship, effective patterns of clinical decision-making, teamwork, and collaboration emerged. In narratives, clinicians spoke of advocacy and clinical risk taking and on how these constructs influenced clinical practice at the MGH. Analysis of these themes helped establish a set of professional behaviors and attributes that act as developmental milestones, which have now been implemented as a component of the professional practice model.

The theoretical foundation of the Clinical Recognition Program is the Dreyfus Model of Skill Acquisition. Developed by Dreyfus and Dreyfus (1986), this model described how, in the acquisition and development of a particular skill, individuals pass through the five stages: novice, advanced beginner, competent, proficient, and expert. The word *stage* is crucial as it relates to the recognition program at the MGH because it reinforces the idea that clinicians must master each stage or level of development before progressing to the next.

Central to the Clinical Recognition Program is the reflective process, which allows individuals to incorporate theory with practice, shaping clinical practice over time. This process helps individuals understand their experience and integrate information in a meaningful way. Reflective practitioners committed to lifelong learning have enabled us to advance and sustain excellence in patient care.

Innovation and Entrepreneurial Teamwork

Innovation and entrepreneurial teamwork are critical to the creation of a professional practice environment that embraces change. As nurses and health care clinicians, we need to innovate and make certain that the delivery of patient care and structures that support it change to meet the changing populations we serve. Several key assumptions guide the work at the MGH with regard to innovation:

- Our employees are our biggest assets.

- Innovation takes great leaders.

- Imagination is necessary and fun for innovation to occur.

- Collaborative decision-making is a core value.

- A professional practice environment is the foundation on which we will build our future.

- Patient-centered care is the key.

Together, questions about beliefs, values, and traditions and how these will affect innovation are addressed. These clinicians must also address the designing of the ideal environment for innovation, the changes that need to occur for the success in regard to this ideal environment, and the best way to capture insights from practitioners at the bedside.

Patient Centeredness

Patient centeredness is the most critical piece of the revised professional practice model and is strategically placed in the center, touching all other components. The ability to efficiently and effectively care for patients and families requires the support of an array of resources, programs, and processes. At the MGH, the professional practice model now embraces the six pillars of quality and safety described by the Institute of Medicine (IOM) (2001):

1. **Safety:** We will work to ensure no needless death, injury, or suffering of patients and staff.

2. **Effectiveness:** Our care will be based on the best science, informed by patient values and preferences.

3. **Patient centeredness:** All care will honor the individual patient and the respective patients' choices, culture, social context, and specific needs.

4. **Timeliness:** We will waste no one's time and will create systems to eliminate unnecessary waiting.

5. **Efficiency:** We will remove all unnecessary processes or steps in a process and streamline all activities.

6. **Equity:** Our work will ensure equal access to all.

Evaluation of Our Professional Practice Model

Evaluation of the professional practice model is truly integrated into our practice environment; we use two methodologies, internal and external. Internally, we have administered our Staff Perceptions of the Professional Practice Environment Survey to nurses and clinicians across patient care services every 12 to 18 months since 1997. This tool:

- Provides an assessment of eight organizational characteristics (see Table 2.1) determined to be important to clinician satisfaction

- Allows clinicians the opportunity to participate in setting the strategic direction for patient care services

- Trends key information

- Provides feedback on strategic goals

- Identifies frequency, preparation, and access to resources in managing common patient problems

- Identifies opportunities to improve the environments for clinical practice (see Table 2.2)

TABLE 2.1: Patient Care Services, Organizational Characteristics, and Definitions

ORGANIZATIONAL CHARACTERISTIC	DEFINITION	SOURCE
Autonomy	The quality or state of being self-governing and exercising professional judgment in a timely fashion	Aiken, Sochalski & Lake, 1997
Clinician-MD Relations	Relations with physicians that facilitate exchange of important clinical information	Aiken, Sochalski & Lake, 1997
Control Over Practice	Sufficient intra-organizational status to influence others and to deploy resources when necessary for good patient care	Aiken, Havens & Sloan, 2000
Communication	The degree to which patient care information is related promptly to the people who need to be informed through open channels of communication	Shortell, Rousseau, Gillies, Devers & Simons, 1991
Teamwork/ Leadership	A conscious activity aimed at achieving unity of effort in the pursuit of shared objectives	Zimmerman et al., 1993

continues

TABLE 2.1: *continued*

ORGANIZATIONAL CHARACTERISTIC	DEFINITION	SOURCE
Conflict Management/ Handling Disagreements	The degree to which managing conflict is addressed using a problem-solving approach	Zimmerman et al., 1993
Internal Work Motivation	Self-generated motivation completely independent of external factors such as pay, supervision, and co-workers	Hackman & Oldham, 1976
Cultural Sensitivity	A set of attitudes, practices and/or policies that respects and accepts cultural differences	The Cross Cultural Health Care Program, 2000

TABLE 2.2: Patient Care Services Survey: Issues and Strategies

STAFF PERCEPTIONS SURVEY ISSUE (BY SURVEY YEAR)	INTERVENTIONS/OUTCOMES
Need for recognition of clinical work (1998)	The chief nurse charged the Professional Development Committee within Collaborative Governance with the responsibility to design an interdisciplinary clinical recognition program. The first-of-its-kind interdisciplinary clinical recognition program was implemented in 2002.
Requests for additional educational opportunities (1998)	The Center for Clinical & Professional Development was expanded to include orientation, training, and continuing education opportunities for clinical and support staff.
Concerns identified with supplies and linen (2000)	Established Materials Management/ Nursing Task Force.

STAFF PERCEPTIONS SURVEY ISSUE (BY SURVEY YEAR)	INTERVENTIONS/OUTCOMES
Need for more inservices on various cultures to deliver culturally competent care (2001)	The Culturally Competent Care Lecture Series was launched to augment the day-long culturally competent care curriculum offered. Developed unit/department culturally competent care resource manuals.
Request for increased nursing director availability (2001)	Nursing director span of control was analyzed and reduced where appropriate.
Need to enhance communication (2002)	Numerous communication strategies employed: made increased use of e-mail to improve communication; created the "Fielding the issues" column in departmental newsletter, *Caring Headlines*, to present timely information in a question-and-answer format.
Concerns identified regarding support from the Department of Food and Nutrition (2002-2003)	Food and Nutrition/Nursing Task Force established.
Request for assistance regarding public speaking and talking to the media (2004)	Launched media and public speaking programs through The Center for Clinical & Professional Development.
Request for conflict resolution skills training (2005–2006)	Developed workshops to present information/skills on working with a multigenerational workforce; on negotiation; and on preparing for, and actively engaging in, difficult conversations.
Need to identify strategies to support the aging nursing workforce (2006)	Conducted multi-site qualitative study designed to explore concerns of the aging nursing workforce. Hosted "coming of age" summit on November 15, 2007—a think tank regarding issues facing the aging nursing workforce.

continues

TABLE 2.2: *continued*

STAFF PERCEPTIONS SURVEY ISSUE (BY SURVEY YEAR)	INTERVENTIONS/OUTCOMES
Need to align work of Collaborative Governance Committee with emerging strategic issues (2008)	Redesigned Collaborative Governance Committee communication and decision-making structure to align with strategic goals.
Need to develop tools to facilitate nurse leader's ability to correlate key data, e.g., nurse-sensitive indicators, patient and staff satisfaction data, etc. (2010)	Developed a relational crosswalk of core measures to provide "at-a-glance" information about unit/department-based metrics.

This psychometrically sound tool has been implemented locally, nationally, and internationally (Ives Erickson et al., 2004; Ives Erickson, Duffy, Ditomassi & Jones, 2009).

Externally, MGH applied for Magnet recognition to validate that we have a strong professional practice model. Magnet recognition by the American Nurses Credentialing Center (ANCC) is the highest honor awarded to health care institutions for excellence in nursing services. Grounded in research, this intensive review is the ultimate confirmation that a supportive professional practice model and environment is thriving within an organization.

The updated Magnet recognition model (ANCC, 2008) is comprised of five elements:

- Transformational leadership

- Structural empowerment

- Exemplary professional practice

- New knowledge innovations and improvement

- Empirical outcomes

The heightened focus on demonstrating the outcomes and effects of nurses' work challenges leaders within a Magnet organization to critically review and improve the structure and processes that support care delivery.

For Magnet-recognized organizations or for organizations on the journey to Magnet recognition, the staff perceptions of the Professional Practice Environment scale may be an effective tool to measure baseline and ongoing perceptions of clinicians' impressions of their professional practice model, which is aligned with the five model elements of Magnet recognition. Administration of the survey over time provides a greater understanding of opportunities to enhance clinical practice because outcomes are trended. At the MGH, this information has provided direction about the support structures that are necessary to hardwire the six aims of the Institute of Medicine into practice. At the MGH, the way we think about, organize, and deliver care is evolving as health care delivery and nursing practice are evolving.

Summary

Nursing is the most important discipline in connecting all the pieces of the new care delivery model. At the MGH, we feel that a refined professional practice model is one construct that enables our staff to continue the integration and continued growth of theory as an essential element of practice. For any professional practice model to be effective, nursing leaders must understand, embrace, and master the skills involved in setting up the structure and then leading others through resources and support to achieve the desired state of practice. This practice is a journey nurses and other members of the health care team must take together to chart the future of health care and care delivery.

References

Aiken, L., Havens, D., & Sloane, D. (2000). The Magnet Nursing Services Recognition Program: A comparison of two groups of Magnet hospitals. *American Journal of Nursing, 100*(3), 26-36.

Aiken, L., Sochalski, J., & Lake, E. (1997). Studying outcomes of organizational change in health services. *Medical Care, 35*(Suppl. 11), NS6-18.

American Nurses Credentialing Center (ANCC). (2008). *Announcing a new model for ANCC's Magnet recognition program.* Retrieved from http://cms.nursecredentialing.org/Magnet/NewMagnetModel.aspx

Benner, P. (1984). *From novice to expert: Excellence and power in clinical nursing practice*. Menlo Park, CA: Addison Wesley.

The Cross Cultural Health Program. *Introduction to culture competence*. Retrieved from http://www. xculture.org

Dreyfus, H. L., & Dreyfus, S. E. (1986). Five steps from novice to expert. In *Mind Over Machine* (pp. 16-51). New York, NY: Free Press.

Hackman, J., & Oldham, G. (1976). Motivation through the design of work: Test of a theory. *Organizational Behavior and Human Performance, 16*(2), 250-279.

Institute of Medicine (IOM). (2001). *Crossing the quality chasm: A new health system for the 21st century*. Washington, DC: National Academy Press.

Ives Erickson, J., Duffy, M. E., Ditomassi, M., & Jones, D. (2009). Psychometric evaluation of the revised professional practice environment (RPPE) scale. *Journal of Nursing Administration, 39*(5), 236-243.

Ives Erickson, J., Duffy, M., Gibbons, M., Fitzmaurice, J., Ditomassi, M., & Jones, D. (2004). Development and psychometric evaluation of the professional practice environment (PPE) scale. *Journal of Nursing Scholarship, 36*(3), 279-285.

McClure, M. L., Poulin, M. A., Sovie, M. D., & Wandelt, M. (1983). *Magnet hospitals: Attraction and retention of professional nurses*. Washington, DC: American Nurses Publishing.

Shortell, S. M., Rousseau, D. M., Gillies, R. R., Devers, K. J., & Simons, T. L. (1991). Organizational assessment in intensive care units (ICUs): Construct development, reliability, and validity of the ICU nurse-physician questionnaire. *Medical Care, 29*(8), 703-723.

Zimmerman, J. E., Shortell, S. M., Rousseau, D. M., Duffy, J., Gillies, R. R., Knaus, W. A., … Draper, E. A. (1993). Improving intensive care: Observations based on organizational case studies in nine intensive care units: A prospective, multicenter study. *Critical Care Medicine, 21*(20), 1554-1551.

Chapter 3

Creating Empowering Work Environments to Promote Professional Nursing Practice

Heather K. Spence Laschinger, RN, PhD, FAAN, FCAHS

Ashley L. Grau, MSc

Professional practice models are systems that "support registered nurse control over the delivery of nursing care and the environment in which care is delivered."

(Hoffart & Woods, 1996, p.354)

Introduction

In its report *To Err Is Human: Building a Safer Health System*, the Institute of Medicine (IOM, 2001) estimated that as many as 98,000 hospitalized Americans die each year not as a result of their illness or disease, but as a result of errors in their care. Similar results were found in Canada (Baker et al., 2004). Nurses, representing approximately 54% of all health care workers in the United States (IOM, 2004), have been identified as a critical resource for reducing these types of errors given their around-the-clock responsibilities for patient care.

Indeed, a study of medication errors in two hospitals over a 6-month period found that nurses were responsible for 86% of all interceptions of medication errors made by physicians, pharmacists, and others involved in providing medications for patients before the error reached the patient (Leape et al., 1995). This finding highlights the importance of ensuring that the required conditions are in place to support excellent professional nursing practice, and that nurses have the autonomy to make clinical decisions and act on behalf of their patients to their full scope of practice.

Supportive professional nursing practice environments are facilitated by empowering workplaces that provide nurses with control over both the *content* and *context* of nursing practice (Laschinger & Havens, 1996; Manojlovich, 2007). While empowerment research in nursing has largely focused on empowering providers of care (nurses), ongoing health care reforms have demanded increased efficiency in already resource-constrained environments, generating attention for models focusing on empowering consumers of care (patients). Segal (1998) suggests that empowered patients require the "confidence and competence to act on the information and a capacity to influence the services they access. This requires an understanding of their own health, of the available service options and acceptance of responsibility for decisions about their own health care." (p. 37) Nurses are a key resource for patient empowerment, and it is reasonable to expect that empowered nurses practicing to their full scope would be best positioned to empower patients for optimal health outcomes.

This chapter begins by outlining theory and research demonstrating the importance of professional nursing practice to nurse and patient outcomes. We then examine the value of creating empowering work environments that support professional nursing practice and theoretical models testing these propositions.

Finally, we finish with a review of strategies that nurses can implement to empower their patients for successful and sustainable patient outcomes.

Professional Practice Models and the Environment

Professional nursing practice models proliferated in the 1980s in clinical settings to create an infrastructure to facilitate professional nursing practice. Development of these models took on greater importance following massive hospital restructuring initiatives in the 1990s, during which program management models resulted in the disappearance of distinct nursing departments in hospital settings. The lack of a distinct nursing department within organizations forced nursing to more clearly articulate the role of professional nursing practice within the patient care delivery system and to create structures to ensure that clinical decision-making and nursing governance were visible within the organization. (An illustration of a professional practice model is described in Chapter 2, "Professional Practice Model: Strategies for Translating Models into Practice.")

The work of Kramer and Schmalenberg (1988a, 1988b) and McClure, Poulin, Sovie, and Wandelt (1983) in the 1980s describing "Magnet hospital" work environment characteristics in the United States has informed much of the theory and research on effective professional practice environments. The Magnet Model (ANCC, 2008) assumes that positive outcomes will follow:

- Transformational leadership practices

- Structurally empowered work environments

- Exemplary professional practice

- New knowledge, innovations, and improvements in nursing care

Hospitals with Magnet status meet a set of criteria designed to measure the strength and quality of nursing practice environments and when in place have demonstrated the ability to attract and retain talented nurses through increased nurse retention and satisfaction and decreased burnout and turnover (Aiken, Sochalski & Lake, 1997; Lacey et al., 2007; Laschinger, Finegan, Shamian & Wilk, 2004; Upenieks, 2003a, 2003b). These hospitals also have higher rates of patient care quality, safety, and satisfaction (Aiken et al., 1997; Aiken, Smith & Lake, 1994; Armstrong & Laschinger, 2006; Clarke, Sloane & Aiken, 2002; Havens & Aiken, 1999; Laschinger & Leiter, 2006; Neisner & Raymond, 2002; Rosenberg, 2009).

A major outcome of this body of research was the widespread adoption of the Magnet Hospital model as a standard of excellence for professional practice environments in nursing. As a result many hospitals aspire to Magnet Hospital status through the American Nurses Credentialing Center (ANCC) Magnet Recognition Program. Most professional practice models in use today include concepts similar to those described in the Magnet model (Ives Erickson & Ditomassi, 2011). One model integrating theory and research from both nursing and the management literature to describe workplace conditions that support professional practice is the Nursing Worklife Model proposed by Leiter and Laschinger (2006) and further developed by Laschinger and colleagues (2004).

Nursing Worklife Model

The Nursing Worklife Model (NWM), originally described by Leiter and Laschinger (2006), is a framework derived from the Magnet hospital research describing work environments that support professional nursing practice and influence nurse and patient outcomes. In this model, five worklife factors identified by Lake (2002) as characteristics of effective professional nursing practice environments interact with each other to affect nurse and patient outcomes. The five worklife factors are as follows:

1. Effective nursing leadership

2. Staff participation in organizational affairs/policy

3. Adequate staffing resources for quality care

4. Support for a nursing (versus medical) model of patient care

5. Effective nurse/physician relationships

The pattern of relationships among Lake's five qualities of professional nursing work environments forms the basis of the NWM (see Figure 3.1 on the next page). Leadership is the starting point, with direct paths to (or influence on) staffing/resource adequacy and policy involvement, as well as the quality of nurse/physician relationships. Both policy involvement and nurse/physician relationships influence the extent to which a nursing model of care (in contrast to a medical model) is emphasized in the delivery of nursing care, which in turn influences perceived staffing/resource adequacy, and ultimately nurse and patient outcomes.

In the initial examination of the NWM (Leiter & Laschinger, 2006), the relationship among these factors and their link to outcomes focused on nurse burnout. In this study, Leiter and Laschinger (2006) found support for the proposed interrelationships among these factors in a large sample of Canadian nurses. Nursing leadership was found to be the driving force of the model, strongly influencing the other professional practice environment factors, which in turn influenced the degree of burnout. In further analysis, Laschinger and Leiter (2006) expanded the model by linking professional practice characteristics to nurse-assessed adverse events. They found that burnout played a mediating role in this relationship. The results suggest that qualities of the work environment influence adverse events to the extent that they contribute to feelings of exhaustion, cynicism, and personal efficacy.

Manojlovich and Laschinger (2007) extended the model to demonstrate the role of structural empowerment in promoting supportive professional practice environments and subsequent outcomes, specifically nurses' job satisfaction. In their study, nurses who reported higher levels of structural empowerment (access to support, resources, information, and opportunities to learn and grow) were more likely to report better leadership on their units and greater access to elements of support for professional practice in their work environments. The

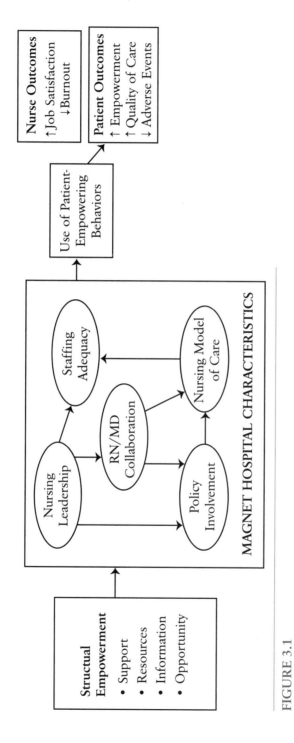

FIGURE 3.1

The Expanded Nursing Worklife Model.

pattern of relationships among Lake's five factors was replicated in this study, providing further empirical support for the original NWM. Laschinger (2008) further replicated and extended these findings in a Canadian sample by linking structural empowerment and professional practice characteristics to both job satisfaction and nurse-assessed patient care quality.

These findings highlight the importance of empowerment in creating supportive professional practice environments through its influence on the leadership component of the NWM. Thus, structural empowerment can be seen as an important precursor to the process of creating supportive professional practice environments. Kanter's theory of structural power in the organization (Kanter 1977, 1993) offers an actionable approach to creating work environments that empower nurses to accomplish their work in meaningful ways. This model has been tested extensively in the nursing population, and numerous studies have linked structural empowerment to the extent to which nurses perceive their work environments to be supportive of professional nursing practice (Laschinger, Almost & Tuer-Hodes, 2003; Manojlovich & Laschinger, 2007; Ives Erickson, Duffy, Ditomassi & Jones, 2009). Kanter's model is described in detail in the following section.

Structural Empowerment

Kanter's (1977, 1993) theory of structural empowerment is grounded in the notion of *power*, not as a form of domination, but as the ability to get things done. Any organization has a limited quantity of power. Thus, when power is monopolized by the few, the many are left *powerless*, preventing them from being able to act effectively. However, when this power is shared and the many become *empowered*, the system becomes more effective and more gets accomplished.

Power is a dynamic structure created through formal and informal systems within the organization. *Formal* power results from positions that are visible, flexible, and central to the organization, whereas *informal* power is acquired through connections inside and outside the organization, such as relationships with sponsors, peers, and other coworkers. These types of power facilitate access to four empowerment structures within the workplace:

1. Opportunities to learn and grow

2. Information

3. Support

4. Resources required for the job

Kanter suggests that managers are essential in developing empowering conditions and providing employees with access to these structures.

Empowering Conditions of Structural Empowerment

Access to *opportunity* provides individuals with the chance to advance within the organization and to develop their knowledge and skills. Access to *information* refers to the knowledge that is necessary to carry out job activities in a meaningful way, which includes technical knowledge and expertise related to the core roles of employees and information concerning what is going on in the larger organization. Access to *resources* is having the ability to obtain the materials, money, and rewards necessary for achieving job demands and having sufficient time to accomplish work. Access to *support* relates to sources that function in a way to maximize effectiveness, such as positive feedback from superiors in an organization.

Structural empowerment has been linked to supportive professional practice environments in several studies (Laschinger et al., 2003; Manojlovich & Laschinger, 2007). Furthermore, when nurses work in environments that are structurally empowering and supportive of professional practice they have been shown to have higher job satisfaction (Laschinger et al., 2003) and lower turnover intentions (Lavoie-Tremblay, Paquet, Marchionni & Drevniok, 2011; Nedd, 2006). Further studies have shown that structural empowerment is strongly related to nurses' autonomy (Sabiston & Laschinger, 1995) and control over their practice environment (Laschinger & Havens, 1996, 1997; Manojlovich, 2005). These findings provide empirical links between empowerment and key elements of professional nursing practice. (Refer to Chapter 13, "Mastering the Hospital Work Environment: Development,

Validation, and Revision of the Professional Practice Environment Scale." Chapter 13 provides an in-depth discussion of the Revised Professional Practice Environment [RPPE] scale, which has been designed to measure these linkages.)

Leadership and Structural Empowerment

Nursing leaders are instrumental in creating structurally empowering workplace conditions for their employees. Indeed, strong leadership has been shown to be a predictor of staff nurses' perceptions of structural empowerment on their units (Laschinger, Finegan & Wilk, 2009, 2011). Structural empowerment has also been linked to

- The five leader empowering behaviors described in Thomas and Velthouse's (1990) leadership model (Conger & Kanungo, 1988; Greco, Laschinger, & Wong, 2006; Laschinger, Wong, McMahon & Kaufmann, 1999)

- Perceptions of manager emotional intelligence (Lucas, Laschinger & Wong, 2008; Young-Ritchie, Laschinger & Wong, 2009)

- Authentic leadership (Wong & Laschinger, 2011)

- Transformational leadership styles (Laschinger, Wong & Grau, 2012)

Empirical support for the influence of leadership on structural empowerment and research linking empowerment to the leadership component of the nursing work–life model suggest a reciprocal relationship between leadership and empowerment.

Finally, Abdelrazek et al. (2010) found a link between frontline managers' structural empowerment and their supervisors'/senior nurse leaders' leadership characteristics (interpersonal skills, achievement orientation, and political savvy) in their study of Swedish and Egyptian nurses. These findings remind us that for managers to be effective in empowering their staff, they themselves need to be empowered. Health care organizations should provide nursing leaders with resources that enable them to redesign nursing work environments and care processes to optimize professional nursing practice, which in turn, will reduce the likelihood of medical errors (IOM, 2004). Armstrong and Laschinger (2006) and Armstrong, Laschinger, and Wong (2009) showed that nurses felt more empowered in work environments with positive patient safety cultures. Armellino, Griffin, and Fitzpatrick (2010) found a similar relationship in a study of 257 nurses in a large tertiary hospital in the United States. These findings— together with research linking structural empowerment to positive professional practice environments and nurse care quality—make the case for supporting efforts to create empowering nursing practice environments.

Empowering Nurses: Implications for Nursing Administrators

Management strategies for empowering nurses and improving their access to the empowerment structures have been described in the literature (Laschinger, Gilbert, Smith & Leslie, 2010; Laschinger & Shamian, 1994). See Table 3.1. Though these theory-derived strategies have been informally validated in focus group discussions with practicing nurses and managers, large systematic intervention studies to validate these strategies in actual work settings are rare.

TABLE 3.1: Nurse-Empowering Behaviors

COMPONENT OF KANTER'S THEORY	EXAMPLES OF NURSE-EMPOWERING MANAGEMENT BEHAVIORS
Access to Information	Practice open communication
	Share information
	Communicate goals of management
	Communicate current and proposed future state of the organization
	Provide timely information
	Communicate using various means (e.g., e-mail, websites, online newsletters)

COMPONENT OF KANTER'S THEORY	EXAMPLES OF NURSE-EMPOWERING MANAGEMENT BEHAVIORS
Access to Support	Adopt an interactive, coaching, and facilitating leadership style
	Provide specific, timely feedback
	Provide recognition and applaud achievements
	Encourage autonomy
	Encourage collaboration and collegiality among staff
	Provide support
	Provide links to helpful people when needed
Access to Resources	Assure adequate time and resources to accomplish work
	Assure supplies are accessible and responsibly used
	Involve nurses in evaluation of supplies to assure quality
	Develop a plan for equipment replacement and preventive maintenance strategies
	Develop proposals to obtain funding for new equipment and equipment sharing
	Promote staff involvement in resource decisions
	Encourage interpretation of workload data as a necessary part of decision-making
Access to Opportunity to Learn and Grow	Encourage/facilitate advanced educational preparation
	Participate in training and development sessions
	Request secondment or job exchange to expand skills
	Negotiate expanded role/function in current job
	Add new challenges and developmental tasks
	Establish career ladders based on skill rather than status
	Participate in special task forces or important organizational committees

continues

TABLE 3.1: *continued*

COMPONENT OF KANTER'S THEORY	EXAMPLES OF NURSE-EMPOWERING MANAGEMENT BEHAVIORS
Informal Power	Provide opportunities to network with colleagues through task forces, work groups
	Build networking skills initially at the unit level through team-building exercises
	Broaden networking to include agency-wide and extra-organizational contacts
	Develop interdisciplinary networking opportunities
	Encourage collegiality
Formal Power	Increase recognition of the staff nurse role as central and relevant
	Develop a comprehensive job analysis of professional nursing practice
	Define outcomes of nursing practice and align with organizational goals
	Encourage nurses to positively view their contribution to patient care and education
	Provide opportunities for nurses to showcase their skills
	Provide opportunities to develop skills
	Promote participative management and autonomous work units

One exception is a recent a study from Laschinger, Leiter, Day, Gilin-Oore, and Mackinnon (in press), demonstrating the effectiveness of a unit-based workplace civility intervention on improving perceived access to components of structural empowerment, particularly access to support, post intervention in comparison to a control group. To our knowledge this is the first study to demonstrate the ability of a focused intervention to make a change in structural empowerment.

Empowering Patients: Structural Empowerment and Practice Environments

Building on more than a decade of research on the importance of structural empowerment in creating supportive professional practice environments, Laschinger et al. (2010) expanded the empowerment model to include patient empowerment. They reasoned that empowered nurses would be more likely to use patient-empowering behaviors, which in turn would result in greater patient empowerment and subsequently better health outcomes.

Evidence for the influence of patient empowerment on health outcomes has been demonstrated across a range of health problems in both chronic and acute settings. Patient empowerment strategies have been shown to improve chronic pain management (Helme et al., 1996) and improve self-care and health outcomes in diabetes patients (Cox, Gonder-Fredrick, Julian & Clark, 1994; Hanefeld et al., 1991; Mazzuca et al., 1986). A recent study from Bartlett and Coulson (2011) found that online empowerment strategies significantly predicted patients' feelings of being informed, increased confidence with their physician, acceptance of their illness, confidence in their treatment, optimism and hope for the future, and enhanced self-esteem and social well-being. Segal (1998) explains that clients experience enhanced well-being when they feel supported and encouraged to accept responsibility for their own health outcomes and are given a role in decisions about their treatment plan because of an improved sense of control and self-care practices and an increased use of a variety of health services.

Nurses spend more time with patients than any other health care provider, making them the most viable source of patient empowerment in current health care environments. Nurses must themselves receive the support and resources required to commit to patient empowerment strategies, reinforcing the important role of strong nursing leadership. The following section details numerous strategies nurses can use to improve patient access to sources of empowerment within their own environments. See Table 3.2.

TABLE 3.2: Patient-Empowering Behaviors

COMPONENT OF KANTER'S THEORY	EXAMPLES OF PATIENT-EMPOWERING NURSE BEHAVIORS
Access to Information	Provide relevant information coupled with clear answers to patient questions
	Conduct nursing tasks only after explaining actions
	Dispense medications and treatments only after explaining what they entail
	Use information technology creatively
	Familiarize patients with their surroundings
Access to Support	Ascertain how patient beliefs, thoughts, and feelings might affect nursing efforts
	Ask what patients need to obtain from their interactions with health care providers
	Describe your caregiver role and support patients' right to be the decision-maker
	Respect patient choices
	Offer encouraging remarks for achieving specific health goals
	Address patient complaints and call bell triggers quickly
	Work quietly at night to allow patients to rest
	Provide a supportive environment by assuming a partnership approach
Access to Resources	Facilitate access to clinical and community resources
	Facilitate patients' access to interdisciplinary team members
	Help patients identify their own resources, self-care abilities, and internal strengths
	Create patient-centered practices that incorporate self-management support
	Provide patients with time necessary to accomplish personal activities (e.g., personal hygiene, eating, etc.)

COMPONENT OF KANTER'S THEORY	EXAMPLES OF PATIENT-EMPOWERING NURSE BEHAVIORS
Access to Opportunities to Learn and Grow	Provide learning opportunities at appropriate level (jargon free)
	Provide scenarios to create opportunities to practice new skills
	Help patients to use knowledge and skills to manage their own health problems
	Supplement self-management support for patients with information technology
Informal Power	Establish partnerships with families
	Promote strong alliances between patients and members of the health care team
	Develop strong relationships with family and friends in the community
	Work with patients to identify strategies for developing supportive alliances
	View patients as important allies in the health-producing process
Formal Power	Adopt a flexible approach to managing care that fosters self determination
	Negotiate a mutually agreeable schedule
	Encourage patients to make decisions about care
	Acknowledge that more than one way to accomplish mutually defined goals exists
	Allow patients to decide when to eat and drink and what activities to engage in
	Refrain from using dominant postures or talking down to patients during visits
	Attend to patients only with permission
	Be visible and available to respond to patient needs

The professional practice model is designed to foster patient-centered care and facilitate a practice environment where nurses come to know their patients and provide the needed resources and knowledge to facilitate their control over health and illness. The nurses' awareness of principles and strategies to enhance patient empowerment impacts on nurse and patient satisfaction with care outcomes.

Patient-Empowering Behaviors

Empowering nurses to empower their patients can help facilitate a healing space that enables nurses to fulfill the physical, emotional, and spiritual healing needs of their patients. When the organization and nursing administration work together to create healing environments, both nurses and their patients benefit. Nursing environments that support nurses in their work with patients result in satisfied engaged nurses who are better able to provide a high quality of care based on their knowledge and expertise. Consequently, patient care is enhanced, resulting in greater nurse and patient satisfaction. In this section we describe nurse-patient interactions that exemplify how Kanter's (1977; 1993) empowerment theory might be translated to the patient care process, as originally described by Laschinger et al., (2010). We begin this section with a discussion of informal and formal power.

Informal Power

Informal power develops out of supportive relationships and an individual's network of alliances. This kind of power can be fostered in patients when nurses support the development of relationships between patients and members of their health care team as well as other professionals in their community. Positive working relationships between the patient and their health care professionals can lead to quick access to care when needed (Thorne, 2006). Furthermore, strong associations with family and friends in the patient's own community will lead to more informal support of daily resources for the management of health care issues.

The role of the nurse in developing and identifying strategies to develop these informal supportive alliances is an important empowering behavior of health care professionals (Funnell & Anderson, 2004). Furthermore, because the nurse/patient relationship is inherently collaborative, nurses must view patients as important allies in the health producing process (McWilliam et al., 1997; Paterson 2001).

Formal Power

In Kanter's model (1977, 1993), formal power is acquired through the high visibility, relevance, and flexibility of one's jobs activities (Brown & Kanter, 1982). Nurses who are able to take a flexible approach with their patients' management of care, compared to imposing a rigid schedule on their activities, can promote empowerment. By allowing patients to initiate and perform chosen activities, encouraging patients to make decisions about their care, and responding promptly to patients' needs, nurses can begin to shift the focus of power to the patient (Aujoulat, d'Hoore & Deccache, 2007; McWilliam et al., 1997).

Yet, many nurses struggle with the process of integrating patient-empowering skills into their care. McWilliam, Ward-Griffin, Sweetland, Sutherland, and O'Halloran (2001) found that when nurses concentrate on the daily routine of nursing care, opportunities to implement empowerment strategies are often neglected, negatively affecting patient feelings of autonomy and self-determination (Aujoulat et al., 2007). Faulkner (2001) suggests simple acts such as refraining from using dominant physical postures or talking down to patients during interactions, which aid feelings of patient empowerment and autonomy over their own health. Formal power strategies for patients helps create a relationship where nurse and patient work collaboratively towards optimal quality of care.

Providing Access to Information

Nurses are well placed to collaborate with patients when they require additional information to address particular health problems. For example, patients might lack clinical knowledge that relates to an identified problem. By providing ongoing information about the costs and benefits of therapeutic and behavioral options, nurses can increase patient access to information as a source of empowerment. Central to providing health information is the patients' participation in identifying health knowledge gaps. According to Faulkner (2001), information that is relevant to a particular health concern, together with clear answers to questions, is an example of empowering nursing care.

Nurses working in clinical settings often provide care for patients unfamiliar with health care environments, which might result in feelings of powerlessness within the system. Virtanen, Leino-Kilpi, and Salantera (2007) suggest that powerlessness might be avoided by engaging in empowering discourse with the patient, which involves maintaining a mutual respect for each other's (the nurse's and patient's) current health knowledge and collaborating to create mutually satisfying health goals.

Further suggested by Faulkner is that nurses should work to familiarize their patients with their clinical surroundings and routines on first contact. Additionally, nurses should carry out care practices only after explaining why they are needed, which helps prevent patient perceptions of a power imbalance (Faulkner, 2001). A similar approach is suggested by McWilliam and colleagues (2001) for home-care settings, identifying the need for flexible, client-driven approaches to nursing care. Nurses in their qualitative study felt the home setting allowed them to respond to clients as individuals and provided appropriate needs-based health teaching to a greater degree than in the hospital setting (McWilliam et al., 2001).

Nurses might also be aware of other possible sources and means for patient access to health information (Pellino et al., 1998). For example, nurses can work to empower their patients by using information technology, such as providing access to reliable Internet websites or conducting consultations through confidential e-mail (Grol, 2001). Working with the patient to identify and access desired health information is a part of professional practice that supports patient-centered care and is consistent with Kanter's (1977, 1993) concept of access to information, a critical element for empowerment.

Providing Patients Access to Knowledge

Active patient participation in care planning is essential if patients are to gain new knowledge and skills in the management of their own health and well-being. A variety of strategies can be used to support this development. Funnell and Anderson (2004) suggest that organizations supplement self-management support for patients with information technology, such as decision-support algorithms, reliable online health information, electronic health records, and care plans. Exploring scenarios and/or role-playing with nurses can create opportunities to practice new skills, such as dealing with changes in health or stress.

Delivery of knowledge and expectations around self-care should be tailored to the patient's understanding and ability to perform skills. Unnecessary jargon should also be avoided. The inclusion of family members might be beneficial, because they can play a role in support and care provision. Building on existing knowledge and combining previously gained skills with new information can help strengthen family and patient self-efficacy in health management. Continued encouragement and support from health care providers along with the creation of partnerships with the patient and family are vital for lasting patient skill development and knowledge application (Funnell & Anderson, 2004).

Providing Access to Support

As health care professionals who provide the majority of hands-on patient care, nurses are invaluable for the support of patients and their families in the management of health and illness or injury. As a fundamental component of empowerment, access to support plays an important role in helping patients meet and maintain their health goals. Funnell and Anderson (2004) suggest that support can be provided, first, by listening to patient-identified fears and concerns; second, by determining the patient's beliefs, thoughts, and feelings that might hinder or support nurse efforts; and third, by asking about the patient's expectations of and needs from the health care provider. Nurses should ensure they clearly identify their role as a collaborator in the care process and acknowledge patients' rights to make their own decisions on care (Funnell & Anderson, 2004).

Nurses are key players in creating stronger support networks for patients (Leino-Kilpi, Maenpaa & Katajisto, 1999). Because of the intimate nature and numerous interactions required in the provision of patient care, nurses have the opportunity to initiate ongoing dialogue with patients and families. This communication allows for the exploration of sources of social and physical support currently in the patients' life, with the identification of any additional supports needed. In addition, nurses can support atmospheres conducive to health and healing by working to promptly address care needs and concerns, respecting patient choices, offering encouragement, and addressing learning needs for the achievement of specific health goals (Faulkner, 2001; Leino-Kilpi et al., 1999). These sources of support are similar to Kanter's (1977, 1993) component of access to support for accomplishing goals in different settings.

Providing Access to Resources

Comprehensive quality patient care includes nurses providing access to resources that address health problems or improve care for their patients. Introducing patients to alternative resources within their community as well as introducing patients to interdisciplinary team members to achieve optimal health is beneficial to the continuity of care. Ensuring patients have access to the resources necessary to achieve optimal health is consistent with Kanter's (1977, 1993) theory and is an essential element in the empowerment process.

Kanter's theory of empowerment suggests benefits of resources being available to patients and health care providers. The benefits to patients include better communication with providers, greater satisfaction with care, and improved physical and psychosocial outcomes and emotional well-being. The benefits to providers include achievement of recommended standards of care, improved outcomes, and greater professional satisfaction (Funnell & Anderson, 2004).

Another feature of access to resource is resource allocation, so that nurses allow patients the time necessary to accomplish personal activities on their own to provide a sense of autonomy and control (e.g., sufficient time for eating, dressing, etc.). Allowing patients extra time to achieve goals, enhances their overall sense of empowerment and control over their own care and facilitates decisions about the care that best fit their daily lives (Aujoulat et al., 2007). Building on patients' existing skills and personal resources might help nurses in assisting their patients in identifying resources, self-care abilities, and internal strengths.

Summary

Manojlovich (2007) points out that the key concepts articulated in Kramer and Schmalenburg's (1993) work on features of supportive professional practice environments are consistent with structural empowerment. This chapter has presented a discussion around the essential elements needed to enhance the nurse-patient environment of care. Several studies have shown that structural empowerment is associated with perceptions of support for professional nursing practice and, subsequently, positive nurse and patient outcomes. This research suggests that empowering work environments can have an important impact on professional nursing practice by strengthening practice environments that foster both nurse and patient empowerment, thereby ensuring high-quality, safe patient care in today's challenging health care settings.

References

Abdelrazek, F., Skytt, B., Aly, M., El-Sabour, M.A., Ibrahim, N., & Engstrom, M. (2010). Leadership and management skills of first-line managers of elderly care and their work environment. *Journal of Nursing Management, 18*(6), 736-745.

Aiken, L. H., Smith, H. L., & Lake, E. T. (1994). Lower Medicare mortality among a set of hospitals known for good nursing care. *Medical Care, 32*(8), 771-787.

Aiken, L. H., Sochalski, J., & Lake, E. T. (1997). Studying outcomes of organizational change in health services. *Medical Care, 35*(11), NS6-NS18.

American Nurses Credentialing Center (ANCC). (2008). Magnet recognition program new model. Retrieved from http://www.nursecredentialing.org/Documents/Magnet/NewModelBrochure.aspx

Armellino, D., Quinn Griffin, M. T., & Fitzpatrick, J. (2010). Structural empowerment and patient safety culture among registered nurses working in adult critical care units. *Journal of Nursing Management, 18*(7), 796-803.

Armstrong, K., & Laschinger, H. K. S. (2006). Structural empowerment, magnet hospital characteristics, and patient safety culture: Making the link. *Journal of Nursing Care Quality, 21*(2), 124-132.

Armstrong, K., Laschinger, H. K. S., & Wong, C. (2009). Workplace empowerment and magnet hospital characteristics as predictors of patient safety climate. *Journal of Nursing Care Quality, 24*(1), 55-62.

Aujoulat, I., d'Hoore, W., & Deccache, A. (2007). Patient empowerment in theory and practice: Polysemy or cacophony? *Patient Education and Counseling, 66*(1), 13-20.

Baker, G. R., Norton P. G., Flintoft, V., Blais, R., Brown, A., Cox, J., ... Tamblyn, R. (2004). The Canadian adverse events study: The incidence of adverse events among hospital patients in Canada. *Canadian Medical Association Journal, 170*(11), 1678-1686.

Bartlett, Y., & Coulson, N. (2011). An investigation into the empowerment effects of using online support groups and how this affects health professional/patient communication. *Patient Education and Counseling, 83*(1), 113-119.

Brown, J. C., & Kanter, R. M. (1982). Empowerment: Key to effectiveness. *Hospital Forum, 25*(3), 6-7, 9, 11-12.

Clarke, S. P., Sloane, D. M., & Aiken, L. H. (2002). Effects of hospital staffing and organizational climate on needlestick injuries to nurses. *American Journal of Public Health, 92*(7), 1115-1119.

Conger, J., & Kanungo, R. (1988). The empowerment process: Integrating theory and practice. *Academy of Management Review, 13*(3), 471-482.

Cox, D. J., Gonder-Frederick, L., Julian, D. M., & Clark, W. (1994). Long-term follow-up evaluation of blood glucose awareness training. *Diabetes Care, 17*(1), 1-5.

Faulkner, M. (2001). A measure of patient empowerment in hospital environments catering for older people. *Journal of Advanced Nursing 34*(5), 676-686.

Funnell, M. M., & Anderson, R. M. (2004). Empowerment and self-management of diabetes. *Clinical Diabetes, 22*(3), 123-127.

Greco, P., Laschinger, H. K. S., & Wong, C. (2006). Leader empowering behaviours, staff nurse empowerment and work engagement/burnout. *Nursing Leadership, 19*(4), 41-56.

Grol, R. (2001). Improving the quality of medical care: Building bridges among professional pride, payer profit, and patient satisfaction. *Journal of the American Medical Association, 286*(20), 2578-2585.

Hanefeld, M., Fischer, S., Schmechel, H., Rothe, G., Schulze, J., Dude, H., ... Julius, U. (1991). Diabetes intervention study: Multi-intervention trial in newly diagnosed NIDDM. *Diabetes Care, 14*(4), 308-317.

Havens, D. S., & Aiken, L. H. (1999). Shaping systems to promote desired outcomes: The magnet hospital model. *Journal of Nursing Administration, 29*(2), 14-20.

Helme, R. D., Katz, B., Gibson, S. J., Bradbeer, M., Farrell, M., Neufeld, M., & Corran, T. (1996). Multidisciplinary pain clinics for older people. Do they have a role? *Clinics in Geriatric Medicine, 12*(3), 563-582.

Hoffart, N., & Woods, C. Q. (1996). Elements of a nursing professional practice model. *Journal of Professional Nursing, 12*(6), 354-364.

Institute of Medicine (IOM). (2001). *To err is human: Building a safer health system.* Washington, DC: National Academy Press.

Institute of Medicine (IOM). (2004). *Keeping patients safe: Transforming the work environment of nurses.* Washington, DC: The National Academies Press.

Ives Erickson, J., & Ditomassi, M. (2011). Professional practice model: Strategies for translating models into practice. *Nursing Clinics of North America, 46*(1), 35-44.

Ives Erickson, J., Duffy, M. E., Ditomassi, M., & Jones, D. (2009). Psychometric evaluation of the Revised Professional Practice Environment (RPPE) scale. *Journal of Nursing Administration, 39*(5), 236-243.

Kanter, R. M. (1977). *Men and women of the corporation.* New York, NY: Basic Books.

Kanter, R. M. (1993). *Men and women of the corporation* (2nd ed.). New York, NY: Basic Books.

Kramer, M., & Schmalenberg, C. (1988a). Magnet hospitals: Part I: Institutions of excellence. *Journal of Nursing Administration, 18*(1), 13-24.

Kramer, M., & Schmalenberg, C. (1988b). Magnet hospitals: Part II: Institutions of excellence. *Journal of Nursing Administration, 18*(2), 11-19.

Kramer, M., & Schmalenberg, C. (1993). Learning from success: Autonomy and empowerment. *Nursing Management, 24*(5), 58-64.

Lacey, S. R., Cos, K. S., Lorfing, K. C., Teasley, S. L., Carroll, C. A., & Sexton, K. (2007). Nursing support, workload, and intent to stay in magnet, magnet-aspiring and non-magnet hospitals. *Journal of Nursing Administration, 37*(4), 199-205.

Lake, E. T. (2002). Development of the practice environment scale of the nursing work index. *Research in Nursing & Health, 25*(3), 176-188.

Laschinger, H. K. S. (2008). Effect of empowerment on professional practice environments, work satisfaction, and patient care quality: Further testing the nursing worklife model. *Journal of Nursing Care Quality, 23*(4), 322-330.

Laschinger, H. K .S., Almost, J., & Tuer-Hodes, D. (2003). Workplace empowerment and magnet hospital characteristics. *Journal of Nursing Administration, 33*(7/8), 410-422.

Laschinger, H. K. S., Finegan, J. E., Shamian, J., & Wilk, P. (2004). A longitudinal analysis of the impact of workplace empowerment on work satisfaction. *Journal of Organizational Behavior, 25*(4), 527-545.

Laschinger, H. K. S., Finegan, J., & Wilk, P. (2009). Context matters: The impact of unit leadership and empowerment on nurses' organizational commitment. *Journal of Nursing Administration, 39*(5), 228-235.

Laschinger, H. K. S., Finegan, J., & Wilk, P. (2011). Testing a multi-level model of staff nurse organizational commitment. *Journal of Healthcare Management, 56*(1), 81.

Laschinger, H. K. S., Gilbert, S., Smith, L., & Leslie, K. (2010). Towards a comprehensive theory of nurse/patient empowerment: Applying Kanter's empowerment theory to patient care. *Journal of Nursing Management, 18*(1), 4-13.

Laschinger, H. K. S., & Havens, D. S. (1996). Staff nurse work empowerment and perceived control over nursing practice: Conditions for work effectiveness. *Journal of Nursing Administration, 26*(9), 27-35.

Laschinger, H. K. S., & Havens, D. S. (1997). The effect of workplace empowerment on staff nurses' occupational mental health and work effectiveness. *Journal of Nursing Administration, 27*(6), 42-50.

Laschinger, H. K. S., & Leiter, M. P. (2006). The impact of nursing work environments on patient safety outcomes: The mediating role of burnout engagement. *Journal of Nursing Administration, 36*(5), 259-267.

Laschinger, H. K. S., Leiter, M. P., Day, A., Gilin-Oore, D., & Mackinnon, S. (in press). Building empowering work environments that foster civility and organizational trust: Testing an intervention. *Nursing Research.*

Laschinger, H. K. S., & Shamian, J. (1994). Staff nurses' and nurse managers' perceptions of job-related empowerment and managerial self-efficacy. *Journal of Nursing Administration, 24*(10), 38-47.

Laschinger, H. K. S., Wong, C., & Grau, A. L. (2012). Authentic leadership, empowerment and burnout: A comparison in new graduates and experienced nurses. *Journal of Nursing Management.* doi: 10.1111/j.1365-2834.2012.01375.x

Laschinger, H. K. S., Wong, C., McMahon, L., & Kaufmann, C. (1999). Leader behavior impact on staff nurse empowerment, job tension, and work effectiveness. *Journal of Nursing Administration, 29*(5), 28-39.

Lavoie-Tremblay, M., Paquet, M., Marchionni, C., & Drevniok, U. (2011). Turnover intention among new nurses: A generational perspective. *Journal for Nurses in Staff Development, 27*(1), 39-45.

Leape, L., Bates, D., Cullen, D., Cooper, J., Demonaco, H., Gallivan, T., ... Vander Vleit, M. (1995). Systems analysis of adverse drug events. *Journal of the American Medical Association, 274*(1), 35-43.

Leino-Kilpi, H., Maenpaa, I., & Katajisto, J. (1999). Nursing study of the significance of rheumatoid arthritis as perceived by patient using the concept of empowerment. *Journal of Orthopaedic Nursing, 3*(3), 138-145.

Leiter, M. P., & Laschinger, H. K. S. (2006). Relationships of work and practice environment to professional burnout. *Nursing Research, 55*(2), 137-146.

Lucas, V., Laschinger, H. K. S., & Wong, C. (2008). The impact of emotional intelligent leadership on staff nurse empowerment: The moderating effect of span of control. *Journal of Nursing Management, 16*(8), 964-973.

Manojlovich, M. (2005). The effect of nursing leadership on hospital nurses' professional practice behaviors. *Journal of Nursing Administration, 35*(7-8), 366-374.

Manojlovich, M. (2007). Power and empowerment in nursing: Looking backward to inform the future. *OJIN: The Online Journal of Issues in Nursing, 12.* Retrieved from http://www.nursingworld.org/MainMenuCategories/ANAMarketplace/ANAPeriodicals/OJIN/TableofContents/Volume122007/No1Jan07/LookingBackwardtoInformtheFuture.aspx

Manojlovich, M., & Laschinger, H. K. S. (2007). The nursing worklife model: Extending and refining a new theory. *Journal of Nursing Management, 15*(3), 256-263.

Mazzuca, S. A., Moorman, N. H., Wheeler, M. L., Norton, J. A., Fineberg, N. S., Vinicor, F., ... Clark, C. M. (1986). The diabetes education study: A controlled trial of the effects of diabetes patient education. *Diabetes Care, 9*(1), 1-10.

McClure, M. L., Poulin, M. A., Sovie, M. D., & Wandelt, M. A. (1983). *Magnet hospitals: Attraction and retention of professional nurses.* Kansas City, MO: American Nurses Association.

McWilliam, C. L., Stewart, M., Brown, J. B., McNair, S., Desai, K., Patterson, M. L., ... Pittman, B. J. (1997). Creating empowering meaning: An interactive process of promoting health with chronically ill older Canadians. *Health Promotion International, 12*(2), 111-123.

McWilliam, C. L., Ward-Griffin, C., Sweetland, D., Sutherland, C., & O'Halloran, L. (2001). The experience of empowerment in in-home services delivery. *Home Health Care Services Quarterly, 20*(4), 49-71.

Nedd, N. (2006). Perceptions of empowerment and intent to stay. *Nursing Economics, 24*(1), 13-19.

Neisner, J., & Raymond, B. (2002). Nurse staffing and care delivery models: A review of the evidence. Retrieved from www.kpihp.org/kpihp/frmContent.aspx?CMS_Entry_Id=235&Content_Type=F

Paterson, B. (2001). Myth of empowerment in chronic illness. *Journal of Advanced Nursing, 34*(5), 574-581.

Pellino, T., Tluczek, A., Collins, M., Trimborn, S., Norwich, H., Engelke, Z. K., & Broad, J. (1998). Increasing self-efficacy through empowerment: Preoperative education for orthopedic patients. *Orthopedic Nursing, 17*(4), 48-59.

Rosenberg, M. C. (2009). *Do Magnet-recognized hospitals provide better care?* Paper presented at the October 2009 American Nurses Credentialing Center Magnet Conference, Louisville, KY. Abstract retrieved from http://hdl.handle.net/10755/182328

Sabiston, J. A., & Laschinger, H. K. S. (1995). Staff nurses work empowerment and perceived autonomy. *Journal of Nursing Administration, 25*(9), 42-50.

Segal, L. (1998). The importance of patient empowerment in health system reform. *Health Policy, 44*(1), 31-44.

Thomas, K., & Velthouse, B. (1990). Cognitive elements of empowerment: An 'interpretive' model of intrinsic task motivation. *Academy of Management Review, 15*(4), 666-681.

Thorne, S. (2006). Patient-provider communication in chronic illness: A health promotion window of opportunity. *Family and Community Health, 29*(1 Suppl.), 4S-11S.

Upenieks, V. V. (2003a). Recruitment and retention strategies: A magnet hospital prevention model. *Medsurg Nursing*, suppl, 21-27.

Upenieks, V. V. (2003b). The interrelationship of organizational characteristics of magnet hospitals, nursing leadership, and nursing job satisfaction. *The Health Care Manager, 22*(2), 83-98.

Virtanen, H., Leino-Kilpi, S., & Salantera, S. (2007). Empowering discourse in patient education. *Patient Education and Counseling 66*(2), 140-146.

Wong, C. A., & Laschinger, H. K. S. (2012). Authentic leadership, performance, and job satisfaction: The mediating role of empowerment. *Journal of Advanced Nursing.* doi: 10.1111/j.1365-2648.2012.06089.x. First published online July 05, 2012.

Young-Ritchie, C., Laschinger, H. K. S., & Wong, C. (2009). The effects of emotionally intelligent leadership behaviour on emergency staff nurses' workplace empowerment and organizational commitment. *Nursing Leadership, 22*(1), 70-85.

Chapter 4
Scope of Work—
Care at the Bedside

Thomas Smith, DNP, RN, NEA-BC

[The purpose of nursing is]... to find the ways to know a person, as a human being in difficulty—and to help that person to stretch his or her capabilities and exercise innate capacities.

–Hildegard Peplau, 1965

Today, the role of the nurse providing direct care to patients requires added knowledge within a broad range of new science and related competencies. Many of these competencies encompass the complexities of clinical care, evidence-based practice, communication, collaboration, and teamwork.

Nurses are knowledge workers "who synthesize[s] a broad array of information and knowledge from a wide variety of sources and bring[s] that synthesis to bear on nursing work" (Porter O'Grady, 2003). Bedside nurses cannot achieve this level of practice alone. Nurse leaders in clinical settings support nurses providing direct care by creating work environments that advance autonomous, empowered professional nursing practice. Leaders also involved in education are designing educational programs that provide students with the theoretical, clinical, and leadership knowledge required to engage in the full scope of bedside work.

Since the founding of modern nursing, bedside care has embodied the essence of care delivery by a professional nurse. Today, bedside care is often discussed in relation to direct patient care, a term that encompasses the practice of both registered nurses (RNs) and advanced practice registered nurses (APRNs), all involved in the delivery of care of patients, families, communities, and populations. Nurses provide direct care in a variety of settings, including hospitals, clinics, long-term care facilities, schools, homes, workplaces, and battlefields. In fact, nursing care occurs anywhere nurses are present and in a position to use the knowledge and competencies within their scope of practice to care for others. As expressed so elegantly by Henderson (1961) and Peplau (1965), the direct care of patients, regardless of setting or context, represents the core of nursing practice.

> "The unique function of the nurse is to assist the individual, sick or well, in the performance of those activities contributing to health or its recovery (or to peaceful death) that the person would perform unaided given the necessary strength, will, or knowledge. And to do this in such a way as to help the individual gain independence as soon as possible."
>
> –Virginia Henderson, 1961

This chapter focuses on a discussion of nurses' scope of work; the dimensions of direct care; and the roles and responsibilities of nurse leaders, educators, and specialists needed to guide and empower bedside nurses with the knowledge, competencies, and tools essential to deliver excellent patient care. In addition, it explores the impact of health care in the future, its potential impact on nurses and patients, and the steps needed to assure that patients derive maximum benefit from the unique knowledge of professional nurses.

Scope of Work and Definition of Direct Care

Professional nurses across health care settings and populations establish and affirm the primacy of the nurse-patient relationship and strive to attain the primary goals of nursing: to optimize health, prevent illness and injury, alleviate suffering, and advocate for patients' needs (American Nurses Association [ANA],

2003). Though the provision of direct patient care is central to nursing practice, nurses providing bedside care have always assumed additional responsibilities as part of the role as caregiver.

In the early days of so called "hospital nursing," these additional activities might have included such things as meal preparation, equipment cleaning, and housekeeping. Today's nurses have to incorporate patient and staff education, teaching and mentoring colleagues, leading care redesign, delivering primary care to individual patients, participating in organizational governance and decision-making, evaluating and designing innovations to advance nursing practice, and a broad range of other activities in the definition of professional nursing.

Scope of Work

Like health care in general, the scope of work for the professional nurse is constantly changing in response to societal requirements and advances in science and knowledge (ANA, 2010a). At the beginning of the 20th century, hospitals as places of care and healing were still new concepts. The majority of nurses were employed as private duty nurses, caring for patients in their homes and hospitals (Whelan, 2011). For the hospitalized patients unable to afford a private duty nurse, nurses on the hospital staff or nursing students (especially if the hospital had a school of nursing) provided most of the care. Private duty nurses, hospital nurses, and students worked long hours to address patients' care needs. Though housekeeping tasks were often part of their work assignment, the majority of nursing work involved caring for patients directly, including activities such as administering treatments, preparing patients for surgery and caring for them post-operatively, dressing wounds, and attending to patients' personal needs (King, 1987; Rosenberg, 1987).

Over the years, the scope of nursing practice has steadily broadened, increasing in complexity as advancements in science led to new ways of treating disease and managing care. The advent of sulfa drugs in the 1930s and penicillin in the 1940s refocused nurses' work on medication administration, so this activity became an increasingly important aspect of the nurse's role. In addition, increased use of intravenous lines, oxygen therapy, and the iron lung and practices such as earlier ambulation after surgery further expanded nurses' responsibilities and added to the complexity care of patient care (Fairman & Lynaugh, 1998).

NOTE

In response to changing roles and responsibilities of the nurse, along with the growing practice demands and knowledge requirements, sociologist Esther Lucile Brown wrote an influential report titled Nursing for the Future *and presented it to the National Nursing Council (Brown, 1948). In this report, Brown identified that nurses acquire "a body of scientific nursing knowledge which is based upon and keeps pace with general scientific advancement" (p. 73). Brown strongly encouraged the nursing profession to consider requiring a baccalaureate degree for entry to professional nursing practice.*

By the 1950s, new options for treating heart disease and improving the management of chronic conditions associated with aging were being developed. As a result, many of the patients being admitted to hospitals were older adults and often seriously ill or unstable for at least part of their hospital stay. To respond to this challenge, nurses had to incorporate close monitoring and surveillance of these individuals into their care delivery. At this time, most hospitals used functional or team nursing models to organize the delivery of nursing care. In these approaches to care, nurses were assigned one or more discrete tasks to complete for a group of patients on the care unit (e.g., the medication nurse) while much of the personal care was provided by ancillary staff (Lynaugh & Brush, 1996). This manner of delivering care drew nurses away from the bedside and failed to address the needs of seriously ill patients who required the continuous monitoring by a nurse. In the 1950s and 1960s, a response to this challenge emerged as the first critical-care units were developed. These units were usually created within existing space, and rather than offering new technology and treatment options, they provided patients with the constant surveillance by a nurse (Fairman & Lynaugh, 1998).

Throughout the latter half of the 20th century, the complexity and scope of bedside nursing continued to expand, fueled by the introduction of new and more sophisticated technologies and treatment options. Hospital-based schools of nursing were increasingly difficult to operate, restrictions by accrediting bodies (e.g., National League for Nursing) limited student nurses' clinical hours, and hospital-based schools of nursing began to decline. This trend gave way to an increase in educational opportunities in community college and university-based nursing programs.

> **NOTE**
>
> *Recognizing the increasing complexity of the professional nurse's role and the importance of comprehensive educational preparation, the American Nurses Association (ANA) in 1965 proposed the baccalaureate degree as the minimum preparation for practice as a professional nurse. This proposal was ultimately endorsed by the National League for Nursing (NLN) in 1982 (ANA, 1965; Lynaugh & Brush, 1996). Though endorsed by these groups, baccalaureate education as a minimum requirement for professional nursing practice remains a challenge for professional nursing today.*

Specialty Nursing

In the 1970s, specialty nursing practice emerged, focusing on areas such as critical care, oncology, nephrology, emergency, and perioperative nursing. Graduate nursing education at the master's level was identified as necessary preparation for many practices within specialties including roles as clinical nurse specialists (CNSs), nurse practitioners (NPs), nurse midwives, and registered nurse anesthetists. By clarifying core elements of a curriculum and identifying required theoretical and clinical knowledge, master's level programs in nursing fostered development of specialty roles and helped distinguish a nurse specialist from a generalist in nursing practice. Clinical specialization also offered nurses a way to advance and expand their role and knowledge while still engaging in direct patient care (Lynaugh & Brush, 1996). Nursing specialty organizations (e.g., cardiovascular nursing, oncology nursing society, and so on) began to form and provided a way for specialty groups to develop standards for specialty practice, to provide education and staff development, and to promote optimal patient care for specialty populations.

Primary Nursing

One of the most important changes in bedside nursing practice that occurred in the late 1960s and 1970s was the emergence of primary nursing. This model was viewed as a replacement for more traditional functional and team nursing. Within this approach to nursing care delivery, patients were assigned to one nurse who was responsible and accountable for planning and providing the patient's care throughout a hospital stay (Manthey, 1973). Through primary nursing, nurses could exercise independent clinical decisions about their nursing care, gain greater autonomy and clinical authority for practice decisions, and assert their role in direct patient care. By spending more time directly with patients, nurses came to know their patients, gained a deeper understanding of their patients' needs and responses to illness, and served more ably as patient advocates.

Primary nursing served as the foundation for the relationship-based models of nursing care delivery currently used in many health care settings. Like primary nursing, these models value and support the therapeutic relationships between patients and families and groups while also emphasizing the importance of collaborating with intra-professional colleagues on the patient care team (Clifford, 1991; Manthey, 2006).

Nursing Care at the Bedside: Today

Today, the scope of work for all nurses in direct care is reflected in the ANA definition of nursing (see the sidebar). The definition addresses disciplinary boundaries and informs the scope of professional practice.

DEFINITION OF NURSING (ANA, 2003)

Nursing is the protection, promotion, and optimization of health and abilities, prevention of illness and injury, alleviation of suffering through the diagnosis and treatment of human response, and advocacy in the care of individuals, families, communities, and populations.

Standards of Care

Though each state in the United States has also established its own *nurse practice act* highlighting specific requirements, expectations, and practice parameters for nurses within that particular state, the ANA definition of nursing applies to all nurses, regardless of their level of experience or whether they assume general or specialty practice. Further, direction and guidance regarding nurses' scope of work is provided by the ANA Standards of Practice, which identifies nursing competencies pertaining to each component of the nursing process, and the Standards of Professional Performance, which outline competencies pertaining to collaboration, education, ethics, evidence-based practice, and other elements that distinguish professional practice (see Figure 4.1) (ANA, 2010a).

Although all direct care nurses share the same scope of practice, the depth and breadth to which individual nurses engage in implementing their practice depends on their specific clinical role, place of employment, education, and level of professional and self-development (ANA, 2010b). For example, APRNs possess specialized knowledge and skills gained through their educational preparation that enable them to assume significant role autonomy, including responsibility for health promotion, the diagnosis and treatment of patient conditions, use of complex clinical decision-making algorithms, and leadership for organizations and environments of care (ANA, 1996; APRN Joint Dialogue Group, 2008; Hamric, 2009).

Scope of Practice

The ANA standards and definition of nursing clarify and confirm nurses' obligations to patients and provide a description of the role and expectations of direct care nurses. Using the nursing process as a framework, direct care nurses assess patients and use relevant patient data; analyze their findings to identify potential problems and diagnoses; define expected outcomes; and develop and implement an evidence-based, individualized nursing plan of care that is continually evaluated and revised based on changes in the patient's condition and response to treatment (ANA, 2010a). The key tenets of nursing practice are the centrality of caring; use of the nursing process to provide individualized care; and partnership with patients, families, support systems, and other care providers

Standards of Practice

1. Assessment

2. Diagnosis

3. Outcomes identification

4. Planning

5. Implementation

    a. Coordination of care

    b. Health teaching and health promotion

    c. Consultation (graduate-level prepared specialty nurse or APRN)

    d. Prescriptive authority and treatment (APRN)

6. Evaluation

Standards of Professional Performance

1. Ethics

2. Education

3. Evidence-based practice and research

4. Quality of practice

5. Communication

6. Leadership

7. Collaboration

8. Professional practice evaluation

9. Resource evaluation

10. Environmental health

FIGURE 4.1

American Nurses Association: Standards of
Professional Nursing Practice (ANA, 2010a).

to plan and provide nursing care that promotes achievement of optimal patient outcomes (ANA, 2010a).

Competencies

The different expectations for general care and advanced practice registered nurses are reflected in the ANA Standards of Practice and Standards of Professional Performance (see Figure 4.1 earlier in this chapter), which outline baseline competencies for all nurses and additional competencies for APRNs and graduate-level prepared specialty nurses (ANA, 2010a).

For example, the Standards of Practice identifies 12 competencies. Standard 1 (Assessment) includes two competencies:

- Uses appropriate evidence-based assessment techniques, instruments, and tools

- Synthesizes available data, information, and knowledge relevant to the situation to identify patterns and variances

Two additional competencies are specified for APRNs and specialty practice nurses:

- Initiates and interprets diagnostic tests and procedures relevant to the health care consumer's current status

- Assesses the effects of interactions among individuals, family, community, and social systems on health and illness

The additional competencies reflect the expanded knowledge base and accountabilities associated with these roles.

Autonomy and Professional Practice

Autonomy, or the capacity of a nurse to determine her or his own actions within the full scope of nursing practice, is a hallmark of professional nursing practice. The degree to which a nurse can practice autonomously is related to level of competency (ANA, 2010b). Benner (2001) has studied variations in bedside nursing practice related to competency. Using nurses' experience-based narratives, Benner described various competency levels of clinical nurses ranging from novice to expert and identified how these levels manifest in nurses' discretionary clinical judgment and ability to anticipate and prevent negative patient outcomes.

Benner's work has provided a seminal and influential framework for many nurse leaders responsible for systems redesign of nurses' professional development. It highlighted the value of using narratives to help nurses "uncover the knowledge embedded" in their clinical practice (Benner, 2001) and to learn from other nurses' patient care experiences. This reflective process has proven effective in evaluating staff development and growth.

Safety and Quality

In recent decades, the scope of work of bedside nurses has expanded beyond the nurses' primary role of providing direct care to patients. In particular, nurses involved in direct care are significant contributors to improving patient care and promoting safety. As frontline clinicians, nurses engage in continuous patient surveillance and can identify potential problems and risk factors to prevent adverse events or respond quickly should they occur (Institute of Medicine [IOM], 2003a). Nurses work to enhance safety for patients and families. In addition, nurses also have critical knowledge about care systems and related processes that help position them as critical members of performance improvement teams.

Decision-Making

In many organizations, the role of bedside nurses is further broadened with the implementation of shared or collaborative governance models. By active participation in these initiatives, direct care nurses can help shape policies, inform standards and decisions affecting nursing care, and gain control over nursing practice (Hess, 2004). Implementing collaborative governance structures within health care infrastructures advances a professional practice environment, acknowledges and promotes the professional role of nurses, and supports nurse accountability for practice standards and nursing quality. In addition, active participation in a collaborative governance committee structure can improve the integration of an evidence-based approach to care and enhance decision-making in the workplace.

Advanced Practice Nursing

The role of APRNs, including CNSs, advanced nurse practitioners (ANPs), nurse midwives, and nurse anesthetists, prepared at the graduate level and within a specialty area, has expanded significantly in recent decades. Though direct clinical practice is the central competency of the APRN role, core competencies including expert coaching and mentoring; teaching and guidance of patients, families, and other care providers; consultation and collaboration with clinical partners as well as professional and systems leadership; ethical decision-making; and research (Hamric, 2009) complement expert care delivery. Many organizations rely on clinical nurse specialists to maintain and monitor standards of nursing practice, provide mentoring and clinical guidance to bedside nurses, and lead and participate in systems improvement efforts.

ANPs promote patient, family, and population care in hospitals and communities. With a focus and competence in health promotion and care of complex patient populations, nurse practitioners are often utilized to lead and participate in disease management initiatives and the coordination of care across the health system continuum. The role of the APRN is enhanced in today's health care environment where groups such as the IOM in their *The Future of Nursing* report (2010) recommend that all nurses be able to practice to the full scope of their practice ability.

Communicating Nursing's Work

Communicating nursing practice to other care providers has taken many forms, including a narrative description of nursing practice (Benner, 2001) and patient responses and use of other sources of documentation including flow sheets for monitoring patient responses to treatments. Methods of codifying and documenting the unique contributions of nurses also began to appear in the 1970s. This work was initially advanced with the classification of nursing diagnoses by the North American Nursing Diagnosis Association (NANDA) (Gebbie & Lavin, 1974; NANDA International, 2012). Later, other classifications emerged. These classifications are discussed in more depth in Chapter 5, "Nurse-Patient Relationship: Knowledge Transforming Practice at the Bedside." The impact of nursing languages within the nursing workforce is one way to communicate the scope of nurses work, cost out care, and link nursing care to patient outcomes (Jones, Lunney, Keenan & Moorhead, 2011).

Supporting Bedside Practice— The Role of Nurse Leaders

Efforts to define and effectively support bedside nursing practice have a long history. In her report for the National Nursing Council in 1948, Brown lamented bedside nurses' lack of autonomy and urged hospitals to find ways of allowing nurses more time with individual patients while also providing them a greater voice in organizational planning and policy formation.

Two decades later, the National Commission for the Study of Nursing and Nursing Education (1970) offered recommendations for improving nursing education, practice, and retention, including "establishing conditions, through organizational and staffing practices, that will give nurses an opportunity to provide optimum care to their patients, including individual planning and implementation of the care plan" (p. 292). Though many organizations struggled to establish such "conditions," others met with success. Among them were hospitals identified in the original Magnet Hospital study conducted by the American Academy of Nursing in the early 1980s (McClure, Poulin, Sovie & Wandelt, 1983).

The Magnet hospital study reflected ongoing concern about regularly occurring nurse shortages. To address this issue, the researchers studied organizations that managed to attract and retain nurses despite shortages, and they identified factors that enabled these hospitals to succeed. These organizational characteristics, still highly relevant today, included:

- A participative management style

- Strong and supportive leadership

- A patient-centered philosophy of care that is made explicit in day-to-day operations

- A decentralized structure that gives nurses a sense of control over their work environment

- Nursing involvement in the hospital committee structure

- A professional practice model that emphasizes accountability and nursing autonomy

- Adequate staffing and the availability of specialists and other consultative resources

- Continuing education and professional development opportunities

Since the Magnet hospital study, other nurse researchers have affirmed the relationship between the quality of the work environment and lower levels of nurse burnout (Aiken, Clarke & Sloane, 2002; Harwood, Ridley, Wilson, & Laschinger, 2010; Laschinger, Finegan & Wilk, 2009) and better patient outcomes (Aiken, Clarke, Sloane, Lake & Cheney, 2008). In the last decade, professional nursing organizations have built on these findings to develop programs and guidelines for nurse leaders seeking to improve patient care and the practice environment for nurses. Examples include:

- The Standards for Establishing and Sustaining Healthy Work Environments developed by the American Association of Critical-Care Nurses (AACN, 2005)

- The Magnet Recognition Program created by the American Nurses Credentialing Center (ANCC, 2012)

- The Transforming Care at the Bedside (TCAB) initiative developed by the Institute for Healthcare Improvement (IHI) and the Robert Wood Johnson Foundation (IHI, 2012)

These programs provide a blueprint for nurse leaders committed to creating work environments supportive of nurses in direct care. Essential elements of these environments include transparency and effective communication between nurse leaders and direct care nurses, involvement of direct care nurses in decision-making about issues influencing nursing practice, intra-professional collaboration, support for professional development and advancement, and a culture of respect.

Assuring that nurses have consistent access to needed resources is critical. This includes the presence of adequate nurse staffing and availability of the information and education required to maintain clinical competency. Consistent access to required resources also means having experts available at the bedside to support and guide nurses through challenging patient situations and to support them in advancing their clinical nursing practice. Preceptor and peer mentoring programs help to assure that direct care nurses have access to clinical guidance and expertise, along with professional development opportunities for experienced nurses.

In today's complex care environment, graduate-level prepared specialty nurses and APRNs also serve an important role. In addition to helping manage the care of complex and vulnerable populations, nurse specialists and APRNs provide critical education and support to bedside nurses and play a leadership role in facilitating change and innovation (Lewandowski & Adamle, 2009).

The Role of Academic Settings and the Importance of Academic-Practice Partnerships

Attaining excellence in bedside nursing practice requires the leadership of deans and faculty in schools of nursing and administrative leadership in clinical settings. Within the report titled *The Future of Nursing*, the IOM highlighted the important role of nurse faculty in preparing students for independent clinical practice (IOM, 2010). The report urged schools of nursing to develop strategies to help students gain the knowledge and skills that can enable them to lead and shape future environments of care. By providing students with the knowledge needed to excel in clinical practice environments, faculty were also exhorted to ensure that students could adapt to changes in science, technology, and care delivery, and could gain an understanding of care management, intra-professional teamwork, quality improvement methods, use of information technology, and system-level change management.

Many schools of nursing have redesigned their curricula in response to the challenges and opportunities of nurses in direct care practice. For example, some schools are using curricula and teaching strategies developed through the Quality and Safety Education for Nurses (QSEN) initiative (QSEN, 2012). Launched in 2005, QSEN convened nurse experts from schools of nursing to develop curricula and strategies for helping nurses attain competency in six key areas defined by the IOM (2003b):

- Patient-centered care
- Teamwork and collaboration
- Evidence-based practice
- Quality improvement
- Safety
- Informatics

In addition to defining competencies for each area, QSEN currently serves as a clearinghouse for teaching strategies regarding quality and safety developed by school of nursing faculties across the United States.

Partnerships

Developing partnerships between schools of nursing and practice settings helps to bridge the gap between what students are taught in school and what they need to know in practice (Kirschling & Ives Erickson, 2010). Academic-practice partnerships have led to a wide range of innovations in practice and teaching-learning experiences. A few examples include shared implementation of evidence-based guidelines (Virani & Grinspun, 2007); development of simulation scenarios for students and nurses in critical care, medical-surgical nursing, obstetrics, and other specialty areas (Kirschling & Erickson, 2010); and the creation of dedicated education units (DEUs), in which bedside nurses play a significant role in the clinical education of students (Edgecombe, Wotton, Gonda & Mason, 1999; Glazer, Ives Erickson, Mylott, Mulready-Shick & Banister, 2011; Moscato, Miller, Logsdon, Weinberg & Chorpenning, 2007).

Though more needs to be implemented to foster effective partnerships between the academic and practice settings, initiatives such as these mentioned offer promise and a template for innovative approaches to educating future nurses and translating knowledge into professional practice settings that enhance high-quality, safe, cost-effective, patient-centric care.

Looking to the Future

Nursing practice will continue to change and evolve as the health care delivery system is transformed. Several years ago, Porter-O'Grady (2003) noted that more than half the patients who entered the health care system required personal health services for no more than four or five hours. This is different from the time, not so long ago, when patients entered the hospital a day or two in advance of surgery simply to prepare for the procedure. The shift to shorter, ambulatory-based interventions has important implications for patients and for direct care nursing practice, says Porter-O'Grady. Patients must now take a more active role in their own health care, while direct care nurses must change how they approach their practice.

Today's direct care delivery models extend beyond the boundaries of the hospital and into the communities. Increasingly, patients experience contact with the nurse before and after hospitalizations. Instead of managing all aspects of a patient's care in one episode of care, nurses find ways to support and empower patients to own and direct their care over time and across settings. The continued development of transitional care models that promote opportunities for nursing care outside of the acute care setting are opening up new ways of implementing care at the bedside. These innovations are promoting safe, effective quality care while seeking to reduce costs accrued through hospital admissions and emergency department visits.

Summary

Though change is often challenging, it also promotes opportunity. As suggested by this discussion and advanced by the IOM (2010), direct care nurses of the future will assume more visible roles across the full spectrum of care and treatment—including health promotion and disease prevention, chronic disease management, support of patients' recovery from illness in the community, and preventing or limiting injury and disability. Because of their knowledge and experience providing direct patient care, bedside nurses are uniquely qualified to be full partners in designing future health care delivery systems, as envisioned by the IOM and others. During this era of health care transformation, direct care nurses must embrace and implement changes in their practice so that patients benefit from the nurses' wisdom and expertise, which improves the health of the communities the nurses so ably serve.

References

Aiken, L. H., Clarke, S. P., & Sloane, D. M. (2002). Hospital staffing, organization, and quality of care: Cross-national findings. *Nursing Outlook, 50*(5), 187-194.

Aiken, L. H., Clarke, S. P., Sloane, D. M., Lake, E. T., & Cheney, T. (2008). Effects of hospital care environment on patient mortality and nurse outcomes. *The Journal of Nursing Administration, 38*(5), 223-229.

American Association of Critical Care Nurses (AACN). (2005). AACN standards for establishing and sustaining healthy work environments: A journey to excellence. *American Journal of Critical Care, 14*(3), 187-197.

American Nurses Association (ANA). (1965). Education for nursing. *American Journal of Nursing, 65*(12), 106-111.

American Nurses Association (ANA). (1996). *Scope and standards of advanced practice registered nursing.* Washington, DC: Author.

American Nurses Association (ANA). (2003). *Nursing's social policy statement.* Silver Springs, MD: Nursesbooks.org.

American Nurses Association (ANA). (2010a). *Nursing scope and standards of practice* (2nd ed.). Silver Springs, MD: Nursesbooks.org.

American Nurses Association (ANA). (2010b). *Nursing's social policy statement.* Silver Springs, MD: Nursesbooks.org.

American Nurses Credentialing Center (ANCC). (2012). *ANCC Magnet Recognition Program.* Retrieved from http://www.nursecredentialing.org/Magnet.aspx

APRN Joint Dialogue Group. (2008). *Consensus model for APRN regulation.* Chicago/Washington, DC: Author.

Benner, P. (2001). *From novice to expert: Excellence and power in clinical nursing practice* (Commemorative ed.). Upper Saddle River, NJ: Prentice-Hall.

Brown, E. L. (1948). *Nursing for the future: A report prepared for the National Nursing Council.* New York, NY: Russell Sage Foundation.

Clifford, J. (1991). An interview with Joyce C. Clifford. Interview by Carmella A. Bocchino. *Nursing Economics, 9*(1), 7-17.

Edgecombe, K., Wotton, K., Gonda, J., & Mason, P. (1999). Dedicated education units: 1. A new concept for clinical teaching and learning. *Contemporary Nurse, 8*(4), 166-171.

Fairman, J., & Lynaugh, J. E. (1998). *Critical care nursing: A history*. Philadelphia, PA: University of Pennsylvania Press.

Gebbie, K. M., & Lavin, M. (1974). *Classification of nursing diagnoses: Proceedings of the first national conference*. St. Louis, MO: C. V. Mosby.

Glazer, G., Ives Erickson, J., Mylott, L., Mulready-Shick, J., & Banister, G. (2011). Partnering and leadership: Core requirements for developing a dedicated education unit. *Journal of Nursing Administration, 41*(10), 401-406.

Hamric, A. B. (2009). A definition of advanced practice nursing. In A. B. Hamric & J. A. Spross (Eds.) *Advanced Practice Nursing: An Integrative Approach* (pp.75-94). St. Louis, MO: Saunders Elsevier.

Harwood, L., Ridley, J., Wilson, B., & Laschinger, H. K. (2010). Workplace empowerment and burnout in Canadian nephrology nurses. *Canadian Association of Nephrology Nurses and Technicians, 20*(2), 12-17.

Henderson, V. (1961). *Basic principles of nursing care* (p. 42). London, UK: International Council of Nurses.

Hess, R. G. (2004). From bedside to boardroom: Nursing shared governance. *The Online Journal of Issues in Nursing, 9*(1). Retrieved from http://nursingworld.org/MainMenuCategories/ANAMarketplace/ANAPeriodicals/OJIN/TableofContents/Volume92004/No1Jan04/FromBedsidetoBoardroom.aspx

Institute for Healthcare Improvement (IHI). (2012). *Transforming care at the bedside*. Retrieved from http://www.ihi.org/offerings/Initiatives/PastStrategicInitiatives/TCAB/Pages/default.aspx

Institute of Medicine (IOM). (2003a). *Keeping patients safe: Transforming the work environment of nurses*. Washington, DC: National Academies Press.

Institute of Medicine (IOM). (2003b). *Health professions education: A bridge to quality*. Washington, DC: National Academies Press.

Institute of Medicine (IOM). (2010). *The future of nursing: Leading change, advancing health*. Washington, DC: National Academies Press. Retrieved from http://www.iom.edu/Reports/2010/The-Future-of-Nursing-Leading-Change-Advancing-Health.aspx

Jones, D. (2007). A synthesis of philosophical perspectives for knowledge development. In C. Roy & D. Jones (Eds.), *Nursing Knowledge Development and Clinical Practice* (pp. 163-176). New York, NY: Springer Publishing.

Jones, D., Lunney, M., Keenan, G., & Moorhead, D. (2011). Standardized nursing languages: Essential for the nursing workforce. *Annual Review of Nursing Research: Nursing Workforce Issues, 28*, 253-294.

King, M. (1987). *The Peter Bent Brigham Hospital School of Nursing: A history, 1912-1985*. Boston, MA: Brigham and Women's Hospital.

Kirschling, J. M., & Ives Erickson, J. (2010). The STTI Practice-Academe Innovative Collaboration Award: Honoring innovation, partnership, and excellence. *Journal of Nursing Scholarship, 42*(3), 286-294.

Laschinger, H. K., Finegan, J., & Wilk, P. (2009). New graduate burnout: The impact of professional practice environment, workplace civility, and empowerment. *Nursing Economics, 27*(6), 377-383.

Lewandowski, W., & Adamle, K. (2009). Substantive areas of clinical specialist practice: A comprehensive review of the literature. *Clinical Nurse Specialist, 23*(2), 73-90.

Lynaugh J. E., & Brush, B. L. (1996). *American nursing: From hospitals to health systems.* Malden, MA and Oxford, England: Blackwell Publishers.

Manthey, M. (1973). Primary nursing is alive and well in the hospital. *American Journal of Nursing, 73*(1), 83-87.

Manthey, M. (2006). Leadership for relationship-based care. *Creative Nursing, 12*(1), 10-11.

McClure, M. L., Poulin, M. A., Sovie, M. D., & Wandelt, M. A. (1983). *Magnet hospitals: Attraction and retention of professional nurses.* Kansas City, MO: American Nurses Association.

Moorhead, S., Johnson, M., & Maas, M. (Eds.). (2004). *Nursing outcomes classification* (3rd ed.). St. Louis. MO: Mosby/Elsevier.

Moorhead, S., Johnson, M., Maas, M., & Swanson, E. (2008). *Nursing outcomes classification (NOC)* (4th ed.). St. Louis, MO: Mosby/Elsevier.

Moscato, S. R., Miller, J., Logsdon, K., Weinberg, S., & Chorpenning, L. (2007). Dedicated education unit: An innovative clinical partner education model. *Nursing Outlook, 55*(1), 31-37.

NANDA International. (2012). *NANDA-I history: 1973-1979.* Retrieved from http://www.nanda.org/AboutUs/History/1973to1979.aspx

National Commission for the Study of Nursing and Nursing Education. (1970). Summary report and recommendations. *American Journal of Nursing, 70*(2), 279-294.

Peplau, H. E. (1965). The heart of nursing: Interpersonal relations. *Canadian Nurse, 61,* 273-275.

Porter-O'Grady, T. (2003). Nurses as knowledge workers. Interview by Kathy Malloch. *Creative Nursing, 9*(2), 6-9.

Quality and Safety Education for Nurses (QSEN). (2012). *About QSEN.* Retrieved from http://www.qsen.org/about_qsen.php

Rosenberg, C. E. (1987). *The care of strangers: The rise of America's hospital system.* Baltimore, MD: The Johns Hopkins University Press.

Virani, T., & Grinspun, D. (2007). RNAO's Best Practice Guidelines Program: Progress report on a phenomenal journey. *Advances in Skin & Wound Care, 20*(10), 528-535.

Whelan, J. C. (2011). *Private duty nursing.* University of Pennsylvania School of Nursing website, Nursing History and Health Care. Retrieved from http://www.nursing.upenn.edu/nhhc/Pages/PrivateDutyNursing.aspx

Chapter 5

Nurse-Patient Relationship: Knowledge Transforming Practice at the Bedside

Dorothy A. Jones, EdD, RNC, FAAN

If we are to move toward a more holistic and healthy world, then we must discover a way of unifying statements of objective science with our own personal vision of the world, and we must do this without diluting the authenticity of either approach.

(Peat, 1991, p. 47)

The advances in knowledge are the basis for dealing effectively with the challenge to transform nursing practice.

(Roy, 2007, p. 25).

Introduction

As the complexity of the practice environment increases, the demand for a better educated workforce, responsive to changing demographics, diversity of the population and increased regulatory and health policy mandates, is essential

(Aiken & Patrician, 2000; Institute of Medicine [IOM], 2010). Currently, changes within the health care environments, including reduced hospital stays and challenges associated with recovery outside of the acute care settings, have left consumers feeling unprepared to manage their health and feeling "abandoned" by the current a health care system (Flanagan, 2009). Demands to document care electronically are seen as important innovations to improve communication across disciplines, reduce errors, and promote a culture of safety for patients and their families. Within the milieu of interdisciplinary practice comes the need for evidence-driven care and outcomes attributed to disciplinary contributions.

This chapter focuses on the importance of relationship-based care and nurses knowing their patients to enhance recovery from illness, foster and sustain health promotion, optimize prevention strategies, and reduce cost while maintaining quality, effectiveness, safety, and patient/family-centric patient care. Uncovering the patient experience using a problem solving or a process dialogue approach is addressed along with a discussion on how nurses at the bedside come to understand the meaning of illness to the patient. Discussions also focus on nursing's being with patients and families during significant life transitions and how the caring presence of the nurse facilitates positive change (Newman et al., 2008). Documentation is addressed as a mechanism to communicate care and provide evidence that gives voice to nursing's contributions to care across patient groups.

Patient-Centric Care

Patient-centered care is a core goal of health care reform. To achieve this requires:

- Visionary leadership
- Clear strategic direction
- Patient-family involvement in care planning
- Professional practice environment impacting staff and patient outcomes
- Evidence-driven care
- Cost-effective quality focus
- Technology to support the infrastructure (Shaller, 2007)

Nurses have a unique perspective on the nature of person and the delivery of care that is patient/family/community centered. This perspective is driven by knowledge and grounded in the basic assumption that the relationship between the nurse/patient/family and is the central focus of the discipline (Newman, 2008). Table 5.1 addresses characteristics identified as critical to implementing care that is patient centric.

TABLE 5.1: Key Attributes of Patient-Centered Care (Shaller, 2007)

KEY ATTRIBUTES
Education and shared knowledge
Involvement of family and friends
Collaboration and team management
Sensitivity to non-medical and spiritual dimensions of care
Respect for individual needs and preferences
Free flow and accessibility to information
ADDITIONAL ATTRIBUTES (WATSON, 1999; NEWMAN, SMITH, PHARRIS & JONES, 2008; WILLIS, GRACE & ROY, 2008)
Relationship between the nurse and patient/family—key to knowing the person
Intentional presence of the care provider with another—a mutual process
Understanding the pattern of the whole
Knowing self in relation to another
Search for meaning
Uncovering truth, enabling choice, and promoting transformation through action
Caring
Power as participation in change
Reflection, relaxation, and balance—essential to insight and self-discovery
Creating an environment to support professional practice and a healing space

Relationship-Based Care

The relationship between the nurse, patient, family, and even community is viewed by many as core to optimal nursing practice (Roy & Jones, 2007). The process embodies what some refer to as the "mystery" of professional practice. It is that unspoken dynamic that occurs between the nurse and patient and is built on a sense of trust. The relationship between the patient and nurse is embedded in a partnership that promotes the integration and sharing of knowledge and creates an environment for patient/family experiences and perceptions to be discussed and validated.

Within this relationship, the nurse comes to know the individual as a whole person and views illness as part of health (MacLeod, 2011; Smith, 2011). The intentional presence of the nurse with another directs the nurse's attention on the human experience within the context of the environment and life process as perceived by the patient and family. The practice environment enables the nurse at the bedside to come to know the person while actualizing the professional role to its fullest.

Nurse-Patient Relationship

Nursing's unique position to take the lead in coordinating relationship-centered care is also being called for by voices outside of nursing (IOM, 2010; Roy, 2007). Dossey and Keegan (2013) suggest that the focus of this relationship between the nurse/patient/family and community is grounded in knowledge, skills, and values that center around "self-awareness, patient experiences of health and illness, developing and maintaining a caring relationship and effective communication" (p. 17). The presence of the nurse in partnership with the patient focuses on discovery and meaning and understanding of the life pattern, responses to illness, and perception about health (Jones, 2006; Jones & Flanagan, 2007; Picard & Jones, 2005).

Effective relationships are guided by intentional presence, effective communication, and active listening between the individual and provider. "The nurse-patient relationship is dynamic, evolving, and a transforming partnership grounded in trust and truth" (Roy, 2007, p. 29). "It is the nature of the nurse-patient relationship that unites the practice of nursing as it occurs in myriad settings throughout the world at every moment of every day" (Newman et al., 2008, p. E17).

Knowing the Person

"Knowing the patient encompasses the complex processes whereby the nurse acquires understanding of a specific patient as a unique individual, which enhances clinical decision-making" (Whittemore, 2000, p. 75). A significant body of literature has been written about knowing the person and its impact on care outcomes. Findings from the literature describe how nurses come to know the patient and the impact expertise has on nurses' decisions about care (Benner, Tanner & Chelsa, 1996; Jenny & Logan, 1992; Radwin, 1996). Watson and Smith (2004) discussed the importance of a caring relationship, describing it as the hallmark of the discipline. Jones (2006) and others (Chase, 2001; Dossey & Keegan, 2013; Willis, Grace & Roy, 2008; Newman et al., 2008) have discussed how patients' perceptions of feeling known by their nurse and intentional presence of the nurse within the nurse-patient relationship (Doona, Chase & Haggerty, 1999) enhance patient satisfaction with care.

Development of measures to evaluate the impact of knowing the person and the nurse-patient relationship have been linked to outcomes such as quality care and patients' perceptions of nurse caring (Della Monica, 2008; Radwin, Alster & Rubin, 2003; Wolf, Zuzelo, Goldberg, Crothers & Jacobson, 2006). In a qualitative study reported by Somerville (2009, p. 39), patients felt known by their nurse when they were "recognized as a unique human being, felt safe within the care environment, experienced a connection with the nurse they perceived as meaningful and felt empowered by the nurse to actively participate in their care." This study led to the development of the *Patients Perceptions of Feeling Known by Their Nurse Scale* (PPFKNS) (Somerville, 2009). Psychometrics of the instrument yielded results that reported the PPFKNS was a reliable, valid four-component scale with alpha coefficient for each component ranging between 0.90–0.96 (2009, p. 41) and therefore a reliable measure used to evaluate patients "being known" by the nurse.

The inclusion of nurse-sensitive outcome measures to evaluate knowing the patient, grounded in a nursing framework, gives nurses at the bedside a more effective way to capture the essence of nursing care resulting from the nurse-patient relationship (Della Monica, 2008; Wolf et al., 2006). Within this relationship, the focus of nursing care moves nursing practice beyond "tasks" and activities performed on behalf of managing the illness to a place where the nursing actions are informed by knowledge and focus on understanding the whole person and partnering with them to identify problems and patterns that compromise health (Newman, 2008). To effectively come to know the person, nurses must have the time, support, and resources to help patients make new choices and take new actions that promote health and prevent illness.

Intentional Presence

"The authentic presence between the patient and nurse is a transformation for both. Presence is a matter of consciousness and reflected in holistic beings that are both nurses and patients" (Chase, 2001, p. 323). **Presence** is a process of human–to–human interaction that creates the opportunity for dialogue and unfolding meaning. **Intentional presence** is an opportunity for the nurse to witness verbal and non-verbal expressions and responses occurring in the encounter between the nurse and patients. The literature discusses intentional presence as "genuine dialogue, commitment, full engagement and openness, free-flowing attentiveness and transcendent oneness" (Smith, 2011). Having the time to "be" with patients and their families and actively listen to fears, hopes, and concerns is critical to uncovering meaning. Empowering patients, families, and communities to become "knowing participants in change" (Barrett, 2003) can transform the patient experience and potentially impact healing, recovery, and even end-of-life care.

The purposeful attention to intentional presence while caring for patients is a conscious one and central to effective nursing care. Taking the time to hear the patient's messages increases the nurse's awareness concerning what is important to the person and family, an insight critical to promoting patient health. In addition, nurses are expert observers of patient responses. This skill promotes responsiveness and facilitates immediate actions that save and restore lives. The observational skill of the nurse is an "intuitive" response and linked to overall nursing expertise (Benner, 1984). The nurse describes this as "just knows something is wrong" and responds immediately to the event. Other scholars suggest that intuitive knowing is based on the nurse's expertise and ability to respond to a complex set of cues that is the result of clinical expertise. After repeated exposures to caring for the patient, the nurse accumulates knowledge about the patient's pattern of responses to health and illness and is able to quickly make judgments (Gordon, 1994).

Nurses at the bedside need time to come to know the patient beyond their disease and the symptoms associated with illness. Establishing a connection with the patient, grounded in trust and authenticity, enables the nurse to recognize truth and react to the moment, "going beyond the scientific data to being with the patient" (Doona et al., 1999). The exemplar to follow reveals the experience of a nurse at the bedside and the impact being intentionally present can have on care outcomes.

EXEMPLAR: INTENTIONAL PRESENCE AND THE NURSE AT CARE AT THE BEDSIDE

A staff nurse at Massachusetts General Hospital related a story that articulates the reality of intentional presence within the care environment. A female patient had just received a diagnosis of breast cancer. Since her conversation with the physician, the patient had been withdrawn, crying, and unresponsive to the attempts of many nurses to engage in a conversation.

One of the staff nurses, enrolled in a master's program had read about "intentional presence" and the potential impact it could have on changing the outcome of a patient encounter. She decided to work with the patient and entered the room, greeting the patient, and sat at the bedside to inquire about "How things were going?" The patient said, "Okay," and quietly lay in the bed offering little dialogue.

The nurse moved about the room completing her work and decided to "just sit and be" with the patient for a while. She thought that by "being present and available" she might bring a new opportunity for the patient to respond when

> *she was ready. After a prolonged time with no conversation, the nurse stood up and said she would be back a little later and to contact her if she needed anything.*
>
> *As the nurse moved to open the door, the patient quietly said, "Did you hear that I have cancer?" The nurse slowly turned and said, "Yes, I did," and returned to the bedside. The dialogue that followed lasted over an hour, often interrupted with tears, a hopeful smile, or a caring touch. The patient unburdened her concerns and fears. The nurse listened, supported, and helped her explore choices and facilitate decisions.*

In the preceding exemplar, the nurse is intentionally present and establishes a way to "be with" the patient. Using silence, the nurse manages to be in the moment with another person, provide a sense of comfort and trust, and communicate to the patient that at that moment the patient is the nurse's most important concern. In this scenario, the nurse had no preconceived ideas about the encounter but was available and open to whatever happened. Newman calls this being in the "temporal present" (Newman, 2008, p. 59). Others have referred to this as a caring, spiritual moment where the self and another are connected (Capasso, 1998; Jonsdottir, Litchfield & Pharris, 2003; Quinn, 1996; Roy & Jones, 2007; Watson, 1999). When the nurse is able to create a safe space, the patient may feel free to disclose their concerns and express fears freely. The patient and the nurse in the exemplar were mutually present and available; aware; and ready to listen, gain insight, and uncover new possibilities.

Uncovering Meaning

According to Willis et al, "meaning is a human's arrived-at understanding of life experiences and their significance that comes from processing those experiences" (2008, p. E34). Responses to meaning as interpreted by the person can lead to reactions expressed as behaviors or even physical bodily responses. Making meaning from an individual's exposure to information from the environment of which they are a part involves a process and the interpretation of an event or events. Often on the basis of this interpretation the individual will make choices and take action that can influence health and life experiences. "Without meaning, our society would fall apart" (Bohm, 1993, p. 150).

Developing a sustaining relationship with the patient creates opportunities to reflect on, interpret, and make sense (meaning) of life processes, events, and new information given to the patient during hospitalization or a clinic visit (e.g., a new medical diagnosis). Nurses at the bedside are often present during conversations between the patient, family, and another provider. When the physician, as an example, discusses a health problem or related treatment options with the patient and family they may become overwhelmed. The patient often feels left to decide a course of action on their own. It is not unusual for the patient to ask the nurse for information and added clarity around a proposed treatment following their conversation with a physician. The nurse who knows the patient can not only provide the requested information but also can help the patient reflect on the impact of their choices on such things as lifestyle, quality of daily activities, and life goals. Nurses help the patient make decisions and take actions that are meaningful and reflect who they are as a person (Flanagan, 2005).

Patients remember "their nurse" and the partnership built on trust. Nurses share profound moments with patients and families, from happy experiences associated with the birth of a child to helping patients manage a new illness or a family cope with the death of a loved one. The nurse is the one constant connection throughout these experiences, journeying with the patient through the changes and challenges of health and illness. Nurses who are present and available to the patient share a rare gift. They become part of a transforming experience that holds unique meaning for each individual (Jones, 2006; Willis et al., 2008). While focusing on what the patient believes is the most important to them, the nurse uses knowledge within the context of the nurse-patient relationship to uncover the meaningful whole. By "stepping into the whole through the parts" (Newman, 2008, p. 41) the nurse comes to know the whole person. As patient and nurse awareness is increased, insights are revealed and the emerging pattern creates opportunity for new dialogue, choice, and action (Pharris, 2002). The exemplar to follow provides the use of the dialogue as an effective approach to behavior change.

EXEMPLAR: CHANGING AND SUSTAINING NEW BEHAVIOR USING PROCESS DIALOGUE

Nurses working with patients to reduce and eliminate smoking behaviors might enter the discussion through a response to behavior: smoking. As the dialogue with the patient focuses on the meaning of smoking to the patient, the discussion quickly shifts away from the smoking behavior to the role this response plays in the life of the whole patient. Telling the patient about the negative effects of smoking might not be enough to change the individual's smoking behavior. Even if the patient were to stop smoking, often without addressing this change within the context of the whole, patients might find it difficult to sustain the new behavior (Berry, 2004).

As shown in the preceding exemplar, when the nurse can use experiences to discuss things that are meaningful to the patient, the nurse has an opportunity to move beyond the behavior and uncover meaning of the smoking, for example, as a response to life stressors. Within the context of knowing the whole is where change can be introduced and hopefully sustained.

Environment of Care: A Healing Space

The environment within which the nurse and patient are present is critical to the care experience, which includes healing, recovery, change, and transformation. Nurses at the bedside are central to creating an environment that promotes the nurse-patient relationship within the context of the patient's life experiences.

Working in a professional practice environment that provides a comfortable, quiet space for healing fosters an opportunity for mutual process to occur between the nurse and patient. Attention to environmental stimuli (e.g., excessive noise, changing temperature, overhead paging) can be identified during patient rounding and discussions with the patient. Selecting alternative mechanisms, for example, to use when contacting the nurses can help minimize noise and create an environment of care that is responsive to recovery. Additional interventions focusing on the use of complementary healing modalities (e.g. relaxation, reflection, stress management) create opportunities to attend to the patient with the healing environment (Coakley & Mahoney, 2009; Flanagan, 2005).

Approaches to Uncovering the Whole

Knowing the patient and developing an environment of care that is designed to foster patient recovery is critical to nurses effectively delivering holistic patient care. There are multiple approaches that can be used by nurses to understand the person's response to illness and the behaviors they engage in to promote a healthy lifestyle. By recognizing patterns that are supportive of positive health or put the patient at risk, nurses can design care that is sensitive to patient goals while optimizing health and preventing illness.

The Health/Illness Experience

Using disciplinary knowledge at the bedside gives nurses an opportunity to describe the patient response to illness and health within a disciplinary perspective. Two approaches—problem solving and process/dialogue—assist nurses in understanding the patient and their health experiences within the context of the whole person and their environment. A **problem-solving approach** is a deductive process that involves data collection using a more systemized approach (e.g., systems review or functional health patterns) to assemble information. Though some might consider the process linear, others argue that as new data becomes available judgments are continually revised and care re-evaluated (Gordon, 1994). The **process/dialogue approach** is an inductive process that evolves for the nurse-patient dialogue and leads to the uncovering of a pattern of the whole. As patients become aware of behaviors that threaten health, the nurse and patient mutually address new actions that can be taken to change behaviors and transform health.

Problem Solving and Decision-Making

"The problem-solving perspective includes reference to humans as holistic, bio-psychosocial beings interacting (functioning) within the environment and shaped by age, developmental stage, health status and culture (and ethnicity)"

(Jones, 2007, p. 165). Within a problem-solving approach, nurses use empirical measures, such as height and weight, along with subjective and objective data to evaluate functional health and responses to illness. Nurses obtain data through a systemized approach to assessment and synthesize data to identify (deductively) a problem. The naming of the problem (nursing diagnosis) and identification of the probable cause (related factors) direct interventions designed to eliminate or relieve the originating problem and reduce risk. The social policy statement articulates nursing as the "diagnosis of responses to actual and potential health problems...actions nurses take to improve conditions and evaluate the effectiveness on an intervention" (American Nurses Association, 2004, p. 7).

Clinical Decision-Making and Reasoning

Clinical decision-making involves a process of collecting, analyzing, and synthesizing information, as discussed in this chapter, within a nursing framework. The outcome of the clinical decision-making process is a clinical judgment (nursing diagnosis). Arriving at a clinical judgment involves generating a tentative hypothesis based on and supported by evidence.

While nurses engage in a process of deductive reasoning, based upon data (cues), to arrive at a nursing diagnosis, physicians and some advance practice nurses (APNs) engage in a similar process to identify and validate the presence of a medical diagnosis. The accuracy of the diagnosis informs the intervention, and the effectiveness of nursing action occurs on measurable care outcomes. If a diagnosis (judgment) is made prematurely (premature closure) or with limited data, diagnostic accuracy and patient outcomes can be compromised (Gordon 1982; Gordon 1994; Gordon, 2010; Lunney, 2009). Figure 5.1 depicts the multiple approaches nurses use to arrive at a clinical judgment including problem solving, expert knowledge, clinical wisdom, and intuitive knowing (inference).

Critical thinking is exemplified by the clinical/diagnostic reasoning. It has been defined as "reflective thinking in that one questions one's thinking process to determine if all possible avenues have been explored and if all conclusions that are being drawn are based on evidence" (Chase, 2004, p. 45). Critical thinking helps the diagnostician appreciate the need for continued data collection,

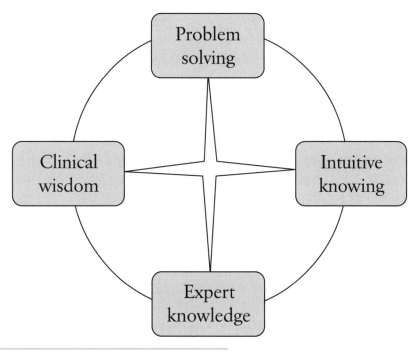

FIGURE 5.1

Components influencing clinical decision-making and problem-solving process.

validates decisions, and supports a process that all nurses at the bedside need to engage in when trying to solve problems. It requires knowing the patient and patterns of responses to illness and having knowledge about existing evidence and review of judgments by other professionals to ensure optimal care and best practices.

Intuitive Knowing, Inference, and Expertise

Authors including Benner (1984) and Gordon (1982, 1994) have discussed **intuition** in relation to clinical expertise and as a component of assessment. Often knowing an individual's "usual response to illness and recovery is linked to knowledge and linked to being able to see beyond" or, as Gordon suggests, being able to "extend the picture, synthesize the picture or create a picture" (1982,

p. 143). This process is often linked to generating **inferences** about a behavior (crying), or a problem (nursing diagnosis), or thoughts (often unspoken) about a life situation. The expert or seasoned clinician often sees the "big picture" and is able to "grasp" the whole with limited data and infer meaning. A **clinical inference** is described as a "deliberative, conscious reasoning leading from observation to judgment (Gordon, 1982, p. 143). Inferences are often associated with a response appearing to be outside of the so-called "norm." The nurse who walks into a patient's room might describe having "a gut feeling" that something is just not right. Upon further investigation, this reaction is easily validated by further assessment.

Nurse **expertise** has been described in relation to behaviors associated with clinical experiences and knowledge. Benner and Tanner (1987) discuss five levels of expertise (novice to expert) that included movement from beginning knowledge and skills, to becoming competent in the use and application of these attributes, then becoming proficient, and finally expert. Within the context of decision-making, the more novice nurse might experience challenges responding to and synthesizing patient information easily, resulting in multiple or inaccurate diagnoses (Lunney, 2009). The novice might use limited data (cues) to make a decision when additional data might be needed, resulting in a new decision or diagnosis.

With time, experience, and mentoring this situation can be overcome. Residency programs for new graduates were developed to provide needed time to foster knowledge application and to increase accuracy in decision-making and expertise in coming to know the whole person. The nurses at the bedside are acute observers of patients' reactions and responses to illness. This responsiveness to the patient ensures quality, safe, and effective care. Clinical wisdom has also been linked to expertise suggesting that the more experienced nurse knows the whole patient, is intentionally focused on the patient's experience, and is able to notice changes in patients' behavior and address those inconsistencies promptly (Litchfield, 1999). The following example provides a common patient scenario and reflects the nurse's ability to fully assess a problem before deciding to act on the basis of limited information.

EXEMPLAR: CLINICAL DECISION-MAKING AND
NURSE EXPERTISE

A nurse goes to see a patient who recently had surgery several days earlier. As she enters the room, the patient appears sad and is crying. The nurse assumes the patient is in physical pain and asks if she would like pain medication. The more experienced nurse, however, might seek to know the whole situation and talk further with the patient about her behavior. With additional information the nurse finds out that the crying is linked to the fact that the patient just got off the phone with a family member and was upset about the conversation. The nurse's response then seeks to provide comfort using a different strategy.

Assessment: Problem Solving

Within the problem-solving approach to care, nurses at the bedside need to have a systemized approach to data collection. A nursing assessment using an organized approach to data collection is a way to come to know the person and generate a clinical judgment. It involves the collection analysis and synthesis of disciplinary and other biomedical and behavioral knowledge data to arrive at a clinical judgment (diagnosis).

To date, nursing lacks a standardized approach to assessment. In some clinical settings nurses follow a systems review, others a checklist, and some use a focused assessment (e.g., pain) or a risk assessment (e.g., falls or medical risks). These approaches are often incomplete or focused on a presenting problem or chief complaint. Linking assessment to knowing the person requires a more in-depth approach to come to understand the total patient experience. Assessment formats that seek to establish the nature of an individuals responses over time, including perceiving the person's health status and changes in "usual" health patterns, are essential to clinical decision-making. The process involves an organized systematic approach, different from a medical assessment, and is a way to

- Generate clinical information (cues) responsive to nursing autonomous practice

- Synthesize data

- Generate a clinical judgment (nursing diagnosis)

- Select interventions

- Produce measurable evidence that informs outcomes

To date a common, standardized nursing approach to data collection has been the use of the Functional Health Pattern Assessment Framework (FHP) (Gordon, 1982; Gordon, 2008). The FHP assesses an individual's function within 11 pattern areas to determine a patient's perception of function and overall health.

Functional Health Pattern (FHP) Assessment

The Functional Health Pattern (FHP) framework is defined as optimal level of functioning for an individual, family, or community (Gordon, 1994; Gordon, 2008). The FHP describes client strengths and function, lifestyle management, and overall health status. Data generated for each pattern provides cues (evidence) to guide clinical judgments. Data from each pattern synthesis is expressed as a nursing diagnosis. The FHP assessment framework provides a systematic, structured approach to assessing patients (families and communities). Table 5.2 provides a list of the 11 functional patterns with definitions.

TABLE 5.2: Functional Health Pattern Assessment (Gordon, 1994, 2008)

PATTERN	DESCRIPTION
Health Perception— Health Management	Describes individual's (family, community) perceived pattern of health and well-being; also describes perception of how health is managed and health behaviors practiced routinely to prevent illness and promote health. Identification of behaviors that place an individual's health at risk (e.g., smoking, use of alcohol, drugs) are also evaluated. Pattern assessment can include demographics that address allergies, medical prescriptions, perceptions associated with personal safety, etc.

PATTERN	DESCRIPTION
Nutritional—Metabolic	Describes an individual's food and fluid intake, along with metabolic indicators of intake including body temperature, height, weight, and body mass. Assessment includes reporting about hair, nails, and mucus membranes; condition of teeth and gums; and pattern of skin healing. Access to food supply and patterns/rituals around eating can be explored.
Elimination	Describes individual's perceived regularity of excretory function (bowel, bladder, and skin) and the times per day/week, mode, quantity, and quality of excretion. Use of laxatives or devices to control excretion and changes in routine or usual pattern are explored.
Activity/Exercise Tolerance	Describes the individual's perceived pattern of activity and exercise, including quantity and quality of activity. Pattern assessment includes work activity, leisure time, activities of daily living requiring energy expenditure (e.g., bathing, cooking, cleaning, shopping), and exploration of how the person responds to these activities.
Sleep/Rest	Describes the individual's perceived quantity and quality of sleep during a 24-hour period, nighttime routines (including the use of sleep aids and medications), interrupted sleep (urinary frequency), energy level when awake, and periods of relaxation.
Cognitive/Perception	Describes perceived sense of taste, smell, touch, hearing, and vision, along with cognitive ability (language, memory, decision-making) and pain perception/tolerance and usual pattern of pain management.
Self-Perception/ Self-Concept	Perception of one's self, including attitudes about one's self, intellectual abilities, body image, sense of personal identity, self-esteem, worth, and emotional pattern.

continues

TABLE 5.2: *continued*

PATTERN	DESCRIPTION
Role-Relationship	Describes pattern of perceived role engagements and relationships. In addition, perceptions linked to role satisfaction/dissatisfaction, major roles (work, family, social situations), and related responsibilities are explored.
Sexuality—Reproductive	Describes reproductive pattern as well as satisfaction/dissatisfaction with one's sexuality.
Coping/Stress-Tolerance	Describes perceived usual pattern of coping with stress (e.g., identification of potential stressors, response to stress), ability to control/manage stress, and includes supports and other resources used to manage stress.
Value/Belief	Describes perceived goals, values, beliefs (including spiritual and religious beliefs), meanings, choices, and decisions. Includes importance and conflicts with values and beliefs and health.

Exploration of each functional pattern by the nurse is accomplished using a variety of questions to understand an individual's function and perception of their response(s) in health and illness. To assess all 11 FHPs, nurses engage in purposeful questioning and branching (or expanded questions) to obtain an unfolding picture of functional health. Data collected reflects an individual's (family, community) perceptions of function along with objective (measurable) data. Each pattern is evaluated separately by the nurse and evaluated across patterns. All 11 of the functional patterns need to be assessed before a clinical judgment (nursing diagnosis) is made. Table 5.3 provides examples of questions that can be asked to evaluate an FHP.

TABLE 5.3: Sample Questions for Assessment of Selected Functional Health Patterns (Gordon, 1994, 2008; Jones & Lepley, 1986)

HEALTH PERCEPTION, HEALTH MANAGEMENT

1. On a scale of 1–10 how would you rate your current health?
2. What do you do on a regular basis to maintain your health?
3. How does your present health compare to your health one year ago?
4. Do you smoke?
5. What non-prescription medications do you use on a regular basis?
6. Do seasonal changes affect your health? Describe.
7. Do you feel your age has influenced your current health status?

NUTRITIONAL METABOLIC PATTERN

1. Report the foods consumed over a 24-hour period.
2. Patient's height and weight?
3. Is it easy for you to access food?
4. Do you usually prepare your own meals?
5. Do you usually eat three meals a day? at a similar time?
6. Do you feel satisfied at the completion of each meal?
7. Do you snack during the day?
8. Are you satisfied with your current weight? If not, what would you like to change?
9. Does your level of perceived stress affect you eating behavior? Describe.

SLEEP REST PATTERN

1. How many hours do you sleep each night?
2. Do you have any usual routines prior to going to sleep?
3. Do you take medications to fall asleep?
4. How easy is it for you to fall asleep?
5. Is your sleep interrupted? Why?
6. If your sleep is interrupted, is it easy for you to return to sleep?
7. Do you feel rested when you awake?
8. Do you take a nap during the day?
9. Have you noticed a change in your sleep pattern? Why do you think this is occurring?

FHPs describe information about the patient experience within the context of a holistic assessment. This information can be used to identify and validate clinical judgments (diagnosis), foster knowledge synthesis (mid-range theory), and generate testable diagnoses or identify new phenomena. The FHP assessment framework has been used with multiple nursing theories (Gordon, 1982, 1994, 2008) and with a variety of populations, age groups, and health conditions.

Within the context of the FHP assessment framework are two types of assessments nurses can use with patients and groups:

1. A *full assessment* involves a comprehensive assessment of all 11 health patterns and takes about 30 minutes to 1 hour to complete. A series of questions is used by the provider to uncover patient information (Gordon, 1994, 2004; Herdman, 2012-14; Jones & Lepley, 1986) and evaluate each pattern.

2. A *partial assessment* refers to data collected within several patterns that have been selected to assess at a given point in time. For example, pattern data related to the nutritional metabolic pattern or activity/exercise might be evaluated for a patient with obesity. What is important to remember is that within the FHP framework this assessment database is considered incomplete without data from all 11 patterns.

Screening the Functional Health Patterns

A **screening assessment** can be used to quickly assess screen responses to all 11 FHPs and guide further nursing assessment. Screening assessments are often used in response to challenges with time and patient availability. The Functional Health Pattern Assessment Screening Tool (FHPAST) was designed as a measure for use in research (Barrett & Jones, 1999; Jones, Flanagan & Duffy, 2012). The FHPAST captures all 11 FHPs and can be completed in 5–10 minutes by the patient or a designee (e.g., family member or nurse). Findings from a psychometric evaluation of the 57-item FHPAST indicate the presence of three subscales. The tool is a reliable, construct-valid tool that can be used in research to measure functional health. The FHPAST could help isolate actual or potential patient problems, provide information about changing health status, or help identify risk or readiness for health. Sample screening assessment questions from the FHPAST include:

- I feel good about myself.

- I have difficulty controlling my anger.

- I feel safe.

- I am happy with my life.

- I have enough energy for daily activities.

- I am comfortable with the role I play in my family.

- Health is important to me.

- I feel rested when I am awake. (Jones, Flanagan & Duffy et al., 2012)

Following an assessment of the patient's health using a framework such as FHPs, the nurse analyzes and synthesizes the data and arrives at a clinical judgment or nursing diagnosis. As the nurse identifies related factors from the assessment data to support the diagnosis selected or seeks to obtain more information to increase the accuracy of the diagnosis identified.

Nursing Diagnosis

A nursing diagnosis is "a clinical judgment about an individual, family, or community experiences/responses to an actual or potential health problem/life processes. A nursing diagnosis provides the basis for the selection of nursing interventions to achieve outcomes for which the nurse has accountability" (Herdman, 2012-14, p. S15). According to the North American Nursing Diagnosis Association-International (NANDA-I) website, a diagnosis can be an actual/potential diagnosis, a risk diagnosis, a syndrome, and a health promotion/wellness nursing diagnosis that have been researched, tested, validated, and approved for inclusion in the NANDA–I Classification of Nursing Diagnosis (Herdman, 2102-14). A nursing diagnosis contains a label (name/concept), a definition, related factors or cues that support the presence of a diagnosis, and/or risk factors.

The process of accepting and classifying nursing diagnosis is a complex one and effectively managed by a committee infrastructure within NANDA-I. Currently NANDA-I uses 13 domains and 47 classes to organize nursing diagnoses. Clinicians at the bedside have made significant contributions to the development, testing, and refinement of more than 140 nursing diagnoses. Accuracy (Lunney, 2009) of each nursing diagnosis and the language used to modify it (axes) are guiding nursing decisions and interventions. Nursing diagnoses development has given nurses a language to communicate their practice and content to inform the science. The NANDA-I classification is used globally and discussed at regular meetings held by NANDA-I. Nurses from around the world participate in the development, testing, and refinement of nursing diagnoses. The Diagnosis Development Committee (DDC) within NANDA-I meets regularly to review submissions and discuss advances and challenges around the use and implementation of nursing diagnoses. The NANDA-I classification contains data that can be coded for use in the electronic health record and provides a direct link to the judgments made by the nurse that impact health care outcomes.

Nursing Interventions

An **intervention** is defined as "any treatment, based upon clinical judgment and knowledge that a nurse performs to enhance patient/client outcomes" (Bulechek, Dochterman & Butcher, 2008). Nursing interventions are activities that occur in response to a clinical judgments (nursing diagnosis), identified by the nurse as requiring direct or indirect nursing action. The Nursing Interventions Classification (NIC) contains a comprehensive listing of research-based interventions and independent and collaborative activities developed by nurse leaders at the Center for Nursing Classification and Clinical Effectiveness (CNC), University of Iowa. NIC actions are used in the delivery of patient care or might be linked to indirect activities that are part of a nurse's role (e.g., consultation and collaboration with other disciplines). The NIC includes 542 interventions (Bulechek et al., 2008; CNC), each of which is located in 1 of 7 domains and grouped into 30 classes. The NIC interventions have been mapped to NANDA-I and Nursing Outcomes Classification (NOC) outcomes (Johnson et al., 2003). Each intervention contains a label name, a definition, a set of activities that are used to implement the intervention, and references. The NIC data has been coded for use in the electronic health record and describes the autonomous and collaborative actions taken by the nurse to impact health care outcomes.

Nursing Outcomes

"An outcome is a measurable individual, family, or community state, behavior or perception that is measured along a continuum and is responsive to nursing interventions" (Morehead, Johnson, Mass & Swanson, 2008). NOC provides a research-based, comprehensive classification of patient/client outcomes. NOC was developed to evaluate nursing actions taken to address a nursing diagnosis. The classification lists 330 NOC outcomes organized in 7 domains and 34 classes (classification-center@uiowa.edu).

Each outcome contains a definition, evaluation indicators, rating scale for each indicator, and references. NOC is designed to measure patient progress on a predetermined basis (hourly or daily, for example) and make changes to the plan of care based upon evaluation data to achieve a desired goal. Examples of scales used to rate the status of outcome are:

- 1 = extremely compromised to 5 = not compromised

- 1 = never demonstrated to 5 = consistently demonstrated

The NOC has been coded for use in the electronic health record and provides visible, measureable evidence around nurse-sensitive contributions to health care outcomes.

Advantages of Standardized Nursing Languages

"If you cannot name it, we cannot control it, practice it, research it, teach it, finance it, or put it into public policy" (Clark & Lang, 1997). Though this message was delivered years ago, its importance resonates today. The development of standardized languages first began in 1973 (Gebbie & Lavin, 1973) with a group later to be called the North American Nursing Diagnosis Association (NANDA). The goal of the group was the naming and classifying of nursing phenomena of concern (American Nurses Association [ANA], 2004).

As a discipline, nurses have been working to communicate their practice to others. The 2012 celebration of NANDA-I's 40th Anniversary highlighted that much work had been accomplished to advance nursing and standardized languages. The depth of research and development reported was overwhelming and had global scope and reach. As nursing continues to debate the value of standardized nursing languages (SNLs) in education, practice, and research, the work moves forward. Recently, renewed attention to the patient's electronic health record (EHR) has revitalized the need to publically document evidence to communicate nursing practice in an electronic format.

The American Nurses Association (ANA) Nursing Information and Data Set Evaluation Center (NIDSEC) has approved multiple data sets, classifications, and taxonomies for inclusion in information system vendors. NANDA-I, NIC, and NOC, along with other SNLs, such as the Home Health Care Classification (HHCC) (Saba, 1992) and the Omaha System (Martin & Scheet, 1992), have been approved. NANDA-I, NIC, and NOC, the largest and most developed nursing languages, are included in the National Library of Medicine's thesaurus for a Unified Medical Language, and in the Cumulative Index to Nursing Literature and mapped into a SNOMED (Systemized Nomenclature of Medicine) RT. NANDA-I, NIC, and NOC have also been approved for use by Health Level 7 (HL7) Terminology.

The use of SNLs by nurses at the bedside has accelerated in recent years, prompted by legislation and health care reform activities. Within some health care systems across the United States, such as SNOMED RT, and internationally, such as International Classification of Nursing Practice (ICNP) (Coenen, 2001), SNLs have been integrated into a variety of information systems. Widespread use is evolving. A review of literature discussing the integration of nursing SNLs in the workplace suggests that "the integration of SNLs into the patient record offers nurses an opportunity to describe the focus of their practice through the identification of nursing diagnosis, interventions and outcomes" (Jones, Lunney, Keegan & Moorhead, 2011, p. 253-54). The review also presents multiple research strategies that have been used to develop, test, and refine SNLs to teach, further research, evaluate, and use in practice to communicate nursing care. Contributions of SNLs are summarized in Table 5.4.

TABLE 5.4: Contributions of Standardized Nursing Language (SNLs)

Support nursing knowledge development and delineate the substantive content of the discipline (e.g., concept isolation, concept development, generation of mid-range theory)

Promote the continued development, testing, and refinement of concepts and content essential to the discipline

Relate social policy mandate and standards of nursing care with clinical decision-making, nursing assessment, diagnosis, outcomes, and interventions

Link judgments about the patient experiences with care outcomes and nursing's response (interventions) to address concerns

Use across populations, specialties, settings, age groups, cultures, and ethnic groups to describe individual, family, and community responses to health and well-being as well as illness

Provide a language to articulate (voice) nursing's contribution to care outcomes, a language to articulate nursing practice

Link evidence for achieving successful patient/organizational outcomes/indicators with nursing knowledge-based interventions

Enable nurses to identify frequently occurring problems associated with individuals and groups and intensify nursing assessment and management of risk and commonly occurring nursing diagnosis (e.g., risk for falls, ineffective pain management, anxiety, ineffective individual/family coping)

Integrate SNL easily into information systems used to document information in the EHR

Code SNL data to cost out nursing care encounters, capture evidence, determine nurse-patient ratio, and acknowledge patient complexity on nurse staffing and time in caring

Advances research, development, testing, and validation of SNLs using multiple methodologies

Translate and use SNLs globally to create an international body of knowledge that can be used in global research and dialogue

Develop, test, and refine multiple theoretical frameworks and research methodologies to extend and refine nursing knowledge

Contribute to the development of predictive models related to cost, quality, and nursing practice

Figure 5.2 focuses on the interaction of SNLs within the nurse-patient environment of care. It proposes that the knowledge of the discipline (e.g., concepts defined and the diagnosis) are essential to care delivery. The use of SNLs in practice gives voice to the discipline, facilitates documentation, and communicates evidence to influence outcomes. The development, testing, and refinement of SNLs promote a nursing language that can be used to inform education and influence practice. Nursing diagnosis contributes knowledge for practice, can be refined and tested through research, and gives voice when communicating the discipline to others. The model provided in Figure 5.2 can be used to articulate diagnoses, interventions, and outcomes and their impact on patient care.

Process/Dialogue Approach

Knowledge linked to health, mutual processes, patterning, caring, consciousness, presence, resonance, and meaning provides the framework for nursing within the context of a process dialogue. This approach promotes "the nature of a relationship that is transformative for both nurse and patient" (Newman et al., 2008). Benner used the narrative as a way of "understanding the patient experience as an evaluation of a nurse's growth and professional development" (Benner, 1984). Understanding an experience from the patient's perspective creates a different dialogue and understanding of the content expressed in the dialogue (Newman et al., 2008, p. E16).

Understanding Health and the Pattern of the Whole

Appreciating a process dialogue approach to care is a mutual one, relying heavily on the nurse-patient relationship, intentional presence, and an implicit grasp of the whole (Newman, 1994; Newman 2008). The dynamic interaction of person and their environment and experiencing the unfolding whole is inherent in the process (Cowling, 2000; Endo, 1998; Litchfield, 1999). Within the process both the nurse and the patient recognize insights that inform choices, actions, and transformation. Data from the dialogue informs an unfolding pattern of the whole (Flanagan, 2009; Newman, 2008; Picard & Jones, 2005).

Environment of Health Care

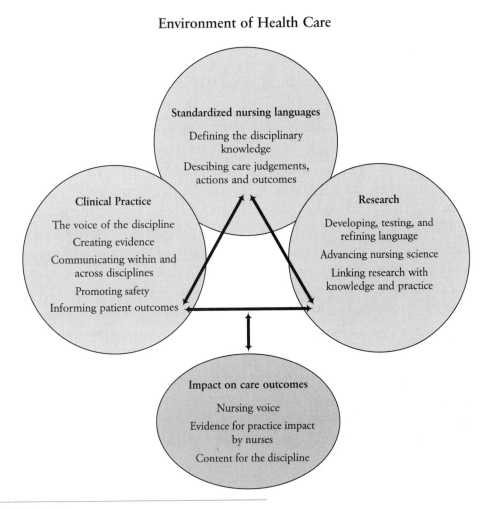

Standardized nursing languages

Defining the disciplinary knowledge

Descibing care judgements, actions and outcomes

Clinical Practice

The voice of the discipline

Creating evidence

Communicating within and across disciplines

Promoting safety

Informing patient outcomes

Research

Developing, testing, and refining language

Advancing nursing science

Linking research with knowledge and practice

Impact on care outcomes

Nursing voice

Evidence for practice impact by nurses

Content for the discipline

FIGURE 5.2

Interface of Standardized Nursing Language (e.g., NANDA-I, knowledge development, clinical practice, and evidence for research) (Jones, 2012).

The nurse-patient encounter allows for the uniqueness and wholeness of the pattern to emerge (Newman, 1994). The experience is guided by an "invitation to participate" (Picard & Jones, 2005) in the dialogue. The patient is in control of the discussion and how the information unfolds. The nurse becomes an active participant in the process, moving with the patient through the process (Barron,

2005). Establishing a safe space for creating the dialogue is important to the nurse at the bedside. The intentional presence of the nurse allows for silence and freedom of expression, and refocusing of the dialogue emerges. Cowling (2000) uses pattern appraisal as a way to appreciate wholeness within the lived experiences of another.

Newman (1994, 2008) uses the frame of Health as Expanding Consciousness (HEC) as praxis to actualize pattern recognition. Uncovering the underlying pattern of the whole requires the full intentional presence of the nurse. The patient and nurse engage in a mutual process of actively listening and attending to the other. Each participant provides clarity as requested and new ideas as the conversation progresses. The nurse can open the dialogue in a variety of ways, including responding to a patient concern or a request for information. Another approach is using an opening question such as "Tell me about the people and events in your life that have been meaningful to you." The patient begins the story, and as it unfolds, the nurse participates in the dialogue and also seeks clarification as needed. The goal is to "grasp meaning" and come to know the pattern of the whole (Newman, 2008, p. 89-91).

Following the dialogue the nurse can present the patient with a construal or configuration that depicts relationships and patient experiences that informs the evolving pattern. This patient has an opportunity to reflect on the data and provide clarification and validation. The nurse seeks to engage in the experience, working with the patient to uncover meaning, identify opportunity for new choices and actions, and support the person with knowledge and assistance in response to the patient's responses. The process is a mutual one and expressed within the context of the nurse patient/family/community relationship (MacLeod, 2011; Ruka, 2005).

A patient experience that focuses on pattern moves away from the medical disease and illness and incorporates them as part of the whole experience. Data provided by the patient occurs within this context and focuses on the patient's story. Emerging from dialogue with the patient, each story is unique, and the pattern expressed is validated with the possibility that new insights and meanings might emerge, resulting in increased awareness of new possibilities, choices, and actions to improve health and personal transformation.

Advantages to the Process Dialogue Approach

Educational experiences using a more structured assessment (e.g., the FHPs) paired with an opportunity to uncover a pattern in a less structured way offer the learner the opportunity to see the benefit of both approaches on uncovering and discovery of knowledge for the patient and nurse (Newman, 2008). Powerful articles by leaders at the bedside (Capasso, 1998; Jonsdottir, Litchfield & Pharris, 1993), including change and sustaining healthy behaviors (Berry, 2004), living with chronic illness (Flanagan, 2009; MacLeod, 2011), promoting health through family and community engagement (Pharris, 2002; Rosa, 2009; Ruka, 2005), all describe the role of patient choice and nurse action to promote a mutual transformation, all realized within the process dialogue approach to care.

Researchers using HEC as praxis reported the value of the nurse-patient relationship in uncovering patterns, promoting holistic health, and promoting change and mutual growth. The following exemplars offer insight to the value of intentional presence, "being there," and mutual relationship.

EXEMPLARS: RESEARCH AND HEC

Capasso: Discovering and Uncovering the Whole

Capasso's work (1998) provides a clear link to entering an experience through a part ... to find the whole. Dr. Capasso, a clinical nurse specialist and wound care specialist, was participating in a home visit with a patient recovering from a wound that was not closing. On a particular visit, the patient suddenly said "I don't know why but I feel like telling you something that I have never told anyone ... even in deep analysis. My adoptive father sexually abused me when I was 9 years old (p. 67)." In the quiet of the patient's home, the patient began to sob.

Capasso, not sure of how to respond, simply went to the patient and hugged her. Further discussion ensued, and the patient was offered a referral to a therapist for more follow-up. Capasso continued to change the dressing and observed the wound.

On a return visit one week later Capasso noted "obvious improvement" in the wound as she removed the dressing. She reported this to the patient who told her of her a renewed interest in participating in interventions Capasso suggested earlier. She said, "You know you really helped me last week" (p. 68). For Capasso, this was a defining moment that facilitated intentional presence, connectedness, provider availability, and mutual trust.

Ruka: The Family Role in Sustaining the Pattern of the Whole

Ruka (2005) came to know the elderly patients with Alzheimer's disease by conducting a pattern analysis with the nursing home residents' families. The creation of a healing and responsive environment, use of complementary therapies (e.g., therapeutic touch, pet therapy), and redesigning and innovating care practices (e.g., the "comfort Zone"—a new bathing tub) designed to reduce the stress of activities for the patient's enhanced patient responsiveness. Nurses introduced life stories and photos obtained from the family to recall happy events when patients became agitated and promoted a healthy environment for the patients, the families, and staff.

MacLeod: Uncovering Spousal Response Pattern to Recovery and Chronic Illness

MacLeod's (2011) experiences focused on the spouses (wives) of patients following cardiac surgery. In visits with the wives at home, MacLeod uncovered how the patient's recovery also changes the life of the caregiver.

Wives disclosed that there was a significant period of adjustment and an uncertainty about what would happen during this time between discharge from the hospital and entering a rehabilitation program 6 weeks later. The wives expressed fears associated with "not knowing," changes in their lifestyles, and roles and responsibilities along with social isolation. Participants described limiting family and friends coming to visit for fear that they might compromise the patient's recovery. Spouses felt alone with no one to talk to who truly understood what was happening to them.

"By giving the caregivers the opportunity to reflect on their lives ... new realizations regarding the influence their life experiences had on the current experience began to emerge" (MacLeod, 2011, p. 253). As they talked with the nurse, new understandings and meanings about the caregiving experience were expressed. The importance of relationship with the nurse, along with availability and active listening and opportunities for reflection, were important for the nurse, the caregiver, and the patient to move forward.

Experiences such as these are transformative and speak to the impact that nurses have on a variety of caring experiences. Within the caregiving role nurses help patients bring awareness, choice, and new actions. Change is a process, and time is critical to developing a truly patient-centric health care system. Nurses are in a key position and have the needed knowledge to make this happen.

Implications for Advancing Nursing Leadership at the Bedside

Nursing is currently in a critical position to redesign health care and reform the way health is defined (Newman et al., 2008). Knowledge acquired to date and the way it is used in practice seeks to address health in a way that gives a new perspective on patients' engagement in taking actions to improve health and sustain new behaviors in a way that acknowledges patient's involvement in change that is transformative.

Figure 5.3 focuses on the iterative nature of knowledge development and its impact on care. As nurses, we can connect to the process at any point. As an example, research produces the needed evidence to inform education and shape practice. In turn, the questions that need to be studied can emerge from

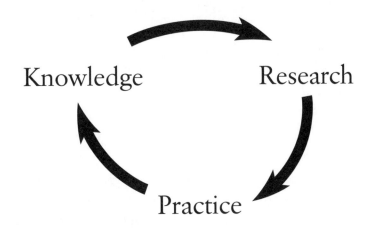

FIGURE 5.3

Care at the bedside and knowledge development: An iterative process.

the challenges in clinical practice. Researchers can provide the methodologies to uncover new knowledge around these concerns. This knowledge can stimulate new research, advance education, and cycle back to impact patient care.

Nurses need to look to the practice environment for the questions and in turn bring the answers back to the place where they originated, continuing to build the science, impact health promotion, and inform policy. For Willis and colleagues (2008, p. E 29) "nursing practice shapes nursing knowledge." Current shifts in practice and the number of doctorally prepared nurses in practice roles appear to support this belief.

Educators must provide students with a disciplinary framework to guide care and help articulate their practice. Knowledge acquisition should focus from within and across other disciplines. By learning to distinguish nursing practice outcomes from other disciplines and recognizing opportunities to complement and collaborate with other providers, nurses can give voice unique contributions to patient care. This can reduce disciplinary blurring and promote the values needed to enhance patients' and staff's satisfaction with care.

Nursing Leadership at the Bedside: Organizational Commitment to Excellence

Nurses at the bedside and beyond are "thirsty for a meaningful practice, one that is based upon nursing values and knowledge, one that is relationship centered ... and brings a missing dimension to our current health care" (Newman et al., 2008 p. E25). Today, both the consumers and health care providers worry about the shift in care away from the person to a focus on health care as a business. The fear is that care will become less than personal and turn more automated and increasingly mechanistic.

Although this concern might be the view of many, others suggest that "nursing is in a position to shape the future stage of evolution of the universe" (Roy, 2007). To accomplish this, nursing leaders across academic and health care settings and policy environments must influence (Adams, 2009) care environments and promote new opportunities for nurses to develop, implement, evaluate, research, test, and refine the delivery of patient/family-centric care across acute care, primary care, and community settings. Nurses need to use disciplinary and other related knowledge to come to know the patients as people, their perceptions of the experiences associated with health and illness, and the impact of life experiences on current and future health choices and actions.

Summary

The intentional presence of the nurse and the ability to create an environment of care that promotes healing and caring can yield care outcomes attributable to nursing. Nurses at the bedside must "be empowered to discover new opportunities to participate fully and creatively in shaping our future" (Tarnas, 2002). Collaboration with other disciplines can bring patient-centric care to a new level and allow the best of all science to advance care that is patient-centered. Facilitating this can be fully realized in outcomes that reduce cost, promote quality and safety, and increase provider and patient satisfaction with health care. Shalala (2009) states, "To successfully transform the way health care is structured and delivered in our country, it is absolutely essential to actively engage nurses for their leadership and unique expertise." Leadership at the bedside working to advance care within a professional practice environment can make this a reality.

> Knowing who we are in the context of society and other related discipline is essential for our own health and well-being and essential for our own ability to help others. (Chinn, 1999, p. 14)

References

Adams, J. M. (2009). *The Adams Influence Model (AIM): Understanding the factors, attributes and process of achieving influence*. Saarbrüken, Germany: VDM Verlag.

Aiken, L., & Patrician, P. (2000). Measuring organizational traits of hospitals: The revised nursing work index. *Nursing Research, 49*(3), 146-153.

American Nurses Association (ANA). (2004). *A social policy statement*. Washington, DC: Author.

Barrett, E. A. M. (2003). Update on a measure of power as knowing participation in change. In O. L. Strickland & C. DiIorio (Eds.), *Measurement of nursing outcomes: Focus on patient/client outcomes, Vol. 4* (pp. 21-39). New York, NY: Springer.

Barrett, F., & Jones, D. (1999). Development and testing of the functional health pattern screening assessment tool. In M. Rantz & P. LeMone (Eds.), *Proceedings from the 13th North American Nursing Diagnosis Association*. Glendale, CA: CINAHL Information System.

Barron, A. M. (2005). Suffering, growth and possibility: Health as expanding consciousness in end-of-life care. In C. Picard & D. Jones, *Giving voice to what we know: Margaret Newman's theory of health as expanding consciousness in nursing practice, education and research*. Sudbury, MA: Jones and Bartlett.

Benner, P. (1984). *From novice to expert: Excellence in clinical nursing practice*. Menlo Park, CA: Addison Wesley.

Benner, P., & Tanner, C. (1987). Clinical judgment: How expert nurses use intuition. *American Journal of Nursing, 87*(1), 23-31.

Benner, P., Tanner, C. A., & Chelsa, C. A. (1996). *Expertise in nursing caring: Clinical judgment and ethics*. New York, NY: Springer Publishing Co.

Berry, D. (2004). An emerging model of behavior change in women maintaining weight loss. *Nursing Science Quarterly, 17*(3), 242-252.

Bohm, D. (1993). Science, spirituality, and the present world crisis. *ReVision, 15*(4), 147-152.

Bulechek, G., Butcher, H., & Dochterman, J. (2008). *Nursing intervention classification (NIC)*, (5th ed.). St. Louis, MO: Mosby Elsevier.

Capasso, V. A. (1998). The theory is the practice: An exemplar. *Clinical Nurse Specialist, 12*(6), 226-229.

Center for Nursing Classification and Clinical Effectiveness (CNC). University of Iowa. classification-center@uiowa.edu

Chase, S. K. (2001). Response to The concept of nursing presence: State of the science. *Scholarly Inquiry for Nursing Practice: An International Journal, 15*, 323-327.

Chase, S. K. (2004). *Clinical judgment and communication in nurse practitioner practice*. Philadelphia, PA: F.A. Davis.

Chinn, P. (1999). Do we know who we mean when we say "we"? *Advances in Nursing Science, 14*(1), vi.

Coakley, A. B., & Mahoney, E. K. (2009). Creating a therapeutic and healing environment with a pet therapy program. *Complementary Therapies in Clinical Practice, 15*(3), 141-146.

Coenen A. (2003). The International Classification for Nursing Practice (ICNP®) Programme: Advancing a Unifying Framework for Nursing. *Online Journal of Issues in Nursing, 8*(2).

Cowling, W.R. III. (2000). Healing as appreciating wholeness. *Advances in Nursing Science, 22*(3), 16-32.

Della Monica, N. (2008). *Development and psychometric evaluation of the nurse caring patient scale*. (Doctoral Dissertation). Boston College (Publication No ATT3310341).

Doona, M. E., Chase, S. K., & Haggerty, L. A. (1999). Nursing presence: As real as a Milky Way bar. *Journal of Holistic Nursing, 17*(1), 54-70

Dossey, B. M., & Keegan, L. (2013). *Holistic nursing: A handbook for practice* (6th ed.). Burlington, MA: Jones and Bartlett Learning.

Endo, E. (1998). Pattern recognition as a nursing intervention with Japanese women with ovarian cancer. *Advances in Nursing Science, 20*(4), 49-61.

Flanagan, J. (2005). Creating a healing environment for staff and patients in the pre surgery clinic. In C. Picard & D. Jones (Eds.), *Giving voice to what we know: Margaret Newman's theory of health as expanding consciousness in nursing practice, education and research* (pp. 53-63). Sudbury, MA: Jones and Bartlett.

Flanagan, J. (2009). Patient and nurse experiences of theory-based care. *Nursing Science Quarterly*, 22(2), 160-172.

Gebbie, C., & Lavin, M. (1973). *Proceedings from the first national conference to classify nursing diagnosis*. St. Louis, MO: C.V. Mosby.

Gordon, M. (1982). *Nursing diagnosis: Process and application*. New York, NY: McGraw-Hill.

Gordon, M. (1994). *Nursing diagnosis: Process and application*. New York, NY: McGraw-Hill.

Gordon, M. (2008). *Assess notes: Nursing assessment and diagnostic reasoning*. Burlington, MA: Jones and Bartlett.

Gordon, M. (2010). *Manual of nursing diagnosis*. Philadelphia, PA: F. A. Davis.

Herdman, T. H. (Ed.), (2012-14). *NANDA-I Nursing diagnosis: Definitions and classification*. Oxford, UK: Wiley Blackwell.

Institute of Medicine (IOM). (2010). *The future of nursing: Leading change, advancing health*. Washington, DC: National Academies Press.

Jenny, J., & Logan, J. (1992). Knowing the patient: One aspect of clinical knowledge. *Image: Journal of Nursing Scholarship, 24*(4), 254-258.

Johnson, D. E. (1965). Today's action will determine tomorrow's nursing. *Nursing Outlook, 12*, 38.

Johnson, M., Bulecheck, G., Butcher, H., McCloskey Dochterman, J., Mass, M., Moorhead, S., & Swanson, E. (2006). *NANDA, NOC, and NIC linkages. Nursing diagnoses, outcomes and intervention*, (2nd ed.). St. Louis, MO: Elsevier Health Sciences.

Jones, D. (2006). Health as expanding consciousness. *Nursing Science Quarterly, 19*(4), 330-332.

Jones, D. (2007). A synthesis of philosophical perspectives for knowledge development. In C. Roy & D. A. Jones (Eds.), *Nursing Knowledge Development and Clinical Practice* (pp. 163-176). New York, NY: Springer Publishing.

Jones, D., Duffy, M., & Flanagan, J. (in press). Psychometric functional health pattern screening assessment tool (FHPAST). *Journal of Nursing Knowledge, 1*.

Jones, D., & Flanagan, J. (2007). Guest editorial. *International Journal of Nursing Terminologies and Classifications*, Winter-Feb/March.

Jones, D., & Lepley, M. (1986). *Health assessment manual*. New York, NY: McGraw-Hill.

Jones, D., Lunney, M., Keegan, G., & Moorhead, S. (2011). Standardized nursing languages: Essential for nursing workforce. In A. Debisette and J. Vessey (Eds.), *Annual Review of Nursing Research, Volume 28: Nursing Workforce Issues, 2010* (pp. 253-294). New York, NY: Springer Publishing.

Jonsdottir, H., Litchfield, M., & Pharris, M. (1993). Partnerships in practice. *Research Theory and Nursing Practice International Journal, 17*(1), 51-63.

Lang, N. M., & Clark, J. (1997). The international classification for nursing practice: Classification of nursing outcomes. *International Nursing Review, 44*(4), 121-124.

Litchfield, M. (1999). Practice wisdom. *Advances in Nursing Science, 22*(2), 62-73.

Lunney, M. (2009). *Critical thinking to achieve positive health outcomes: Nursing case studies and analysis* (2nd ed.). Ames, IA: Wiley Blackwell.

MacLeod, C. (2011). Understanding the experiences of spousal caregivers in health as expanding consciousness. *Advances in Nursing Science, 24*(3), 245-255.

Martin, K. S., & Scheet, N. J. (1992). *The Omaha System: Application for community health nursing.* Philadelphia, PA: Saunders.

Moorhead, S., Johnson, M., Mass, M., & Swanson, E. (2008). *The Nursing Outcomes Classification, (NOC).* St. Louis, MO: Mosby Elsevier.

Newman, M. A. (1994). *Health as expanding consciousness* (2nd ed.). Sudbury, MA: NLN Press.

Newman, M. A. (2008). *Transforming presence: The difference that nursing makes.* Sudbury, MA: Jones and Bartlett.

Newman, M. A., Smith, M., Pharris, M., & Jones, D. (2008). Focus of the discipline revisited. *Advances in Nursing Science, 31*(1), E16-27.

Peat, F. D. (1991). *The philosopher's stone: Chaos, synchronicity, and the hidden order of the world.* New York, NY: Bantam Books.

Pharris, M. (2002). Coming to know ourselves as community through a nurse partner relationship with adolescents convicted of murder. *Advances in Nursing Science, 24*(3), 21-24.

Picard, C., & Jones, D. (2005). *Giving voice to what we know: Margaret Newman's theory of health as expanding consciousness in nursing practice, education and research.* Sudbury, MA: Jones and Bartlett.

Quinn, J. (1996). Therapeutic touch and a healing way. *Alternative Therapies, 2*(4), 69-75.

Radwin, L. (1996). "Knowing the patient": A review of research on an emerging concept. *Journal of Advanced Nursing, 23*(6), 1142-1146.

Rosa, C. (2009). Recognizing health with pregnant Cambodian American women by finding meaning in relationship. *Advances in Nursing Science, 32*(4), 322-337.

Roy, C. (2007). Global application of the cosmic imperative for nursing knowledge development. In C. Roy & D. A. Jones, (Eds.). *Nursing knowledge development and clinical practice* (p. 321). New York, NY: Springer Publishing.

Roy, C. & Jones, D. A. (2007). *Nursing knowledge development and clinical practice.* New York, NY: Springer Publishing.

Ruka, S. (2005). Creating balance: Rhythms and patterns in people living with dementia in nursing homes. In C. Picard & D. Jones, (Eds.), *Giving voice to what we know: Margaret Newman's theory of health as expanding consciousness in nursing practice, education and research.* Sudbury, MA: Jones and Bartlett.

Saba, V. K. (1992). The classification of home health care nursing: Diagnosis and interventions. *Caring Magazine, 11*(3), 50-57.

Shalala, D. (2009). *Future of health care.* Presentation given at Robert Wood Johnson Foundation Forum.

Shaller, D. (2007). Patient-centered care: What does it take? *Health policy, health reform, and performance improvement, 74*, 1-3.

Smith, M. (2011). Integrative review of research related to Margaret Newman's theory of health as expanding consciousness. *Advances in Nursing Science, 24*(3), 256-272.

Somerville, J. (2009). Development and psychometric testing of patient's perception of feeling known by their nurse scale. *International Journal of Human Caring, 13*(4), 38-43.

Tarnas, R. (1998). The great initiation. *Noetic Sciences Review, 47*, 24-31.

Watson, J. (1999). *Postmodern nursing and beyond*. Edinburgh, UK: Churchill Livingstone.

Watson, J., & Smith, M. (2004). Caring science and the science of unitary human beings: A trans-theoretical discourse for nursing knowledge development. In P. Reed, N. Crawford Shearer, & L. Nicoll (Eds.), *Perspectives on nursing theory* (pp. 449-461). New York, NY: Lippincott Williams and Williams.

Whittemore, R. (2000). Consequences of not "knowing the patient." *Clinical Nurse Specialist, 14*(2), 75-81.

Willis, D. G., Grace, P. J., & Roy, C. (2008). A central unifying focus of the discipline: Facilitating harmonization, meaning, choice, quality of life, and healing in living and dying. *Advances in Nursing Science, 31*(1), E29-40.

Wolf, Z., Zuzelo, P., Goldberg, E., Crothers, R., & Jacobson, N. (2006). The caring behaviors inventory for elders: Development and psychometric characteristics. *International Journal of Human Caring, 10*(4), 49-59.

Chapter 6
Nursing's Moral Imperative

Pamela Grace, PhD, RN, FAAN
Ellen M. Robinson, PhD, RN

What then is your duty? It is what the day demands.

(Goethe, Sprüch in Prosa, 3.151)

Introduction

An underlying assumption of this book is that nurses *should* be prepared and able to facilitate good patient care. Furthermore, when unable to adequately address a patient's problems or concerns, regardless of the reason, nurses then have the further responsibilities to investigate barriers and take steps to remove them. The term *should* implies an ethical obligation or imperative to act in ways that promote good patient care. But what is the foundation for asserting that nurses have an ethical responsibility and what is the strength of the assertion? Do nurses have an ethical duty if their action choices are limited by external circumstances?

This chapter describes the ethical nature of nursing and health care practice; discusses some of the obstacles to ethical practice at the bedside; and provides strategies to strengthen nurses' knowledge, skills, and confidence in recognizing the ethical content of their everyday work and acting accordingly. Additionally, the collaborative roles of bedside nurses in leading efforts to initiate policy and/ or practice changes when the same types of ethical issues keep re-occurring will be discussed. These types of actions facilitate what is called *preventive ethics*. **Preventive ethics** is the idea that many, but not all, complex issues that arise in clinical care could have been effectively addressed earlier if the emerging issues were recognized at or around the time of their inception.

NOTE

As a point of clarity, the terms ethical *and* moral *will be addressed as synonymous within the context of this chapter. Though they are often taken to denote slightly different human characteristics and attitudes in everyday life, they actually have very similar root meanings but come from different languages. Because actions taken in health care and in health care practice are aimed at furthering a human good, the ethical action can also be considered the morally correct action (Grace, 2009).*

Origins of Nurses' Ethical Responsibilities

As a profession responsive to the needs of society nurses play a key role in activities that advance the human good. The origins of ethical responsibilities of nursing are rooted in professional membership, the delivery of a crucial human service.

Professional Membership

Ethical responsibilities are assumed when one becomes a member of a profession, such as nursing, that offers the promise of providing a necessary human good for individuals in the society. A "good" in this sense means some action or gift that helps the individual achieve or regain a sense of well-being or lessens the impact of the harms inevitably experienced in the course of living.

Not all nurses, however, see themselves as being members of a profession or as having an ethical responsibility for the choices they make. And in some countries nurses are not encouraged to act with any autonomy. Like earlier European and U.S. nurses, these nurses might see their main purpose as following the orders or directives of others, such as physicians and supervisors, and they might even realistically be afraid for their own safety if they do otherwise.

However, the evolution of nursing as a vocation, and more recently in developed countries as a profession, provides a model for nurses in developing countries to follow as they strive for more independence in their caregiving activities.

Nursing: A Crucial Human Service

You could argue that the strength of ethical responsibilities attached to professional role varies depending on the purposes of the discipline. However, those professions that provide services of a "grinding, life-or-death sort of importance" (Windt, 1989, p. 7) have strong associated responsibilities. (We give our reasons for asserting this shortly.) Windt explores the relationship of obligation and the service professions, particularly those of law and medicine. Membership in such professions is accompanied with ethical responsibilities to actually provide the service that has been in a sense "promised" via implicit or explicit codes of conduct and ethics.

Elsewhere, Grace (1998, 2001) defended the idea that nursing in developed countries is a profession that similarly provides a human service of critical importance to the well-being of individuals and society. This conception of nursing is supported in the codes of ethics for nurses of various countries and in the International Council of Nurses (ICN) Code of Ethics for Nurses (ICN, 2006), which represents the thinking of nurse scholars and practitioners from 130 member countries. (The purpose and nature of codes of ethics is discussed in more detail later in the chapter.)

Both the American Nurses Association (ANA) and the ICN also recognize the broader societal responsibilities of nurses to address environmental causes of ill health. It might seem unrealistic that nurses working within health care institutions have such broad responsibilities, but because nurses might be the first and only ones to recognize that some health issues arise because of unjust societal arrangements that make people especially vulnerable, nurses' responsibilities might extend beyond the immediate patient care situation (ANA, 2008; ANA, 2010; ICN, 2012). Nursing as a profession exists because of a societal need for the services that nursing provides. In turn the nursing profession is granted by society certain privileges because of the services provided. This places obligations upon nurses and the profession to ensure that it continues to provide needed services.

Professions and Ethical Responsibility

Professional associations and other groups note that certain crucial professions have associated responsibilities. Nursing is a crucial profession for society because of the nature of services it provides. This expectation has implications for the actions of the nursing profession as a whole and those of its individual members. Some might object that nursing is not really a profession but rather a job that requires a certain level of technical proficiency, but not necessarily independent judgments. We present an argument to the contrary.

Though it is not settled exactly which groups constitute a profession because no universally accepted defining criteria exist, some generally accepted characteristics demarcate service professions from other technical, craft, or business-oriented groups. Since Flexner's project in 1915, which was established to determine what might be needed to improve the education of physicians, some characteristics of service professions have generally been agreed as necessary for privileging the profession with control over its own practices. "Flexner … proposed that professions have an extensive and specialized knowledge base, take responsibility for developing and using their knowledge, have a practice or action orientation that is used for the good of the population served, and autonomously set standards for and monitor the actions of their members" (Grace, 2009, p.40).

Lisa Newton (1988) makes an even stronger proposition that

> (T)he professional must respond … if practices in his (sic) field are
> inadequate at any stage of the rendering of the service: if the client
> the ultimate consumer is unhappy; if he is happy but unknowing,

badly served by shabby products or service; or if he is happy and well served by the best available product but the state of the art is not adequate to his real needs. (p. 48)

For Newton, then, professions such as nursing, medicine, and law have anticipatory and reflexive as well as service roles. She is highlighting the fact that people, all things being equal, do not have the knowledge to evaluate the services received or what might be needed in the future. This lack of knowledge can render people vulnerable to their health care needs.

Designating a group of persons who do a particular sort of work as a profession—more importantly as a critical or crucial (to the society) service profession and ceding control and regulation of activities to the particular professional body—is a matter of strong interest to society and its members. This is because professions are also granted by society a certain amount of autonomy over the knowledge development and practice activities of their members. Society does so expecting that the profession knows what is and what is not required for good practice. Practice activities aim to achieve the profession's ultimate goals. These goals have unsurprisingly remained fairly constant and are aligned with those of other health care professionals. However, nursing's perspective on how to achieve these goals has changed and developed in concert with scientific innovations and sociopolitical movements. Internationally, nursing is proposing goals that are designed "to promote health, to prevent illness, to restore health and to alleviate suffering" (ICN, 2006).

Fiduciary Nature of Critical Service Professions

The downside of granting service professions the freedom to control their own practice is that those in need of the profession's services are forced to trust that the focus of services remains on them and their needs (as related to the purposes of the profession) and is not distorted by human greed or self-interest. In this sense, those requiring services are vulnerable to what is needed from a professional and are dependent on the level of integrity of the profession and its members to be responsive to unmet health care needs. Patient expectations and the accompanying vulnerability heighten the obligation of nurses, as service professionals, to stay focused on the patient's well-being as primary.

Society has an interest in the appropriate development of professionals because these professionals have specialized knowledge and skills not readily available to the rest of society. Moreover, a dimension of trust exists between the patient and professional that must be addressed. Society trusts that professions will provide the services that they say they will provide. In addition, consumers rely on each profession to keep the best interests of the individual in mind and not be distracted by ideas of profit, self-interest, or expediency. Contemporarily, we now face worries about the shift to business models of health care delivery and the ability of professions to continue to focus on patient good over economic interests. Though cost-effectiveness is a critical factor in health care delivery, the ostensible reason for the shift to a business model is that more persons can have their health care needs met if more resources are available and waste is reduced.

In the United States, major injustices remain present in the way health care is funded and who has access to services both prior to a hospitalization and on discharge. Such issues are beyond the scope of this chapter. Addressing these challenges, except to say, as professionals, nurses do have responsibilities to collaborate on policy and social issues that create problems for their populations of concern. However, internationally many commonly shared issues face nurses at the bedside, some related to access to care, but many more that are not. Several common and serious problems along with related strategies to address them are discussed later in the chapter. The problems discussed along with the ways to address them are, for the most part, applicable internationally.

The Nature of Professional Responsibility for Good Practice

What, then, does professional responsibility for ethical practice—a practice that aims to further the goals of the profession related to individuals and society— mean for nurses at the point of care? Often these nurses are not entirely free to practice as their clinical judgment directs. An exploration of this question ideally provides nurses with some clarity about their responsibility for, rationale for, and motivation to persist in getting patients what is needed for those patients' optimal care in the face of challenges.

As noted earlier health care-provider relationships are sometimes described as fiduciary in nature. What this means is that they are based in the idea of a differential power relationship that exists between the provider and the patient (Grace, 1998; Pellegrino, 2001; Spenceley, Reutter & Allen, 2006; Zaner, 1991). Patients are vulnerable and because of a lack of knowledge, skills, or capacity must "trust" that health care providers will act in their best interests, which in turn fortifies the existing responsibility to strive to meet the goals of the profession.

Nursing's responsibility to strive to meet professional goals of good care often seems increasingly difficult to honor. Yet, where nurses do not take an active role in their practice, patients are unlikely to receive optimal care. One reason for this is that nurses, especially in institutional settings, tend to be the clinicians who spend the most time with patients. Patients in turn are most likely to confide in nurses contextual information about their beliefs and values and ask for clarification about their illness or proposed procedures and interventions.

Collaborative and Independent: The Dual Roles of Bedside Nurses

The nursing profession can be considered somewhat unique in its role obligations, in that collaboration with medicine, to carry out the "goals of medicine," has historically been part and parcel of nursing's role in patient care. The needs of society have required such collaborations because each discipline has attended to different yet overlapping aspects of a patient's condition. Though the collaboration is for the most part beneficial for the patient, the nature of the two roles and the tendency for a power differential to exist have also contributed to the role confusion for nurses and thus, at times, a lack of clarity around nursing's distinct professional goals.

Gordon (1994) has offered a clear way of conceptualizing nursing's work through a model that accounts for nursing's collaborative and independent practice. In the collaborative realm, nurses are providing assessment and interventions that emanate from the medical assessment (e.g., patient history and physical examination). The "database" reflects medical data that contributes information important to the broader nursing understanding of the whole person and their unique individual response to health and illness. Nursing's perspective is on care of the person as a contextual being inseparable from his or her life circumstances (Grace, 2009). Thus, the physical status of the patient is an important piece of the human puzzle of who this person is and of understanding the person's responses to illness and related needs. The independent contributions of the professional nurse focus on autonomous actions within a scope of practice for which they are accountable. The collaborative responses to patient needs as determined by monitoring, surveillance, and physician orders are linked to "doing" the collaborative part of the practice. The following exemplar provides a case that addresses independent and collaborative nursing practice.

EXEMPLAR: DISTINCTION BETWEEN COLLABORATIVE AND INDEPENDENT NURSE ACTIONS

A 56-year-old man named Jim Brown was admitted to the Cardiac Care Unit (CCU) with an anterior wall ST elevation myocardial infarction. His severe left ventricular dysfunction resulted in low cardiac output, hypotension, and acute tubular necrosis (ATN). In the first 72 hours post event, vasoactive medications were needed to decrease afterload and maintain a reasonable blood pressure. In addition, continuous venous-to-venous hemofiltration (CVVH) was in place to treat fluid overload in the setting of failing renal function.

Critical-care nursing professionals, educated to provide care for patients such as Jim (e.g., acute pathological processes, often involving multiple organ systems), provided care relative to his medical diagnosis and complications that occurred while the patient was in the CCU. The diagnosis and management of Jim's myocardial infarction (MI) was complicated by cardiogenic shock and its sequelae fall. Though the management of the MI was within the domain of medicine, nurses functioned effectively to provide care and monitoring to Jim as his cardiogenic shock evolved and as he received complex medications and technologies. The minute-to-minute decisions about titrating medications per Jim's physiological responses required specialty knowledge and skill. Nurses have historically done and continue to do this work well, even as medications and technologies actually increase in complexity. It is part of their role in collaborating with other disciplines.

Collaborative Practice

Such work, as just discussed, occurs within the "collaborative domain" of professional nursing practice—the aspect of nursing practice where nurses work closely with physicians to ensure that the patient's medical diagnoses are carefully assessed and treated. The administration and monitoring of medications and technologies that aim to treat failing physiological processes are clearly within the realm of nursing's collaborative role. Professional role structures in nursing and medicine have actually served the public effectively through this model, which places acutely ill hospitalized patients under the care of nursing and nursing services 24 hours per day, 7 days a week.

Nurses' presence in hospitals, indeed the existence of hospitals, permit ongoing assessments and monitoring of the patient's response to such treatments, improvements or declines in condition. Medicine in fact could not fulfill its goals without the active participation of nurses, and many patients would either not survive or have their healing impeded without nursing's services in this regard. In intensive care settings, the percentage of a nurse's time in the collaborative domain might be as high as 90% of their work effort.

Preparing for Collaboration with Other Disciplines

To fulfill the collaborative role obligation, nurses must be educated and knowledgeable in the human sciences, including pathophysiology and pharmacology. In addition, nurses in this situation also begin to evaluate the patient/family response to this experience, coming to know the individual as a person and attempting to address fears, uncertainty, and concerns associated with the critical nature of the health problem(s) described. They assess the patient within the context of a nursing assessment and seek to uncover the meaning of the illness and its impact on lifestyle. They focus on knowing the person and their experience and consult and collaborate with other providers (e.g., social work, chaplaincy, and so on) to bring to the bedside a holistic perspective to the health care experience.

Nursing's Independent Role: The Focus of Nursing-Specific Actions

As described in the preceding exemplar, nursing's role is not complete or fully professionalized within the collaborative domain alone. Gordon (1994) describes the independent domain of nursing as the unique contribution of nursing as a profession—the aspect of practice that bears the characteristics of a profession, such as autonomy and control over practice. Nurses assess and intervene for the person, sick or well, in determining through a nursing assessment a person's "response" to physiological and pathological processes in health and illness.

The question for professional nursing, in this exemplar is:

> Who is Jim, the person, and how is he responding, as a human being, to this pathological state of myocardial infarction?

Perhaps Jim is the breadwinner of a family of six and is worried about his spouse and children. Perhaps Jim has health risks such as obesity or an elevated cholesterol level because of poor nutritional habits. Maybe Jim coped with his work stress by smoking. Perhaps his wife is struggling with a newly defined role returning to the workforce to support her children and spouse, now with, at best, symptomatic heart failure. Perhaps Jim is truly frightened and afraid that he might die. His family might be as well.

The patient and family response to Jim's experience (e.g., fear) is part of the phenomena of concern to professional nursing and is within nursing's independent (autonomous) domain of practice. The unique contribution of professional nursing described as the independent domain of nursing then is its impact to the health and well-being of individuals, families, community, and society. Nurses need to know something about the patients' stories to help them regain health or achieve relief from suffering, regardless of whether the suffering is physiological, psychological, or existential in nature. Willis, Grace & Roy (2008) have identified from nursing literature, historic and contemporary, a central unifying focus for the discipline that has developed over time—that of "facilitating humanization, meaning, choice, quality of life, and healing in living and dying" (E28).

Collaborative and Independent Roles: Reconciling Domains

Nurses in their practice settings are often simultaneously implementing both aspects of their role in the collaborative and independent domains (see Figure 6.1). However, the value of the independent domain work might not be as visible or quantifiable to hospital administrators or other management personnel as the collaborative work, especially when nursing's autonomous role is now well documented. Institutional systems might highly value the collaborative aspect of care, while not accounting adequately for nursing's independent role functions. Yet, often the independent role functions contribute the most to the ostensible reason that health care institutions exist—"healing" and "curing" patients. Nurses who understand the broader nature of their role will try to continue to fulfill the collaborative and independent aspects of their roles and goals, sometimes at their own expense, because they see this as required to meet the patient's (and family's) total care needs (Rodney et al., 2009).

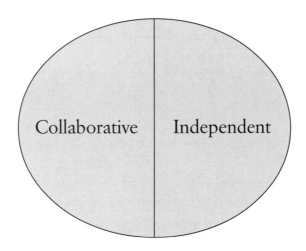

FIGURE 6.1

Nursing's disciplinary contribution: collaborative and independent domains of nursing practice (Gordon, 1982).

Gordon (2010) has argued that the independent domain of the nurse's practice is, in fact, the domain that professionalizes nursing. This makes sense in that independence in clinical practice means sole accountability for the judgments made and the actions undertaken. The professional aspect of nursing involves promoting nursing goals and purposes, directs nursing-specific research, and fosters the implementation of educational programs. Disciplinary or knowledge-development activities are aimed at describing the phenomena of concern for nursing and effective interventions and good outcomes. One helpful framework to categorize the phenomena of concern to nursing—in the independent role domain of the profession—is captured by the Functional Health Pattern assessment and associated nursing diagnoses (Gordon, 1994, 2010), as described in Chapter 5 of this book.

Gordon, among others, asserts that both aspects of nursing's roles, the collaborative and independent, provide ethical obligations because they are both important in achieving patient goals and meeting patients' real needs. Arguably, other professions also have independent and collaborative obligations as well. Medicine, in institutional settings, cannot optimally fulfill its goals without effective collaboration with nurses and members of other health professions such as physiotherapy, occupational therapy, and so on.

Professional Advocacy

Grace (2001) has discussed professional advocacy as an ethical obligation to ensure professional goals are met (in this case, nursing goals), including the need to address underlying causes of ill health. Gadow (1990), in her discussion of existential advocacy, describes the role of the nurse as understanding the "unique meaning which the experience of health, illness, suffering, or dying is to have for that individual" (p. 59). Though neither author specifically distinguishes the collaborative and independent domain of nursing practice as other writers have, implicit in their descriptions of advocacy is the idea that to understand what the patient's personal (as a particular, unique human being) and physiological needs are and what actions are needed to meet them, nurses need both collaborative and independent actions.

As an illustration of this point, in the previous exemplar a nurse caring for a critically ill patient on CVVH and vasoactive drugs is acutely aware of that patient's physiological responses to these interventions. Is the patient's mental status better? Are uremic and fluid overload signs and symptoms lessening as a result of the CVVH? Or, conversely, for the patient who has been receiving vasopressors for extended periods, are there adverse effects to the peripheral vascular system that might lead to a need for amputation? The "objectively" ill body, in cardiogenic shock, might, through monitoring devices and therapeutic interventions, show improvement and be perceived as a success in terms of medical goals.

Existential Advocacy

But, nursing is also concerned with the possibility (risk) of deleterious physiological side-effects (responses), such as need for amputation of fingers and toes, long-term hemodialysis, and other sequelae causing an emotional and psychological toll that either outweigh the benefit of surviving or need further nursing interventions to support patient coping and adaptation. In either case the nurse's role is to discover what the patient desires and wants as far as possible and articulate this in a collaborative setting. The nurse does this either directly via what Gadow (1990) terms *existential advocacy* or by gathering data from those who know the patient. This is an example of how nursing's knowledge, skill, and expertise in both the collaborative and independent domain can actually facilitate optimal care for the particular patient. Moreover, this is an ethical responsibility of nurses as argued by Grace (2001). However, not all nurses feel confident or able to articulate their particular knowledge of the patient in interdisciplinary arenas, and this is a problem for nurse education, continuing education, and nursing leadership to address.

The problem of moral distress and its potential effects on caregiving activities as experienced by nurses who know what the actions in a particular case should be but are unable to carry them out are discussed in the following section, along with strategies for strengthening nurse's advocacy, or speaking up in behalf of the patient. Gadow's existential advocacy depends on the idea of an interrelationship between nurse and patient made possible by the time spent in direct care with the person. She notes the ethical responsibility of the nurse is to help the patient be clear about what they need and are willing to accept in the context of their lives, beliefs, and desires. Advocacy, as conceptualized by Grace (2001), captures the nurse's responsibility to meet the individual patient's real needs and to address underlying structural, institutional, or societal issues that obstruct nurses in providing their services and meeting nursing goals.

Moral Distress

Many obstacles impact effective ethical practice at the bedside. These include issues around skill and knowledge development, interpersonal conflicts, communication, and economic and institutional factors among others. The effects of persistent barriers to good practice have two important effects:

1. Suboptimal patient care

2. The experience of "moral distress" (Jameton, 1984)

These unresolved effects contribute to inadequate care because they often result in conscientious nurses, as well as other providers, leaving the setting or even the profession (Ulrich et al., 2007). Residual effects, termed *moral residue* by Webster and Bayliss (2000), can also cause nurses to distance themselves from experiencing further distress, including distancing themselves from patients.

Moral distress is the troubling feeling people experience when they know what ought to be done but either cannot carry the action through, or in collaborative situations, prevail on others to do so. Chambliss (1996) studied nurses working in critical-care settings over a 7-year period. He noted that when nurses (and others) feel powerless in a situation they tend to become "numb" to the ethical content of future situations and might not act even when it is ethically required. Findings from studies in moral and cognitive psychology support the idea that inaction, distancing, and escape are human responses to feelings of powerlessness (Doris et al, 2010).

Moral Distress and Powerlessness

Others have documented problems associated with nurses feeling powerless. Besides the issue of ceasing to respond to unethical practices, some nurses leave the setting or seek other types of employment (Austin, 2012; Corley, 2002; Corley, Minick, Elswick & Jacobs, 2005; Hamric, 2012; Mohr & Mahon, 1996). Another aspect of modern health care is the shift toward a business model of health care delivery that can refocus care from patient to the economic bottom line. Austin (2012) notes that "if healthcare environments are not understood as moral communities but rather as simulated marketplaces, then health professionals' moral agency is diminished and their vulnerability to moral distress is exacerbated."

Austin further warns that increases in reports of moral distress should serve as a warning signal about the toxic nature of health care. An antidote to experiences of moral distress is taking positive action to resolve the issue or address the communication problem. Strategies to fortify nurses' capacity for moral agency (acting to promote what is needed for patient or family good, that is, demonstrating leadership activities at the bedside) are provided later.

Obstacles to Ethical Practice at the Beside

Providers encounter additional common problems that can lead to moral distress, including physician dominance, family demands, and ineffective nurse leadership. These issues, discussed in the following sections, can impact nursing care at the bedside.

Physician Dominance

Though it was once a theme that nurses noted as a source of moral distress, physician dominance as an obstacle to good patient care appears to be lessening in the United States. At least this is true in those institutions that have achieved Magnet status. Magnet status (refer to discussion in the Introduction and Chapter 3) is granted to hospitals that are recognized for "quality patient care, nursing excellence and innovations in professional nursing practice" (American Nurses Credentialing Center [ANCC], 2012). This gives institutions incentives to foster more egalitarian environment.

Physician dominance is a problem because it inhibits the free flow of communication. When nurses are unable to have their perspective on patient needs respected and considered, patients suffer. In our collaborations with nurse ethicists across the country, we have validated that certain clinical areas are "high risk" in terms of difficult nurse-physician relationships. High-risk clinical settings tend to be cardiac surgery, transplant surgery, and oncology. Increasingly, patients and their surrogates in these areas are articulating what is desired in the way of care and what limits of care are acceptable. Nurses, social workers, therapists, and intensive care physicians are advocates for patients and families in seeking ways to have these wishes sought and honored.

However, physicians whose focus might exclusively be on the management of the patient's disease process can lose sight of the impact that such disease processes can have on a person's pain, distress, and quality of life. Recent work (Schwarze, Bradley & Brasel, 2010) highlights the issue that some surgeons undertaking high-risk surgeries might assume they have made a bargain with patients or have gained their "buy-in" in terms of persevering with treatment post-operatively even if things are not going well. These authors describe the phenomena of "buy-in" as the patient's obligation to go along with the surgeon's timeframe to get such patients "successfully through complex surgeries."

For many patients, consenting to complex surgeries can result in a prolonged recovery period, sometimes with complications, that are anticipated and can be overcome. But it is also true that some patients might endure complications that will change the course of their lives in a way that diminishes quality of life for them, and thus, they or their responsible surrogates would judge that "too much to bear." In such circumstances, the focus on surgical success can lead to an unwillingness to consider withdrawing life support or redirecting care to comfort measures.

More work needs to be done to increase nurses' understanding of patient and families' perspectives on these issues and achieving conciliation between the two points of view. Increasingly, in our experience, surgeons in these areas of practice are responding more readily to the concerns of patients and their surrogates, whose voices are most often brought to the table via nurses and social workers.

Family Demands in the Face of "Litigation Anxiety"

Increasingly, nurses, physicians, and health professionals are faced with a new phenomenon in health care as patients near end of life, described as "family/surrogate demands for life sustaining treatment." This can often occur when a consensus exists among nurses, physicians, and other health professionals that the patient's condition cannot improve, and it is certain that he or she will die from the disease process and its accompanying sequelae.

A defining characteristic of such patient's situation is directly linked to the reality that they cannot live apart from life support, cannot return home from the hospital or chronic care setting, and cannot participate in their lives in a meaningful way. In such cases, health professionals believe that the patient is often experiencing too much pain and too many symptoms that cannot be quelled to allow the patient to engage, even if the patient had the capacity to do so. Many of these patients lack decision-making capacity because of their underlying disease processes.

In these cases, nurses, physicians, and health professionals access ethics consultation, but, even with that, the resolution processes can be prolonged, at times involving the courts (Paris, Billings, Cummings & Moreland, 2006). Catlin et al. (2008) argue that conscientious objection might be an effective nurse strategy in such cases. At the Massachusetts General Hospital (MGH), nurses have reported that they are able to stay with the case, caring for the patient and working with the surrogate, when they believe that a process with ethics committee and administrative support is in place and is moving towards resolution (Keith Perleberg, personal communication, 2005).

These patient experiences highlight a swing from a beneficence-based ethics expressed insufficiently as a paternalistic (i.e., attending to the best interests of the patient from the health care provider perspective) approach to care, to one that promotes autonomy (i.e., facilitating and respecting the patient's choice) expressed insufficiently through consumerism. The principles of beneficence and autonomy, when used appropriately to clarify a situation, permit a situation analysis that is most likely to increase patient benefit and minimize harms (Beauchamp & Childress, 2010).

Nursing Leadership: Barriers to Ethical Practices

The professional obligations of nurse leaders include advocating for, and supporting the best practices of, nurses for whom they are providing leadership. This is necessary to facilitate good nursing care. Difficult cases might require the interventions of a nurse leader, particularly in placing ethics consults or setting limits with challenging physicians and/or families. For ethical practice to flourish, nurse leaders need to understand nursing practice, as described previously, and comprehend the language of ethics. In addition, leaders must recognize when barriers to ethical patient care exist and work within their domain to remove them. The case described in the following sidebar exemplifies these points.

EXEMPLAR: LEADERSHIP ROLE IN REMOVING BARRIERS TO ETHICAL PRACTICES

Nurses and house officers were caring for a 78-year-old woman who was post-operative day 45 after cardiac surgery. Based on her clinical situation, they had come to believe that continued aggressive life-sustaining treatment was disproportionately burdensome to her and could not benefit her—they did not believe that it would ever be possible for her to leave the ICU alive. The cardiac surgical attending physician, however, was firm in his belief that the patient could overcome complications of her underlying disease, consisting of respiratory, renal, and hepatic failure.

A night nurse contacted the nurse ethicist via e-mail, requesting an ethics consult, but asked that she remain anonymous, as she feared retribution from the surgeon. The nurse ethicist contacted the nurse director, with the night nurse's permission, and asked the nurse director to place the consult. The nurse director spoke with the surgeon, and explained the request that she would make, without naming the individual nurse; rather she presented the concern as a collective concern of nursing.

The surgeon responded by calling a team meeting, followed by a family meeting, at which time the family readily agreed that their loved one should be taken off life support, after they understood that she would not be able to recover to return home. Her return home was an enduring value to this 78- year-old woman, who was much loved as spouse, mother, and grandmother.

This is an example of support from nursing leadership that is absolutely expected for good ethical care. In such a case, the barrier to ethical care for this patient or, put another way, the source of moral distress was the surgeon's purported belief and un-approachability.

No dilemma existed in the case presented. Unfortunately, the patient had sustained complications because of her underlying disease postoperatively and was nearing the end of her life. Often, the family relies upon the surgeon to convey the patient's status. In this case, and after the surgeon had provided his report, the family was able to gather around the bedside of this beloved woman, and life support was terminated. She died peacefully in their presence.

Reasons for Lack of Moral Agency

Nurses do not feel they are adequately prepared to overcome barriers to good practice for many reasons. Additionally, the confidence and motivation of nurses to address such problems might vary with their emotional state; energy levels; familiarity with the setting; personnel or co-workers; and skills, knowledge, or motivation to address the ethical challenges being presented. In a previous work and based on contemporary literature, Grace (2009, p. 79) divided the factors interfering with good care as *agent-related* and *environmental*.

Agent-related factors include such things as:

- Level of moral development
- Sensitivity to the ethical content of practice
- Ability to be self-reflective and reflect on practice
- An understanding of practice responsibilities, energy levels, and emotional stability

- Confidence in one's judgments

- Lack of ability to connect or empathize

- External or internal locus of control (perceptions of one's effectiveness)

- Fear of disapproval or job loss

- Knowledge, experience, and skill related to the situation

This is by no means an exhaustive list.

Environmental factors are any factor that emerges from the setting, situation, or context within which the issue has arisen. They include such things as:

- Peer pressure

- Pressure from those perceived in some way as being one's superiors

- Social or institutional culture and customs

- Economic, time, and resource constraints

- Competing demands from others

- Fear of legal retribution

- Conflicts of interest

- Threats

Ethical challenges exist in health care as the complexity of care delivery grows. Though there are multiple constraints that nurses have to address, there are also ways to promote effective ethical practice at the bedside.

Strengthening Ethical Practice at the Bedside: Leadership Strategies

Leadership in ethical practice at the bedside can be, and perhaps should be, provided by nurses. Essentially ethical leadership does not mean nurses have to have in-depth knowledge of ethical theory or ethical literature. It does mean that nurses understand the scope of their professional responsibilities to further nursing's goals. Also, nurses will find it helpful to understand the "language of ethics" and know where to access resources because both of these skills permit clear articulation of aspects of a particularly troubling case or issue and to assist the patient and family (or other surrogates) in getting the needed care or in their decision-making about what care is acceptable to them. Additionally, the nurse's ability to recognize the development of impending issues and defuse these is a leadership activity as is policy development for recurring or intractable issues that arise. Leadership at the bedside also means joining with others to change unit or institutional practices that do not serve patients well.

The discussion that follows provides some examples of leadership at the bedside. These examples specifically relate to how nurses at the MGH influence good patient care and what their involvement is in addressing ethical issues. These are models that can be emulated in other institutions, both in the United States and in other countries.

Collaborative Governance Structure

When an organization makes a commitment to good patient care, nurses are enabled to practice to the full extent of their roles and ethical obligations. Their focus is more likely to remain on achieving nursing goals for the patients in their care rather than acting as "physician advocate" or "bureaucratic advocate"— models of the nurse-patient relationship described by Murphy (1983). At the MGH, structures to support ethical patient care exist and professional advocacy (Grace, 2001) is encouraged.

A collaborative governance model (discussed in Chapter 2) has as one of its committees the Ethics in Clinical Practice Committee (EICPC). Since inception in 1997, this committee has continued to be co-chaired by practicing health professionals in direct care roles. The committee co-chairs are developed and supported by persons with ethics and leadership expertise. One of the two co-chairs is always a professional nurse. The committee has approximately 40 members and includes nurses and other health or allied disciplines (e.g., social workers, chaplains, physical, occupational, speech language and respiratory therapists, and physicians). The goals of the committee focus on the education of its own members and provision of educational opportunities for professionals in patient care services and for the lay public, with the ultimate purpose of delivering optimal (ethical) care that is patient-oriented.

This committee has been a favorite of nurses and allied health disciplines throughout the years. The structure provides a place for nurses and health professionals to come together to discuss and learn from past cases. Members of the committee will sign up to present a case, and often a panel presentation of involved professionals across units and disciplines will be invited to attend. An example of such a case is presented in the following sidebar.

EXEMPLAR: CASE PRESENTATION AT ETHICS COMMITTEE MEETING

This case involved a high-spirited, ambitious young man, named Pedro, who had migrated to the United States from an underdeveloped country in Central America. This 28-year-old man was proud of his heritage and cared about the family that he had left behind. He worked the night shift in a factory and saved much of his earnings for his family back home.

Unfortunately, he was in a car accident and sustained a devastating traumatic-anoxic brain injury, leaving him in a persistent vegetative state. His cousin, with whom he worked at the factory, was devastated and tried to speak on his behalf. His sister, whom the young man "followed to America" was inconsolable. Both the sister and cousin believed that Pedro would not want his life sustained on a ventilator, with medically supplied nutrition and hydration. However Pedro's mother, who was back in their home country and could not obtain a visa, was unable to agree to remove life support. The patient continues in a chronic care facility, 2 years later, with return visits from time to time to the acute care setting for treatment of pneumonia and other conditions of the immobile body.

When the members of the EICPC heard such a case presentation, they learned the latest evidence regarding disorders of consciousness and applied the principles of ethics and an ethic of care in the context of a real case. An ethic of care brings focus to relationships between the patient's mother and the cousin/ sister; it was precisely the thought of fracturing this relationship that health care professionals believed would bring more harm to the situation.

Unit-Based Ethics Rounds

Another structure that supports nursing ethics leadership at the bedside is unit-based ethics rounds. Unit-based ethics rounds are a venue that are organized and led by MGH nurses, in collaboration with other professionals, such as social workers, chaplains, speech therapists, physicians, and ethicists. Started back in the 1980s by a nurse ethicist consultant, these rounds serve as mechanism for nurses to process the ethical aspects of care.

Currently, ethics rounds have become increasingly widespread throughout the hospital and are now hosted on about 20 units. The rounds in many areas have expanded to inter-professional discussions and are generally held on a monthly basis. Similar to the goals of the discussions held at the EICPC meeting, the goal at an ethics rounds discussion is to ensure the presence of those who were involved in the case being discussed at the rounds. Units have adopted various modalities for conducting ethics rounds. The following sidebar provides an example of a case discussion during ethics rounds.

EXEMPLAR: UNIT-LEVEL CASE PRESENTATION DURING ETHICS ROUNDS

The MGH neonatal intensive care unit (NICU) has an interprofessional model that is scheduled into the physicians' teaching rounds. All disciplines are invited to attend, and the rounds are co-led by a nurse (a graduate of the Clinical Ethics Residency for Nurses [CERN] discussed later) and a physician. Nursing ethics experts are present at the rounds, as well as a variety of other professionals from social work, chaplaincy, pharmacy, respiratory therapy, and case management. At these ethics rounds, for the most part current, cases and sometimes a topic of interest in clinical ethics are discussed.

The ethical issues in a case are grappled with, or various perspectives related to the topic in question are discussed. In either case, the goal is to keep moral spaces open; that is, a nonjudgmental discussion where people are free to discuss their feelings and thoughts (Walker, 1993). For example, having the space to ask the questions:

- *How do health professionals care for a Trisomy 18 premature infant, when the parents "want everything done"?*

- *What does the empirical literature have to contribute to decision-making?*

- *How are the infant's best interests assessed?*

- *Does parental bonding with such an infant that allows for periods of time that the infant can sit in the arms of the parents provide benefits to the infant that outweigh the burdens of daily d-saturation episodes that sometimes even require chest compressions?*

These are but some of the ethical questions about which nurses and other disciplines grapple at NICU ethics rounds.

Nursing Ethics Education: Clinical Ethics Residency for Nurses

Clinical ethics education is an exciting and dynamic component of MGH patient care services (PCS). A five-year collaboration initiated by MGH's Nurse Ethicist Ellen Robinson and involving Clinical Ethics Director from Brigham and Women's Hospital (BWH), Martha Jurchak; Dr. Libby Tracy from Dana Farber Cancer Institute (DFCI); and Boston College ethics faculty Pamela Grace resulted in an annual day-long interdisciplinary ethics education program. From this annual program and contemporary nursing ethics literature came the realization that more needed to be done to facilitate nurses' abilities to address ethical issues in practice.

As a result, a grant was developed for the purpose of increasing ethics education and confidence in ethical decision-making within MGH and BWH. A Division of Nursing Health Resource Service Administration Grant was awarded to MGH (Robinson, Grace & Jurchak, 2010) in July 2010 until 2013 to support the wider dissemination of ethics knowledge throughout the system. The grant provides funding for a Clinical Ethics Residency Program for Nurses (CERN) to occur each year for three years. Nurse applicants to the CERN program from MGH, BWH, and Northshore Medical Center are plentiful, and evaluations of the program to date have revealed the positive impact of the residency program and the personal transformation this experience has had on the nurse participants.

In the Clinical Ethics Residency Program, nurse residents receive 98 hours of contact time. The curriculum focuses on online learning, classroom and simulation laboratory learning, and a clinical mentorship. This program is led by the MGH nurse ethicist in collaboration with the BWH ethicist, the Boston College William F. Connell Professor of Nursing Ethics, and the MGH Clinical Pastoral Education Director. Along with the didactic aspects of the program, communication skills are taught, practiced, and reinforced through the leadership of the Clinical Pastoral Education Director, a certified systems centered practitioner (Agazarian, 2010), to support the communication and skill development part of the learning, including simulation and role-play.

Finally, when CERN graduates have the opportunity to participate in a clinical mentorship experience, they can apply their knowledge and skills to an ethics-related clinical experience. One nurse has successfully utilized her skills in facilitating ethics rounds on her unit. This staff nurse assists fellow staff nurses in preparing a case for presentation, assembles relevant experts, and on the day of the rounds facilitates the discussion. Several cases have already been presented.

Most recently, two nurses on the unit presented the case of a prisoner who had been admitted after having engaged in severe self-injurious behavior. These nurses presented ethical issues that they encountered in the case, namely, the challenge of balancing the patient's very sad background and his lack of inner resources to soothe himself with the restrictive environment, including the limitation of soothing medications that his prisoner status required. A psychiatric clinical nurse specialist and nurse ethicist provided commentary, and all staff present took part in a discussion.

CERN residents who have completed the residency attend continuation sessions, to stay engaged in clinical ethics and further develop their skills.

Connell Ethics Fellowship

Recently, the family of the late William F. Connell funded the "Connell Ethics Fellowship," which is administered through PCS Institute for Patient Care (Ives Erickson, 2012). The goal of the Connell Ethics Fellowship is to prepare committed and experienced health professionals who are educated at the graduate level to develop and refine their clinical ethics expertise. The Connell

Ethics Fellowship is a one-year intensive training in clinical ethics under the supervision of a senior clinical nurse ethicist, with participation from renowned ethics faculty. The fellowship provides opportunities to acquire historical, philosophical, and empirical knowledge related to ethical problems in health care in an acute care setting. Mentoring in clinical ethics problem solving, consultation, facilitation, and scholarship is included with opportunities to advance nursing ethics at the bedside. The knowledge and skill acquired by the fellows will contribute to overall ethics capacity in MGH PCS and the hospital and community at large. A desired outcome is that the fellow, upon completion of the program, will be identified as a health professional with clinical ethics expertise at the MGH.

Hospital Ethics Committees with Nurses as Co-Leaders

The MGH provides several additional opportunities to advance nurses' involvement in ethics. These include participation in the Optimum Care Committee and the Pediatric Ethics Committee and collaboration with academic partners.

Optimum Care Committee

The MGH Optimum Care Committee, the oldest ethics consultation committee in North America, is co-chaired by the PCS nurse ethicist and two physicians from Medicine/Palliative Care and Psychiatry, respectively. Membership on this committee includes staff nurses, social workers, chaplains, allied health professionals, community members, and physicians. The committee's primary work is policy development and ethics consultation in times of conflict within or between families and interdisciplinary teams.

Anyone can place an ethics consult, and nurses who identify conflict are consistently supported by their nurse directors, clinical nurse specialists and co-chair, and nurse ethicist to do so. Having the nurse ethicist in a leadership role on this committee strengthens the clinical position of nursing ethics within the organization.

Pediatric Ethics Committee

The MGH Hospital for Children has a longstanding ethics committee, which has as its goals education, policy development, and consultation. The Pediatrics Ethics Committee is chaired by a physician ethicist in pediatrics and co-chaired by a pediatric nurse leader. As with the Optimum Care Committee, the Pediatric Ethics Committee has inter-professional membership, including staff nurses.

Academic Partnerships and Resources

At the MGH, the opportunity to collaborate and participate with the academic programs is offered through programs at universities such as Boston College and Harvard Medical School. For example, at the Harvard Medical School Division of Medical Ethics, the Associate Director is a nurse ethicist who is an international leader in ethics and health care. She is a leader in the Boston area on issues related to nurse's voice in ethics and has created a place at the table for nursing and other disciplines through her leadership role at Harvard. For example, a monthly forum called the Harvard Ethics Consortium is a place where over the years many MGH nurses and other professionals from the MGH have presented their challenging cases and hear the commentary of well-known ethicists on the case. Opportunities such as this strengthen inter-professional leadership and voice of nurses.

Additionally, close collaboration between schools of nursing, like the Boston College William F. Connell School of Nursing (BCCSON), has brought nursing ethics faculty from BCCSON to the clinical area. Involvement of faculty in projects such as CERN, ethics rounds, and the Connell Ethics Fellowship and collaborations between the MGH nurse ethicist and staff nurses foster shared learning partnerships between staff and students. In many parts of the United States and other developed countries, other faculty in other disciplines have an interest in ethics. For example, departments of philosophy, theology, and sociology can provide ways of thinking and knowledge that can serve as a resource for clinicians in analyzing ethical issues both at the bedside and when confronted with unjust societal ethical challenges.

Summary

This chapter has focused on foundations for asserting that nurses have a moral imperative to uphold their professional promises to society about the services that can be provided. These services are predicated upon meeting the goals of the profession related to promoting health and relieving suffering. Institutional health care settings, regardless of state or country, tend to present problems for nurses and others in fulfilling patient care goals. Nurses are in the ideal position within the health care team to advocate for the patient's care wishes. In addition, nurses can assist patient and family members in their decision-making autonomously and in collaboration with other health providers.

Nurses are in leadership positions when caring for patients. Their holistic perspective on the patient as person living (or dying) within the contexts of their life experiences, values, and significant others places them in the ideal role to promote ethical patient care and, when that ethical care is in jeopardy, to initiate appropriate actions. Strengthening nurses' ethical leadership abilities is an obligation of nurse leaders, nurse educators, and nursing ethics experts. Ethical actions at the bedside benefit from ongoing education endeavors, engagement on ethics committees, and active participation in unit ethics rounds. These all represent multiple opportunities to facilitate a widened perspective on the ethical issues and gain an increased familiarity with ethics language. We need to remember that all health care professionals share the same goals around the delivery of ethical patient care. Each discipline provides a different ethical perspective on issues, but all disciplines are committed to care that is ethical and respectful of the patient and families.

References

Agazarian, Y. M. (2010). *Systems-centered theory and practice: The contribution of Yvonne Agazarian* (Edited by SCTRI). Livermore, CA: WingSpan Press.

American Nurses Association (ANA). (2008). *Guide to the code of ethics for nurses: Interpretation and application*. M. Fowler (Ed.). Silver Springs, MD: Nursebooks.org.

American Nurses Association (ANA). (2010). *Nursing's social policy statement: The essence of the profession* (3rd ed.). Silver Springs, MD: Author.

American Nurses Credentialing Center (ANCC). (2012). *Magnet recognition*. Retrieved from http://www.nursecredentialing.org/Magnet.aspx

Austin, W. (2012). Moral distress and the contemporary plight of health professionals. *HEC Forum*, 24(1), 27-38. doi: 10.1007/s10730-012-9179-8

Beauchamp, T. L., & Childress, J. F. (2010). *Principles of bioethics* (6th ed.). New York, NY: Oxford.

Catlin, A., Volat, D., Hadley, M. A., Bassir, R., Armigo, C., Valle, E., ... Anderson, K. (2008). Conscientious objection: A potential neonatal nursing response to care orders that cause suffering at the end of life? Study of a concept. *Neonatal Network, 27*(2), 101-108.

Chambliss, D. F. (1996). *Beyond caring: Hospitals, nurses, and the social organization of ethics.* Chicago: University of Chicago Press.

Corley, M. C. (2002). Nurses' moral distress: A proposed theory and research agenda. *Nursing Ethics, 9*(6), 636-650.

Corley, M. C., Minick, P., Elswick, R. K., & Jacobs, M. (2005). Nurse moral distress and ethical work environment. *Nursing Ethics, 12*(4), 381-390.

Doris, J. M., & the Moral Psychology Research Group. (2010). *The moral psychology handbook.* New York, NY: Oxford.

Gadow, S. (1990). Existential advocacy: Philosophical foundations of nursing. In T. Pence, & J. Cantrall (Eds.), *Ethics in nursing: An anthology.* New York: National League for Nursing. (Reprinted from *Nursing image and ideals,* 1980.)

Gordon, M. (1982). *Nursing diagnosis: Process and application.* New York, NY: McGraw-Hill.

Gordon, M. (1994). *Nursing diagnosis: Process and application.* St. Louis, MO: Elsevier Health Sciences.

Gordon, M. (2010). *Manual of nursing diagnosis.* Sudbury, MA: Jones and Bartlett.

Grace, P. J. (1998). *A philosophical analysis of the concept "advocacy": Implications for professional-patient relationships.* University of Tennessee-Knoxville, Hodges Library Thesis 986.G73. Retrieved from http://proquest.umi.com. Publication No. AAT9923287, Proquest document ID 734421751.

Grace, P. J. (2001). Professional advocacy: Widening the scope of accountability. *Nursing Philosophy, 2*(2), 151-162.

Grace, P. J. (2009). *Nursing ethics and professional responsibility in advanced practice nursing.* Sudbury, MA: Jones and Bartlett.

Hamric, A. B. (2012). Empirical research on moral distress: Issues, challenges, and opportunities. *HEC Forum, 24*(1), 39-49. doi: 10.1007/s10730-012-9177-x

International Council of Nurses (ICN). (2006). *The ICN code of ethics for nurses.* Geneva, Switzerland: Author. Retrieved from http://www.icn.ch/images/stories/documents/about/icncode_english.pdf

International Council of Nurses (ICN). (2012). Retrieved from http://www.icn.ch/about-icn/about-icn/

Ives Erickson, (2012, February 2). Generous gift supports ethics and research programs. *Caring Headlines,* 2-3.

Mohr, W. K., & Mahon, M. M. (1996). Dirty hands: The underside of marketplace health care. *Advances in Nursing Science, 19*(1), 28-37.

Murphy, C. P. (1983). Models of the nurse-patient relationship. In C. P. Murphy & H. Hunter, *Ethical problems in the nurse-patient relationship* (pp. 8-24). Boston, MA: Allyn & Bacon, Inc.

Newton, L. (1988). Lawgiving for professional life: Reflections on the place of the ethical code. In A. Flores (Ed.), *Professional ideals* (pp. 47-56). Belmont, CA: Wadsworth.

Paris, J. J., Billings, J. A., Cummings, B., & Moreland, M. P. (2006). Howe v. MGH and Hudson v. Texas Children's Hospital: Two approaches to resolving family-physician disputes in end of life care. *Journal of Perinatology 26*, 726-729.

Pellegrino, E. D. (2001). Trust and distrust in professional ethics. In W. Teays & L. Purdy (Eds.), *Bioethics, justice, and health care* (pp. 24-30). Belmont, CA: Wadsworth. (Reprinted from *Trust and the professions: Philosophical and cultural aspects* by E. D. Pellegrino, R. M. Veatch, & J. P. Langan [Eds.], 1991, Washington, DC: Georgetown University Press).

Robinson, E. M., Grace, P., & Jurchak, M. (2010). Clinical ethics residency for nurses (CERN). *HRSA Grant # D11HP18974.*

Rodney, P., Varcoe, C., Storch, J. L., McPherson, G., Mahoney, K., Brown, H., ... Starzomski, R. (2009). Navigating towards a moral horizon: A multisite qualitative study of ethical practice in nursing. *Canadian Journal of Nursing Research, 41*(1), 292-319.

Schwarze, M. L., Bradley, C. T., & Brasel, K. J. (2010). Surgical "buy-in": The contractual relationship between surgeons and patients that influences decisions regarding life-supporting therapy. *Critical Care Medicine, 38*(3), 843-848.

Spenceley, S. M., Reutter, L., & Allen, M. N. (2006). The road less traveled: Advocacy at the policy level. *Policy, Politics, and Nursing Practice, 7*(3), 180-194.

Ulrich, C. A., O'Donnell, P., Taylor, C., Farrar, A., Danis, M., & Grady, C. (2007). Ethical climate, ethics stress, and the job satisfaction of nurses and social workers in the United States. *Social Science & Medicine, 65*(8), 1708-1719.

Walker, M. U. (1993). Keeping moral space open: New images of ethics consulting. *Hastings Center Report, 23*(2), 33-40.

Webster, G. C., & Baylis, F. (2000). Moral residue. In S. B. Rubin & L. Zoloth (Eds.), *Margin of error: The ethics of mistakes in the practice of medicine* (p. 208). Hagerstown, MD: University Publishing Group.

Willis, D. G., Grace, P. J., & Roy, C. (2008). A central unifying focus for the discipline: Facilitating humanization, meaning, choice, quality of life, and healing in living and dying. *Advances in Nursing Science, 31*(1), E28-E40.

Windt, P. Y. (1989). Introductory essay. In P. Y. Windt, P. C. Appleby, M. P. Battin, L. P. Francis, & B. M. Landesman (Eds.), *Ethical issues in the professions* (pp. 1-14). Englewood Cliffs, NJ: Prentice Hall.

Zaner, R. M. (1991). The phenomenon of trust and the physician-patient relationship. In E. D. Pellegrino, R. M. Veatch, & J. P. Langan (Eds.), *Ethics, trust, and the professions* (pp. 45-67). Washington, DC: Georgetown University Press.

Chapter 7

Innovations in Care Delivery

Jeanette Ives Erickson, RN, DNP, FAAN
Marianne Ditomassi, RN, DNP, MBA

"As everyone at MGH well knows, there's no such thing as "the status quo" in health care. Change is the order of the day—every day. Technology changes. The economy changes. Patients change. And we change. I am reminded of the quote by German poet/ playwright, Bertolt Brecht, "Because things are the way they are, things will not stay the way they are." We can all attest to the truth of that statement.

(Ives Erickson, September 1, 2011, p. 2).

Introduction

This is an exciting time in the evolution of care delivery and a great time to be a nurse influencing the future of the nurse-patient relationship. Today's dynamic health care environment is an opportune time to creatively design and trial new care delivery models that hardwire patient safety across the trajectory of care and better integrate patients and their families into decision-making. At Massachusetts General Hospital (MGH), 12 inpatient units were asked to address issues and implement a core set of interventions with the shared objective of making care delivery more effective, efficient, and affordable for patients and families.

In this chapter we describe the process undertaken to address the changing health care landscape at the system-wide level of Partners HealthCare and specifically at MGH. The work was done recognizing that the best way to be responsive to change is being creative, innovative, and always remaining open to new ideas. Rising costs and a volatile national economy demand that hospitals run more efficiently, while continuing to provide exceptional care to achieve patient outcomes. This chapter is a call to action for creativity in the face of a dynamic agenda for change (Ives Erickson, October 20, 2011).

In response to these challenges, Partners HealthCare initiated a system-wide strategic planning process to ensure the continued success of Partners entities including health centers, two academic medical centers, four community hospitals, a graduate school for Allied Health Professionals, and a very large continuing care network. This work was launched at a time when national health care reform and a troubling economic climate were on the forefront of health care delivery, nationally. The planning process that emerged rendered two main areas of focus:

1. **Care redesign** efforts were realized by convening a multidisciplinary team to identify new approaches to care while focusing on conditions and episodes rather than traditional procedures, visits, and admissions. Examples of the medical conditions selected include colon cancer, coronary disease, stroke, diabetes, and primary care.

2. **Patient affordability** focused on comprehensive efforts to reduce direct patient care costs, improve patient flow, enhance managing human resources, and reduce overhead expenses.

Under the heading of patient affordability, the initial innovations focused on opportunities to reduce costs within inpatient settings, the emergency room, and perioperative settings. During the initial review of existing practices, the Partners System saw standardization emerge as a common theme essential to achieving potential cost savings. This involved standardization and consistency of supplies used and new products accessed across the Partners System along with the articulation of shared rules for adopting new technology.

This discussion ultimately led to the exploration of a new care delivery model. Ives Erickson (2012), co-chairperson of this effort, believed that designing a new patient care delivery model especially focused on the delivery of care to patients with specific health problems would allow the organization to be more cost-effective and to develop more efficient practices with the real goal of improving patient care. "Redesigning care will require transformational change—change that cannot occur at the risk of our patients" (Ives Erickson, January 5, 2012, p. 2).

The belief that change can be "designed, tested, evaluated, and replicated" on Innovation Units led to an organization-wide opportunity for all clinicians to step forward with ideas to enhance quality and safety. Just as the name implies, Innovation Units were specifically created to test, change, and measure outcomes. The framework was to design, implement, re-calculate, re-group, adapt, or abandon the ideas altogether. The interventions on Innovation Units are geared toward improving clinical outcomes, enhancing patient and staff satisfaction, and reducing costs and lengths of stay (Ives Erickson, January 5, 2012, p. 2).

Bohmer and Lee state,

> The knowledge of how to configure structures and processes to attain the best possible clinical outcomes will become health care organizations' most important asset. In outcome-oriented organizations, production knowledge—how to go about improving patients' outcomes—is as much an organizational property as an individual one. Hence, organizational learning is critical and requires deliberate action. Evaluating experience and using it to inform ways of improving clinical outcomes is the new mindset. (2009, p. 533)

Care Delivery Models

Jost, Bonnell, Chacko, and Parkinson (2010) define a nursing care delivery model as an infrastructure for organizing and delivering care to patients and families. Models need to be evolving and reality-based, as they serve to organize the allocation of nursing resources (Jost et al., 2010). In a transforming health care environment, maintaining care delivery models that stand the test of time is an unending challenge.

Partners HealthCare System's pursuit of an effective care delivery model began in 1996 when the corporation engaged Health Workforce Solutions (HWS), a human resources consulting firm, in the development of a long-term recruitment and retention strategy to meet future patient care demand. Integral to the long-term workforce question was an underlying research query:

1. What new innovative care delivery models are being tested across the United States that have the potential to change or reinvent care delivery?

2. What promise do these models hold?

3. What roles do nurses play within the new care delivery models?

4. How do these new models impact quality of care?

5. Are the models cost-effective?

6. Can the new model be replicated or adapted to different regions or markets?

These six key questions formed the basis for HWS's initial research into care delivery models (Kimball, Joynt, Cherner & O'Neil, 2007). Their research led to the identification of five common elements to be included in new care delivery models, as follows:

- An elevated nursing role from traditional care delivery to serving as a coordinator of care for patients and families.

- Sharpened focus on the patient and family and strategies to promote greater patient and family involvement.

- Smoothing of patient transitions and handoffs through the use of specialized tools for assessment, teaching, communication, and measurement.

- Leveraging of technology to enable care model redesign. Examples include electronic medical records, cell phones, bar-coding systems for inventory, and medication to name just a few.

- Recognizing the importance of producing measurable results.

The common elements pointed toward the value of patient-centered care, which can be realized or enhanced within the context of a new and innovative patient care model. The focus on the patient and family to improve communication with renewed attention to safety and resource use that are not only cost effective and of high quality but also can enhance overall patient, family, and staff satisfaction with care during hospitalization was the goal.

MGH Innovation Units

The elements identified by Kimball et al. (2007) serve as the underpinnings of MGH's current Innovation Units. The core principles behind these innovation units are:

- Care is patient- and family-focused, evidence-based, accountable, autonomous, coordinated, and continuous.

- Clinicians are intentionally present and know their patient.

- Care is provided by designated nurses and physicians who assume accountability to ensure continuity.

- Continuity of team care delivery is a basic precept.

- Each patient has the opportunity to participate in the planning of his/her care.

- Technological advancements create opportunities for improved communication and efficiency.

The launching of the Innovation Units was initiated by Chief Nursing Officer (CNO) Jeanette Ives Erickson of MGH. It began with a call for applications to become an Innovations Unit. Interested units submitted proposals, articulating areas for improvement and specifically speaking to strategies that they believed would enhance continuity of care, promote interdisciplinary rounds, embrace patient and family relationship-based care, and develop tactics to enhance efficiency. Twelve Innovation Units were selected to participate in this inaugural work and spanned the practice areas of pediatrics, general medicine and surgery, vascular surgery, orthopedics, oncology, obstetrics, psychiatry, and three intensive care units (neonatal, cardiac, and surgery).

Interdisciplinary leadership and staff working on the selected Innovation Units began the work of redesign on the Innovation Units with a series of three retreats. At these meetings, a framework was presented to staff in an effort to help align the units around enhancing the patient's journey. A continuum of care diagram (see Figure 7.1) was used to illustrate the process of care before, during, and after hospitalization. The schematic highlights the "gaps" found along the continuum of care to be closed with care delivery redesign.

To address these gaps, the 12 MGH Innovation Units identified interventions that they believed were central to the new work of care redesign. They included the following interventions:

- Introduction of *relationship-based* care

- Implementation of the *attending nurse* role

- Development of strategies to enhance *handover communications*

- Develop *welcome packets for patients and families*

- Initiate new strategies to enhancing *pre-admission data collection*

- Create opportunities for each discipline to articulate the contributions of care throughout the patient experience specifically to share each discipline's *domains of practice* and *interdisciplinary rounds*

- Support the inclusion of *technology* within the care delivery experience

- Create strategies to enhance *discharge planning* and patient/family readiness

- Implement discharge *follow-up phone calls*

These interventions are described in detail in the following sections.

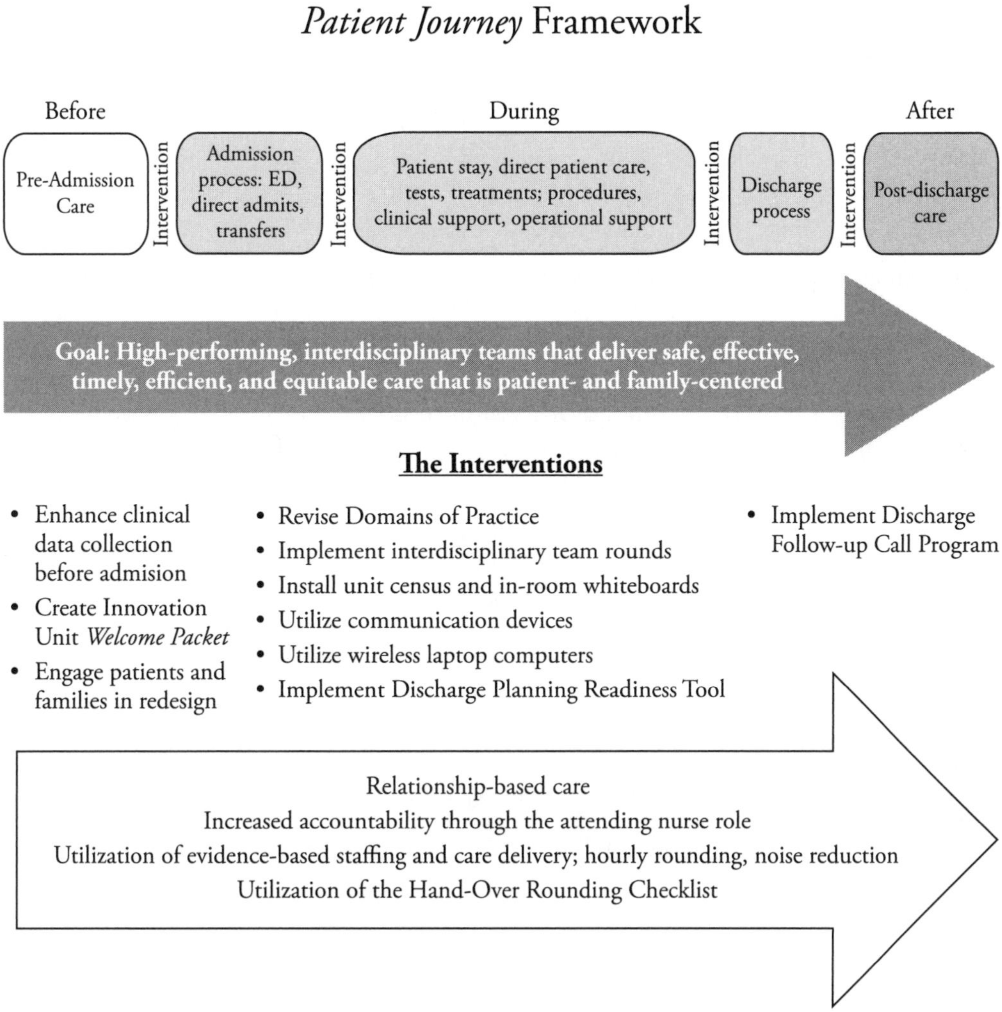

Patient Journey Framework

Before

During

After

Pre-Admission Care

Intervention

Admission process: ED, direct admits, transfers

Intervention

Patient stay, direct patient care, tests, treatments; procedures, clinical support, operational support

Intervention

Discharge process

Intervention

Post-discharge care

Goal: High-performing, interdisciplinary teams that deliver safe, effective, timely, efficient, and equitable care that is patient- and family-centered

The Interventions

- Enhance clinical data collection before admision
- Create Innovation Unit *Welcome Packet*
- Engage patients and families in redesign

- Revise Domains of Practice
- Implement interdisciplinary team rounds
- Install unit census and in-room whiteboards
- Utilize communication devices
- Utilize wireless laptop computers
- Implement Discharge Planning Readiness Tool

- Implement Discharge Follow-up Call Program

Relationship-based care
Increased accountability through the attending nurse role
Utilization of evidence-based staffing and care delivery; hourly rounding, noise reduction
Utilization of the Hand-Over Rounding Checklist

FIGURE 7.1

Patient Journey Framework—Continuum of Care
(© MGH Patient Care Services, 2011).

Relationship-Based Care

Relationship-based care is more than an intervention; it's a philosophy, a way of thinking about care delivery. Relationship-based care stresses three important tenets: a) the caregiver's relationship with the patient and family; b) the caregiver's relationship with his or her colleagues; and c) the caregiver's relationship with himself/herself, known as self-awareness (Koloroutis et al., 2004). In an organization that provides relationship-based care, every member of the team:

- Knows the patient as a person and has access to information across the continuum (an extended discussion of nurses knowing the patient is found in Chapter 5, "Nurse-Patient Relationship: Knowledge Transforming Practice at the Bedside")

- Participates in coordination of care, knows who's responsible, and reviews the plan daily with the patient, family, and team

- Builds the plan of care around the patient's goals and expectations

- Coordinates patient care and teaching with essential information needed and provides time to evaluate learning

- Aligns support around patient populations rather than transactions

- Has the opportunity to reflect on care delivery and learns lessons from the past

According to Koloroutis et al. (2004, p. 4), "We experience the essence of care in the moment when one human being connects to another. When compassion and care are conveyed through touch, a kind act, through competent clinical interventions, or through listening and seeking to understand the other's experience, a healing relationship is created. This is the heart of relationship based care."

The Attending Nurse Role

At the heart of the Innovation Unit model is the introduction of an innovative nursing role, the attending registered nurse (ARN). Within the context of the

MGH model, the ARN functions as a clinical leader and coordinator managing care of patients on a single unit from admission to discharge. The ARN interfaces with the interdisciplinary team, the patient, and the family to foster continuity and responsiveness to issues that can promote effectiveness, safety, quality, and efficiency. Components of the ARN role are outlined in Table 7.1.

TABLE 7.1: Components of the Attending Registered Nurse (ARN) Role

Facilitates care with entire health care team. Is a consistent contact for patients, families, and the health care team throughout the patient's care.	Identifies and resolves barriers to promote seamless handovers, interdisciplinary collaboration, and efficient patient throughput.
Ensures that the team and the process of care sustain a continuous, caring relationship with patients and families that might begin before admission and continue after discharge.	Coordinates meetings for timely, clinical decision-making and optimal handovers across the continuum of care.
Develops a comprehensive patient care assessment and plan using the principles of relationship-based care.	Communicates with patients and families around the plan of care, answers questions, teaches and coaches.
Develops and revises patient care goals with the clinical team daily.	Organizes care-team huddles that include the attending nurse and physician, house staff, staff nurses, and other disciplines.
Serves as a role model for interdisciplinary problem-solving.	Meets with family on a continuous basis regarding the plan of care, disposition, goals of treatment, palliative care, and end-of-life issues.

Enhancing Handover Communication

Time constraints require nurses to share essential information quickly, but nurses self-report that the information they provide and receive during patient handover situations is highly variable from nurse to nurse (Hardey, Payne & Coleman, 2000; Hays, 2003; Shendell-Falik, Feinson & Mohr, 2007). Research has shown that up to two-thirds of sentinel adverse events in hospitals are related to communication problems (Haig, Sutton & Whittington, 2006).

This intervention responds to the need to relay patient information from caregiver to caregiver, from caregiver to patients and families, and from the hospital to other organizations or to the patient's home quickly, accurately, and timely. The process relies heavily on the SBAR (Situation, Background, Assessment, and Recommendations) communication tool that "prompts" caregivers to provide complete information during handovers (Beckett & Kipnis, 2009). This intervention should be thought of not as the introduction of a new tool, but as an implementation of a new standard of practice. Effective communication handoffs promote safety, efficiency, and effective outcomes.

Welcome Packets

When patients have input into clinical communications, organizations see a reduced risk of fragmentation of care, miscommunication-related adverse events, and a greater likelihood of continuity of care (Haggerty et al., 2003; Kravitz & Melnikow, 2001; Wong, Yee & Turner, 2008). Innovation Unit welcome packets (see Figure 7.2) were designed by staff and contain two key components: a patient and family notebook and a discharge envelope. This intervention was developed to introduce patients and families to the Innovation Unit; assist the patient and family in becoming actively involved in the patient's care; identify patient education needs; and help plan for discharge. These goals are accomplished by staff who encourage patients and families to use the notebook each day and take notes and write down questions about their care. Patients and families also have the opportunity to write down questions and concerns to discuss with the nurse and team members prior to patient discharge.

Staff also reviews the *discharge checklist* throughout the hospital stay so that patients are better prepared for discharge. The *discharge checklist* is designed as an envelope and ensures that one place exists to store important patient education information, include the patient notebook, and discharge instructions. The checklist is available for patients and families to take home.

Patient & Family Notebook
...for sharing information to guide your care

 MASSACHUSETTS
GENERAL HOSPITAL

DISCHARGE INFORMATION

We want to help make your discharge from MGH go as smoothly and safely as possible. This envelope has important information inside about caring for yourself after you leave the hospital. Please take it with you when you leave.

We hope the list below will help you plan ahead so that you are ready when it is time to leave the hospital. Please go over any questions or problems with your nurse, who is always ready to help.

Patient/Family Checklist
Expected Discharge Date:

Things I will need when I leave the hospital:

- ☐ Clean, comfortable clothes
- ☐ Keys to my house/apartment
- ☐ Everything I brought with me to the hospital
- ☐ Doctor's note for employer, school, other (as needed)
- ☐ A ride home (likely before 10:00am)
- ☐ My prescription card and a way to pay for medications that I may need before I get home
- ☐ Instructions about how to care for myself at home:
  - What to eat and drink
  - List of activities I should or should not do
  - Medications
  - Special supplies or equipment
  - List of follow up appointments
  - Plan for visiting nurse or other home care services
  - Other:

Things I will need once I get home:

- ☐ Things I am able to eat and drink
- ☐ Prescriptions/medications
- ☐ Someone to help me in my home
- ☐ Special equipment or supplies
- ☐ Visiting nurse or other home care services

 MASSACHUSETTS
GENERAL HOSPITAL

FIGURE 7.2

Patient & Family Notebook and Discharge Envelope (© MGH Patient Care Services, 2012).

Enhancing Pre-Admission Data Collection

One goal of the Innovation Units is for nurses to better understand the patients and related health problems they face before and while they are being cared for. To ensure continuity and accurate information-gathering for all patient populations, a new Admitting Face Sheet was developed. This sheet includes the patient's anticipated discharge date and projected disciplinary disposition to better inform interdisciplinary care planning. This data contains information about the patient that reinforces the focus on discharge planning and begins upon the patient's admission to the hospital.

Domains of Practice and Care Contributions

With implementation of interdisciplinary rounds, it becomes essential for all professional providers to have an increased understanding of all the disciplinary domains of practice involved with the health care team. Towards that end, each discipline was charged with reviewing and updating their domains of practice. This information was shared in various forums to heighten awareness and understanding of each discipline's scope of practice. Identifying domains of practice is designed to optimize resources and contributions from all members of the health care team and utilize professional knowledge within the boundaries of licensure, certification, and scope of work.

Interdisciplinary Team Rounds

O'Leary, Sehgal, Terrell, and Williams (2012) cite that interdisciplinary team rounds have been used for many years as a means to assemble team members in a single location (Cowan et al., 2006; Curley, McEachern & Speroff, 1998; O'Mahony, Mazur, Charney, Want & Fine, 2007; Vazirani, Hays, Shapiro & Cowan, 2005). Recent studies evaluating the effectiveness of structure interdisciplinary rounds (O'Leary et al., 2011b; O'Leary et al., 2010) combine a structured format for communication with a forum for daily interdisciplinary meetings. Though no effect was reported on length of stay or cost, structured interdisciplinary rounds have resulted in significantly higher ratings around the quality of collaboration and teamwork and a reduction in the rate of adverse events (O'Leary et al., 2011a).

Prior to launching the Innovation Units, no formal mechanism existed for daily communication between and among all members of the care team. Interdisciplinary rounds is an effective strategy that brings all members of the team together on a daily basis to identify obstacles to the progression of care, create a more holistic approach to care delivery, and ensure that issues are shared and addressed in a timely manner.

Early feedback on this intervention suggests that a majority of clinicians agreed with the interdisciplinary rounding intervention and reported an improvement in daily work and efficiency. One staff member noted,

> Interdisciplinary rounds keep everyone on the same page. We identify the target discharge date and discuss the post-hospital plan. Having everyone together at the same time, we all hear the same information and can align our schedules accordingly in a way that's best for the patient. It has definitely improved communication. (Sabia, 2012)

Supporting Technology

Efficient, well-coordinated care depends on the staff's ability to communicate effectively. Having the right tools makes communication faster and easier. Technological advances facilitate staff communication in fast-paced clinical settings. The staff members working on the Innovation Units are equipped with specially programmed phones and portable, wireless laptops to make access to and dissemination of information more efficient. And in-room whiteboards and electronic whiteboards at nurses' stations enhance the ability to know the patients and coordinate their care.

Discharge Planning and Readiness

An array of tools is contained in a Discharge Planning toolkit designed to proactively facilitate planning for patients' discharge. The expectation is that from the moment a patient is admitted, staff begin to work with patients, family, and team members to identify potential barriers and/or risks that might delay the discharge process. More specifically, each patient is known to the nurse and interdisciplinary team, and responses to the care experience are carefully documented throughout the patient's hospitalization. In addition, measures, tools, and checklists have also been implemented to ensure that each patient has a plan of care and a proposed length of stay that matches their medical necessity and is enhanced by effective communication, documentation, and optimal system functioning.

Also, screening tools support the identification of patients who are at high risk for readmission. The implementation and assessment of these evaluation measures have been the result of collaborative efforts with representative caregivers from across the care continuum. Nurses from acute, non-acute, and home care settings have all had an active voice in defining the concept of discharge readiness and to recognize when it is not present and actions needed to ensure timely discharge.

Discharge Follow-Up Phone Call Program

Cochran, Blair, Wissinger, and Nuss (2012) highlight that the transition following hospital discharge involves communication and transfer of complex information at a time when patients and families are stressed and vulnerable. Effective communication might include a discussion around information about diagnostic test results, discharge, and medication instructions and follow-up care planning (Mistiaen & Poot, 2006).

In an effort to reduce hospital readmissions, manage care effectively outside of the acute care setting, and ensure patients' understanding of discharge instructions, a discharge follow-up phone call program was implemented on all Innovations Units. This intervention provides a way to ensure that patients can manage their care at home and understand discharge instructions, to communicate the staffs' care and concern for patients after they leave the hospital, and to enhance patients' impression and overall satisfaction with the hospital experience.

Follow-up calls are made 24-48 hours after discharge. Evidence suggests that the phone call can be used to gather data, facilitate symptom management, and clarify instructions for the patient and family (Jones, Duffy & Flanagan, 2011). This research found that patients who received follow-up phone calls at 24 and 72 hours after discharge experienced improved symptom management, decreased anxiety, and better physical function within the first 72 hours post discharge. Patients commented that even when they had a problem, "I knew my nurse would be calling this afternoon, so I waited for her." Continued monitoring of the discharge phone calls continues to be assessed through measures of patient satisfaction responses and relevant quality and readmission data.

Education and Communication

To create an environment of success, consistent understanding of the principles, concepts, and interventions guiding innovation is essential. The Norman Knight Nursing Center for Clinical & Professional Development (Knight Center) at MGH worked to create an educational plan to accompany the "rollout" of the Innovation Units. Based on feedback from planning retreats and other forums, the Knight Center designed a two-hour workshop was designed to provide staff on Innovation Units with a comprehensive overview of the selected redesign interventions. Online modules were created to review information about handover procedures (SBAR), hourly safety rounds, discharge readiness, the discharge follow-up phone call program, and effective use of welcome packets.

In addition, Knight Center professional development specialists were assigned to provide onsite coaching, mentoring, and unit-based education to staff on the Innovation Units as needed. Additional content areas included a focus on the operationalization of the attending nurse role, conflict resolution and management, and discharge planning.

Also, an Attending Nurse Working Group was created to address the concerns associated with role implementation and meets weekly for one hour. This forum is used as a "think tank/support group" for attending nurses as they get more immersed in their new role.

In addition, a leadership workshop was offered to nursing directors, clinical nurse specialists, and medical leadership to foster a better understanding of each professional's contribution and the role they play in leading innovation and supporting staff as they embark on the implementation of a new model of care delivery and professional practice environment.

Finally, to facilitate the communication of key information about the MGH Innovation Units initiative, a web-based Innovation Unit portal page was designed. This site provides easy access to Innovation Unit profiles and contacts, toolkits to implement various interventions, dashboard metrics, best practices, news features, and relevant literature. For access to the portal, visit http://www.mghpcs.org/Innovation_Units/index.asp.

Outcomes and Evaluation

The success of Innovation Units is being measured by a series of predetermined metrics related to length of stay, patient satisfaction, staff satisfaction, quality and safety, and certain nursing-sensitive indicators. A mixed-method, multidimensional approach to evaluating outcomes will be used and facilitated by nurse scientists in the Yvonne L. Munn Center for Nursing Research and the Department of Quality and Safety within Patient Care Services (PCS). Measures obtained pre, during, and post implementation of the Innovation Unit interventions are ongoing and have provided an opportunity to make corrections that might lead to revisions of earlier assumptions. Table 7.3 provides examples of both qualitative and quantitative measures used during all phases of the evaluation process.

Metrics are displayed by each Innovation Unit on a dashboard that categorizes data in the following areas: quality and safety, infection control, patient satisfaction, staff satisfaction, and throughput and efficiency. The same metrics are also captured and displayed for non-Innovation Units to allow for comparison between like units.

TABLE 7.3: Evaluation Measures: Pre, During, and Post Implementation

QUANTITATIVE	QUALITATIVE
Culture of Safety Survey	Focus groups: staff, patients, families
Patient Satisfaction Survey data	Observations
Patients Perceptions of Feeling Known (PPFKN) survey	Clinical narratives
Revised Perceptions of the Practice Environment (RPPE) scale	Journaling
Quality indicators	
Length of stay	
Readmission rates	
Cost per case mix	
Staff retention	

Early Results of Care Redesign and Innovation

In the initial evaluation phase of the program, project leaders determined that it was not feasible to create new databases that would capture a significant amount of data from external hospitals transferring patients to the MGH. Though this effort would have enhanced the development of the initial nursing plan of care, MGH abandoned the idea, knowing that they would be implementing a system-wide enterprise clinical system in the near future to capture the data electronically. Data linked to the patient experience of care alerted MGH to the fact that unit-level noise, thought to be reduced with a more organized system of interdisciplinary rounding, did not prove to be true. The patient data has led to the implementation of noise-reduction campaign pilots on four of the Innovation Units to increase quiet space in the environment of care. Simple signage stating "Shh, Children are healing" has promoted unit quiet hours and has improved patient satisfaction.

The biggest impact on care redesign has been associated with the implementation of the ARN role. Anecdotally, ARNs are sharing that redundancies are being eliminated and reporting major shifts in discharge by time of day and length of stay. In addition, patients and families have indicated that the liaison role played by ARNs during their hospital and post-discharge is helpful. A more detailed discussion of the influence of the ARN role is discussed in Chapter 12, "Transformative Leadership."

Summary

Redesigning patient care delivery models and introducing change and innovation is a long and involved process and requires constant monitoring. To accomplish this all parties involved in the change must continue to view care redesign as a priority. All must remain committed to keeping the staff participating in the work as informed, motivated, and involved as possible. Innovation Unit staff should be engaged in dialogue and identify those interventions to be adopted, adapted, or abandoned.

What we learned during this care redesign experience is that no shortcuts and no simple, easy solutions exist for managing health care costs. The answer lies in working smarter and more efficiently. Kouzes and Posner's writings aptly sum up the essence of the Innovation Unit effort,

> Great leaders are great learners. Exemplary leaders are pioneers at taking the initiative in searching for innovative ways to improve their own work, that of their teams, and their organizations. Rejecting the status quo, they experiment and take risks, treating the inevitable mistakes as important learning opportunities and creating a safe environment in which others can learn from failures as well as from successes. (2010, p. 119)

References

Beckett, C. D., & Kipnis, G. (2009). Collaborative communication: Integrating SBAR to improve quality/ patient safety outcomes. *Journal for Healthcare Quality, 31*(5), 19-28.

Bohmer, R. M. J., & Lee, T. H. (2009). The shifting mission of health care delivery organizations. *NEJM, 361*(6), 551-553.

Cochran, V. Y., Blair, B., Wissinger, L., & Nuss, T. D. (2012). Lessons learned from implementation of post discharge telephone calls at Baylor Health Care System. *Journal of Nursing Administration, 42*(1), 40-46.

Cowan, M. J., Shapiro, M., Hays, R. D., Afifi, A., Vazirani, S., Ward, C. R., & Ettner, S. L. (2006). The effect of a multidisciplinary hospitalist/physician and advanced practice nurse collaboration on hospital costs. *Journal of Nursing Administration, 36*(2), 79-85.

Curley, C., McEachern, J. E., & Speroff, T. (1998). A firm trial of interdisciplinary rounds on the inpatient medical wards: An intervention designed using continuous quality improvement. *Medical Care, 36*(8 suppl), AS4-AS12.

Haggerty, J. L., Reid, R. J., Freeman, G. K., Starfield, B. H., Adair, C. E., & McKendry, R. (2003). Continuity of care: A multidisciplinary review. *British Medical Journal, 32*, 1219-1221.

Haig, K., Sutton, S., & Whittington, J. (2006). The SBAR Technique: Improves communication, enhances patient safety. *Joint Commission's Perspectives on Patient Safety, 5*, 1-2.

Hardey, M., Payne, S., & Coleman, P. (2000). "Scraps": Hidden nursing information and its influence on the delivery of care. *Journal of Advances in Nursing, 32*(1), 208-214.

Hays, M. M. (2003). The phenomenal shift report: A paradox. *Journal of Nursing Staff Development, 19*(1), 25-33.

Ives Erickson, J. (2011, September 1). Innovation units: Driving change with creativity and forward thinking. *Caring Headlines*, 2-3.

Ives Erickson, J. (2011, October 20). Affordable care and cost-containment go hand in hand. *Caring Headlines*, 2-3.

Ives Erickson, J. (2012, January 5). Facing the future with ingenuity and innovation: Focusing on consistency, continuity, and coordination of care. *Caring Headlines*, 2-3.

Jones, D., Duffy, M. E., & Flanagan, J. (2011). Randomized control trial testing the efficacy of a nurse coached intervention (NCI) in arthroscopy patients. *Nursing Research, 60*(2), 92-99.

Jost, S. G., Bonnell, M., Chacko, S. J., & Parkinson, D. L. (2010). Integrated primary nursing: A care delivery model for the 21st century knowledge worker. *Nursing Administration Quarterly, 34*(3), 208-216.

Kimball, B., Joynt, J., Cherner, D., & O'Neil, E. (2007). The quest for new innovative care delivery models. *The Journal of Nursing Administration, 37*(9), 392-398.

Koloroutis, M., Manthey, M., Felgen, J., Person, C., Kinnaird, L., Wright, D., & Dingman, S. (2004). *Relationship-based care: A model for transforming practice.* Minneapolis, MN: Creative Health Care Management.

Kouzes, J. M., & Posner, B. Z. (2010). *The truth about leadership: The no-fads, heart of the matter facts you need to know.* Marblehead, MA: John Wiley & Sons.

Kravitz, R. L., & Melnikow, J. (2001). Engaging patients in medical decision-making. *British Medical Journal, 323*(7313), 584-585.

Mistiaen, P., & Poot, E. (2006). Telephone follow-up, initiated by a hospital-based health professional, for post discharge problems in patients discharged from hospital to home. *Cochrane Database System Review, 18*(4), CD004510.

O'Leary, K. J., Buck, R., Fligiel, H. M., Haviley, C., Slade, M. E., Landler, M. P., & Wayne, D. B. (2011a). Structured interdisciplinary rounds in a medical teaching unit: Improving patient safety. *Archives of Internal Medicine, 171*(7), 678-684.

O'Leary, K. J., Haviley, C., Slade, M. E., Shah, H. M, Lee, J., & Williams, M. V. (2011b). Improving teamwork: Impact of structured interdisciplinary rounds on a hospital unit. *Journal of Hospital Medicine, 6*(2), 88-93.

O'Leary, K. J., Sehgal, N. L., Terrell, G., & Williams, M. V. (2012). Interdisciplinary teamwork in hospitals: A review and practical recommendations for improvement. *Journal of Hospital Medicine, 7*(1), 48-54.

O'Leary, K. J., Wayne, D. B., Haviley, C., Slade, M. E., Lee, J., & Williams, M. V. (2010). Improving teamwork: Impact of structured interdisciplinary rounds on a medical teaching unit. *Journal of General Internal Medicine, 25*(8), 826-832.

O'Mahony, S., Mazur, E., Charney, P., Want, Y., & Fine, J. (2007). Use of multidisciplinary rounds to simultaneously improve quality outcomes, enhance resident education, and shorten length of stay. *Journal of General Internal Medicine, 22*(8), 1073-1079.

Sabia, S. (2012, February 16). Interdisciplinary rounds: Ensuring all disciplines are on the same page. *Caring Headlines*, 12.

Shendell-Falik, N., Feinson, M., & Mohr, B. J. (2007). Enhancing patient safety: Improving the patient handoff process through appreciative inquiry. *The Journal of Nursing Administration, 37*(2), 95-104.

Vazirani, S., Hays, R. D., Shapiro, M. F., & Cowan, M. (2005). Effect of a multidisciplinary intervention on communication and collaboration among physicians and nurses. *American Journal of Critical Care, 14*(1), 71-77.

Wong, M. C., Yee, K. C., & Turner, P. (2008). *Clinical handover literature review.* eHealth Services Research Group, University of Tasmania, Launceston, Australia.

Chapter 8
Promoting Diversity in the Workplace

Linda Burnes Bolton, RN, DrPh, FAAN
Deborah Washington, RN, PhD

To unpathed waters, undreamed shores.

–William Shakespeare

Introduction

Nursing is a profession on the move. The emerging dominance of a multilingual, multiethnic society in the United States creates a new context for nursing practice. The Patient Protection and Affordable Care Act is slated to add millions of people to the health care system in the coming years (http://www.familiesusa.org). Distinct populations contained in that extraordinary number place an unprecedented demand on present-day nursing and its domains of knowledge and practice.

Spurred most specifically by attention to issues of multiculturalism, gender, and age, nursing faces its next evolution as a clinical presence in the American health care system. New knowledge and perspectives are needed to deliver care that is relevant to disparate social groups and vulnerable populations. In today's health care environment, nursing leaders need to respond to the dynamic cultural changes occurring within American society to promote safe, high-quality, patient-centered care for all.

Background

Many adages attach importance to diversity in nursing. These involve such ideas as promoting a workforce that reflects the population it serves; increasing the diversity in nursing leadership to strengthen mentoring opportunities for minority nurses; enhancing and defining the competencies needed to deliver the care required within a pluralistic society; and, in the absence of significant diversity in nursing, a purposeful reflection on the state of the profession and its demographics.

Fundamental to these important observations is an unchanged commitment to high-quality care of all patients and families. This commitment requires a refocusing of nurses' attention on the social profile of care recipients. Two factors account for this new reality: a) attention to an unfamiliar cross section of individuals and families from diverse cultures and languages, now increasingly more prevalent within our health care settings; b) the emergence of new derivations of care from within a wider social context and based in cultural perspectives and gaps between clinicians and patients that are culturally different.

Care at the bedside is challenged to keep pace with this current and evolving reality. The responsive bedside nurse must seek creative and innovative ways to respond to new questions that address the care of diverse, potentially vulnerable patient and family populations. This chapter will address the historical and social context for the relevance of diversity to nursing. Cultural influences and the preparation of nurses from diverse backgrounds needed to address changes in the delivery of equitable, accessible, and affordable health care across groups will be explored. The importance of capturing the diverse patient's narrative will be included in the discussion as a strategy to know the patient and crucial information needed to provide care to patients and their families. Development of care delivery models and the leadership needed to prepare nurses who reflect the population currently seen across patient care settings will also be explored.

Diversity in Nursing

The circumstances surrounding the vision for contemporary nursing in a diverse society originated from a long legacy of predicted changes within the demographics of America. The forecasted increases in pluralism, the development of minority-majority urban centers, and the growth of non-European based immigration have created a shift in the cultural groups living within the United States.

These changes present new opportunities to address the emerging demographics in the United States and their impact on health. Diversity is a complex construct requiring the need for closer examination of conventional ideas defining excellence in the patient experience and anticipated outcomes linked to the care of a diverse patient group. Preparation for this expected shift will demand changes in health policy, the national research agenda, and the academic preparation for nurses beginning their careers in the 21st century.

Milestones: Diversity and Nursing Preparation

The history of diversity in nursing typically reflects the social mores of a given era. For example, state laws once presented challenges around inclusion of nurses on the basis of race and ethnicity, resulting in the need for ethnic minorities to establish their own nursing organizations (Barbee, 1993). Additional pressures against the inclusion of men in nursing met with similar opposition and were equally resisted. A review of history provides object lessons that can inform the future of nursing, diversity, and the human struggle for recognition and visibility within the profession. The following details help to chronicle these events and offer concrete evidence of the challenges experienced by nurses from diverse backgrounds.

- History recognizes Linda Richards as the first trained nurse in America, completing her education in 1873. (http://www.aahn.org/gravesites/richards.html)

- In 1879, Mary Eliza Mahoney was recorded as the first African American registered nurse in the United States. Under the school quota system existing at the time, Mahoney was the only Black nurse allowed to enroll in a nursing program that year. (http://www.minoritynurse.com)

- At various points in nursing's history, men were either barred from admission to schools of nursing or were not given the imprimatur of inclusion in the profession. In 1866 the Alexian Brothers instituted the first hospital-based nursing program for men to address this issue directly. (http://www.alexianbrothershealth.org/about/history/)

- It was not until 1923 that the first Native American registered nurse, Susie Walking Bear Yellowtail, graduated from a nursing school. (http://www.nurses.info/personalities_susie_yellowtail.htm)

These select examples represent the historically marginalized presence of non-White groups and men in professional nursing. Historically, limitations to full participation in professional nursing for those from non-White cultural backgrounds took many forms. Interpersonal and institutional racism are two examples of how restrictions were manifested. They included segregated hospitals (Dittmer, 2009), discrimination against Black doctors by White professional associations (Watt, 2008), and the use of unknowing research subjects in clinical investigations (Washington, 2006). A quote taken from Martin Luther King's 1966 speech presented at the National Convention of the Medical Committee for Human Rights captures the essence of the experience: "Of all the forms of inequality injustice in health care is the most shocking and inhumane."

Nursing as a profession once reflected the European-based population it served. Over the years, other cultural groups from around the world emerged, but the discipline as a whole has failed to reflect the image of a minority-majority American society. We need to explore diversity and larger social issues such as prejudice, bias, and discrimination to fully inform the development of strategic initiatives in nursing that promote inclusion and advance the practice of culturally competent care.

Diversity in Practice

The literature on culturally competent care stresses the benefits of a diverse nursing workforce. The presence of nurses in settings that reflect a cultural match between nurse and patient tends to increase patient satisfaction. Professionals that represent ethnic and cultural similarities also possess the affinity that facilitates a connection based in culture and language. This cultural congruence between patient and clinician is shown to advantage the patient experience (Adams & Price-Lea, 2004; Laveist & Nuru-Jeter, 2002).

In 2008, a survey of nurses (Health Resources and Services Administration, 2008) reported professional demographic information that highlighted a measure of progress towards increasing the presence of ethnic minorities and men. Prior to 2000, approximately 6% of nurses were male. Survey data indicated an increase to 10% after 2000. Likewise, data provided in the report revealed an increase in minority nurses from 13% to 17%, trended over an eight-year period as marked from the beginning of the millennium (http://bhpr.hrsa.gov).

According to the report, the percentage of non-White/Hispanic nurses in 2000 was 12.5% and remained stable at 12.2% in 2004. In 2008, however, a marked increase to 16.8% was reported. By comparison, the percentage of minorities by race, as reported within the general population of the United States, provided an interesting context. For example, in the 2000 census Blacks represented approximately 12% of the larger population. Given that "Hispanic" is not a race category, the numbering of the latter is complicated. However, it was estimated that non-White/Hispanics made up approximately 16% of the population at the time of the 2000 census (http://www.infoplease.com/spot/hhmcensus1.html).

Increases in minority groups have significant meaning, especially when you consider that at the beginning of the century 1 out of 8 Americans was of non-White heritage. However, by the end of the 20th century that ratio dropped to 1 out of 4 (Hobbs & Stroops, 2002).

> **NOTE**
>
> *The aggregated minority population (people of races other than White or those of Hispanic origin) increased by 88% between 1980 and 2000, while the White non-Hispanic population grew by only 7.9% during that 20-year period (Hobbs & Stoops, 2002).*

Perhaps most startling is data reported in the 2010 census. Of significance is the fact that today minority children under the age of 2 are larger in number than White children in that same age group (http://www.cbsnews.com/stories/2011/06/23/national/main20073650.shtml). The implications of these data are enormous. They suggest an approaching generational tide that is ethnically different from the traditional majority. From within this population, future nurses will emerge. This shift will result in a significantly different nursing workforce that will influence the dynamic of the clinical encounter and impact outcomes yet to be measured. We can anticipate that the aging White population will be cared for by the emerging minority populations. Greater incorporation of diversity in nursing now in nursing curricula and clinical preparation will alleviate the need to teach cultural competence to a reversed demographic.

Social Responsibility of Nursing

The intrinsic social contract between nursing and the general public places on us a professional responsibility to develop a workforce with the skills, talents, and abilities to operationalize competence as it relates to nursing practice and a diverse society. The ethical core of the profession demands attention to diversity that is inescapable. This commitment is supported in the ANA *Position Statement on Nurses Role in Ethics and Human Rights* from the American Nurses Association (ANA, 2010) in which specific mention is given to facets of diversity as a principle of human dignity. These identified facets include:

- Institutionalized racism

- Environmental disparities

- Class discrimination

- Sexism

- Ageism

- Heterosexism

- Homophobia

- Physical or mental disability (p. 5)

The ANA further recommends that nursing's role as advocate is both appropriate and needed in exemplary practice.

Population groups that constitute the dimensions of diversity previously mentioned are historically consigned to the margins of quality when viewed through the perspectives of access, affordability, and inclusion. Focusing on diversity in nursing can improve care issues, impacting multiple ethnic and cultural groups. Moving discussions around diversity to the forefront, with the contributions of new voices, can influence the national discourse on health disparities and unequal treatment in care.

Transcultural Nursing

Before demographic shifts in populations occurred, underestimating the knowledge needed to care for the ethnic minority or the foreign-born patient was a possibility. Though care undoubtedly met the highest standards of quality in the universal sense, little evidence indicates that it was being completely addressed outside of Madeleine Leininger's Sunrise Model and Transcultural Nursing (Clark, McFarland, Andrews & Leininger, 2009). Leininger states, "When I started and looked at the journals, the word care was a not a commonly used word. Then within 10 to 15 years, people were advertising care. 'We care for your car.' 'We care for your clothes.' It became an economic value." (p. 237). Leininger's work suggests the need for a concerted concern within nursing to articulate more clearly the importance of culture and ethnicity in care. She further noted a need to include cultural competency as a prominent and noticeable expectation of nursing practice.

Leininger highlights care or caring as an attribute of practice that might require re-examination within the context of a multicultural health care environment. Nursing care, as an economic value, can be linked to patient satisfaction with inclusion of cultural background as a parameter for evaluation. Currently, the meaning of care delivery and patient responses to those actions has often been associated with the perspectives of White, Anglo-Saxon Protestants as the template population. Within the context of a changing population demographic in health care, a changing world view is needed.

Over the years, for example, nursing education and the content of curriculum is tacitly oriented to the values, beliefs, and cultural orientation of the White majority (Allen, 2006). Understanding this reality explicitly has far-reaching importance for the future of nursing as a renewed discipline, brought up-to-date and relevant within the social and changing context of its practice. The larger social environment sets expectations and responsibility on the profession. Principles associated with care at the bedside continue to evolve in alignment with population changes. In the hands of the staff nurse and with visionary leadership guiding the discipline, a mono-cultural health care system is transitioning to care appropriately described as multicultural.

Creating Culturally Sensitive Care at the Bedside

A conscientious effort applied to education, skill, and competency acquisition and the development of innovative practice environments conducive to experiential learning can provide evidence of a discipline exerting effort to be responsive to a present-day society that is both multilingual and multiethnic. As outlined by Siantz & Meleis (2007):

> implementing a vision that integrates cultural competence into nursing education and practice must further consider (a) building sustainable policies that support the increase of diversity in nursing through partnerships, (b) expanding interdisciplinary models to transform health care organizations, (c) applying business principles that will strategically support diversity, (d) integrating rural and urban perspectives, (e) promoting research that evaluates curricular

models of diversity for a global society and market, and (f) evaluating the benefits of cultural competence in health care. (p. 87S)

The development a culturally sensitive caring environment for patients requires the preparation of all providers to support diversity and the unique needs of patients from different cultural groups. Nurses at the bedside have a unique role in advancing this agenda.

The Concept of Equitable Health Services

Many ways to discuss representations of diversity exist beyond race/ethnicity, gender, and age. Equally important to this dialogue are additional elements such as physical and cognitive ability, sexual orientation, socioeconomic status, and spirituality. All of the aforementioned representations of diversity require great skill and knowledge to enlarge the meaning of consistent quality in the prevention and treatment of illness in addition to wellness management. These aspects of diversity are a more comprehensive vision of the whole person. To take a perspective that would parse the personhood of each human being to accommodate a new model of assessment, for example, would be an error. The maxim that the "whole is better than the sum of its parts" is the relevant thought to ponder in this regard.

Clinicians need to be aware of their role in advancing a diversity agenda and must be sensitive to the provision of equitable care. The American Nurses Association Code of Ethics for Nurses (http://www.nursingworld.org/codeofethics) does not exempt the practicing nurse from providing care appropriate to the uniqueness of any individual. Through its various provisions the Code of Ethics covers important principles such as nursing judgment and the significance of care provided to culturally diverse communities. The ability of the larger health care system, organization, or even the individual practitioner to guarantee adherence to this code requires vigilance. For example, nurses who lack knowledge about diverse groups unintentionally circumvent the code because their cultural illiteracy prevents the cognitive dissonance that serves to alert individual nurses that something is amiss in the quality of information or the effects of interventions.

Equity in health services to the populations, as already noted, addresses the need for a humanistic approach to care delivery. It embodies the need to consider in detail those outcomes of care that reflect the uniqueness of each person and who they are as individuals or groups to be cared for rather than placed within the context of a socially stigmatized or disadvantaged group.

The associated concept of unequal treatment has gained increased emphasis within the lexicon of health care after the groundbreaking 2003 report from the Institute of Medicine (IOM) on unequal treatment in health care (http://www. iom.edu/Reports/2002/Unequal-Treatment-Confronting-Racial-and-Ethnic-Disparities-in-Health-Care.aspx), which delineated disparities in health outcomes between comparative ethnic groups. In the executive summary of the report it was noted, "Even among the better-controlled studies, the vast majority of published research indicates that minorities are less likely than whites to receive needed services, including clinically necessary procedures, even after correcting for access-related factors, such as insurance status" (http://www.iom.edu/~/media/Files/Report%20Files/2003/Unequal-Treatment-Confronting-Racial-and-Ethnic-Disparities-in-Health-Care/DisparitiesAdmin8pg.pdf).

This added greater complexity and controversy to the significant national discussion that followed the published report.

Nurses' Role in Equal Treatment of All Patients

Nurses at the bedside need to increase their knowledge about unequal treatment (e.g., comparatively less preventive care provided to ethnic minorities) and develop the ability to detect what comprises evidence of unequal treatment (e.g., inadequate and differential practices related to ethnic groups). To decidedly pose the question about the existence of unequal treatment at the bedside is an exercise in reflective practice. This includes awareness of systemic issues and attention to individual performance.

The nurse at the bedside must be conscious about care that is too generalized and applied too broadly so that the care at the bedside will not become outdated or invalid. In addition, an individual's performance must be challenged by a combination of subjective and objective elements. The evaluation and evaluator of these elements should reflect the knowledge at the forefront of the discipline. Diversity requires a reappraisal of those factors previously considered norms. The concept of cultural competence suggests the institution of new reference points against which other factors can be assessed.

Affordability and Access to Care

Affordability and accessibility to care became key words linked with a national agenda designed to eliminate disparities and unequal treatment. Although identified as the seminal work on disparities and related ideologies, the Institute of Medicine (IOM, 2002) report on unequal treatment failed to align consensus on theories, strategies, and definitions for concepts such as equity and inequality. Braveman (2006) does provide a thoughtful frame of reference that corresponds with deep-seated ideas integral, though not yet apparent in every respect, to diversity in nursing and health care:

> A health disparity/inequality is a particular type of difference in health or in the most important influences on health that could potentially be shaped by policies; it is a difference in which disadvantaged social groups (such as the poor, racial/ethnic minorities, women, or other groups that have persistently experienced social disadvantage or discrimination) systematically experience worse health or greater health risks than more advantaged groups. (p. 180)

This statement helps to link the relevance of sociological norms and their application to a more complete understanding of health care in relation to diversity. Health care as a right or privilege is linked to social conventions. The challenge of these norms is their systemic and interpersonal effect on clinicians and patients and families. The ability to improve professional nursing's response to a self-differentiating, contemporary patient population now requires an examination of its fundamental ideologies, methods of care, and the appropriate design of institutional structures supporting the work of relief from and prevention of illness. Action taken at the bedside is the primary determinant of the patient experience with quality, safety, and a sense of inclusion.

Diversity at the Bedside: Capturing the Patient Narrative

There is value in the unasked question. The literature is replete with studies of linguistic populations and ethnic minorities that highlight the disconnection between their experiences of care when contrasted with that of the dominant cultural group (http://www.rwjf.org/files/research/Disparities_Survey_Report. pdf). This difference in perception or reality is typically characterized by time spent in the clinical encounter, the quality of information provided, and the undesirable qualities of the cross-cultural relationship. Most of this research-based information is seldom told from the perspective of the nurse-patient encounter. However, this perspective is critical to inform not only care delivery but also to acknowledge the significant meaning attached to the patient and their experiences.

Cultural congruence between patient and clinician is often put forward as a possible solution to this range in experiences. However, reliance on such solutions negates the ethics basic to the practice of nursing, suggests the inadequacy of educational preparation, or makes any nurse ineligible to take care of any patient. To pose the question of the value of cultural competence is to explore the vision for the future of nursing as it relates to understanding the characteristics of expertise at the bedside, support for evidence and evaluation of its presence as an observable phenomenon, and inclusion of feedback from those affected.

Cultural competence implies the elimination of negative effects on care modified by personal considerations. The level of quality in the care experience of the patient from a diverse background requires mutual understanding, trust, and shared agreement between nurse and patient. Current inexplicable differences in both care experience and outcomes necessitate a more developed and multifaceted access by nursing to the diversity-related experience of consumers and their contact with systems of care and its providers.

Patient satisfaction through the lens of culture has unique characteristics. Approach and admittance to that narrative is hindered by a still-developing understanding of the manner in which diversity is shaping nursing. Roadblocks

Roadblocks to the Narrative of the Diverse Patient

- Desire to maintain a relationship with care provider

- Difficultly in being honest about affronts

- Power boundaries between care provider and patient or group

- Protecting reputation as a desired patient by avoiding attributes that evoke stereotypes

- Care environment not time/place for "that" discussion

- What am I willing to put up with?

FIGURE 8.1

Dilemmas of the minority patient in the clinical encounter.

to knowing a person and their stories are encrypted within social themes that intrude on the clinical encounter (see Figure 8.1).

An initial critique of the roadblocks to the narrative of the diverse patient would seem to include themes shared in common with any relationship involving a power differential. Each theme taken separately might, in reality, have crossover value. In combination they represent the unique social experience of the ethnic minority patient that can impact the health care experience of that patient (see Table 8.1).

Challenges to building rapport within the larger society between those who are culturally and socially dissimilar do not disappear in the health care setting. Patients and families manage problematic encounters by placing priority on access rather than service. Encounters that merit fears of retaliation, exhibit power differentials, stand as proof of status, and lessen adverse effects on reputation are managed through well-honed survival skills of those who carry the social histories of the disenfranchised.

TABLE 8.1 : Characteristics of Roadblocks to the Ethnic Minority Narrative

CHARACTERISTICS	OPERATIONAL DEFINITION
Relationship maintenance	Tolerating a personal reduction in worth or character verbally or behaviorally imposed by a clinician and based in social stigma.
Difficulty being honest about affronts	A false statement based in semantic ambiguity that hints at negative personal opinions and beliefs about an ethnic group.
Power boundaries	The inferred possession of control over others or the limits of that control within a relationship.
Being a desired patient	The mindful management by the ethnic minority patient of the clinical encounter so that conventional perceptions by the clinician are less likely to manifest.
"That" discussion	Racism as a perceptible construct in the clinical encounter.
Putting up with	Intentional design and purpose to the reciprocal relationship between clinician and patient that explicitly acknowledges cultural differences. This generally includes addressing missteps and a lack of culture-based knowledge.

Importance of the Diverse Patient Narrative

Cultural competence enables an understanding that some patient-centered initiatives might not be culturally feasible. For example, "speaking up" or "speaking out" is a desired attribute when viewed as an indication of patient and family engagement in care. However, this type of behavior might not be appropriate across all cultures (Charles, Gafni, Whelan & Obrien, 2006). Age, gender, level of education, and socioeconomic status also matter (Arora & McHorney, 2000). The ability to bridge these contradictions in expectations of patient engagement requires insight into the meaning of a positive health care experience through the eyes of the patient from a diverse background.

A combination of circumstances currently drives reassessment of nursing as a discipline within the new health care system on the horizon. They include the changed status quo of the discipline as one increasingly important in the new scenario of care delivery, access, and cost containment. One of the resulting challenges that must be addressed is a corps of practitioners lacking experience with both the change in scenario of patient population and the future of the discipline. The traditional stance of the profession that caring is the essence of its being might benefit from inclusion of multiculturalism as it pursues national agreement on the meaning of the concept. Finfgeld-Connett (2008) posits that characteristics of caring include interpersonal sensitivity, respect for each person, personalized care, and attention to cultural differences. The universality of these components is worthy of further research. The value of the narrative for patients from various cultural groups provides insight into their unique perceptions of and responses to health and illness. See Figure 8.2.

- Reflects the patient and their experience

- Contains crucial information unique to the individual and provides meaning about responses and behaviors

- Might provide new knowledge that creates firsts in the field of nursing inquiry

- Identifies limits of care delivery within a multicultural, multilingual health care system

- Can create new models of practice, not a redesign or an overhaul of the old

- Points out gaps in care and offers distinctive ways to address the care of cultural minority patients following adverse events

---

FIGURE 8.2

Value of the patient narrative and cultural diversity.

Narrative Reflects Crucial Information about Patients and Their Experience

The patient narrative contains knowledge unique to the person, that person's experience, and responses to an experience as a cultural entity. Each patient as a unique entity presents a new personification of what might be deemed familiar. The ability to avoid overgeneralization is a test of the nurse's ability to individualize and not group experiences or responses.

Might Provide New Knowledge

As an ethnic minority, subpopulations grow, acculturate, and change the larger society. The combination of their coexistence and the integration of values, beliefs, and practices within society can remain hidden as they develop and evolve. It becomes essential to design data-collection strategies that uncover such unique cultural modifications as part of more sophisticated, truly holistic nursing assessments when patient care is evaluated.

Can Create New Models of Practice

The current blueprint for patient care is becoming obsolete. It is based on a conceptual framework that has less of the requisite knowledge, pedagogies, art, and indispensible abilities to produce solutions for a multicultural society in which no one group dominates as the standard. What is required by obligation or convention in the definition of nursing as an expression of the profession requires reevaluation. The discipline is defined by a larger vision of practice, and the stated aims and objectives of the profession reflect a stance that is universal.

Nursing is not properly characterized nor should it be constrained by that which is oriented locally or practiced as what is commonly encountered. To do so would be to limit the size and scope of nursing as a field of study. More specifically, the nursing metaparadigm of person, health, environment, and nursing is a useful roadmap to the future. Gunther & Alligood (2002) make the point, "Activities and behaviors of nurses identified in the literature as correlating with high-quality care are learned during formal education and/or developed in nursing practice" (p. 355). As a global discipline, features of nursing such as quality in care are not bounded by geography.

Limits of Care Delivery Within a Multicultural, Multilingual Health Care System

Reports on health disparities result from cumulative evidence. Each nurse at the bedside represents a cohort capable of leveling such variations. Taking up the challenge to understand cultural competence as more than the ability to work with an interpreter exemplifies the search for skills, qualities, and standards that identify when care is delivered well to ethnic minorities. Such care involves knowing the person and their unique responses and behaviors in the face of illness and health and creating the expectation of a mutual engagement cognizant of nurse and patient as members of a larger social environment that can influence the clinical relationship.

Gaps in Supports for Cultural Minority Patients and Adverse Events

The well documented distrust of African Americans related to the health care system might influence their capacity to manage adverse events (http://www.ncbi. nlm.nih.gov/pmc/articles/PMC1497556/pdf/12815086.pdf). Though Hispanics are typically included in research questions related to health care access, insurance coverage, and unequal treatment (Lillie-Blanton, Brodie, Rowland, Altman & McIntosh, 2000), the specific topic of distrust is seldom studied outside the Black experience. This response by patients and families might be linked to past fears and concerns of the ethnic group and past experiences with health care systems.

Experience with institutional and interpersonal racism compromise belief in positive intentions and the application of excellence as a standard of care for the ethnic minority patient. Mistrust categorizes all adverse events as preventable and leaves little room for human error. The ability to build relationships characterized by authenticity, beyond doubt or reproach, necessitates understanding of cultural nuances and knowledge within each clinical encounter between the nurse and the patient and family.

The Future of Nursing: the Paradigm of the "New" Nurse for Unprecedented Times

Recent events in health care redesign and reform (IOM, 2001) have resulted in nursing taking stock of gaps in knowledge related to socially marginalized groups and educational preparation of students who will be expected to provide the highest caliber of safe and equitable care. For example, the predicted graying of Americans as the boomer generation reaches the age of retirement is the focus of much national discourse, including what is happening and how is this happening (e.g., growth of elderly population) and the AACN recommendation for curriculum changes, and so on.

The newly emerging language of health care reflects the inclusion of maturing ideas such as cultural sensitivity, a diverse workforce, unequal treatment, disparities, cultural competence, vulnerable populations, and healthy people. National efforts such as the CLAS Standards (Culturally and Linguistically Appropriate Services) from the Office of Minority Health (OMH) and the 2010 Roadmap for Hospitals from the Joint Commission establish diversity as an ideological and strategic asset for needed systemic change in the health care system (http://www.jointcommission.org/Advancing_Effective_Communication/).

Acquisition of the new competencies and skills required for all nurses working within this changing environment of health care are addressed by the reports previously mentioned. Incorporating these competencies into agendas at national nursing conferences will provide needed evidence to reflect the effort being put forward to gain consensus around the competencies and associated behaviors required to enhance cultural diversity in nursing. Then nursing can conduct the research needed and implement the education in nursing programs to assure that diversity is in fact represented in the priorities of the discipline. To date there is limited national evidence to nursing schools as they integrate diversity content into their programs. At best education has been sporadic from school to school resulting in some students exposed to content and some not.

Additionally, commitment to the inclusive work environment is equally scattered and inconsistent and compromises the national ideal of a culturally competent nursing workforce as a standard of the discipline. We will actualize this ideal when cultural competence is more fully integrated into the fabric of professional education and practice and better represents the broader discipline. The confident anticipation of actions that verify the significance of these indicators should drive nursing more dynamically into its future. The significance of the population shift, global issues that affect the nursing profession, international and domestic humanitarian missions, and critical health policy needs should indicate that something different is about to happen in the profession.

Diversity as an Asset to Achieving Institute of Medicine Future of Nursing

As health care reform expands, there is an opportunity to use this period of change to advance the diversity agenda within health care. Developing and implementing recommendations that impact care at the bedside will ensure new opportunities for addressing the unique needs of a diverse population of patients and their families.

Recommendations

The ideals of universal health care in the United States inherently promise access to services that are safe and of the highest quality without regard to who presents for those services. Diversity adds challenging characteristics to those ideals. A polylingual, multiethnic population is vulnerable to gaps in service delivery and design. The current journey towards a new future for the profession and those it seeks to better serve is benefitting from the roadmap outlined by the Future of Nursing discourse. The written document (IOM, 2010) forecasts an unprecedented place and position for a profession rising to a course of events that will ameliorate long-standing problems for the underserved. Specific examples of the models for change are described in the following sections.

Models for Leadership

Significant changes in nursing leadership from the top-down are an imperative for nursing care at the bedside. First, leadership needs to clearly articulate the desired vision. Next, they then need to produce critical evidence to support the need for change in the comprehensive preparation of nurses for competent practice. Following these steps requires communicating with relevant groups so that others can contribute their expertise and commitment to make the *new* vision a reality. Examples of this process are described in the following sections.

Academic Nurse Leaders

Academic nurse leaders have moved from single courses on caring for diverse populations to promoting inclusivity as a core principle underpinning every course in the nursing curriculum. This important transition signals a mainstreaming of diversity in contrast to its previous role as a sidebar of nursing knowledge.

The National League for Nursing (NLN) and the American Association of Colleges of Nurses (AACN) core curricula includes content on diversity. Additionally, the Institute of Medicine study on the Future of Nursing (2010) identifies several exemplars to promote diversity in nursing faculty, clinicians, scientists, executives, and community nurse leaders.

Health Care Organization Nurse Leaders

Chief nurse executives established programs to increase the diversity of the workforce by adopting diversity as an organizational value and allocating resources to educate, develop, and engage nurses to work in community health, disease prevention, and wellness programs. Organizational examples of such initiatives include the American Organization of Nurse Executives (AONE) and American Nurses Association (ANA).

Equally important, ethnic community nurse leaders possess knowledge and skills that serve to motivate the involvement of representatives from diverse populations. These leaders have coached and mentored individuals to consider nursing as a worthy career, individuals steeped in the experiences of the underserved and driven to make the type of differences that will change the health status of those diverse populations. These leaders are referents on the response to the majority population and its assessment and intervention strategies to promote change. Examples of such organizations are the National Coalition of Ethnic Minority Nurse Association Organizations (NCEMA) and the American Assembly for Men in Nursing (AAMN).

Summary

Nursing has stepped into its next chapter, emerging as a contemporary discipline meeting the challenge of benchmarking itself as state of the art. The vision for the future models a profession that has the capacity to adapt itself to a different set of social conditions. The discipline recognizes its fields of knowledge and practice are global and that these domains are not of geography but of relevance to those served. Population trends point to an inescapable and still-developing discussion about the *art* of nursing as the indispensible dimension of a transformative process driven by diversity and associated issues. To strengthen the status of the art and science of nursing is to become aware of inclusion as a revitalized concept and part of an iterative and evolving process of a profession (i.e., nursing) becoming. A profession's ability to navigate the uncharted waters of inclusion points to a deconstruction of excellence and its missing characteristics relating to what is unfamiliar to practice and practitioners. Consequently, quality in patient care at the bedside must frame untried paradigms that will necessarily break with convention.

Diversity and inclusion lead to a compelling discourse on many important considerations. Ethnic minorities, men, and a multigenerational employee base, for example, presently engender questions, raise awareness, and are currently advancing the gradual transformation of a profession readying itself for a future that is relatively near. Growing attention to preparing nurses to acknowledge the whole person and their uniqueness, especially linked to culture and ethnicity, can help identify unique characteristics of each individual and their story. As nurses advance as leaders at the bedside and expand their knowledge about the concepts of diversity and humanistic care, better health care for all can be realized.

References

Adams, V. W., & Price-Lea, P. J. (2004). A critical need for a more diverse nursing workforce. *North Carolina Medical Journal, 65*(2), 98-100.

Allen, D. G. (2006). Whiteness and difference in nursing. *Nursing Philosophy, 7*(2), 65-78.

American Association for the History of Nursing, Inc. *Linda A. J. Richards.* Retrieved from http://www. aahn.org/gravesites/richards.html

American Nurses Association (ANA). (2010). *The nurse's role in ethics and human rights: Protecting and promoting individual worth, dignity, and human rights in practice settings.* Retrieved from http://gm6.nursingworld.org/MainMenuCategories/Policy-Advocacy/Positions-and-Resolutions/ ANAPositionStatements/Position-Statements-Alphabetically/Nursess-Role-in-Ethics-and-Human-Rights.pdf

American Nurses Association (ANA). (2001). *Code of ethics for nurses.* Retrieved from http://www. nursingworld.org/MainMenuCategories/EthicsStandards/CodeofEthicsforNurses/Code-of-Ethics.pdf

Arora, N. K., & McHorney, C. A. (2000). Patient preference for medical decision-making: Who really wants to participate? *Medical Care, 38*(3), 335-341.

Barbee, E. (1993). Racism in U.S. nursing. *Medical Anthropology Quarterly, 7*(4), 346-362.

Braveman, P. (2006). Health disparities and health equity: Concepts and measurement. *Annual Review of Public Health, 27*, 167-194.

CBS News. (2011). *Minorities make up majority of U.S. babies.* Retrieved from http://www.cbsnews.com /stories/2011/06/23/national/main20073650.shtml

Charles, C., Gafni, A., Whelan, T., & O'Brien, M. A. (2006). Cultural influences on the physician-patient encounter: The case of shared treatment decision-making. *Patient Education and Counseling, 63*(3), 262-267.

Clark, P., McFarland, M., Andrews, M., & Leininger, M. (2009). Caring: Some reflections on the impact of the culture care theory by McFarland & Andrews and a conversation with Leininger. *Nursing Science Quarterly, 22*(3), 233-239.

Dittmer, J. (2009). *The good doctors: The medical committee for human rights and the struggle for social justice in health care.* New York, NY: Bloomsbury Press.

Early history of the Alexian Brothers. (n.d.) Retrieved from http://www.alexianbrothershealth.org/about/ history/

Families USA: The Voice for Health Care Consumers. (2009). *At the Crossroads: Is health coverage ahead for America?* Retrieved from www.familiesusa.org/assets/pdfs/health-reform/at-a-crossroads.pdf

Finfgeld-Connett, D. (2008). Metasynthesis of caring in nursing. *Journal of Clinical Nursing, 17*(2), 196-204.

Gunther, M., & Alligood, M. R. (2002). A discipline-specific determination of high quality nursing care. *Journal of Advanced Nursing, 38*(4), 353-359.

Health Resources and Services Administration. (2008). *The registered nurse population: Findings from the 2008 national sample survey of registered nurses.* Retrieved from http://bhpr.hrsa.gov/ healthworkforce/rnsurvey2008.html

Hispanic Americans by the numbers. (n.d.) Retrieved from http://www.infoplease.com/spot/ hhmcensus1.html

Hobbs, F., & Stroops, N. (2002). *Demographic trends in the 20th Century: Census 2000 special reports.* Retrieved from http://www.census.gov/prod/2002pubs/censr-4.pdf

Institute of Medicine (IOM). (2001). *Executive summary. Crossing the quality chasm: A new health system for the 21st century.* Retrieved from http://www.nap.edu/openbook.php?record_id=10027&page=7

Institute of Medicine (IOM). (2002). *Executive summary. Unequal treatment: Confronting racial and ethnic disparities in health care,* 2. Retrieved from http://www.iom.edu/Reports/2002/Unequal-Treatment-Confronting-Racial-and-Ethnic-Disparities-in-Health-Care.aspx

Institute of Medicine (IOM). (2010). *The future of nursing: Leading change, advancing health.* Washington, DC: National Academies Press.

The Joint Commission. (2010). *Advancing effective communication, cultural competence, and patient- and family-centered care: A roadmap for hospitals.* Retrieved from www.jointcommission.org/Advancing_Effective_Communication

King, W. D. (2003). Examining African Americans' mistrust of the health care system: Expanding the research question. *Public Health Reports, 118*(4), 366-367.

LaVeist, T. A., & Nuru-Jeter, A. (2002). Is doctor-patient race concordance associated with greater satisfaction with care? *Journal of Health and Social Behavior, 43*(3), 296-306.

Lillie-Blanton, M., Brodie, M., Rowland, D., Altman, D., & McIntosh, M. (2000). Race, ethnicity, and the health care system: Public perception and experiences. *Medical Care Research and Review, 57*(supplement 1), 218-235.

Making History: Black Nightingales. (2004). Retrieved from http://www.minoritynurse.com

Siantz, M. L., & Meleis, A. I. (2007). Integrating cultural competence into nursing education and practice: 21st century action steps. *Journal of Transcultural Nursing, 18*(1), 86S-90S.

Susie Walking Bear Yellowtail. (2006). Retrieved from http://www.badeagle.com/cgi-bin/ib3/cgi-bin/ikonboard.cgi?act=ST;f=36;t=5814;&#top

U.S. Census Bureau. *Hispanic Americans by the numbers.* Retrieved from http://www.infoplease.com/spot/hhmcensus1.html

Washington, H. A. (2006). *Medical apartheid: The dark history of medical experimentation on black Americans from colonial times to the present.* New York, NY: Doubleday.

Watt, H. (2008). Doctors' group plans apology for racism. *The Washington Post.* Retrieved from http://www.washingtonpost.com/wp-dyn/content/article/2008/07/09/AR2008070902351.html

Chapter 9

Mentorship and Best Practices for Mentorship

Gaurdia Banister, RN, PhD
Susan Gennaro, RN, DSN, FAAN

The greatest good you can do for another is not just to share your riches but to reveal to him his own.

–Benjamin Disraeli

Introduction

Over the years nurse leaders have written about socialization into professional nursing and the demands of the work environment (Kramer et al., 2007). The nurses' transition into a professional career begins after the initial orientation is completed, but nurses also need guidance throughout their careers. As nurses advance in a chosen role, they often require different levels of guidance, insight, and development. Mentors help provide that "safe space" where the expertise, commitment, and knowledge of a more seasoned professional can assist nurses to move from "novice to expert" leaders in patient care or academic excellence. Recently 44% of 1,399 nurses surveyed said that they planned to make a career change within the next three years (AMN Healthcare, 2010). Those nurses seeking new opportunities all share at least one thing in common—they all would be well advised to find a mentor in their new position.

TERMS YOU NEED TO KNOW

Before proceeding any further, you need to have an understanding of the following terms as they relate to this chapter:

Mentoring: The process of transmitting values, skills, and knowledge; providing networking opportunities; teaching needed information; and providing a sounding board for novices learning to negotiate a new role or new environment

Mentor: An experienced person who guides a novice in learning how to negotiate a new role or environment

Mentee: The one being mentored by an expert to facilitate role transition for the novice and enhance professional growth knowledge acquisition, role socialization, consultation, and support

Mentorship: The process of transmitting skills and networking opportunities, values, and information while being an active listener and problem solver as a mentee negotiates a new role or new environment

Coaching: The process by which an experienced person is involved in skill building and some knowledge transfer to a less experienced person

Facilitating nursing leadership at the bedside can be enhanced by the presence of a mentor. The mentor role is critical to transforming both the clinician and patient care overall. Designating mentors to new and advanced clinical scholars provides opportunities for personal and professional growth in a trusting and safe space. Mentors are rewarded by the success of mentees and inspired by their transformation and ability to lead and transform nursing care.

This chapter focuses on the benefits of mentors, and the guidance and leadership provided by experts, seasoned in their field and effective in communicating important information to others. The process of mentorship is discussed with emphasis on the potential outcomes of the experience as well as the functions mentoring play in relation to professional growth and development. Examples of successful mentored projects are provided along with a discussion of opportunities for mentoring experiences on a global level.

Benefits of Mentorship

Mentorship is increasingly important in today's health care environment where the average nurse is more than 40 years of age (Buerhaus, Staiger & Auerbach, 2000) and where patients are living longer with increasingly complex health care demands in an increasingly complex health care system (Reid Ponte, 2004). These demographics make it particularly important that nurse mentors be available for the novice and the more experienced nurses who are returning to the workforce or moving into new areas of practice. There are many demands and challenges presented to the returning or novice nurses within the practice setting that require mentoring and development. When they are not addressed, retention and overall work morale can be compromised. In the expanding and complex world of health care, a trusted guide increases the likelihood of success and helps individuals grow in the midst of dynamic change.

Mentors are helpful for nurses at all stages of their careers. For novice nurses, mentors can help increase confidence, decrease anxiety, and decrease reality shock (Huybrecht, Loeckx, Quaeyhaegens, De Tobel & Mistiaen, 2010). Mentorship can also help mentees learn new skills such as how to juggle multiple roles in a time-efficient manner (Hawkins & Fontenot, 2009). For experienced nurses entering a new field, mentors help with networking, career development, and in finding solutions to new challenges such as adapting to new organizations and enhancing organizational fit (Race & Skees, 2010).

Mentorship is cost effective and enhances job satisfaction (Fox, 2010; Race and Skees, 2010), job performance, and employee motivation (Bray & Nettleton, 2007). Specifically, a number of studies have found that mentorship results in improved nurse retention (Almada, Carafoli, Flattery, French & McNamara, 2004; Fox, 2010; Hale, 2004) and that mentorship leads to decreased orientation and recruitment costs (Hensinger, Minerath, Parry & Robertson, 2005). Fox studied retention of new nurses and estimates that a mentorship program cost her organization $291,000 annually in 2008 and that the mentorship program resulted in a decrease in turnover of 6.29% resulting in a savings of $1,040,153. Given the important role that mentorship can play in organizations, the American Organization of Nurse Executives (2000) and the Canadian Nurses Association (2004) have both recommended that mentoring networks for new graduates be established as one way to improve the work environment.

Positive Outcomes of Mentorship

Mentorship is valuable to mentors and mentees alike. Mentors report that the most valuable outcomes they experience in being mentors are collegiality, reflection, and personal satisfaction (Ehrich, Tennent & Hansford, 2002). In this same study, mentees report that their most valued outcomes of participating in a mentored relationship were receiving support and empathy, getting help with resources including knowledge, and having someone with whom they can problem solve (Ehrich et al., 2002).

Negative Aspects of Mentorship

At times some people who are not well suited to being mentors assume mentorship roles. Darling (1985) calls these people "toxic mentors." Toxic mentors are often those who are not available, are negative, and who do not value the organization and are similarly not valued by organizational colleagues (Gray & Smith, 1999). Darling discusses four types of toxic mentors. These include the following:

- **Avoiders:** Those who are not accessible

- **Dumpers:** Those who see difficult situations but believe that a sink-or-swim attitude is appropriate

- **Blockers:** Those who are withholders of information or blockers of development by supervising too closely

- **Destroyers:** Those who undermine mentees to their face or to others in the group by being belittling or hypercritical (Darling, 1985)

Though organizations need to avoid all toxic mentors, the mentor who is competent as a nurse but who is burnt out and chooses to punish mentees for their enthusiasm for a new organization is of particular concern to organizational health.

Mentorship can have negative outcomes even when mentors are not toxic. For mentors, the extra time that mentorship takes is a negative outcome listed by mentors and mentees alike (Ehrich et al., 2002). Additionally, mentors have identified lack of training, personality mismatches, conflicting roles in terms of advice and assessment, and extra responsibility associated with the mentoring role as negative aspects of mentorship, and mentees cite the difficulty in having critical mentors, in being constantly observed, and encountering a lack of feedback as additional negative outcomes (Ehrich et al., 2002).

The Process of Mentorship

How is mentorship initiated? Mentors and mentees often find each other or might be assigned to each other by an organizational leader. Historically, the mentor and mentee relationship began as self-selected, informal relationships (like the original Mentor who took care of Odysseus' son in Homer's epic *The Odyssey*). As the benefits of mentorship became clear, organizations developed more formal mentorship programs to help women and other minorities benefit from the experience of others (Ehrich, Tennent & Hansford, 2002).

In self-selected mentor/mentee relationships, both the mentor and the mentee have an informal agreement to work together to meet the career goals of the mentee. The length of time to establish this relationship is also mutually determined and flexible (Bally, 2007). In more formal relationships, such as work transitions or orientation, the length of time and goals of the relationship are set by the institution. Whether mentors are assigned or selected, mentors are experienced in an organization or in a clinical area, discipline, or job position and must have time to be able to help their mentees, who have less experience in this same organization, clinical area, or discipline.

It is not unusual for today's nurse scholars to identify mentors early in their career and work with them throughout their career, growing and emerging in their own work as they continue to communicate and be guided by another professional leader. In nursing, interdisciplinary mentors are also being identified outside of the discipline. As health care becomes less siloed, so, too, a nurse mentor might emerge from another discipline (such as a physician, physical therapist, nutritionist, etc.) or job position (teacher, nurse, nurse practitioner, administrator, etc.) (Webb & Shakespeare, 2008).

Mentorship Versus Preceptorship or Coaching

Mentors identify teaching, supporting, and role modeling as three of their main roles (Bray & Nettleton, 2007). They also identify the most difficult aspect as that of assessor or evaluator (Bray & Nettleton, 2007). This component of the mentor role raises questions about the difference between mentorship and preceptorship or coaching (Huybrecht et al., 2010; Race & Skees, 2010).

Preceptorship differs from mentorship in that preceptorship always carries an evaluation component whereas not all mentorship relationships include evaluation. Preceptorship experiences are usually more short term than are mentorship experiences (Race & Skees, 2010). **Coaching** generally focuses on skills that might also be a part of a mentoring relationship, but mentorship is generally broader in its focus than coaching and so includes relational dimensions such as networking and career development (Race & Skees, 2010). See Table 9.1 for a summary of the differences. Examining the difference between mentorship and other roles such as preceptorship is important because it helps identify difficulties inherent in mentorship relationships. Because mentors and mentees genuinely like each other, they might face an inherent conflict in a mentorship relationship that includes a degree of evaluation as part of the relationship. Organizational mentorship programs, by necessity, often do include evaluation, and mentors who are also evaluators report feeling conflict between their obligations as a friend and as an evaluator (Bray & Nettleton, 2007).

TABLE 9.1: Mentorship Versus Coaching Versus Preceptorship

ROLE	ORIGIN OF RELATIONSHIP	LENGTH	MAIN OBJECT OF ROLE
Mentorship	Mutual between mentor and mentee	Long term	Role socialization
			Value transmission
			Networking
			Personal development
Coaching	Assigned by institution	Short term	Skill building
			Evaluation not central
Preceptorship	Assigned by institution	Short term	Skill and knowledge building
			Evaluation component

Part of why evaluation is difficult for mentors is that when a mentee is not thriving, mentors often feel as if they are not being successful in their role as mentor and that they have in some way failed the mentee with whom they are working (Webb & Shakespeare, 2008). Ensuring that organizational support is available for mentors who are also involved in evaluation helps to decrease some of the role conflict in mentor relationships that include evaluation components.

Mentorship as a Global Phenomenon

Mentorship is global. Mulaudzi, Libster, and Phiri (2009) suggest that around the world good mentors offer knowledge and advice, but that even more importantly they provide welcome and support. Good mentors help create a background much as a good family provides the newest members of the community a place to be nurtured. In fact, Malaudzi et al. (2009) suggest that in a discipline where teamwork is so important, mentoring is one way to weave an organizational tapestry so that the newest team member learns about the values and ways of the team in an organized fashion that truly integrates the mentee into the community.

Specific Functions of a Mentor

In studies of the specific roles and functions that mentors fulfill, nurse mentors report that they act most commonly as teachers, supporters, and role models (Bray & Nettleton, 2007). To be successful in filling these roles, Huybrecht et al. (2010) in a study of mentoring found that one of the most important qualities of a mentor was being trustworthy. They found other important characteristics of a good mentor were being patient and enthusiastic and having the ability to give positive feedback (Huybrecht et al., 2010). Webb and Shakespeare (2008) add that a good mentor has a sense of humor and is approachable and friendly.

Although all mentees are subject to some universal requirements (such as learning organizational values), there are often nursing roles that demand more specific mentorship. Advanced practice nurses, for example, might require specific intellectual support in regard to leadership and research skills (Doerksen, 2010). Novice nursing faculty might have more specific mentoring needs regarding new tasks such as managing clinical placement sites (Hawkins & Fontenot, 2010).

Techniques for Enhancing Success in Mentorship Programs

Mentorship can be learned and mentors can be taught that in addition to acting as trusted counselors they also teach, act as a sounding board, give honest feedback, and guide their mentees in the ways of the organization (Butler & Felts, 2006). Inherent in being a successful guide is the understanding that mentors understand and embrace the values of the institution and have an appreciation for the mentees' values including generational differences in professional boundaries and expectations of professional boundaries (Butler and Felts, 2006). Because mentors are often older than mentees, assuring an understanding of generational differences serves as a particularly helpful intervention to promote success of mentorship programs (Fox, 2010). Butler and Felts (2006) also suggest that mentors be taught information on expected competencies and on delegation as these are two other areas in which mentees benefit from support.

Organizational Support for Mentorship

Some characteristics that organizations need to have successful mentorship programs are as follows:

- Organizational recognition of mentors

- Organizational support of mentorship programs

- Clarification of goals

- Evaluation of programs

- Training of mentors (Ehrich et al., 2002)

Healthy organizations also ensure flexibility of scheduling for mentors and mentees (Bally, 2007), because in a busy system the lack of support for the time that mentorship requires is often very detrimental to the mentor/mentee relationship. Specifically, healthy organizations try to ensure that the schedule of the mentor and mentee match in terms of shifts worked as much as possible, provide resources such as lunch or gift cards, offer training for both the mentor and mentee, expect formative and summative evaluation, and provide bonuses for mentors who stay positively engaged in the mentorship process (Fox, 2010).

Careful selection of mentors is important if mentors are assigned. To increase a common understanding between mentors and mentees, Fox (2010) suggests that matching mentors and mentees in terms of educational background is helpful. In organizational mentoring relationships where mentors are not self-selected, mentors and mentees need to be carefully matched, and this match can be based on personality information such as Myers-Briggs scores (Fox, 2010).

Successful Models of Mentorship

You find successful models of mentorship in a variety of settings, but successful models thrive in shared governance environments. These models are discussed in the following sections.

Collaborative Governance

At Massachusetts General Hospital (MGH) within Patient Care Services, a collaborative governance structure is a critical component of the professional practice model that places the authority, responsibility, and accountability for decision-making for patient care with practicing clinicians. **Collaborative governance** is based on the belief that a shared vision, participation in decision-making, and common goals lead to a highly committed and productive workforce; that participation is empowering; and that staff will make appropriate choices when sufficient knowledge is known and communicated (Erickson, Hamilton, Jones & Ditomassi, 2003).

These leadership values are clearly seen in a mentorship model embedded throughout the collaborative governance committee structure. Within this structure there are eight committees and four subcommittees (see Table 9.2). Staff participants are called committee champions and are viewed by committee members and staff as empowered communicators, content experts, and clinical leaders.

Each committee has two co-chairs, a coach, and an advisor. The co-chairs are generally direct care nurses and other clinicians who have excellent clinical skills but might be less experienced in planning and executing the meetings and directing the work of the committee. Each committee has one coach whose role is to provide individual and group development, mentorship, and support to the co-chairs, members, and the committee as a whole. Furthermore, the coach works collaboratively with the co-chairs and the committee champions to enhance their skills, abilities, knowledge, and/or critical thinking. The advisor provides substantive expertise to the committee; serves as a link to the department; and also mentors the staff co-chairs, coach, and committee champions.

TABLE 9.2: Collaborative Governance Committees

COMMITTEE	DESCRIPTION
Diversity Committee	Create an inclusive and welcoming environment for patients, families, and staff alike through professional development, student outreach, and culturally competent care programs.
Ethics Committee	Develop and implement activities and programs to further clinicians' understanding of ethical aspects of patient care and to identify strategies to integrate ethical judgment into professional practice.
Informatics	Assist in providing informatics education, identification of informatics issues, and the development of solutions.
Practice & Quality Oversight	Oversee the work of the four sub-committees by ensuring that each sub-committee not only meets their goals and outcomes but is working together to create an environment where patients receive safe, evidence-based, high-quality care delivered by caring, competent clinicians.
Falls	*Work to eliminate falls through evidence-based practice and in compliance with all regulatory standards. Serve as a resource/consultant to other members of the health care team.*
Pain Management	*Assist in the development and dissemination of materials that give clinicians the knowledge, resources, and skills to address and treat patient's pain. The members serve as a resource/consultant to other members of the health care team.*
Restraint Usage	*Assist in the development and dissemination of materials and information that is evidence-based and in compliance with regulatory statutes to ensure that restraint use is minimal and, if used, implemented appropriately.*

continues

TABLE 9.2: *continued*

COMMITTEE	DESCRIPTION
Skin Care	*Ensure that clinicians have the knowledge, resources, and skill to maintain skin integrity and prevent and treat hospital acquired pressure ulcers.*
	Collaborate to develop and update guidelines and resources that reflect the state of the science to ensure prevention and treatment of pressure ulcers and other wounds.
	Serve as a resource/consultant to colleagues to ensure that all members of the team have the knowledge necessary to effectively eliminate skin breakdown.
	Collaborate with unit/department leadership on tracking, analyzing, and problem solving occurrences of skin breakdown.
Policy, Procedure & Products	Review and approve all policies and procedures so that they are properly vetted and consistent with the evidence.
	Review and approve all products brought to the practice setting to ensure they are properly trialed and vetted with recommendations for dissemination.
Patient Education	Support clinical staff in developing their role in patient education activities that reflect the diverse patient population served.
Research & Evidence-Based Practice Committee	Disseminate new knowledge derived from clinical research and support clinicians' implementation of evidence-based research. The committee fosters collaboration across disciplines in research efforts to support bedside clinicians in providing optimal care.
Staff Nurse Advisory	A forum for communication between leadership and clinical staff in nursing, OT/PT, and social work.

One example of this mentorship is provided by nurse F, a member of one of the collaborative governance committees. She comments that she is what she is today because of the mentorship and coaching she received on the committee from the co-chair, coaches, and advisors who enthusiastically supported her development.

EXEMPLAR: MENTORSHIP

The mentoring enabled me to build leadership skills to become a chairperson of the committee, to explore my career interests further, and ultimately to begin to serve as a mentor to other nurses. The mentorship that I have experienced can be divided in three distinct, chronological phases that loosely parallel my development as a nurse.

The first phase occurred during the first two years of my membership on the Collaborative Governance Committee. As a newly graduated nurse, I joined the committee seeking to learn more about clinical research and apply evidence to my developing nursing practice. The leaders of collaborative governance shared their clinical and research knowledge during meetings. After meetings, they asked me about the clinical decisions I faced as a new nurse and then encouraged my clinical inquiry. These leaders became mentors because they developed a personal interest in my growth as a person and clinician.

During the second phase of mentorship, I had begun to establish myself as a leader of the committee but lacked many of the necessary skills to be effective at accomplishing the objectives of the group and encouraging member participation. My mentors met with me before committee meetings and suggested techniques to try while facilitating the group. They provided valuable feedback after each meeting but more importantly had me reflect on my strengths and areas for improvement. Although I am able to understand their motivation now, I did not comprehend at the time that they were developing my self-awareness and independence. My mentors were ensuring that I am able to succeed autonomously.

I believe I am currently in the third phase where I am beginning to mentor other clinicians. This phase has been the most rewarding for me because I am able to witness how my support helps a clinician succeed. My own mentors still serve as a critical part of my professional development; they offer me advice as to how to succeed as a mentor. Recently I spent time meeting with a clinician who is preparing to conduct her first community needs assessment. I helped her focus her goals through thoughtful inquiry. As I was speaking with this clinician, I heard the words of my mentors echoing out of my mouth and could not help but reflect that I was assuming their role for a new nurse.

Each time I had the opportunity to take on a new leadership role I experienced initial feelings of self-doubt; I was uncertain if I would be able to thrive in the role as the previous occupant had. My mentors always seemed to understand that emotional axis I was teetering on and provided the right amount of reassurance while simultaneously pushing the limits of my comfort zone.

Note: This narrative was provided with the permission of Katherine Fillo, RN, Staff Nurse Bigelow 11, Medicine and Patient Education Nurse, the Maxwell & Eleanor Blum Patient and Family Learning Center, Massachusetts General Hospital.

This example expresses the value of mentoring for the staff nurse and the professional growth that emerges across the mentee's professional career from these important opportunities. As the role of the mentor continues to expand, another issue is addressing the health care needs of patients from diverse backgrounds and the development and advancement of staff seeking new roles within health care delivery.

Diversity and Mentoring

Another program that highlights the value and power of mentorship is the Clinical Leadership Collaborative for Diversity in Nursing (CLCDN) at the MGH, which was launched in 2007. This action occurred in response to growing evidence that greater racial diversity among health care providers is an effective means of decreasing health care disparities among diverse patient populations (Sullivan Commission on Diversity, 2004). The CLCDN was created to increase the number of diverse nurses within the Partners Healthcare System of which the MGH is a founding member. In collaboration with the University of Massachusetts Boston College of Nursing and Health Sciences, the CLCDN program aims to ease the transition from student to nurse through capstone experiences, mentoring, and employment opportunities. Applicants who identified themselves as American Indian/Alaska Native, Asian, Black/African American, Hispanic/Latino, or Native Hawaiian/Other Pacific Islander were encouraged to apply.

As in other mentorship programs mentors are chosen based on criteria to facilitate collaboration, and in this case mentors are nurse leaders from any of the Partner's in Health care sites that are from underrepresented ethnic or racial minorities. Mentors undergo training sessions outlining the role of the mentor in relation to the mentee. The role includes serving as a professional role model; providing a listening ear and constructive feedback; identifying professional development opportunities such as attending educational programs, committee meetings and clinical activities; problem solving with the mentee when difficult or challenging situations arise; and encouraging the mentees ambitions to return to graduate school, pursue leadership roles, and more. In addition, the mentors receive continuing education and leadership development, recognition by the leadership and their peers, and opportunities to participate in teambuilding activities with the other mentors and mentees.

In formal and informal sessions, CLCDN mentors and mentees identify ways to achieve academic excellence, and develop clinical and leadership skills. What is unique about this program is that it also focuses on helping mentees manage the racial, ethnic, and cultural issues that arise in the clinical environment. In 2011, a survey of the mentors was conducted asking how important the CLCDN is for them and their professional development.

EXEMPLAR: DIVERSITY AND MENTORING

It is crucial for us to understand different cultures and culturally competent nursing practices. Cultural subconscious bias exists, and it may influence trusting relationships and care. The CLCDN [mentorship program] allows us to share issues and stories which are culturally challenged and culturally rewarded. This provided me with the opportunity to share some of my professional experiences in the nursing workplace with my mentee, with the hopes that he would profit from my successes and NOT repeat my failures. It allowed me to further enhance my leadership skills, my teaching skills, and to work with like-minded individuals who understand that minority students often need more support to navigate through both the clinical and political issues and concerns of the hospital systems.

Note: This narrative was provided with the permission of Gaurdia Banister, author of a report on the Clinical Leadership Collaborative for Diversity in Nursing (CLCDN), March 10, 2012.

Potential mentoring opportunities exist across health care environments. In addition to organizational leadership, another group that has played a key role in mentoring staff at the bedside has been the clinical nurse specialist (CNS). In particular, those CNSs working at the bedside have been influential in promoting and developing staff and advancing the health care for patients and their families.

Mentoring and the Clinical Nurse Specialist

Another exemplar on mentorship involves the role of CNS as a mentor in the practice environment. At MGH the CNS is a master's-prepared clinical nurse expert with areas of specialization in quality improvement, analytics, education, consultation, and research. The CNS assists others in achieving desired outcomes through direct and indirect patient care activities. The CNS's spheres of influence include the patient, family, all health care practitioners, and organizational systems. The CNS also assists with providing operating efficiencies and ensuring compliance with hospital and regulatory policies and standards of practice. Serving as coach, mentor, and resource for staff is one of the CNS's key accountabilities. The CNS works synergistically with nursing staff by assisting them in acquiring advanced clinical skills through clinical discussions and role modeling. One CNS with expertise in geriatrics describes her experience with mentoring a staff nurse, Nurse S, on a medical unit.

EXEMPLAR: CNS AS MENTOR

During the geriatric team meetings, Nurse S showed strong interest in learning more about gerontological nursing. I encouraged Nurse S's professional development through multifaceted mentoring strategies. We began by discussing her vision for improving the care of older adults on her unit and how she might inspire a shared vision among her colleagues. This included seeking appropriate opportunities for her professional development and encouraging her to experiment and take risks with the understanding that I was there to support and assist as needed. As she became more confident, Nurse S gradually assumed more initiative to help implement practice changes on her unit. We worked on developing her presentation skills as well as team-building and communication skills. These mentored experiences helped to transform her from a passive participant to a well respected geriatric nurse expert and unit leader.

I encouraged her to broaden her network and geriatric knowledge. The hospital provided support for Nurse S to join our geriatric team and attend a national gerontological nursing conference. As she grew in her role, she took the lead in helping to plan our geriatric team meetings and eventually lead our discussions. We worked together, with the unit leadership team, to strategically plan and goal set. This provided Nurse S with an opportunity to see the bigger picture and further develop her communication and leadership skills.

I provided Nurse S with mentored opportunities to develop her presentation skills. As she developed her knowledge and confidence she assumed more of a leadership role in implementing some of our geriatric initiatives. We worked together on several structured projects to promote participation among the staff.

When asked about her experience in being mentored, Nurse S stated,

"The geriatric specialist has encouraged me to push myself to try new things I never thought possible. I have always loved caring for older adults, but now it's a passion. As a mentor, she has shown me that I can do anything, even return to school after 25 years to get my Adult-Geri NP! I can't wait until I graduate in May so I can follow her lead as a change maker in the care of this special population. With her mentoring, I have presented at the hospital and around the country on geriatric topics and have my first article published in this month's issue of The Journal of Gerontological Nursing!*"*

Note: This narrative was provided with the permission of Deborah A. D'Avolio, PhD, APRN-BC Geriatric Specialist, Nurse Scientist, and Susan Gage, RN, staff nurse on Ellison 16, Medicine, at Massachusetts General Hospital.

While significant mentoring can occur in health care setting mentoring opportunities, experiences can also play an important role in advancing student learning, especially within academic environments. Learners exposed to mentors throughout their academic careers grow and develop professionally from their counsel and often continue to collaborate with their mentors.

Mentoring in Academic Settings

In academic settings mentorship also thrives where you find collaboration, shared values, and shared governance. Mentorship starts at faculty orientation where faculty with special knowledge and skills are introduced to incoming new faculty and where the mission and values of the organization are well explicated. Department chairs are generally an important focus of mentorship because their role is to identify and strengthen the skills of department members. Through regular meetings, planning, and clear goal settings, the department chair can help novice staff advance in their career and help the more experienced faculty move into new forums at the national and international level, learning to mentor others along the way.

For example, at Boston College the associate deans for specific academic programs (e.g., the Associate Dean for Research), the dean, and the department chair work collaboratively to ensure that all faculty have the resources they need to thrive in their multiple roles as educators, researchers, and practitioners. A variety of unique opportunities have been established throughout the year such as "Think Tanks" for researchers to develop skills in presenting and developing new research ideas, all designed to advance the development of the faculty. Mock grant review meetings help researchers in grantsmanship, as do other special programs such as grant boot camps. Additional forums such as specialty meetings provide knowledge about academic skills such as test taking, evaluation, advising, and so on also occur throughout the year.

No matter what the academic institution, the complexity of the many roles required of faculty makes it essential that all mentors communicate regularly. Just as it is with mentorship in practice sites, evaluation of academic mentorship is essential to ensure that mentorship is helping the mentee to meet goals and is not confusing or counterproductive.

Summary

Whether in academic or clinical settings mentorship is essential and organizationally desirable, but does require resources of time, teaching, skill building, and money. The rewards from mentorship clearly outweigh the initial investment because mentorship is truly an investment in an organization's future and ultimately in the profession's future. The rewards for mentors include satisfaction in seeing their abilities transferred to others, and the rewards for mentees are increasing the ability to thrive in an organization. With good mentorship everyone wins. The effectiveness of mentoring facilitates the professional nurse's development and fosters the growth of new leaders to become active participants in the mentoring of other professionals.

References

Almada, P., Carafoli, K., Flattery, J. B., French, D. A., & McNamara, M. (2004). Improving the retention rate of newly graduated nurses. *Journal for Nurses in Staff Development, 20*(6), 268–273.

AMN Healthcare. (2010). *2010 survey of registered nurses.* Retrieved from http://www. healthleadersmedia.com/page-1/NRS-246272/Half-of-Nurses-Plan-Career-Change-Says-Survey

American Organization of Nurse Executives (AONE). (2000). *Perspectives on the nursing shortage: A blueprint for action.* Washington, DC: Author.

Bally, J. M. (2007). The role of nursing leadership in creating a mentoring culture in an acute care environment. *Nursing Economics, 25*(3), 143-149.

Bray, L., & Nettleton, P. (2007). Assessor or mentor? Role confusion in professional education. *Nurse Education Today, 27*(8), 848-855.

Buerhaus, P. I., Staiger, D. O., & Auerbach, D. I. (2000). Implications of a rapidly aging registered nurse workforce. *The Journal of the American Medical Association, 283*(22), 2948-2954.

Butler, M. R., & Felts, J. (2006). Tool kit for the staff mentor: Strategies for improving retention. *The Journal for Continuing Education in Nursing, 37*(5), 210-213.

Canadian Nurses Association (CNA). (2004). *Achieving excellence in professional practice: A guide to preceptorship and mentoring.* Ottawa, Ontario: Author.

Darling, L. A. (1985). What to do about toxic mentors. *Journal of Nursing Administration, 15*(5), 43-44.

Disraeli, B. (n.d.) *The Quotations Page.* Retrieved from http://www.quotationspage.com/quote/2140.html

Doerksen, K. (2010). What are the professional and mentorship needs of advanced practice nurses? *Journal of Professional Nursing, 26*(3), 141-151.

Ehrich, L., Tennent, L., & Hansford, B. (2002). A review of mentoring in education: Some lessons for nursing. *Contemporary Nurse, 12*(3), 253-264.

Erickson, J. I., Hamilton, G. A., Jones, D. E., & Ditomassi, M. (2003). The value of collaborative governance/staff empowerment. *Journal of Nursing Administration, 33*(2), 96-104.

Fox, K. C. (2010). Mentor program boosts new nurses' satisfaction and lowers turnover rate. *Journal of Continuing Education in Nursing, 41*(7), 311-315.

Gray, M., & Smith, L. N. (1999). The professional socialization of diploma of higher education in nursing students (Project 2000): A longitudinal qualitative study. *Journal of Advanced Nursing, 29*(3), 639–647.

Hale, R. (2004). *Mentorship of nurses: An assessment of the first year of licensure.* (Doctoral dissertation.) Lamar University, Texas, USA.

Hawkins, J. W., & Fontenot, H. (2009). What do you mean you want me to teach, do research, engage in service, and clinical practice? Views from the trenches: The novice, the expert. *Journal of the American Academy of Nurse Practitioners, 21*(7), 358-361.

Hensinger, B., Minerath, S., Parry, J., & Robertson, K. (2005). Asset protection: Maintaining and retaining your workforce. *Journal of Nursing Administration, 34*(6), 268-272.

Huybrecht, S., Loeckx, W., Quaeyhaegens, Y., De Tobel, D., & Mistiaen, W. (2011). Mentoring in nursing education: Perceived characteristics of mentors and the consequences of mentorship. *Nurse Education Today, 31*(3), 274-278.

Kramer, M., Maguire, P., Halfer, D., Brewer, B., & Schmalenber. (2011, August 4). Impact of Residency Programs on Professional Socialization of Newly-Licensed Nurses. *Western Journal of Nursing Research,* 1-38.

Mulaudzi, F., Libster, M., & Phiri, S. (2009). Suggestions for creating a welcoming nursing community: Ubuntu, cultural diplomacy and mentoring. *International Journal of Human Caring, 13,* 45-51.

Race, T. K., & Skees, J. (2010). Changing tides: Improving outcomes through mentorship in all levels of nursing. *Critical Care Nursing Quarterly, 33*(2), 163-174.

Reid Ponte, P. (2004). The American health care system at a crossroads: An overview of the American Organization of Nurse Executives monograph. *The Online Journal of Issues in Nursing, 9*(2). Retrieved from www.nursingworld.org/MainMenuCategories/ANAMarketplace/ANAPeriodicals/OJIN/TableofContents/Volume92004/No2May04/NurseExecutivesMonograph.aspx

Sullivan Commission on Diversity. (2004). Missing persons: Minorities in the health professions. A report of the Sullivan Commission on Diversity in the Healthcare Workforce.

Webb, C., & Shakespeare, P. (2008). Judgments about mentoring relationships in nursing education. *Nurse Education Today, 28*(5), 563-571.

Chapter 10

Evidence/Knowledge-Driven Practice

Susan M. Lee, PhD, RN, NP-C
Lynda Brandt, MS, RN-C

The essence of nursing practice at Massachusetts General Hospital is caring. Our every action is guided by knowledge, enabled by skill, and motivated by compassion. Patients are our primary focus, and the way we deliver care reflects that focus every day. We have a practice environment that has no barriers, is built on a spirit of inquiry, and reflects a culturally competent workforce supportive of the patient-focused values of this institution. Evidence-based standards of practice guide the decision-making and activities of the Department of Nursing.

–MGH Philosophy of Nursing

DISCLAIMER

This project is/was supported by funds from the Division of Nursing (DN), the Bureau of Health Professions (BHPr), the Health Resources and Services Administration (HRSA), and the Department of Health and Human Services (DHHS) under D11HP14632, Retooling for Evidence-Based Nursing Practice, for $899,129. The information or content and conclusions are those of the author and should not be construed as the official position or policy of, nor should any official endorsement be inferred by, the DN, BHPr, HRSA, DHHS, or the U.S. Government.

Introduction

In the 22 years since the term *evidence-based practice (EBP)* was first coined by Gordon Guyatt of McMaster University (DiCenso, Guyatt & Ciliska, 2005), evidence-based practice has become the standard of practice in the United States. Its rise to prominence was fueled by two landmark reports by the Institute of Medicine:

- *To Err is Human: Building a Safer Health System* (Institute of Medicine [IOM], 1999) cited the now familiar statistic that 44,000 to 98,000 people die in hospitals each year due to preventable medical errors.

- *Crossing the Quality Chasm* (IOM, 2001) noted the wide gulf that exists between scientific knowledge and the care that is actually delivered to patients.

In this chapter we describe the overall vision for implementation of an evidence-based practice plan at Massachusetts General Hospital (MGH) and identify critical decision points and their outcomes.

Evidence-based practice (EBP) is the conscientious and judicious use of current best research evidence in conjunction with clinical expertise and patient values to guide health care decisions (IOM, 2001). It is known, more simply, as a method of clinical decision-making (Titler, 2008a), considered to be an essential core competency required by all clinicians in the 21st century (American Association of Colleges of Nursing [AACN], 2008; National Advisory Council for Nurse Education and Practice [NACNEP], 2008) and is designated as an essential requirement for practice (American Nurses Credentialing Center [ANCC], 2012; The Joint Commission [TJC], 2011).

Overall Vision and Implementation of EBP at MGH

The MGH is proud of its 200-year history as a Harvard-affiliated, academic medical center, espousing a four-pronged mission of practice, education, research, and community. Notably, MGH is the recipient of more funding from the National Institutes of Health than any other independent hospital in the United States. For many years, nurses have participated in clinical trials as well as translational research activities, such as the Institute for Healthcare Improvement's *100,000 Lives Campaign* (Berwick, Calkins, McCannon & Hackbarth 2006) and recently in the *State Action on Avoidable Rehospitalizations* (STAAR, 2009) initiative, which has been effective in engaging clinicians across the care continuum in avoiding readmissions through targeted interventions.

Recent organizational developments, namely the creation of the Institute for Patient Care and the Yvonne L. Munn Center for Nursing Research, along with international visibility and Magnet redesignation, have provided the impetus for looking more closely at developing new strategies to advance nursing practice at MGH. To this end and within this infrastructure, MGH developed a strategic goal to advance an agenda of EBP within the clinical practice environments. The emphasis of this goal was to create a learning environment that advances staff's critical thinking, decision-making, and communication skills and provides the opportunity to link care outcomes to nursing practice data. Though nurses used evidence-based strategies to implement patient care-related activities, we recognized that the ability to inform the entire MGH nursing workforce with an EBP framework would significantly impact the quality of care and reduce health care disparities.

Well before the formal dedication of the Yvonne L. Munn Center for Nursing Research in 2008, nurses were engaged in the conduct of research at MGH. Since that time, nursing research has assumed greater prominence and with a higher degree of rigor, thanks in part to the research infrastructure of the Center.

For at least a decade, EBP was advanced by a group of clinical nurse specialists who were engaged in projects designed to answer pressing clinical questions. Four years ago, the chief nursing officer accelerated the work by sending two nurse scientists from the Yvonne L. Munn Center for Nursing Research, along with one clinical nurse specialist, to participate in advanced EBP training at the Advanced Practice Institute conducted by EBP expert Marita Titler, PhD, RN, FAAN, and her team located at University of Iowa Hospitals and Clinics in 2008 (Cullen, Titler & Rempel, 2011). Upon returning to MGH, the nurses implemented a comprehensive plan to strengthen overall EBP capacity. To intensify the efforts, the nurses sought and received external funding.

Retooling for Evidence-Based Nursing Practice Project

In 2008, the *Retooling for Evidence-Based Nursing Practice* (REBNP) Project was funded by the Division of Nursing, Bureau of Health Professions, Health Resources and Services Administration, and United States Department of Health and Human Services under D11HP14632 in the amount of $899,129. The overall aim was to strengthen evidence-based nursing capacity by developing, implementing, and evaluating a professional development program based upon the Iowa Model of Evidence-Based Practice to Promote Quality Care (Iowa Model) (Titler et al., 2001).

The three goals of the REBNP Project were as follows:

1. To strengthen all levels of the nursing workforce by teaching knowledge, skills, and competencies of EBP through multimodal continuing education programs

2. To provide opportunities for nurses to participate in mentored evidence-based practice projects that would improve the quality of care and patient outcomes

3. To build infrastructure to support and sustain EBP in our complex academic medical center

The REBNP Project was implemented by a grant team that included two doctorally prepared nurses, two master's-prepared nurses, and a medical librarian. The grant staff reviewed the major EBP models, selecting the Iowa Model because it aligns EBP priorities with organizational goals. Recognizing that the *process* of EBP is the same, regardless of the EBP model chosen, we concluded that the Iowa Model offered distinct advantages, specifically the algorithm format that guides the process across various decision points.

The EBP Curriculum

The REBNP Project consisted of sequential, multimodal education that was offered to nurses in all roles at MGH. The initial courses were live and included one-hour sessions designed to establish a common language around EBP and to stimulate interest (see Figure 10.1).

After attending these courses (shown in Figure 10.1 on the left), nurses could take more in-depth online courses or more intensive, live training sessions spanning 2–3 days. Krugman (2011) confirms our approach by noting that multiple strategies deployed at the same time create *activity volume*, which generates high levels of interest. These live sessions were offered for the first year. Following this, online learning was created for two contact hours using our education platform, HealthStream. Over time the number of online course offerings increased to three. Nurses choosing to participate in the intensive courses (shown in Figure 10.1 on the right) were required to take one 100-level class and complete EBP 200 online. One of the benefits of sequential education was that every nurse attending the intensive courses had a foundational knowledge of EBP. Although additional content was provided through a content review, time and money were saved by having the students begin with some baseline knowledge.

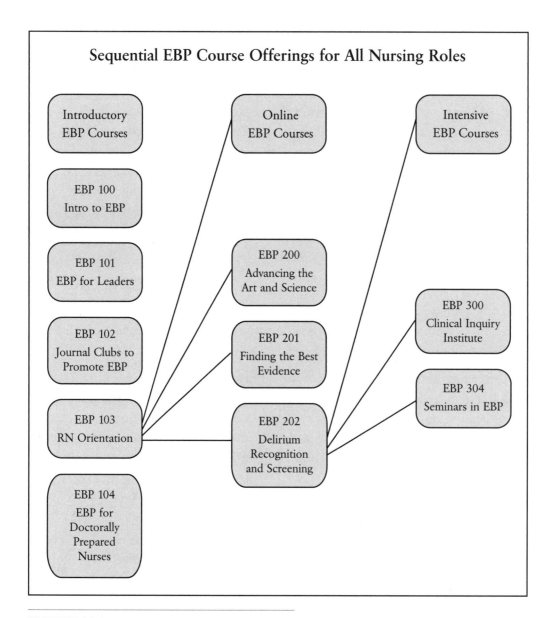

FIGURE 10.1

The REBNP Project consisted of sequential, multimodal courses awarding contact hours in EBP progress from one-hour, live sessions (shown on the left), followed by more intensive online courses (shown on the right). The Clinical Inquiry Institute, an intensive three-day course designed to prepare clinical nurse specialists to become EBP mentors, was sustained with ongoing, monthly seminars for further skills development.

Developing EBP Mentors

Excellence in care at the bedside is driven by the clinical nurse specialist (CNS). MGH employs 65 CNSs, many of whom are unit-based. This means that every nurse at the bedside is only steps away from receiving expert guidance in patient care. CNSs are well-versed in the most recent evidence for their patient populations and have extensive clinical expertise based upon advanced theoretical knowledge and many years of related nursing experience. For this reason, selected CNSs were chosen to focus on the activities of the REBNP Project with the expectation this knowledge could be shared with the larger CNS cohort in the hospital to build EBP capacity among all CNSs at MGH. Heitkemper and Bond (2004) confirmed that the role of the CNS is most associated with translating research findings into practice.

Using a train-the-trainer model, the project developers ensured that a cadre of well-prepared EBP mentors would be available to sustain EBP after the funding period ended. An intensive, three-day training, called the *Clinical Inquiry Institute (CII)*, was provided for the CNSs and was attended by several nurse practitioners, nursing directors, and the acute care documentation team, the latter of whom were building an evidence-based platform for electronic nursing assessment. In total, 51 nurses received training as EBP mentors. Prior to taking the CII, all attendees were required to attend a live, introductory class in EBP and a two-hour online course in EBP and to complete selected readings.

The CII participants were also required to bring a clinical question to the course. We spent two mornings conducting group critiques of the participants' PICO questions, which is the commonly accepted format used to ask EBP questions. Participants welcomed the assistance they received to refine their questions.

NOTE

PICO *stands for patient or problem, intervention, control, and outcome.*

The CII was "very successful" according to the course evaluations and other verbal feedback. Learning the fundamentals of EBP was "more interesting than expected." The idea of being more cautious about what one accepts as evidence was pervasive:

- "I thought I *knew* what EBP was. I thought that finding one convincing article was enough to change practice. Now, I see that I need to assess the *entire* body of knowledge. I will never again endorse a policy after a cursory glance."

Others wrote:

- "As a result of this information, I will be more careful in my critique of literature I plan to use in making changes in practice."

- "I will examine evidence carefully and thoroughly before using it as supportive documentation to make change."

- "I will be checking for evidence on anything I plan to implement, propose, or be involved with and won't feel guilty about taking the time to do it."

The implementation team learned that nurses believed that they knew what EBP was prior to attending, but their beliefs changed after attendance. The CII was "eye-opening," a term used by many participants.

In addition to course evaluation, the CII was also evaluated by creating a longitudinal data set to track attitudes, knowledge, and self-efficacy related to EBP among the project participants. Scores on attitudes toward EBP were initially high, indicating that nurses believed EBP to be very important; the scores remained high throughout the project. We found that knowledge and self-efficacy significantly improved after the CII with no significant degradation over time.

Experiential Learning

Following the CII, monthly seminars were held to reinforce and extend learning. A dedicated group of EBP mentors attended these sessions. Feeling "new" in their skills, they suggested that we undertake a literature review as a group.

The grant team welcomed the opportunity to mentor the group through the EBP process. At that time, a pressing clinical question arose: Staff nurses and some physicians were beginning to question the accuracy of temporal artery thermometers, the standard method of measuring temperatures on inpatient units at MGH. At the same time, there was some indication—gleaned from listserv conversations—that U.S. oncology nurses were questioning the accuracy of the device, as was detected on listserv conversations.

The EBP mentor group initiated a project to determine whether temporal artery thermometers were accurate and precise. The project had a twofold purpose: to answer a clinical question important to the organization and to develop and practice the advanced skills necessary to the EBP process. The project served as an important pilot from which decisions were made that will continue to influence future EBP work.

NOTE

For more information about this project, see the sidebar "EBP Exemplar 1: Temporal Artery Thermometer (TAT)" later in this chapter.

Critique of the Literature

One of the most challenging aspects of the EBP process is critiquing, leveling, and grading the literature. When the EBP mentors group began the critique process during the project, they found just how important finding the right approach to evaluation is. To that end they set a goal to identify a grading taxonomy that would be clear, easy to use, and provide the rigor necessary for confident practice recommendations. The road to finding a system that met our needs was longer than we anticipated and involved epistemic questions that led to some interesting dialogue about the nature of nursing knowledge. Limited nursing literature addresses the issue of leveling and grading nursing evidence. A brief discussion of our experience related to this journey was reported to be "helpful" by others and is included here.

Taxonomy Models

The Agency for Healthcare Research and Quality (AHRQ) reports that more than 120 various systems and taxonomies are available to evaluate health care evidence (AHRQ, 2002). So the second decision we had to make was, "Which taxonomy should we adopt?" Generally, taxonomies meet a specific purpose. For example, a well-known taxonomy is used by the U.S. Preventive Services Task Force (USPSTF, 2012), which grades recommendations from A to D. The highest rating, A, states, "The USPSTF recommends the service. There is high certainty that the net benefit is substantial;" D, the lowest rating states, "The USPSTF recommends against the service. There is moderate or high certainty that the service has no net benefit or that the harms outweigh the benefits." The USPSTF makes recommendations about clinical preventive services to primary care clinicians for adults and children with no signs and symptoms. The recommendations are for screening, counseling, and preventive medical care. This taxonomy, therefore, was not intended for the acute care setting and would not be appropriate for MGH nursing.

The SORT Methodology

Following the Iowa Model, the group had formulated a question, found the evidence, and begun critiquing the literature. The Strength of Recommendation Taxonomy (SORT) taxonomy was recommended to us (Ebell, et al., 2004). The SORT methodology was designed primarily for family medicine literature. It does not consider the results of qualitative research. SORT, as it turns out, was not intended to be a standalone system. The group liked the ease of using SORT when determining the strength of the recommendation, but the group found the focus was too narrow.

The GRADE System

While we were trialing SORT, members of the group were evaluating the Grading of Recommendations Assessment, Development and Evaluation (GRADE) system (Guyatt et al., 2008). This methodology is commonly used among the medical staff at MGH and throughout the health care community and grades evidence and recommendations. Our experience with GRADE was mixed.

We had much discussion and some difficulty reaching consensus for scoring several articles. The team found that the guidance for using GRADE was difficult to follow and unclear in some instances.

However, GRADE does have several strong points: for example, a clear separation between the quality of evidence and strength of a recommendation and acknowledgement of the patient's values and preferences. This was a step in the right direction; however, we still did not have a good approach to evaluate a broad range of evidence that we would use to answer an EBP question. Clearly this would not be a "standalone" system to meet our project goal.

Emerging Ideas on Taxonomy Issues and Evidence

Both SORT and GRADE had strong points, but these systems demonstrated a lower value for qualitative research than the discipline of nursing does. Nursing takes a broader view of evidence for practice, including theory (Fawcett & Garity, 2009). This view is likely related to the fact that the focus of the discipline of nursing is appropriately studied through qualitative methodologies. Using medical taxonomies risks that nursing research gets assigned to some arbitrary low or mid-level points on the evidence pyramid (Grace & Powers, 2009).

The Meaning Pyramids: Grace and Powers (2009) have suggested that EBP is biased toward medical domains of therapy, harm, prognosis, and diagnosis. They propose two additional evidence pyramids: human response and meaning. They effectively argue that one of nursing's core questions stems from "diagnosing and treating *human response* to actual or potential health problems" (*italics added)*. The authors constructed a *human response pyramid* that embraces both quantitative and qualitative human response evidence. Their second evidence pyramid, the *meaning pyramid*, directly addresses the third prong in the definition of EBP—that of patient values. Grace and Powers' meaning pyramid addresses the range of meanings patients bring to health care encounters. Because attributed meaning is a personal experience, the meaning pyramid is non-hierarchical. The ideas of Grace and Powers (2009) were influential in our thinking and an important work in advancing evidence-based nursing practice.

The LEGEND Tool

Another model was introduced to help clinicians synthesize evidence obtained from the literature. The LEGEND tools were designed for point-of-care clinicians and guide the synthesis of evidence from published studies (Clark et al., 2009). Cincinnati Children's Hospital Medical Center developed a comprehensive evidence evaluation system known as Let Evidence Guide Every New Decision (LEGEND) (Clark, Burkett & Stanko-Lopp, 2009).

The MGH team decided to try LEGEND and assess the usability of the system for its project. The team found that the tools provided within this system were straightforward with clear guidance. The algorithm tool includes decision points to help clinicians determine the study design of an article and then find the most appropriate evidence appraisal form by study design and domain (Clark et al., 2009). The appraisal forms are part of the LEGEND system. The ready availability of tools was helpful for clinicians, whether experienced or new to evidence appraisal.

LEGEND proved to be the system that worked best for the MGH project. The study designs were determined using the algorithm tool. Evidence appraisal forms, specific to the study design and domain, facilitated appraisal of individual studies. Guidance for determining the quality of the study can be found in the Table of Evidence Levels within the LEGEND guidelines. After the team determined the quality of the studies, they evaluated the body of evidence using the LEGEND grading tool. This tool allows for some flexibility and individual judgment (Clark et al., 2009).

The EBP mentors reported that this system was best suited to meet the project needs. LEGEND came with clear decision-making tools and covers all aspects of appraisal. Strength of recommendation tools provide a systematic way to discuss findings and reach consensus on practice recommendations stemming from evidence appraisal. The resulting evidence statement provides a clear, informative report on the clinical question, the process of evaluating evidence, and the resulting recommendation.

Summary of the REBNP Project

The REBNP Project shaped our program of EBP at MGH in many ways. Decision points were triggered by questions, such as:

- What constitutes evidence?

- What is our definition of evidence-based practice?

- What model of EBP would best meet our needs?

- What educational offerings will help us attain our goals in terms of content and numbers of nurses reached?

- What nursing roles are critical to advancing the work of EBP?

- Are online courses as effective as live courses?

- What evidence hierarchies will serve to attribute value nursing's core questions?

- How do we convene busy clinicians in the review of evidence?

- How do we sustain the momentum?

- How do we create a lasting infrastructure?

- How do we communicate the importance of reviewing the *entire body* of evidence to arrive at the correct conclusion for clinical decision-making?

Coming to a consensus on each of these questions was a process we undertook as a group; our decisions seemed to best fit our needs. Marshall (2004) helpfully described the steps of implementing an EBP model in an organizational setting. We found that some of these steps were linear, whereas others were iterative.

During the course of the REBNP Project, we presented 121 classes, presentations, and/or consults involving 2,164 attendees, or 1,634 unique nurses locally, nationally, and internationally. We are in the process of evaluating the broad impact of this education across the Department of Nursing.

The goal of EBP is to support our nurses at the bedside so that they have easy accessibility to resources. Figure 10.2 illustrates the staff nurse's access to clinical expertise close to the point of care in the role of the EBP mentor, likely their CNS. The EBP team provided another layer of support, followed by nurse scientists. A typical project also requires support from specialists in the Patient Care Services Quality and Safety Department in the form of baseline data; the Yvonne L. Munn Center for Nursing Research in the form of an institutional review board or methodological assistance; and our onsite Treadwell Library through their medical librarians and extensive online, full-text journal collection.

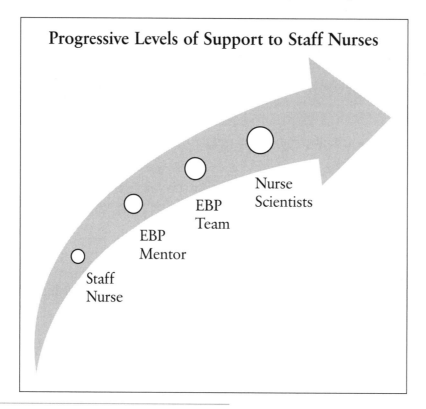

FIGURE 10.2

Staff nurses can access resources and support for assistance with EBP at the unit level and beyond.

What follows are four examples of EBP Projects that were completed during the REBNP Project. Each project is an example of clinical decision-making where little evidence exists.

EBP EXEMPLAR 1: TEMPORAL ARTERY THERMOMETER (TAT)

Elizabeth Johnson, RN, MSN, AOCNS, OCN, and the EBP TAT Group

Background/Problem

Temperature is an important physiologic parameter measured on all patients. Clinicians expect devices used to measure vital signs will provide accurate and precise results. The TAT is the standard device used for temperature measurement on inpatient units at MGH. The TAT is calibrated to measure core temperature to provide consistency between the intensive care and general care units. Frontline oncology nurses asked if the TAT readings were consistently accurate. A clinical nurse specialist and EBP mentor brought this issue to an EBP seminar.

Trigger

Problem-focused trigger and knowledge-focused trigger.

PICO

In the adult inpatient population, does the Exergen temporal artery thermometer (TAT) compared with the pulmonary artery thermistor (PAT) provide a precise and accurate measure of core body temperature?

Process

Following the Iowa Model of Evidence-Based Practice to Promote Quality Care (Iowa Model) the EBP mentor group, assisted by a nurse scientist and medical librarian, conducted a review of the literature and developed an evidence summary. The initial search resulted in few articles that directly compared the TAT and PAT. The search criteria were revised, and a small body of literature remained. The articles were leveled and graded. Using the LEGEND (Let Evidence Guide Every New Decision) format from Cincinnati Children's Hospital Medical Center, a Best Evidence Statement (BESt) was developed.

Findings/Outcomes/Recommendations

The BESt included the following:

1. *The evidence supports the accuracy and precision of the temporal artery thermometer compared to the pulmonary artery thermistor for detection of normal-range temperatures in the adult inpatient population.*

2. *Insufficient evidence and lack of consensus supports a recommendation regarding the precision and accuracy of the TAT for identification of hypothermia and hyperthermia in the adult inpatient population.*

The small body of literature provided a moderate level of evidence. Limited published evidence was available and most studies consisted of small sample sizes. No published studies had adequate power to address the use of the TAT for detection of hypothermia or hyperthermia.

Following the Iowa Model, when insufficient evidence for a practice recommendation exists, conduct of research is indicated. Upon reviewing an existing data set here at MGH, the TAT was found to be accurate and precise in hypothermic patients. Therefore, staff nursing in the Cardiac Surgical Intensive Care Unit will be conducting a study in 2012 that will directly compare the TAT with the PAT, considered to be the gold standard, to determine if the TAT is precise and accurate in the febrile population. The findings of the study will guide the future use of the TAT.

EBP EXEMPLAR 2: AN EVIDENCE-BASED PRACTICE APPROACH TO BEDSIDE HAND-OFFS

Kathryn Whalen, MSN, RN, FAHA

Background/Problem

Kate, an EBP mentor and clinical nurse specialist (CNS) in the progressive cardiac care unit, became concerned when she received several safety reports indicating the IV fluids that were infusing were not the same as what was reported at shift hand-off. Immediately investigating each one, she noted common elements. The existing practice was that hand-offs occurred at the nurses' station with no prescribed format. An added concern was the number of newly licensed and newly hired registered nurses with less experience with hand-offs.

Trigger

Problem-focused trigger.

PICO

On a progressive cardiac care unit, would a structured bedside hand-off format result in fewer safety reports and increased nurse vitality and satisfaction as compared with current practice?

Process

Kate searched the literature and found significant evidence to guide practice change. Using the latest evidence, she created a customized hand-off tool. After obtaining approval to modify the Situation Background Assessment Recommendations (SBAR) format from its author, Kate added a final "T" to allow for additional data and "thank you." The resulting tool became the Situation Background Assessment Recommendations, Thank You (SBART), a tool which is customized to the specific needs of patients with cardiac surgical needs.

Nurses were also asked to do shift hand-off at the patients' bedside to assure completion of the "technical" checks of patients' IVs, central lines, dressings, and other technology. Bedside hand-off also allows the off-going nurse to introduce the new nurse by name, enhancing continuity of care. The new form was piloted in the summer of 2011 and modified based on staff feedback.

Nurses were surveyed before and after the new bedside hand-off using the Healthcare Team Vitality Instrument (Vitality). A t-test was used to compare pre- and post-bedside hand-off scores. A separate analysis of a single-item measure, "Care professionals communicate complete patient information during hand-offs," was also completed.

Findings/Outcomes/Recommendations

Significant evidence indicated that a standard format leads to higher-quality care. In addition, bedside hand-offs, where nurses jointly assess the patient and verify IVs, equipment, and so on, is an early trend with a body of anecdotal literature to support the practice.

Two patient outcomes have been noted:

1. The patients' experience of care has been enhanced. They appreciate the new bedside hand-off because it helps patients and families better understand their clinical course and plan of care. Additionally, patients and families are participating more in planning care and developing goals.

2. Since the inception of bedside hand-offs, the number of safety reports for IV discrepancies has dropped to zero.

Two nurse outcomes have also been noted:

1. The results of the pre- and post-bedside hand-off Vitality scores showed a significant improvement, and the nurses also perceived better communication as a result of the new process.

2. The second nursing outcome is an increased dialogue about the evidence-based practice process and better understanding of translating evidence to practice.

The hand-off project is expanding to include unit-to-unit hand-offs between the Surgical Intensive Care Unit and the Intermediate Care Unit.

EBP EXEMPLAR 3: NURSE PLACEMENT OF ESOPHAGEAL TEMPERATURE PROBE IN THE CARDIAC CATHETERIZATION LAB

Howard T. Blanchard, MEd, MS, RN, ACNS-BC, CEN

Background/Problem

In an effort to improve door-to-balloon (D2B) time for out-of-hospital patients who have a cardiac arrest with return of spontaneous circulation, the ST Elevation Myocardial Infarction (STEMI) Quality Improvement Team worked with emergency medical care providers and the emergency department (ED) to improve patient access to the cardiac catheterization lab (CCL). The improved process allowed ambulance teams to take patients directly to the CCL if it were deemed appropriate by an ED physician. Though this shortened the time to cardiac treatment, it also created a procedural dilemma by having patients arrive to the CCL ready to receive definitive cardiac care but also requiring brain-saving therapeutic hypothermia.

When an out-of-hospital patient arrives directly to the CCL, no core temperature probe is in place to provide feedback to the surface cooling console required for therapeutic patient cooling. Placing or changing a temperature probe in a urinary catheter competes with preparing the patient's groin for the catheterization procedure.

Trigger

Problem-focused trigger.

PICO

Is placement of an esophageal temperature probe by the RN an appropriate alternative to a urinary catheter temperature probe when this probe can already be placed by the RN concurrently with the initiation of patient cooling and the procedure site for cardiac catheterization?

Process

An inquiry from an intensive care unit to a nurse researcher was referred to the evidence-based practice team clinical project specialist. Discussions among the CNSs and the clinical project specialist identified the problem and raised the question of esophageal probe placement by an RN in the CCL to avoid a delay in treatment and enhance patient outcomes. Assisted by a medical librarian, the team performed a literature search.

Findings/Outcomes/Recommendations

The literature review yielded little evidence. The American Association of Critical-Care Nurses produced the key evidence for this project, found in their procedure manual. The team found a procedure for esophageal probe placement and applicable case studies. Although the evidence was scant, it was the "best evidence." A policy was drafted, reviewed, and approved. In July 2011, the policy was used on the first patient to meet criteria with a positive outcome.

EBP EXEMPLAR 4: IMPROVING CONTINUITY OF CARE IN THE NICU

Janet Madden, RN, MS, CCNS

Background/Problem

Janet, an EBP mentor and clinical nurse specialist (CNS) in the neonatal intensive care unit (NICU), has a long-standing commitment to improving continuity of care for the NICU population. Personal observations led her to evaluate the current status of continuity of care and explore potential care delivery models that would improve continuity of care for this fragile population and their families.

Trigger

Problem-focused trigger.

PICO

Will early patient assignment to designated care teams improve continuity of care and parent satisfaction for patients in the neonatal intensive care unit?

Process

Working with a medical librarian, Janet found very little evidence on continuity of care in the NICU population. She found a strong link between a high level of continuity of care and parental satisfaction.

To collect baseline data, Janet used the Continuity of Care Index (CCI) as suggested for use by Martha Curley, PhD, RN, FAAN (Children's Hospital, Boston and University of Pennsylvania), to collect data on nurse staffing patterns for 14 infants over four months in early 2011.

Findings/Outcomes/Recommendations

The CCI indicated the existing model of staffing was not associated with a high degree of continuity of care. The NICU nursing staff was surprised but receptive to the results. Following a discussion with staff, a group of nurses volunteered to form the first care team in the spring of 2011 to pilot the new care delivery model. The results of the pilot demonstrated that the care team model resulted in an improved CCI with high parent satisfaction. Over time, staff members developed care teams with the goal of having the same nurses caring for specific infants and parents as much as possible.

By January of 2012, all neonates were assigned to a care team upon admission. The first month of the fully implemented care delivery model showed some improvement in the CCI and also highlighted some team configurations that required adjustment to reflect the diversity of staff work schedules. Additional adjustments have been made, and the CCI is now a new internal benchmark in the NICU. Janet and her team continue to monitor and evaluate their success.

Summary

EBP, just 20 years old, is still in its infancy—evidence is still difficult to find and distill, advanced research skills are still required to conduct much of the work, and insufficient time is still widely cited as a barrier. Yet, our guiding value must be this: "Have we done all that we can to ensure that current knowledge has reached the bedside?" That is our mandate as leaders in health care settings.

The IOM report *The Future of Nursing: Leading Change, Advancing Health* (IOM, 2011) reiterates the standard of evidence-based practice stating, "The United States has the opportunity to transform its health care system to provide seamless, affordable, quality care that is accessible to all, patient-centered, and *evidence-based* and leads to improved health outcomes" (IOM, 2011, p. S-1) *(italics added)*. The report is a call to action for nursing to take a leading role in health care redesign.

Nurses stand on equal ground with other health care clinicians when we invoke evidence in the clinical setting. Evidence is the great equalizer. Applying best evidence is a moral obligation to our patients. It is our role as nursing leaders to provide our bedside nurses with everything they need to deliver the finest, evidence-based care.

ACKNOWLEDGMENT

We wish to thank Marita Titler, PhD, RN, FAAN, author of the Iowa Model of Evidence-Based Practice to Promote Quality Care, who served as our mentor and guide.

References

Agency for Healthcare Research and Quality (AHRQ). (2002). *Systems to rate the strength of scientific evidence.* (Evidence report/technology assessment: number 47; AHRQ Publication No. 02-E015). Rockville, MD: Author.

American Association of Colleges of Nursing (AACN). (2008). *Revision of the essentials of baccalaureate education for professional nursing practice.* Washington, DC: Author.

American Nurses Credentialing Center (ANCC). (2012). *ANCC Magnet recognition program.* Retrieved from http://www.nursecredentialing.org/Magnet.aspx

Berwick, D. M., Calkins, D. R., McCannon, C. J., & Hackbarth, A. D. (2006). The 100,000 Lives Campaign: Setting a goal and a deadline for improving health care quality. *JAMA, 295*(3), 324-327.

Clark, E., Burkett, K., & Stanko-Lopp, D. (2009). Let Evidence Guide Every New Decision (LEGEND): An evidence evaluation system for point-of-care clinicians and guideline development teams. *Journal of Evaluation in Clinical Practice, 15*(6), 1054-1060.

Cullen, L., Titler, M. G., & Rempel, G. (2011). An advanced educational program promoting evidence-based practice. *Western Journal of Nursing Research, 33*(3), 345-364.

DiCenso, A., Guyatt, G., & Ciliska, D. (2005). *Evidence-based nursing: A guide to clinical practice.* St. Louis, MO: Mosby.

Ebell, M. H., Siwek, J., Weiss, B. D., Woolf, S. H., Susman, J., Ewigman, B., & Bowman, M. (2004). Strength of recommendation taxonomy (SORT): A patient-centered approach to grading evidence in the medical literature. *Journal of the American Board of Family Practice, 17*(1), 59-67.

Fawcett, J., & Garity, J. (2009). *Evaluating research for evidence-based nursing practice.* Philadelphia, PA: F.A. Davis Company.

Grace, J. T., & Powers, B. A. (2009). Claiming our core: Appraising qualitative evidence for nursing questions about human response and meaning. *Nursing Outlook, 57*(1), 27-34.

Guyatt, G. H., Oxman, A. D., Vist, G. E., Kunz, R., Falck-Ytter, Y., Alonso-Coello, P., & Schunemann, H. J. (2008). GRADE: An emerging consensus on rating quality of evidence and strength of recommendations. *BMJ, 336*(7650), 924-926.

Heitkemper, M. M., & Bond, E. F. (2004). Clinical nurse specialists: State of the profession and challenges ahead. *Clinical Nurse Specialist, 18*(3), 135-140.

Institute of Medicine (IOM) Committee on Quality of Health Care in America. (1999). *To err is human: Building a safer health system.* Washington, DC: National Academies Press.

Institute of Medicine (IOM) Committee on the Quality of Healthcare in America. (2001). *Crossing the quality chasm: A new health system for the 21st century*. Washington, DC: National Academies Press.

Institute of Medicine (IOM) of the National Academies. (2003). Greiner, A. C., & Knebel, E. (Eds.). *Health professions education: A bridge to quality*. Washington, DC: National Academies Press.

Institute of Medicine (IOM). (2011). *The future of nursing: Leading change, advancing health*. Washington, DC: The National Academies Press.

The Joint Commission. (2011). *Improving America's hospitals - The Joint Commission's annual report on quality and safety*. Retrieved from http://www.jointcommission.org

Krugman, M. (Ed.). (2011). Evidence-based practice: Strategies for embedding evidence-based practice in your organization. *Journal for Nurses in Staff Development, 27*(2), 100-101.

Marshall, M. L. (2004). Strategies for success. *Clinical Nurse Specialist, 20*(3), 124-127.

National Advisory Council on Nurse Education and Practice (NACNEP). (2008). *Meeting the challenges of the new millennium: Challenges facing the nurse workforce in a changing health care environment. Sixth annual report to the U.S. Department of Health and Human Services and the U.S. Congress.* Author.

State Action on Avoidable Rehospitalizations (STAAR). (2009). *An initiative of the Commonwealth Fund at the Institute for Healthcare Improvement*. Retrieved from http://www.ihi.org

Titler, M. G. (2008a). *Advanced Practice Institute: Promoting adoption of evidence-based practice. (Course Manual)*. Iowa City, IA: Nursing Clinical Education Center, University of Iowa Hospitals and Clinics.

Titler, M. G. (2008b). The evidence for evidence-based practice implementation. In R. Hughes (Ed.), *Patient safety & quality: An evidence-based handbook for nurses.* (AHRQ Publication No. 08-0043). Rockville, MD: Agency for Healthcare Research and Quality.

Titler, M. G., Kleiber, C., Steelman, V. J., Rakel, B. A., Budreau, G., Everett, L. Q., … Goode, C. J. (2001). The Iowa Model of evidence-based practice to promote quality care. *Critical Care Nursing Clinics of North America, 13*(4), 497-509.

U.S. Preventive Services Task Force (USPSTF). Grade definitions. Retrieved from http://www. uspreventiveservicestaskforce.org/uspstf/grades.htm

Watson, J. (2008). *The philosophy and science of caring* (Rev. ed.). Boulder, CO: University Press of Colorado.

Chapter 11

Designing the Infrastructure to Foster Nurse-Led Care at the Bedside

Debra Burke, RN, MSN, MBA
Theresa Gallivan, RN, MS
Dawn Leslie Tenney, RN, MSN
Kevin Whitney, RN, MA, NEA-BC

Good leadership is a conscious enterprise. All that you think, envision, decide and do are guided at some level by what you believe as a leader is and does.

–Marla Salmon ScD, RN, FAAN (2007, p. 2)

Introduction

This chapter discusses how to promote the discovery of the leader within and serves as an effort to improve management within a mentored environment to foster interdisciplinary, high-quality care in the workplace and promote opportunities for enhanced communication, teamwork, and decision-making in clinical practice settings. We describe the tools nurses need to enhance leadership and impact practice by focusing on how the associate chief nurse (ACN) can support and optimize the provision of care at the bedside. The ACN serves as the leader who directly oversees the efforts of nursing directors (NDs), who, in turn, directly oversee a large staff of registered nurses (RNs) and additional patient care staff.

At the Massachusetts General Hospital (MGH), the position of associate chief nurse (ACN) reports to the chief nursing officer (CNO) and, in collaboration with medical staff leadership, is accountable for the day-to-day operations of patient care delivery. The ACN assists the CNO with strategic planning and implementation of quality management, performance improvement, core measures, the patient experience, fiscal management, and staff development programs. The ACN is a strategic contributor to long-term planning and business growth development activities. This key position is also accountable for ensuring that all regulatory and accrediting standards are fully implemented as directed by the CNO.

> **NOTE**
>
> *Please note that the role of nurse director (ND) at the Massachusetts General Hospital is comparable to the nurse manager role in other organizations.*

The Role of the Associate Chief Nurse

Gordin and Trey (2011) assert, "Nurses who can find their inner leader and use it in their practice, at whatever level they contribute to the organization, will find that they are able to positively impact patient care outcomes." For nurses to find that "leadership within," they need to be provided with high-quality management; a workplace where they can be mentored and can develop good working relationships with others within and beyond their discipline; and opportunities for the development of communication, team-building, and problem-solving skills, along with clinical nursing knowledge.

At the Massachusetts General Hospital (MGH), ACNs assist in the design and development of a practice environment that optimizes the delivery of patient care and advances the ND's role through coaching and mentoring. The ACN partners with the NDs to implement the hospital and nursing strategic plans, assuring understanding of and adherence to the mission, vision, value, and standards of nursing practice. Together, ACNs and NDs are responsible for promoting and enhancing a professional practice environment in which clinical nursing practice is optimized and patient outcomes are achieved across the organization.

Today, growing evidence in the nursing literature points to the positive impact healthy work environments can have on staff satisfaction, retention, improved patient outcomes, and organizational performance (Aiken, Clarke, Sloane, Lake & Cheney, 2008; Shamian & El-Jardali, 2007). One of the key elements identified as supporting a healthy work environment is the presence of expert, competent, credible, and visible leadership (Nursing Organizations Alliance, 2004).

ACNs are in a unique position to advance clinical practice and promote staff development. They are the individuals who help translate the goals of the organization and the chief nurse, and they work closely with each ND to develop management and leadership skills that in turn can advance the delivery of care for each provider. ACNs have numerous opportunities to work both one-on-one with NDs, including individual meetings, and in larger group meetings where all NDs meet with the team of ACNs. These meetings not only provide an opportunity for strategic and day-to-day problem solving, but also allow for role modeling around the use of effective problem-solving techniques, strategies to enhance communication, and strategies that have succeeded in improving conflict-management skills.

The primary responsibility of the ACN is to support the ND. Through that relationship the ND, along with the unit-based clinical nurse specialist (CNS), ensures the delivery of optimal care for patients and families. In the end, the ACN and the ND working together are ultimately responsible for ensuring that all patients receive high-quality, cost-effective, safe, responsive, evidence-driven patient care throughout the hospital and related services.

Under the purview of the ACN, NDs delegate responsibility to their respective staff with the expectation that each provider is working to the full extent of their education, experience, and expertise. ACNs are in a pivotal position to articulate the overarching strategic vision and desired outcomes of the patient care services and to empower NDs and their staff to drive the "how-to" tactics needed to translate the vision into action.

ACNs also play a key role both in helping to create a culture where NDs are held accountable for care outcomes and in fostering a strong sense of autonomy in nurses to use their professional knowledge and competence to make these outcomes a reality. At MGH, ACNs support and encourage staff to use creative and innovative approaches in quality improvement activities that enhance safety, recruitment, and retention of new graduate nurses and/or in the adoption and use of new technology as a vehicle for knowledge acquisition. ACNs need to fully encourage and align with the work of the NDs because this support enables decisions to be made by those closest to care delivery (Holmes & Chamberlain, 2010).

The role of the ACN is also one of partnerships, including the development of partnerships with frontline nursing leaders and staff, with physicians and physician leaders, other providers, multidisciplinary and administrative leaders, and other colleagues who collaborate in care redesign and delivery. Through these alliances the best staff and patient outcomes can be realized.

The Selection of Patient Care Leaders

The essential initial step needed in building a team of nurses who can perform at the highest level is to hire the best candidates for each and every position. The hiring of candidates pursuing frontline care delivery leadership positions deserves thought, time, and attention.

Prior to interviewing potential candidates, ACNs need to assess the role and functions played by the patient care unit and determine how that unit fits within current organizational strategies. This knowledge helps to identify unit priorities and inform the candidate selection process. Additionally, the person in charge of hiring should meet with key stakeholders, including physicians and other discipline leaders, to review unit-level outcomes data—including patient satisfaction scores, clinical quality data, human resource and staff satisfaction data, and financial reports—to achieve consensus around the priorities identified and to communicate this information to the candidate pursing the position.

During times of leadership transition, ACNs need to spend time meeting with unit staff to discuss the staff perceptions as to what is needed from new leadership and to discuss the process moving forward. Table 11.1 includes a process used by ACNs to communicate to staff a process for preparing a new leader (director).

TABLE 11.1: Communication Process to Preparing for a New Leader

1. An interim leader/manager has been identified to support the staff through the time of transition.

2. Candidates and their resumes will be available for staff to review, and their input will be solicited to help recruit the most qualified candidates.

3. A representative group of unit staff will be identified by the staff and interim leader to participate in the comprehensive screening process.

4. Other leaders or managers will be identified to participate in the selection process of a new leader.

5. The ACN assumes accountability for the final selection and assures the staff that no one will be hired to the position without the support of the representative staff screening group.

This process of involving staff in the hiring of a new leader serves as an important opportunity for leadership to promote staff development by allowing individuals, in a very real and meaningful way, to speak about their practice, discuss their work environment and changes needed, and identify the leader and/or manager they feel can best help them accomplish unit and personal goals. This opportunity can also help the leadership share with staff the strategic direction of the organization and the role that each caregiver plays in achieving the strategic goals identified. At MGH, staff have expressed the value of participating in the hiring process of new leaders, viewing their participation as a sign of leadership's recognition of, as well as enthusiasm and appreciation for, the role they play in the selection of new leadership. They have also described the experience as providing a renewed commitment toward partnering with and supporting the new leader.

To varying degrees, the process of hiring new staff can be implemented when any position is filled. The primary goal is to make it an inclusive process, where key stakeholders feel they have had a say in who gets hired.

After the Leader Is Hired

NDs that are hired (at the MGH) are invited to participate in designing their own orientation experience. The ACN or hiring manager needs to ensure that the new leader knows that their transition into the organization is a priority. This message can be realized through an active process of scheduling meetings and guiding introductions to key leaders within the institution.

New leaders are encouraged to take advantage of the support provided during this interim period and use their orientation as a time to get to know their staff as a team and as individuals, while also becoming familiar with unit, departmental, and organizational operations and culture. ACNs also recommend that in addition to participating in management orientation and leadership development classes, new leaders attend the orientation program provided for staff nurses. This orientation provides each leader with in-depth information about the expectations and commitments of the unit and the organization for which staff nurses assume accountability.

Role Modeling

The ACN can, and should, lead by example, serving as a role model for the ND. Opportunities for role modeling provided by the ACN are suggested in the following exemplars:

- Managing a conflict between two nurses, or other staff, patients, and providers.

- Having critical conversations, such as those between doctors and nurses, related to the scope of practice and expectation

- Creating the budget for the following year with justification and integration into the plan.

Many times within a week or across months, the ACN and the ND have opportunities to be present at other meetings within the organization. At these meetings, the ACN has the opportunity to role model physician partnering and collaboration with other health professions and departments. In turn, the ND has a chance to demonstrate skills such as actively listening to issues and concerns, presenting strategic initiatives and interpreting them to frontline clinicians, and translating evidence-based practice information into daily unit practice in front of the ACN.

Mentoring

ACNs also need to know their NDs and understand potential areas of growth, personal and organizational strengths, and career interests. Mentoring is a continuous process, and the ACN should capitalize on opportunities to role model as well as to provide feedback and celebrate success. The ACN can offer suggestions and provide direction to issues discussed during meetings. The frequency of meetings depends upon the pairing, scope, and complexity of the clinical area the ND is managing and the level of development of the ND (i.e., novice to expert) (Benner, 1984). On occasion, the ACN might meet with a group of NDs around a common clinical affiliation (e.g., perioperative services or cardiac services). Often, the ACN meets regularly, one-on-one, with each ND. During the one-on-one meetings, the ACN and ND would discuss such issues as:

- Staffing patterns and needs

- Budget: current and future

- Implementing regulatory requirements

- Staff development plans and individual needs

- The professional practice environment and its meaning to patient care

- Throughput processes throughout the patient journey, including access to care and discharge planning

- Clinical decision-making and problem solving

- Quality metrics and indicators being monitored for a unit

- Strategic initiatives and unit goals

- Individual career development

- The advancement of collaborative decision-making

These discussions could create opportunities for mentoring, guidance, and professional growth. In group meetings, the ACN can also review standards of practice, assure consistency in care delivery, discuss team building, identify common goals, and share examples of best practices.

At MGH, both one-on-one meetings and group meetings are provided. The ACNs also meet collectively with all the NDs on a monthly basis where common objectives are discussed (e.g., preparation for regulatory reviews, policy changes, and any new initiatives on the horizon). ACNs at MGH also hold joint meetings with the NDs and unit-based CNSs. These meetings provide an opportunity for the ACN to ensure that the administrative and clinical unit-level leaders are aligned to effectively translate the common objectives and to work with their staff toward the desired outcomes.

Sustaining Support for the ND

Regular coaching and direction from the ACN should be accompanied by assigning all new NDs to a preceptor until the new leaders have identified their own mentor(s). This is a critical priority to assure that a well-planned and well-collaborated support system is developed to enable the new leader to enter the system successfully. This strategy assists new leaders' transitions and also conveys to all who are watching that high-quality patient care remains the core mission and that only in partnership with others will they maintain and build upon the caliber of what is currently in place within the system.

Appreciative Inquiry and Emotional Intelligence

Two tools that nurses at all levels of the organization can use to lead at the bedside are Appreciative Inquiry (AI) and Emotional Intelligence (EI). These tools provide ACNs with ways to evaluate the effectiveness of change within an organization and are an effective way to evaluate the impact of leadership on care delivery.

Appreciative Inquiry

Appreciative Inquiry (AI) is a model for change that promotes the positive, focusing on what works well in organizations. This approach allow leaders, including ACNs, NDs, and staff, to learn about systems and processes through positive questioning to inspire, motivate, transform, and sustain positive change. Havens, Wood, and Leeman (2006) highlight the four phases of the sequential AI process: Discovery, Dream, Design, and Delivery.

Discovery

The first phase, Discovery, is where the leader and team ask questions to determine how and why a process or system is working well. The questioning focuses on three categories of questions: backward, inward, and forward. Backward questions focus on past experiences; inward questions look to define specifically what worked well in the current situation or project; and forward questions provide the opportunity for the team to discuss what could improve the current results even further.

Havens et al. (2006) describe a research project where one of the project goals was to increase communication among health care disciplines. During the Discovery phase, their team asked backward, inward, and forward questions (see Table 11.2).

TABLE 11.2: Questions to Ask During Discovery Phase

DISCOVERY PHASE	QUESTIONS TO ASK
Backward	Is there a time when you collaborated with individuals from another department where all parties treated one another with respect and everyone's expertise was needed to make a difference?
Inward	What was your contribution?
	What was it about you, the hospital, and your coworkers that made it special?
	What did you most value about the interaction with the team members?
Forward	What three wishes do you have to improve the vitality and effectiveness of communication and collaboration in your hospital? What is the one thing that, if done well, would make the most difference to improve collaboration at this hospital?

Dream

The second phase, Dream, is where the leader and team members expand on what was learned during the Discovery phase, including the positive themes that arose during the discussion. At this point in the process, the group further explores tactics they could use in the future to make an already positive outcome even greater. Haven et al. (2006) included the following example of a question utilized during the dream phase: "If you could have it your way with respect to communication and collaboration, what would it look like? What are people saying that demonstrates communication and collaboration at its best?"

Design

The third phase, Design, is the process of making a plan to achieve the ideas discussed during the Dream phase. This process includes incorporating suggested ideas into organizational structures and processes to obtain the desired positive outcomes or changes. The design of new or revised systems should not only outline the process for implementation but also include steps and methods to sustain and evaluate the positive change.

Delivery

The fourth and final phase, Delivery, is where the plan outlined in the Design phase is implemented. The leader and team work together to provide positive feedback on what plans are working and the beneficial results being achieved. This positive feedback assists the team with achieving, reviewing, making any corrections, and sustaining the desired, positive results.

The Benefits of the Appreciative Inquiry Process

The ACNs and nurse leaders at all levels can utilize AI in their practice to design, implement, and sustain positive improvement with the entire care team. The AI process is useful because it focuses on why specific features of a project or practice initiative worked well in the past rather than focusing on the negative or what went wrong. This approach helps the team learn through positive reinforcement and encourages them to feel more positive about their work. In addition, AI enables the team to become more confident participating in the decision-making process and promotes the "ability to improve relationships among coworkers and between managers and employees" (Havens et al., 2006).

Health care institutions, including tertiary academic medical centers, are complex organizations seeking to continuously improve their systems, policies, and procedures to best serve patients and families. As patients, legislators, and regulatory agencies continue to advocate for improvements in the current health care system, ACNs and nurses at all levels of the organization must ensure they are active participants with other health care disciplines to further improve quality and reduce costs. This includes developing innovative models of care that are patient-centered, safe, efficient, and evidence-based. In addition, the introduction of new products and information technology into the health care environment is an important component of advancing health care delivery. AI can help establish clear processes for implementing and sustaining positive change.

Emotional Intelligence (EI)

The second framework, **Emotional Intelligence (EI),** has evolved over the past decade and has been defined by research studies in several ways. Lucas, Lachinger, and Wong (2008) summarized EI as "a set of competencies fundamental to effective leadership and organizational effectiveness." In addition, key EI competencies are described as "self-awareness, self-management, social awareness, and relationship management." Lucas et al. (2008) further incorporate Cummings's (2004) research, which reported that nursing leaders who were well grounded in EI competencies "were seen to develop positive relationships with staff nurses and were better able to manage emotions in the workplace" (Lucas et al., 2008, p. 966).

Mayer and Salovey (1997, p. 35) define EI as "the ability to perceive accurately, appraise and express emotion; the ability to access and/or generate feelings when they facilitate thought; the ability to understand emotion and the ability to regulate emotions to promote emotional and intellectual growth." This definition describes successful leaders as being able to identify or assess the emotions of others, interpret these emotions, and then identify an approach to respond to the situation to achieve a positive outcome.

This research supports the incorporation of the EI results into nursing leadership development and demonstrates that when used appropriately, EI can have a significant impact on the leader's effectiveness and performance and can be a key predictor of leadership success. Lucas et al. (2008, p. 966) noted that in a study conducted by Goleman (1998, 2000) involving 20,000 executives, employing EI was "twice as important as technical skills and cognitive abilities in determining excellence at all levels."

Research has produced evidence that shows when nursing leaders, including ACNs and NDs, are skilled in EI, they are better able to improve outcomes "related to patient safety, nurse retention and consumer satisfaction" (Codier, Kooker & Shoultz, 2008). Understanding one's own emotions, knowing how to control those emotions, being able to assess emotions of others, and making appropriate decisions are signs of a leader who has developed effective communication skills, established positive working relationships with staff, and built trust and buy in (Feather, 2009).

Research findings further support the belief that nursing leaders learn about EI and how they can incorporate EI into their leadership practice through education sessions, continuous feedback from ACNs, and experience. Feather (2009) suggests that EI can help make nursing leaders more effective in their role, which translates to increased quality, increased staff satisfaction, efficient use of resources, and lower costs.

Use of AI and EI

ACNs can utilize both AI and EI in their one-on-one interactions with their ND and team especially when ND meetings focus on unit-level challenges and the unit's performance in the areas of quality, patient satisfaction, and staff satisfaction. The use of outcome measurement tools at the unit level, including dashboards, patient feedback, Hospital Consumer Assessment of Healthcare Providers and Systems (HCAHPS) surveys, and staff engagement surveys, can provide the ACN with objective data about what is working well on the individual ND's unit and then celebrate successes. Both the ACN and the ND can discuss specific information that addresses how a unit has made improvements and why they were successful and then seek to apply similar approaches to address other areas requiring improvement.

For example, at MGH, when the ACN receives a patient compliment letter, the ACN sends a note of appreciation to the ND, CNS, and the care team. This action reinforces the positive performance and assists in motivating the entire team to replicate the desired action in the future. This response can be used to direct attention on what went right and, when necessary, what could be done better.

Another example includes the recent opening of a new intensive care unit (ICU) at MGH. When designing the unit's physical space and determining the capital equipment and other non-capital needs, the ACN, ND, and unit-design team turned to the existing ICUs to identify successful processes that were working well, what capital equipment items were preferred, and what documentation tools were found to be most helpful for patient care and patient safety. This dialogue focused on the positive and contributed to the successful opening of the new unit. This example provides important team insights and allows the team to feel valued while receiving the needed information.

The ACNs can also incorporate EI into their practice during coaching and mentoring and when providing feedback to NDs. Utilizing AI and EI together can result in a more positive way to communicate the ACN's appreciation for the ND's positive performance and reflect on prior opportunities that focused on improvements. Telling a story of how others experienced similar situations and how the ND can use others' experiences to inform current leadership practice can also assist in leadership development. ACNs with strong EI are better positioned to assess the ND's readiness for coaching and feedback and to convey empathy and understanding of any given situation.

In summary, AI and EI can be two important tools ACNs can utilize with their team to improve the practice environment and to achieve excellent results including high-quality care, patient satisfaction, staff engagement, and positive working relationships with NDs and the entire care team.

Management by Walking Around

Management by Walking Around (MBWA), a concept initially described by Peters and Waterman (1982) in the hallmark book *In Search of Excellence*, contains information that is even more critical today. As much as electronic means of communication are ever increasingly part of our workplace, Serrat (2009) describes MBWA as a leadership technique that has stood the test of time.

MGH NDs practice this important leadership skill in a variety of ways. One approach is through patient and family rounding. Not only does this innovation provide leaders with the firsthand experience and observations of patients and families, but also it gets them into patient rooms to see how nursing is being practiced (Lee & Manley, 2008). MBWA helps managers observe excellence in action and provide direct feedback in the moment.

MBWA also assists the ACN with identifying issues of concern in the practice environment. As the quality guru Deming articulates, "If you wait for people to come to you, you'll only get small problems. You must go and find them. The big problems are where people don't realize they have one in the first place" (Hindle, 2008). In this way, the ACN can assist with problem solving along with the unit leadership team and help advocate for resources that might be needed to address issues of concern.

MBWA is a powerful tool for connecting with staff nurses. It is an effective way to hear the voice of staff nurses and ensure that they have the skills and needed resources to complete their work and the encouragement to practice at the highest level of their experience. An unexpected consequence—MBWA might also be an effective strategy to identify future leaders, both clinical leaders and those destined to become management leaders.

Evaluating Effective Leadership

As mentioned previously, ACNs and NDs are responsible for care delivery. Multiple ways exist to evaluate effective leadership and describe a leader's impact on care outcomes. Unit-based data, for example, is submitted to the National Database of Nursing Quality Indicators (NDNQI), comprising information about fall rates including falls with injury, hospital-acquired skin breakdown, infection rates, and so on. The unit-based nursing leadership team and the ACN closely follow these and other indicators, such as patient satisfaction, to alert the team around areas of needed improvement and, when possible, to implement a rapid improvement cycle process. (Patient dissatisfaction with care or increased incidents in falls or infection rates are often an indicator of ineffective leadership.)

Additional measures, including staff satisfaction scores, retention rates and turnover rates, and recruitment of staff can be other outcomes of effective leadership. They can be tracked over time and linked to new innovations and improvements in organizational changes and strategic initiatives at the unit level.

Hill (2011) makes the oft-stated case that nurse satisfaction is directly linked to working conditions, overall environment, positive relationships, and low turnover. Hill further notes that retention of staff supports higher levels of expertise, higher quality, and thus intuitive care. Such retention also creates the opportunity for strong relationships with leadership and coworkers and the opportunity to explore and develop the "leader within."

The latest Institute of Medicine report, *The Future of Nursing: Leading Change, Advancing Health* (2010), underscores the importance of nursing leadership and calls for nurses to be full partners with physicians and other health care professionals in redesigning health care in the United States. The report encourages nurses to "take responsibility for their personal and professional growth by continuing their education and by seeking opportunities to develop and grow their leadership skills." New opportunities for such growth are rich within the patient care delivery leadership level, particularly when those assuming such roles hold the required professional qualifications and the personal attributes to help ensure success.

Opportunities for unintended and damaging consequences also exist when leaders are poorly or prematurely selected to assume roles needed to meet the challenge of effectively leading professional nurses and others in the delivery of high-quality, safe patient care. Ineffective leaders can jeopardize the delivery of care quality. Such leaders increase the potential risk that nurses at the bedside will fail to identify their "leader within" or will fail to have the resources and support they deserve when they do.

Summary

Promoting nurse-led care at the bedside begins with strong nursing leadership throughout the hospital. The ACN plays a key role in role modeling leadership behaviors when addressing a variety of challenging situations within the health care environment. A strong infrastructure that supports the acquisition and development of nursing leadership is required to create a "work environment that facilitates and encourages involvement of the staff in critical thinking to enact professional nursing practice so that the nurse at the bedside makes appropriate patient care decisions" (American Nurses Association [ANA], 2002). Mentoring provided by the ACN can promote the hiring, development, and role implementation of the ND who can implement the goals of the ACN in enhancing care at the bedside and promoting quality interdisciplinary care at the bedside.

References

Aiken, L. H., Clarke, S. P., Sloane, D. M., Lake, E. T., & Cheney, T. (2008). Effects of hospital care environment on patient mortality and nurse outcomes. *JONA, 38*(5), 223-229.

American Nurses Association (ANA). (2002). *Scope and standards for nurse administrators.* Washington, DC: American Nurses Publishing.

Benner, P. (1984). *From novice to expert: Excellence and power in clinical nursing practice.* Menlo Park, CA: Addison-Wesley Publishing Company.

Codier, E., Kooker, B. M., & Shoultz, J. (2008). Measuring the emotional intelligence of clinical staff nurses: An approach for improving the clinical care environment. *Nursing Administration Quarterly, 32*(1), 8-14.

Cummings, G. (2004). Investing relationship energy: The hallmark of resonant leadership. *The Canadian Journal of Nursing Leadership, 17*(4), 76-87.

Feather, R. (2009). Emotional intelligence in relation to nursing leadership: Does it matter? *Journal of Nursing Management, 17*(3), 376-382.

Goleman, D. (1998). The emotionally competent leader. *Harvard Business Review, 41*(2), 36, 38, 76.

Goleman, D. (2000). Leadership that gets results. *Harvard Business Review,* March-April, 82-83.

Gordin, P. C., & Trey, B. (2011). Finding the leader within: Thoughts on leadership and nursing. *Journal of Perinatal and Neonatal Nursing, 25*(2), 115-118.

Havens, D. S., Wood, S. O., & Leeman, J. (2006). Improving nursing practice and patient care: Building capacity with appreciative inquiry. *JONA, 36*(10), 463-470.

Hill, K. S. (2011). Work satisfaction, intent to stay, desires of nurses and financial knowledge among bedside and advanced practice nurses. *JONA, 41*(5), 211-217.

Hindle, T. (2008). *The Economist guide to management ideas and gurus.* London, England: The Economist Newspaper, Ltd.

Holmes, A. M., & Chamberlain, B. (2010). Transforming care at the bedside: The CNO's role. *Nursing Management, 41*(6), 45-47.

Institute of Medicine (IOM). (2010). *The future of nursing: Leading change, advancing health.* Washington DC: National Academies Press.

Lee, S. M., & Manley, B. (2008). Nurse director rounds to ensure service quality. *JONA, 38*(10), 435-440.

Lucas, V., Laschinger, H. K., & Wong, C. A. (2008). The impact of emotional intelligent leadership on staff nurse empowerment: The moderating effect of span of control. *Journal of Nursing Management, 16*(8), 964-973.

Mayer, J. D., & Salovey, P. (1997). What is emotional intelligence? In P. Salovey & D. Sluyter (Eds.), *Emotional development and emotional intelligence: Educational implications* (pp. 3-31). New York, NY: Perseus Books Group.

Nursing Organizations Alliance. (2004). *Principles and elements of a health practice/work environment.* Retrieved from http://www.aacn.org/WD/HWE/Docs/ExecSum.pdf

Peters, T. J., & Waterman, R. H. (1982). *In search of excellence.* New York, NY: Warner Books, Inc.

Salmon, M. (2007). Leadership is inspiring. In T. Hansen-Turtin, S. Sherman, & V. Ferguson (Eds.), *Conversations with leaders* (p. 3). Indianapolis, IN: Sigma Theta Tau International.

Serrat, O. (2009). *Managing by walking around.* International Publications. Paper 148. Retrieved from http://digitalcommons.ilr.cornell.edu/intl/148

Shamian, J., & El-Jardali, F. (2007). Healthy workplaces for health workers in Canada: Knowledge transfer and uptake in policy and practice. *Healthcare Papers, 7.* Retrieved from www.longwoods. com/product.php?productid=18668

Chapter 12

Nurse Leaders: Influencing New Paradigms of Care Delivery

Jeffrey M. Adams, RN, PhD

They always say time changes things, but you actually have to change them yourself.

–Andy Warhol

Introduction

Nurses have a unique role in health care. They comprise the largest professional group of health care providers, with more than 3.1 million nurses in the United States (Health Resources and Services Administration [HRSA], 2008) in contrast with 600,000 licensed physicians (Bureau of Labor Statistics, 2010). According to a 2010 report from the Gallup company, for more than a decade consumers have identified nurses to be the most trusted profession, yet in decisions related to health care reform in the United States, nurses self-identify as less influential than non-nurse executive counterparts (Adams et al., 2008) and even meet the criteria for being categorized as an oppressed group (Freire, 2000).

This chapter highlights the state of nursing within the context of United States health care reform and includes two frameworks that present new options for nurses to use knowledge and power to impact change locally and globally.

Nursing is in a position to dramatically contribute to the direction of health care reform, now and in the future. The available disciplinary knowledge and clinical expertise positions nurse leaders to impact change while interacting with other disciplines to promote lasting health care reform. Nurses must understand and speak to their unique contributions as all of health care looks to define the health care of the future.

Paradigms of Nurses in Health Care

In the book the *Structure of Scientific Revolutions*, the philosopher Thomas Kuhn (1962) brings the concept of paradigms into the common vernacular. By describing the process of scientific knowledge development, Kuhn views all science operating within a specific worldview or paradigm. For example, the geocentric model of cosmology describes the Earth as the center of the universe. In fact, humanity operated within this paradigm until Copernicus found that the Earth actually revolved around the sun.

In Kuhnian language, Copernicus identified an anomaly. As with the Copernican discovery, the continued identification of new anomalies in science leads to an absence of a unified political, social, or scientifically accepted paradigm, with the accompanying struggle to find "the new normal." It is well-documented that during these times post-anomaly, a time Kuhn refers to as a *pre-paradigmatic state* (Kuhn, 1962), you have those who are invested that cling to the original paradigm and those who race to accept or define a changing paradigm. Eventually, through scientific inquiry, a new paradigm emerges and is adopted. This scientific revolutionary process repeats itself as science "advances" in a deductive mechanism.

Kuhn's revolutionary paradigms can also be used to explain the current state of health care in the United States. Within this context, today's health care environment is in a pre-paradigmatic state. For many the existing paradigm used to guide care delivery in the United States is failing. The exponential growth in the cost of care coupled with an increasing demand for quality of services has led to the anomaly where the current model can no longer be sustained.

However, support for the transition from the old paradigm to the new one is significantly challenged, in part because the "new normal" is yet to be well defined. Researchers, practitioners, policy makers, educators, and theorists express many competing disciplinary perspectives about what the future of health care will look like in the United States. The work of the Institute of Medicine (IOM), *The Future of Nursing* report (2010), supports the fact that nurses will be the key to development, implementation, and outcome of a of care delivery solution in the new health care paradigm of the future.

Nursing's Influence

Simultaneous to the changes in the economic/political health care landscape and through efforts including the Future of Nursing campaign (Adams, 2011), nursing as a discipline has positioned itself to accelerate change within its own disciplinary domain.

Since the days of Florence Nightingale (1859), nurses have provided unique and valuable contributions to the well-being of individuals, families, communities, and systems; however, nurses as a group have not been a historically influential group (Sullivan, 2004). In many instances nurses have not been invited to be active participants at key decision-making tables (Adams et al., 2008) or have been identified by the public as not tremendously important players in defining health reform (Robert Wood Johnson Foundation, 2010).

Adams (2012) suggests, "There is no they, it is you, me and us," a proposed way of thinking that nurses must adopt in their individual and collective roles to effectively influence health care for the well-being of all. Thus, nurses have an imperative to seize the current pre-paradigmatic state of health care and be an articulate voice for nursing and its contributions to the future of health care in the United States and beyond.

Knowledge to Influence the Future

For nurses to become key partners in the future of health care, they must make a concerted effort to build upon those established characteristics that consumers expect and history supports. A key strength of the nursing discipline is to integrate interdisciplinary knowledge development when generating theoretical models and frameworks that guide, ground, and offer perspective around a unique disciplinary approach to care. The discussion to follow highlights two such models that can facilitate nursing's approach to informing and influencing changes in health care:

- The Model of the Interrelationship of Leadership, Environments, and Outcomes for Nurse Executives (MILE ONE)

- The Adams Influence Model (AIM)

These models (see Figures 12.1 and 12.2) articulate perspectives toward uncovering the unique value nurses provide. They serve as guides for nurses, influencing dialogue around health care reform in the boardroom and at the bedside. These models are discussed and used to frame exemplars provided by nurses actively participating in change. These examples reflect emerging nursing paradigms that are redefining the roles and structure of health care delivery within an academic quaternary care center in New England and a community hospital in California.

MILE ONE

The MILE ONE model (Figure 12.1) was developed (Adams, 2009) as a literature-based conceptual framework, designed to identify how leadership, systems, and professional practice are intertwined to optimize patient, staff, and systems outcomes. MILE ONE represents each nursing role and organizational project with a focus on nurses' potential to influence within all organizational roles.

The model emphasizes the role administrators play in continually working to empower staff and enhance professional practice environments to promote this goal. When staff working in these positive environments are empowered, it helps foster, identify, lead, and promote change that impacts patients, the workforce, and the organization's outcomes. Improving the quality of outcomes can and will inspire the administrator to push innovative means to enhance the environment, and thus the cycle continues (Adams, Ives Erickson, Jones & Paulo, 2009).

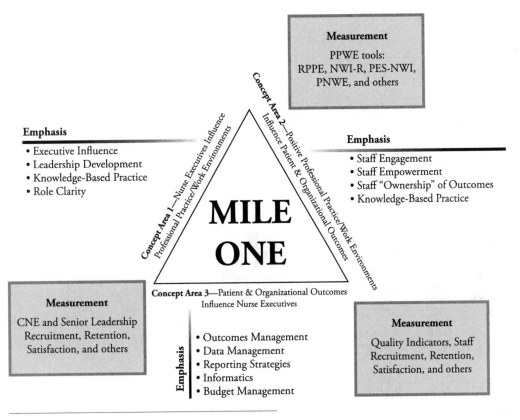

FIGURE 12.1

The MILE ONE model.[1]

1. PPWE (Professional Practice/Work Environment), RPPE (Revised Professional Practice Environment) scale, NWI-R (Nursing Work Index – Revised), PES-NWI (Practice Environment Scale of the Nursing Work Index), PNWE (Perceived Nursing Work Environment) scale

AIM

The Adams Influence Model (AIM) is a conceptual representation of the dynamic interaction between the nurse leader and staff and is validated through research (Adams, 2009). The concept of influence represents an approach to enable nurses to achieve advancement as individuals and as a discipline within the context of health care, one issue at a time.

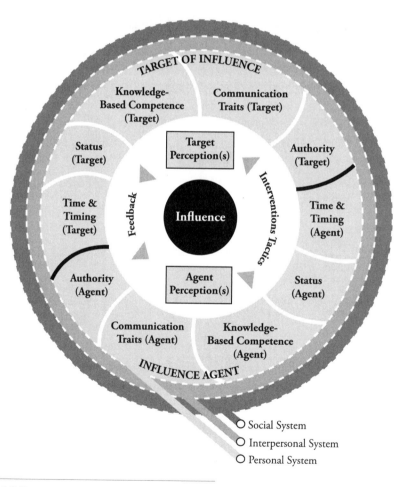

FIGURE 12.2
The AIM model.

The AIM is purposefully depicted as a camera shutter (Figure 12.2), conceptualizing influence as a snapshot that focuses on a single issue to better understand and represent how individuals see the challenge and become influential or powerful as leaders of change. The AIM seeks to builds upon Elizabeth Barrett's (2010) prevailing definition of *power* as "knowing participation in change" and identifies *influence* as the ability of an agent to sway or affect a target about a single issue based on authority, communication traits, knowledge-based competence, status, and use of time and timing (Adams, 2009).

As depicted in Figure 12.2, the AIM draws from the work of Ludwig von Bertalanffy's (1968) open systems theory to represent the constant, dynamic interaction continually occurring between the personal, interpersonal, and social systems, as noted in the outer dotted rings of the model.

The graphic represents the construct of influence as occurring between two sources: an *agent* of influence and a *target* of influence. Both the agent and target possess the influence factors, which include the following:

- Authority

- Communication traits

- Knowledge-based competence

- Status

- Time and timing

Attributes that are affiliated with these factors are shown in Table 12.1. The influence agent and the influence target each possess these factors and attributes, likely in different titrations, given a specific issue of clinical circumstance being addressed.

TABLE 12.1: AIM Influence Factors and Associated Influence Attributes

FACTOR	ASSOCIATED INFLUENCE ATTRIBUTES
Authority	Access to Resources
	Accountability
	Responsibility

continues

TABLE 12.1: *continued*

Communication Traits	Confidence
	Emotional Involvement
	Message Articulation
	Persistence
	Physical Appeal Environment
	Physical Appeal Self
	Presence
Knowledge-Based Competence	Aesthetic Knowledge
	Empirical Knowledge
	Ethical Knowledge
	Personal Knowledge
	Sociopolitical Knowledge
Status	Hierarchical Position
	Informal Position
	Key Supportive Relationships
	Reputation
Time and Timing	Amount of Time to Sell an Issue
	Timing to Deliver the Issue

At the core of the AIM is the process of influence. This process involves agents having perceptions of themselves in relation to targets. These perceptions cause agents to choose specific tactics or approaches (e.g., persuasion, coalitions, pressure, and so on) to influence responses. Similarly, targets also have perceptions of themselves and the agent. These perceptions are also informed by the tactics chosen by agents. Targets then provide feedback to agents, and influence is either achieved or a new process can begin, informed by additional data.

The AIM was initially developed with an emphasis on executive nurse leaders. To date it has appeared in the literature only in relation to facilitating an understanding of nursing administration's influence on professional practice environments (Adams, 2009), as a framework for the chief nurse's practice (Adams & Ives Erickson, 2011; Keys, 2011), and as a guide for strategizing about influence and health policy (Adams, Chisari, Ditomassi & Ives Erickson, 2011). Articulating the influence of the nurse in direct care of patients is an emerging application of the AIM.

The two exemplars to follow offer valuable applications of the AIM to date and might be effective in giving voice and value to nursing's disciplinary perspective and health care reform.

EXEMPLAR 1: APPLICATION OF THE AIM AND DOCUMENTATION USING STANDARDIZED NURSING LANGUAGE IN A CALIFORNIA DISTRICT HOSPITAL

In a California District Hospital, the organization had a need for improved clinical documentation. The leadership reported confidence in the quality of care being delivered (Adams, Denham & Neumeister, 2010), but a visit by The Joint Commission identified a need for improved communication between and among staff and leadership.

The organization sought to achieve this goal by revising and updating organizational policies, practices, and documentation procedures. As reported in many nursing documentation studies, nurses used individual or unit-specific terminology to describe their care. The reporting structures used did not maximize opportunities for data analysis, reporting, decision-making, or articulate the evidence needed to adequately describe the contributions of nursing practice outcomes (Keenan, 2007; Thede & Schwiran, 2011).

As these concerns were addressed, the organization designed an improved approach to documentation and selected a multipronged improvement process. Initially, emphasis was placed on improving the structure and content of nursing documentation. A team of staff nurses was assigned to define and identify the best terminology and infrastructure for communicating nursing practice.

This team, empowered by administrators, discovered that the implementation of a standardized nursing terminology that best supported clinical documentation provided improved communication of care across settings and complemented research (Rutherford, 2008) aligned with the MILE ONE structure. As the process moved forward, it became readily apparent that the inclusion of standardized nursing language, without an opportunity for multidisciplinary input, would be of value to nursing, but might not necessarily optimize the organization's opportunity for quality data.

The team moved to documentation improvement efforts that solicited and incorporated staff nurses' involvement solidified the nurse administrator's convictions for having standardized language utilization, across the disciplines. Linking these decisions to the characteristics used by nurses and administrators within this exemplar helps to validate the AIM. As the end users of the system, knowledgeable staff (knowledge-based competence), when empowered (authority) and recognized for their roles (status), were committed and persistent in promoting change (communication traits) at a time of need (time and timing). Additionally, and potentially most importantly, the efforts of the staff nurses participating in the project described not only influenced change in documentation practices for the discipline, but the nurses themselves articulated an organizational improvement that reflected their commitment to the discipline, patients, and personal development.

Narratives

These experiences as undertaken by nurses participating in change might be best understood through the words of the nurse participants:

> *I've had the opportunity to work closely with other nurses from different units of the hospital that have the same level of care, concern, and dedication to nursing as I do. The uniqueness of our committee has been the innate desire of all of us to improve nursing as a whole within our institution...I credit [this project] for my personal growth as a nurse and as team member of a committee that is playing a vital part of the positive change that is happening at [this hospital]. (D. R.)*

> *Many surprising changes have taken place in my attitude since I became part of the solution... Apathy is contagious, and I may have passed a bit of that on, too...It has truly been a blessing to be a member of [this*

project]... I also have a renewed sense in the professionalism of nursing and how even one nurse can be a catalyst for change. (D. D.)

Without doubt, my participation in [this project] has been the highlight of my nursing career at [this hospital]. What this committee has done for me personally and professionally is immeasurable...Perhaps the most valuable experience I have learned from [this project] is the engagement benefit for the nursing staff. By allowing frontline nurses to participate in this project, not only were we able to identify problems, we were willing to take ownership and provide solutions. (L. M.)

Application of Models

It is evident that nurses participating in the project discussed in this exemplar knowingly participated in change, seized an opportunity, shared through administrative support, and were able to influence important organizational and unit-level change. Their efforts helped influence and improve documentation standards for nursing as well interdisciplinary documentation across the organization. Additionally, these staff leaders were able to articulate the value of nursing and its role in optimizing care delivery within professional practice environments.

EXEMPLAR 2: INNOVATION AND THE ATTENDING NURSE

This exemplar presents an exploration of the nursing role on 12 newly designated Innovation Units (IUs) launched at the Massachusetts General Hospital (MGH). At the MGH, the IUs are designed to empower staff within a highly monitored, operational research test-bed system within the acute care arena. The IUs have implemented the MILE ONE framework. They are structured, empowered, and supported by nursing leadership to influence direct care nurse decision-making while simultaneously implementing new operational innovations, as discussed in Chapter 7. These efforts are designed to further advance the professional practice environments within the IU settings.

One of the "MGH innovations" is the introduction of a groundbreaking new role, referred to as the attending registered nurse (ARN). The development of the ARN role was informed by similar approaches identified in existing literature

(Brown et al., 2005; Fulmer et al., 2011; Watson & Foster, 2003). At the MGH, the ARN role was designed to optimize the influence of the ARN across the unit and with other disciplines. This included working five eight-hour shifts (presence), participating in regular training meetings (empirical knowledge), and connecting with the nursing leadership in regularly scheduled meetings (key supportive relationships), during a period of flux in health care (timing to deliver the issue). Additionally, ARNs are identified as having significant authority (access to resources, accountability, and responsibility) to identify and enact change both for patients and the organization.

The operationalization of these core structures continues to be adjusted to fit the culture and demands of each individual IU. As suggested by existing ARNs in the following narratives, the creation of the ARN provides a new opportunity to articulate the role of nurses at the bedside, while empowering each nurse to lead change in the care delivered by nurses and valued by patient and families.

Narratives

As an attending registered nurse [ARN], one of our primary goals is to increase or strengthen patient relationships; establishing strong patient relationships earlier in the health care process HAS been very successful. I credit the ability to meet some of the patients preoperatively very helpful in this endeavor.

One of my most memorable patient relationship building experiences came from meeting a surgical candidate preoperatively. Throughout the patient's stay, I remained a constant in his care and in keeping him and the family up-to-date. As we had established a bond early on, I was considered the family's "go-to person," someone they relied on and trusted. Whether I gave them new information regarding the plan of care or just stopped in to meet additional family members, my presence was appreciated. The patient was later readmitted for unrelated reasons to a different unit. The family made it a point to inform me that the patient was readmitted and asked if I could go and visit. The work put into establishing an early relationship with the patients during their hospital stay has proven to be most valuable. (M. A.)

When I introduce myself as the attending nurse to patients and families [and]... I get to the part that I will follow up with phone calls; this seems to make me a more influential part of their thinking and care. For patients who have been here for some time, it can be stressful to think about going home. ... I have found that the follow-up phone calls prove beneficial to the patients.

When I call patients at home, even though they know I will call, they are always surprised that I have followed through. The phone calls usually are short and to the point when patients have no questions or issues. They are always thankful to the staff for the wonderful care that they have received and in awe at how respectful and professional staff all are. Where the phone calls are most influential are when the patients do have questions about their discharge or are experiencing difficulties whether major or minor. Additionally, the nurses who have cared for the patients are always curious about how they are adjusting at home. The phone calls just create an additional linkage; they are our patients.

The attending nurse position has opened up a lot of opportunity for me to grow personally and professionally. There is still a lot to learn from the attending nurse experience, but I believe it can be a standard of care. (G. J. C.)

Application of Models

The preceding examples highlight the commitment and strategies two attending nurses use in the development of relationship with and care of patients. Ultimately, however, ARNs are charged to cross traditional organizational boundaries and find solutions that coordinate care throughout the continuum. The ARN role helps to solidify nurses as the lynchpin in promoting cost-effective, high-quality, safe, patient-centric care delivery within an interdisciplinary team. When nurses are put in a position to be influential and empowered, they can optimize their authority, communication traits, knowledge-based competence, and status during this time of change to efficiently identify, implement, and lead innovation in practice.

As with all conceptual models or frameworks, the AIM and MILE ONE provide a structure, a starting point to approach individual, professional, organizational, or societal improvement efforts. The nurses highlighted in the preceding sections cross all care delivery settings. Yet, each provides examples of the actual and potential impact of nursing on care and their abilities to influence change in the boardroom and at the bedside.

Summary

The chapter discussed examples from two different health care settings to exemplify how care redesign can be redefined using disciplinary paradigms that offer a new world of health care. When projects supported by leaders and driven by influential staff nurses are replicated, as evidenced in the exemplars provided, nurses can and will influence the redesign of the new paradigm of care delivery. By using philosophical and theoretical representations such as the MILE ONE and AIM, nurses can house change in knowledge and shape that change to provide a forum for themselves to further articulate a unique approach to care. Within this context, the value and contributions of the discipline can be purposeful and intentional. It promotes out-of-the-box thinking and supports knowing participation in change and redesign of care to enhance the future well-being of patients, communities, systems, and the discipline.

References

Adams, J. M. (2009). *The Adams Influence Model (AIM): Understanding the factors, attributes, and process of achieving influence.* Saarbrüken, Germany: VDM Verlag.

Adams, J. M. (2011). Influencing the future of nursing: An interview with Sue Hassmiller. *Journal of Nursing Administration, 41*(10), 394-396.

Adams, J. M. (2012, May 31). The bucket list: Advancing an international research agenda using administrative data in evaluating leadership and organizations. *Caring Headlines,* 9.

Adams, J. M., Chisari, R. G., Ditomassi M., & Ives Erickson, J. (2011). Understanding and influencing policy: An imperative to the contemporary nurse leader. *AONE: The Voice of Nursing Leadership, 7,* 4-7.

Adams, J. M., Denham D., & Neumeister, I. (2010). Applying the Model of Interrelationship of Leadership, Environments and Outcomes for Nurse Executives: A community hospital's exemplar in developing staff nurse engagement through documentation improvement initiatives. *Nursing Administration Quarterly, 34*(3), 201-207.

Adams, J. M., & Ives Erickson, J. (2011). Applying the Adams Influence Model (AIM) in nurse executive practice. *Journal of Nursing Administration, 41*(4), 186-192.

Adams, J. M., Ives Erickson, J., Jones, D. A., & Paulo, L. (2009). An evidence-based structure for transformative nurse executive practice: The Model of the Interrelationship of Leadership, Environments and Outcomes for Nurse Executives (MILE ONE). *Nursing Administration Quarterly, 33*(4), 280-287.

Adams, J. M., Paulo, L., Meraz-Gottfried, L., Aspell Adams, A., Ives Erickson, J., Jones, D. A., & Clifford, J. C. (2008). *Success measures for the nurse leader: A survey of participants from the 2007 INHL conference.* Boston, MA: The Institute for Nursing Healthcare Leadership.

Barrett, E. A. M. (2010). Power as knowing participation in change: What's new and what's next? *Nursing Science Quarterly, 23*(1), 47-54.

Brown, C. L., Holcomb, L., Maloney, J., Naranjo, J., Gibson, C., & Russell, P. (2005). Caring in action: The patient care facilitator role. *International Journal for Human Caring, 9*(3), 51-58.

Bureau of Labor Statistics, U.S. Department of Labor. (2012, March 29). Physicians and surgeons. *Occupational Outlook Handbook, 2010-11 Edition*. Retrieved from http://www.bls.gov/oco/ocos074.htm

Freire, P. (2000). *Pedagogy of the oppressed* (30th anniversary ed.). New York, NY: The Continuum International Publishing Group.

Fulmer, T., Cathcart, E., Glassman, K., Budin, W., Naegle, M., & Van Devanter, N. (2011). The attending nurse: An evolving model for integrating nursing education and practice. *The Open Nursing Journal, 5*, 9-13.

Gallup, Inc. (2010). *Nurses top honesty and ethics list for 11th year*. Retrieved from http://www.gallup.com/poll/145043/nurses-top-honesty-ethics-list-11-year.aspx#1

Health Resources and Services Administration (HRSA). (2008). *National sample survey of registered nurses*. Retrieved from http://datawarehouse.hrsa.gov/nursingsurvey.aspx

Institute of Medicine (IOM). (2010). *The future of nursing: Leading change, advancing health*. Retrieved from http://www.nap.edu/catalog/12956.html

Keenan, G. (2007). *HIT support for safe nursing care*. Retrieved from www.healthhit.ahrq.gov/portal/server/keenan.ppt

Keys, Y. (2011). Perspectives on executive relationships: Influence. *Journal of Nursing Administration, 41*(9), 347-349.

Kuhn, T. S. (1962). *The structure of scientific revolutions*. Chicago, IL: University of Chicago Press.

Nightingale, F. (1859). *Notes on nursing: What it is and what it is not* (1st American edition). New York, NY: Appleton and Company.

Robert Wood Johnson Foundation. (2010). *Nursing leadership from bedside to boardroom: Opinion leaders' perceptions*. Retrieved from http://www.rwjf.org/pr/product.jsp?id=55091

Rutherford, M. (2008). Standardized nursing language: What does it mean for nursing? *Online Journal of Issues in Nursing, 13*(1).

Schwiran, P., & Thede, L. (2011). Informatics: The standardized nursing terminologies: A national survey of nurses' experiences and attitudes. *Online Journal of Issues in Nursing, 16*(2).

Sullivan, E. J. (2004). *Becoming influential: A guide for nurses*. Upper Saddle River, NJ: Pearson Educational, Inc.

von Bertalanffy, L. (1968). *General system theory*. New York, NY: George Braziller.

Watson, J., & Foster, R. (2003). *The Attending Nurse Caring Model®*: Integrating theory, evidence, and advanced caring—Healing therapeutics for transforming professional practice. *Journal of Clinical Nursing, 12*(3), 360-365.

Chapter 13

Measuring the Hospital Work Environment: Development, Validation, and Revision of the Professional Practice Environment Scale

Mary E. Duffy, RN, PhD, FAAN,
Jeanette Ives Erickson, RN, DNP, FAAN
Marianne, Ditomassi, RN, DNP, MBA
Dorothy A. Jones, RN, EdD, FAAN

So never lose an opportunity of urging a practical beginning,
however small, for it is wonderful how often in such matters the
mustard-seed germinates and roots itself.

–Florence Nightingale

Introduction

Understanding nurses' perceptions about the effectiveness of a professional practice model at the patient care unit level, as well as across the practice environment, can provide important information about professional nursing practice to the chief nursing officer and other executive leadership. Changes and innovations implemented at the point of care can be communicated to the leadership through evaluation and decision-making influenced by data from responsive staff. Developing valid and reliable measures to evaluate the staffs' perceptions of the work environment is an effective way to come to know how nurses are experiencing the professional work environment.

Since the late 1980s, increased attention has been paid to the practice environment in which health professionals, in particular nurses, work. The focus on creating professional practice settings that enhance autonomy and optimize nursing's ability to deliver knowledge-driven, evidence-based care was accelerated by many professional movements, in particular the American Academy of Nursing's (AAN) Magnet report on attraction and retention of professional nurses (McClure, Poulin, Sovie & Wandelt, 1983). The Magnet report acknowledged that the practice environment had the potential to become optimized.

Despite this attention, research initiatives available to evaluate practice environment outcomes have not kept pace with the growing interest in how nurse providers link professional practice environments with optimal patient care. Ives Erickson and colleagues (2004) believe this might be due, in part, to the dearth of reliable and valid measures to adequately assess the various dimensions of the professional practice environment, particularly in acute care settings. In a review of the types of research studies using specific instruments to evaluate practice environments, Lake (2007) confirms this perspective, finding only seven multidimensional instruments in 203 research reports that met inclusion criteria. The need for measures to adequately evaluate professional practice is essential to improving the work environment for optimal patient care by nurses practicing at the bedside.

This chapter provides information related to measuring the professional practice environment through the development, validation, and revision of the Professional Practice Environment (PPE) Scale.

The Nursing Work Index and the Revised Nursing Work Index

The first multidimensional measure of the nursing practice environment was the Nursing Work Index (NWI), developed by Kramer and Hafner (1989). The original NWI consisted of 65 items, anchored by a four-point Likert scale (Strongly Disagree, Disagree, Agree, and Strongly Agree). The instrument was designed to measure those organizational traits reported by the original Magnet hospital staff nurses as characteristic of their professional work environments (McClure et al, 1983).

According to Aiken and Patrician (2000) the original NWI was designed to be an "inclusive list of factors that directly bear on environments conducive to quality care provision and job satisfaction" (p. 149). They conclude that the "NWI is a gauge for measuring the extent to which a nursing care environment may be considered a professional practice environment" (p. 149).

Several years later, the NWI was revised and 10 items deemed not to be significantly related to the elements of a professional practice environment were dropped, reducing the NWI to 55 items. In addition, one item was slightly modified, and one item was added to address team nursing. Items were then grouped into three conceptually derived subscales, namely:

- Autonomy

- Control over the work environment

- Relationships with physicians (Baggs, Ryan, Phelps, Richeson & Johnson, 1992)

This now 57-item scale became the Revised Nursing Work Index (R-NWI). The R-NWI was then psychometrically evaluated and demonstrated satisfactory internal consistency and test-retest reliability, content, and construct validity (Baggs et al., 1992).

In 2002, Lake then reviewed the original 65 NWI items and, along with another nurse researcher and a hospital staff nurse, chose 48 items they believed met the definition of the nursing practice environment. After coding the items so that higher scores represented higher amounts of the constructs being measured, they subjected the scale to factor analysis. Because 3 to 15 subscales might be extracted, they used the following criteria to evaluate each of the models for its ability to produce subscales that:

1. Retained three or more items with a high item-to-subscale correlation, called a *salient loading* (0.40)

2. Produced high internal consistency for salient items (> 0.80)

3. Remained invariant across models

4. Made theoretical sense in terms of parsimony (i.e., mutually exclusive assignment of items to subscales) and compatibility with categories described in the Magnet hospital research (McClure et al., 1983)

The researchers considered the model that extracted five factors using principal axis factoring with Varimax (orthogonal) rotation to be the one satisfying most of the stated criteria. The factor structure retained 31 of the 48 items in the instrument and was called the Practice Environment Scale of the Nursing Work Index (PES-NWI). The five subscales of the PES-NWI are labeled in Table 13.1.

TABLE 13.1: The Subscales of the PES-NWI

SUBSCALES	NUMBER OF ITEMS
Nurse Participation in Hospital Affairs	9 items
Nursing Foundations for Quality of Care	10 items
Nurse Manager Ability, Leadership, and Support of Nurses	5 items
Staffing and Resource Adequacy	4 items
Collegial Nurse-Physician Relations	3 items

Researchers created mean subscale scores and then averaged them to form an overall composite score. The calculated Cronbach's alpha internal consistency reliability scores on all but one subscale, and the composite score ranged from 0.71 to 0.84 and were deemed satisfactory. Only one scale, Collegial Nurse-Physician Relations, failed to make the 0.80 reliability cutoff, and this was most likely because of the small number of items (N = 3) forming the subscale.

Lake (2002) concludes that the R-NWI demonstrated "substantive coherence, multilevel range in hospital context, internal consistency, aggregate reliability and generality to contemporary practice, affirming their conceptual and empirical foundations." Since its development and validation, the PES-NWI has been recommended by key organizations promoting quality care as a measure of the quality of the nursing practice environment (Warshawsky & Havens, 2011).

The Massachusetts General Hospital (MGH) Professional Practice Model

The MGH professional practice model (PPM) builds upon the foundation established by the initial Magnet hospital study (McClure et al., 1983) that articulated the salient elements of professional practice as autonomy, control over practice, and collegial relations with physicians. In addition to incorporating other health care disciplines besides nursing, the MGH model builds on this Magnet foundation and integrates other findings from extant research on organizational behavior and descriptive theory models.

The MGH PPM's core elements are:

- Professional staff leadership and autonomy in practice

- Control over one's practice

- Collaborative governance stressing staff participation in decision-making about patient care and the environment within which care is delivered

- Interdisciplinary communication and teamwork

- Use of a problem-solving approach to handle disagreements and conflict

- Enhanced internal work motivation

- Delivering culturally sensitive, competent care to patients of all ethnic groups (Ives Erickson & Ditomassi, 2011)

(Refer to Chapter 2 for a reprint of this reference.)

Since 1997, components of the MGH PPM have been systematically evaluated regularly (1 year to 18 months) through administration of the Staff Perceptions of the Professional Practice Environment (SPPPE) Survey to all patient care services (PCS) disciplines, namely: ambulatory care, chaplaincy, child life specialists, nursing, occupational therapy, physical therapy, respiratory therapy, social services, and speech/language pathology.

The SPPPE Survey

The SPPPE survey consists of several components including:

1. A set of demographic items (gender, age, educational background, number of years in the discipline, and number of years at MGH)

2. An overall work satisfaction item

3. The Job Enjoyment scale

4. The Professional Practice Environment (PPE) Scale (Ives Erickson et al., 2004) or the Revised PPE (Ives Erickson, Duffy, Ditomassi & Jones, 2009) that were developed and psychometrically evaluated to measure components of the MGH PPM

The survey also includes an open-ended question that offers each clinician the opportunity to share additional comments (positive and negative) they feel are important to communicate to the leadership.

The SPPPE evaluation serves as an effective "report card" to the leadership of the health of the MGH PPE. MGH administrators have reported that these findings continue to help them more fully understand and appreciate those organizational factors that enhance clinical practice and what support structures might be needed to achieve the Institute of Medicine's six aims: patient centeredness, safety, effectiveness, efficiency, timeliness, and equity of care (Institute of Medicine [IOM], 2001).

Development and Psychometric Evaluation of the Original PPE Scale

The MGH PPM guided the development of the first version of the PPE Scale. The original PPE Scale was administered in late 1998 to evaluate the effectiveness of the PCS's new practice environment in supporting clinicians in their delivery of patient care. This 35-item scale was designed to measure eight clinical practice environment characteristics:

- Leadership and autonomy over practice (5 items)
- Clinician-physician relationships (2 items)
- Control over practice (6 items)
- Communication about patients (3 items)
- Teamwork (4 items)
- Conflict management (8 items)
- Internal work motivation (4 items)
- Cultural sensitivity (3 items) (Ives Erickson et al., 2004)

PPE Scale Definitions

The PPE scale has eight subscales, defined in Table 13.2. Seven hospital staff members from across all PCS disciplines were selected as a content validity panel to ascertain how well each item represented the conceptual category it was designed to measure. A final review of the items for readability, clarity and meaning resulted in minor wording changes to several items. Ultimately, all of the items were retained.

TABLE 13.2: PPE Scale Definitions

SUBSCALE	DEFINITION
Leadership and autonomy in clinical practice	The quality or state of being self-governing and exercising professional judgment in a timely fashion (Aiken, Sochalski & Lake, 1997).
Clinician-physician relationships	Those associations with physicians that facilitate exchange of important clinical information (Aiken et al., 1997).
Control over practice	Denotes sufficient intra-organizational status to influence others and employ resources when necessary for good patient care (Aiken & Havens, 2000).
Communication about patients	Defined as the degree to which patient care information is related promptly to the people who need to be informed through open channels of interchange (Shortell, Rousseau, Gillies, Devers & Simons, 1991).
Teamwork	Viewed as conscious activity aimed at achieving unity of effort in the pursuit of shared objectives (Zimmerman et al., 1993).
Conflict management	The degree to which managing conflict is addressed using a problem solving approach (Zimmerman et al., 1993).
Internal work motivation	Self-generated encouragement completely independent of external factors such as pay, supervision, or co-workers (Hackman & Oldham, 1976, 1980).
Cultural sensitivity	A set of attitudes, practices, and/or policies that respects and accepts cultural differences (The Cross Cultural Health Care Program, 2010).

Each PPE item was placed on a four-point Likert scale of SA (Strongly Agree), A (Agree), D (Disagree), and SD (Strongly Disagree). A brief set of instructions was provided to direct hospital staff respondents to circle the letter that best indicated the amount of agreement they had on each item.

Initial Use and Revision of PPE Scale

The resulting 35-item PPE Scale was used from 1999 through 2001 to evaluate the effectiveness of MGH's PPE and observe evidence that suggests changes during this period. Although Cronbach's alpha internal consistency reliability estimates were satisfactory for the overall scale and for six of eight subscales, two scales had problems, namely the internal work motivation subscale as a whole and one item in the conflict management scale.

The problem with the internal work motivation scale was due most likely to the scale being only four items in length and the relative homogeneity of staff responses on these items. To address this problem, four additional items were developed, content validated with the category definition, and then added to the scale.

In the conflict management scale, the problem item contained two ideas rather than one, thus creating possible confusion for respondents. The item was rewritten to contain one idea, thus eliminating the ambiguity on how to respond in the original item. A second item was written to include the other idea removed from the ambiguous item. This revised PPE scale (2002), now 40 items, was used in subsequent psychometric analyses reported in this chapter.

The PPE scale was then psychometrically evaluated as follows:

1. Item analysis

2. Principal components analysis (PCA) with Varimax rotation and Kaiser normalization

3. Cronbach's alpha internal consistency reliability of the resulting eight subscales and total score

The detailed report of this evaluation was published in the *Journal of Nursing Scholarship* by Ives Erickson and colleagues (2004). Only the PCA, Cronbach's alphas of the PPE subscales, and the revised PPE are discussed next.

Principal Components Analysis (PCA) of Original PPE Scale

After item analysis of the 40-item PPE Scale was undertaken with a sample of 849 professional staff, two items were dropped because of item-total correlations below the 0.30 cutoff. The PPE Scale, now 38 items, was next subjected to PCA with iterations and mean substitution of missing values, followed by Varimax rotation and Kaiser normalization.

Initially, nine components had eigenvalues greater than 1.0, accounting for almost 64% of explained variance. The scree test, however, was more parsimonious, suggesting an eight-factor solution. Thus, a second PCA was performed specifying eight factors. The rotated factor matrix revealed a more interpretable solution that confirmed the theoretical view of eight PPE components. All 38 items had significant loadings (> 0.30) on one of the eight components, with very few substantial side loadings. As Table 13.3 reports, the PPE items and their component loadings on the PCA-derived scales explained 61% of initially extracted common variance.

TABLE 13.3: PCA Factor Loadings for the Professional Practice Environment (PPE) Scale

Item ($N = 849$; Scale Cronbach's Alpha = 0.93)	Loading
FACTOR 1: CONFLICT MANAGEMENT (27.5% VARIANCE, CRONBACH'S ALPHA = 0.88)	
22. When staff disagree, they ignore issue, pretending it will go away.	0.77
23. Staff withdraw from conflict.	0.76
28. Disagreements between staff are ignored or avoided.	0.73
25. All staff work hard to arrive at best possible solution.	0.71
24. All points of view considered in finding best solution to problem.	0.69
27. All contribute from their experience, expertise to effect high-quality solution.	0.67
26. Staff involved don't settle dispute until all are satisfied with decision.	0.66

29. Staff involved settle disputes by consensus.	0.31

FACTOR 2: INTERNAL WORK MOTIVATION
(7.7% VARIANCE, CRONBACH'S ALPHA=0.86)

34. I have challenging work that motivates me to do the best job I can.	0.82
32. I feel a great sense of personal satisfaction when I do this job well.	0.76
33. I feel a high degree of personal responsibility for the work I do.	0.74
35. Working on this unit gives me the opportunity to gain new knowledge and skills.	0.72
37. Working in this environment increases my sense of professional growth.	0.62
36. I am motivated to do well because I am empowered by my work environment.	0.56
30. My opinion of myself goes up when I work on this unit.	0.53

FACTOR 3: CONTROL OVER PRACTICE
(5.9% VARIANCE, CRONBACH'S ALPHA=0.82)

8. Enough staff to provide quality patient care.	0.85
10. Enough staff to get the work done.	0.83
6. Adequate support services allow me to spend time with patients.	0.73
7. Enough time and opportunity to discuss patient care problems with other staff.	0.69
11. Opportunity to work on highly specialized patient care unit.	0.36
5. Patient care assignments that foster continuity of care.	0.36
14. Not being placed in a position of having to do things against my professional judgment.	0.32

FACTOR 4: LEADERSHIP AND AUTONOMY IN CLINICAL PRACTICE
(4.9% VARIANCE, CRONBACH'S ALPHA=0.83)

9. A manager who is a good manager and leader.	0.79
1. Leadership supportive to department or unit staff.	0.75

continues

TABLE 13.3: *continued*

12. Manager who backs up staff in decision-making, even in conflict with MD.	0.75
2. My discipline controls its own practice.	0.39
3. Freedom to make important patient care and work decisions.	0.37

FACTOR 5: CLINICIAN-PHYSICIAN RELATIONSHIPS
(4.6% VARIANCE, CRONBACH'S ALPHA = 0.79)

4. A lot of teamwork between physicians and staff.	0.82
13. Physicians and department or unit staff have good relationships.	0.76

FACTOR 6: TEAMWORK (3.8% VARIANCE, CRONBACH'S ALPHA = 0.78)

19. This unit doesn't get cooperation it needs from other hospital units.	0.79
21. Inadequate working relationships with other hospital groups limit effectiveness of work on this unit.	0.76
20. Other hospital units seem to have a low opinion of this unit.	0.69
18. This unit has constructive relationships with other groups in this hospital.	0.65

FACTOR 7: CULTURAL SENSITIVITY
(3.6% VARIANCE, CRONBACH'S ALPHA = 0.78)

39. Staff are sensitive to diverse patient populations whom they serve.	0.87
40. Staff are respectful of their department or unit's diverse health care team.	0.80
38. Staff have access to necessary resources to give culturally competent care.	0.65

FACTOR 8: COMMUNICATION ABOUT PATIENTS
(3.0% VARIANCE, CRONBACH'S ALPHA = 0.80)

16. When patient's status changes, I get relevant information quickly.	0.77
15. I get information on patient's status when I need it.	0.77

The eight components were named because of the way the items loaded:

- Component 1, with eight items, was called **Conflict management** because it contained all of the original disagreement/conflict items.

- Component 2, with seven items, was called **Internal work motivation** because all of the items designed to measure this component loaded together.

- Component 3, called **Control over practice,** had seven items, six of which were the original control items and one original item labeled a leadership and autonomy item (i.e., Not being placed in the position of having to do things against my professional judgment). After examination of this item within Component 3, the research team determined the item did not tap into the construct of control over practice and logically belonged with the other control items.

- Component 4, with five items, was called **Leadership and autonomy in clinical practice.** Four of the original leadership and autonomy over practice items and one item (i.e., A manager who is a good manager and leader), originally thought to be a control over practice item, comprised this component. However, it logically belonged with the other items defining this factor.

- Component 5, with only two items, loaded together as expected and was called **Clinician-physician relationships.**

- Component 6, defined by four items, loaded as expected and was labeled **Teamwork.**

- Component 7, with three items was called **Cultural sensitivity.**

- Component 8, consisting of two items, was called **Communication about patients.**

Reliability Estimation of PCA-Derived Scales in Original PPE Scale

Cronbach's alpha internal consistency reliabilities, shown in Table 13.3, were next computed on the 38-item PPE Scale, producing a standardized alpha coefficient of 0.93. This was followed by computing Cronbach's alpha coefficients for the 8 PCA-derived scales. As Table 13.3 shows, these coefficients ranged from 0.78 to 0.88, as follows:

Component	Coefficient
Conflict management	0.88
Internal work motivation	0.86
Control over practice	0.82
Leadership & autonomy in clinical practice	0.83
Clinician-physician relationships	0.79
Teamwork	0.78
Cultural sensitivity	0.78
Communication about patients	0.80

Each PPE subscale was judged to have sufficient internal consistency reliability for use as an independent measure in subsequent research.

Development of the Revised Professional Practice Environment Scale (RPPE)

After the MGH PCS strategic goals were revised in 2005, the PPE Scale underwent further revision. Nursing leadership reviewed the PPE items, edited them for greater clarity, and added two items to Conflict management (i.e., *Most conflicts occur with members from my own discipline* and *Most conflicts occur with members from other disciplines*). It was hoped that the additional items would help to more clearly pinpoint where conflicts and disagreements originated.

The RPPE scale, now 42 items in length, was the version used in the MGH 2006 SPPPE study. This was the first time the survey was delivered electronically to MGH professional staff, yielding a 61% response rate (N = 1,837). The RPPE was psychometrically evaluated using all PCS staff who had no missing data on the scale (n = 1,550). Because this sample size was significantly larger than the sample used in the original PPE evaluation (N = 849), a random sample cross-validation procedure (Cudeck & Browne, 1983; Ives Erickson et al., 2004) was employed to determine if the eight original components in the RPPE could be derived in one sample and validated in a comparable second sample drawn from the same population of MGH staff. Prior to statistical analyses, the 2006 PCS sample was randomly cut in half, producing two samples:

1. The calibration sample (n = 775), used to derive the underlying RPPE components

2. The validation sample (n = 775), used to confirm the RPPE component structure

If both samples produced the same or very similar results, then additional evidence of construct validity would exist (Li et al., 1998).

Prior to undertaking PCAs on the two samples, descriptive statistics were calculated on the demographic characteristics and examined. These analyses are discussed in detail in the published report of the RPPE psychometric evaluation (Ives Erickson et al., 2009). The two samples were comparable with no significant differences on the demographic characteristics of age, gender, highest educational level, number of years in the profession, and number of years at the MGH. Sample size for both samples (n = 775) was judged to be adequate to undertake PCAs; each sample had an estimated 20:1 case-to-variable ratio (Comrey, 1988; Tabachnick & Fidell, 2007).

Similar to the psychometric evaluation of the original PPE, the RPPE appraisal included:

1. Internal consistency reliability using Cronbach's alpha and item analysis

2. Principal Components Analysis (PCA) using the previously described random sample, cross-validation technique

3. Internal consistency reliability of resulting components using Cronbach's alpha

A description of the PCA is described next.

PCA: Calibration Sample

A PCA with Varimax rotation and Kaiser normalization was next done on the calibration sample (n = 775), stipulating eight components and resulting in a parsimonious and interpretable solution. Thirty-nine (39) of the 42 items loaded greater than the 0.30 loading cutoff on one of the eight components, with very few substantial side loadings. As Table 13.3 shows, the rotated matrix for eight components explained 59.2% of initially extracted common variance.

Component 1, **Conflict management,** had nine items.

Component 2, **Leadership and autonomy in clinical practice,** had five items.

Component 3, **Internal work motivation,** had eight items.

Component 4, **Control over practice,** had five items.

Component 5, **Teamwork,** had four items.

Component 6, **Communication about patients,** had three items.

Component 7, **Cultural sensitivity,** had three items.

Component 8, **Clinician-Physician relationships,** had two items.

Three items did not load significantly (< 0.30) on any component. These items were:

1. Patient care assignments foster continuity of care

2. I am asked to do things against my professional judgment

3. Most conflicts occur with members from other disciplines

PCA: Validation Sample

A second PCA with Varimax rotation and Kaiser normalization was next computed on the validation sample (n = 775) and produced very similar results. Table 13.4 confirms that all eight components comprising the same items in the same order were identical to what was found in the calibration sample PCA (see Table 13.3). The validation sample also showed that the same three items that were dropped because components loadings were < 0.30 in the calibration sample were also eliminated in the validation sample PCA. The shared variance in the validation sample PCA equaled 59.7%, just 0.5% higher than the explained variance in the calibration sample PCA.

TABLE 13.4: PCA Loadings for Varimax-Rotated Factor Matrix for Revised Professional Practice Environment (RPPE) Scale—Validation Sample N = 775

(Cronbach's Alpha Total 39-Item Scale = 0.92)
Component Total Explained Variance 59.7%

COMPONENT 1: CONFLICT MANAGEMENT (25.8% VARIANCE, CRONBACH'S ALPHA = 0.85

20. When staff disagree, they ignore issue pretending it will "go away"	0.76
27. Disagreements between staff are ignored/avoided	0.74
24. All staff work hard to arrive at best possible solution	0.70
26. All contribute from their experience, expertise to effect high-quality solution	0.69
22. Staff withdraw from conflict	0.67
25. Staff involved don't settle dispute until all are satisfied with decision	0.64
23. All points of view considered in finding best solution to problem	0.62
28. Staff involved settle disputes by consensus	0.41
21. Most conflicts occur with members of my own discipline	0.37

continues

TABLE 13.4: *continued*

COMPONENT 2: LEADERSHIP & AUTONOMY IN CLINICAL PRACTICE (7.3% VARIANCE, (CRONBACH'S ALPHA = 0.84)

11. Department head supports staff even if conflict is with a doctor	0.77
1. Leadership supportive to department/unit staff	0.72
2. My discipline controls its own practice	0.69
8. Department head is a good manager & leader	0.67
3. I have freedom to make important patient care & work decisions	0.64

COMPONENT 3: INTERNAL WORK MOTIVATION (6.2% VARIANCE, CRONBACH'S ALPHA = 0.83)

32. I feel a great sense of personal satisfaction when I do this job well	0.81
33. I have challenging work that motivates me to do best job I can	0.81
31. I feel a high degree of personal responsibility for the work I do	0.79
34. Working on this unit gives me opportunity to gain new knowledge & skills	0.68
36. Working in this environment increases my sense of professional growth	0.54
35. I am motivated to do well because I am empowered by my work environment	0.45
29. My opinion of myself goes up when I work on this unit	0.40
30. I feel bad & unhappy when I discover I have performed less well than I should	0.38

COMPONENT 4: CONTROL OVER PRACTICE (5.2% VARIANCE, CRONBACH'S ALPHA = 0.82)

7. There are enough staff to provide quality patient care	0.84
9. We have enough staff to get the work done	0.84
5. I have adequate support services to allow me to spend time with patients	0.63

6. I have enough time & opportunity to discuss patient care problems with other staff	0.62
10. There are opportunities to work on highly specialized patient care unit	0.34

COMPONENT 5: TEAMWORK
(4.4% VARIANCE, CRONBACH'S ALPHA = 0.81)

17. My unit/department doesn't get cooperation it needs from other hospital units	0.81
19. Inadequate working relationships with other hospital groups limit effectiveness of work on this unit	0.79
18. Other hospital units/departments seem to have low opinion of my unit/department	0.72
16. My unit/department has constructive relationships with other groups in this hospital	0.68

COMPONENT 6: COMMUNICATION ABOUT PATIENTS
(4.1% VARIANCE, CRONBACH'S ALPHA = 0.85)

14. I receive information quickly when patient's status changes	0.85
13. Information regarding patient care is relayed without delays	0.82
15. Information on the status of patients is available when I need it	0.75

COMPONENT 7: CULTURAL SENSITIVITY
(3.5% VARIANCE, CRONBACH'S ALPHA = 0.88)

38. Staff are sensitive to diverse patient populations for whom they serve	0.87
39. Staff respect the diversity of their health care team	0.84
37. Staff have access to necessary resources to provide culturally competent care	0.74

COMPONENT 8: CLINICIAN-PHYSICIAN RELATIONSHIPS
(3.2% VARIANCE, CRONBACH'S ALPHA = 0.85)

12. Physicians and staff have good working relationships	0.47
4. There is a lot of teamwork between unit/departments and doctors	0.46

continues

TABLE 13.4: *continued*

DROPPED ITEMS DUE TO FACTOR LOADINGS < 0.30

Patient care assignments foster continuity of care
I am asked to do things against my professional judgment
Most conflicts occur with members from other disciplines

RPPE Cronbach's Alpha Internal Consistency Reliabilities in Both Samples

Prior to computing RPPE mean subscale scores, Cronbach's alpha internal consistency reliabilities for each of the eight PCA-derived components were next computed on both samples' scores. As Tables 13.3 and 13.4 show, subscale reliabilities ranged from 0.80 to 0.87 in the calibration sample and from 0.81 to 0.88 in the validation sample. Thus, the now 39-item RPPE measuring eight components of the professional practice environment was judged sufficiently reliable and valid for use as independent measures in subsequent research. In addition, these findings demonstrate that the RPPE is psychometrically equivalent to its predecessor, the PPE Scale (Buchanan et al., 2005).

Scoring takes place as follows:

- **Mean conflict management subscale:**
  Add items 20, 21, 22, 23, 24, 25, 26, 27 and 28 and divide by 9

- **Mean internal work motivation subscale:**
  Add items 29, 30, 31, 32, 33, 34, 35, and 36 and divide by 8

- **Mean control over practice subscale:**
  Add items 5, 6, 7, 9, and 10 and divide by 5

- **Mean leadership & autonomy in clinical practice subscale:**
  Add items 1, 2, 3, 8, and 11 and divide by 5

- **Mean clinician-physician relationships subscale:**
  Add items 4 and 12 and divide by 2

- **Mean teamwork subscale:**
  Add items 16, 17, 18, and 19 and divide by 4

- **Mean cultural sensitivity subscale:**
  Add items 37, 38, and 39 and divide by 3

- **Mean communication about patients subscale:**
  Add items 13, 14, and 15 together and divide by 3

Development and Psychometric Evaluation of the Chinese PPE (CPPE) in Taiwan

In response to the nurses in Taiwan's need to evaluate changes in the health care system potentially compromising the delivery of safe, timely, and effective care for patients, Chang (2009) began the development of a Chinese version of the original PPE. To answer questions about the nursing work environment, Chang found that instruments to measure nurses' work were not currently available.

The few measures that were available, such as the NWI, the PES-NWI, and the PPE, were rooted in English-speaking countries and had not yet been translated into Chinese. A culturally sensitive instrument that employs the Chinese language was needed to evaluate Taiwanese nurses' practice environments and to link organizational research to outcomes research.

The purposes of Chang's methodological dissertation research were to:

- Translate the PPE Scale from English to Mandarin Chinese

- Evaluate the equivalencies across the translated Chinese version of the PPE Scale (CPPE) with the English version of the PPE Scale

- Adapt the CPPE Scale as needed to produce a culturally sensitive instrument

- Evaluate the psychometric properties of the CPPE Scale in Taiwanese nurses working in acute care settings

- Determine the extent to which selected demographics explain Taiwanese nurses' perceptions of their professional practice environment

In phase I of the study, the 38-item PPE was translated into Mandarin Chinese and evaluated for semantic and content equivalence. As a result of this examination, 10 Taiwanese validation experts suggested that the CPPE have additional items focusing on professional development to increase the cultural sensitivity and comprehensiveness of the measure. An additional 27 items were developed and added to the CPPE, increasing its length to 66 items (Bracken, & Barona, 1991; Marin & Marin, 1991). The CPPE's content equivalence was supported by satisfactory content validity indices.

Phase II consisted of a psychometric evaluation of the CPPE. A cross-sectional survey of 977 Taiwanese nurses working in acute care settings completed the CPPE. A PCA with Varimax rotation and Kaiser normalization was then undertaken on the original 38 PPE items, demonstrating an eight-component solution for 36 of the 38 CPPE items. The Cronbach's alpha coefficient was 0.90 for the total 36-item CPPE and ranged from 0.68 to 0.87 for the eight subscales.

A PCA with Varimax rotation and Kaiser normalization was then run on the 66-item CPPE, producing an 11-component solution for 58 of the 66-item CPPE. The Cronbach's alpha was 0.95 for the total 58-item CPPE and 0.71 to 0.87 for the 11 subscales. Both the 36-item CPPE and the 58-item CPPE demonstrated satisfactory test-retest reliability and concurrent validity.

The psychometric structures of the 36-item CPPE and the 58-item CPPE were different from the original PPE. Both measures were judged to be reliable and valid, but the 58-item CPPE was considered more culturally sensitive to the Taiwanese nurses. The 58-item CPPE was judged useful for measuring the Taiwanese nursing practice environment.

NOTE

For an in-depth discussion of the development and psychometric evaluation with accompanying tables, see Chang's dissertation (2009).

2011 Staff Perceptions of the Chinese Professional Practice Environment

The 2011 study population for the Chinese PPE study consisted of 941 Chinese nurses who provided direct care to patients. Table 13.5 provides response rates by setting. After a back-translation of the English RPPE into Mandarin Chinese, this paper-and-pencil survey was independently administered, and data collection occurred in September 2011. The surveys were sent to research staff in the MGH Yvonne L. Munn Center for Nursing Research, where they were manually entered into SPSS, version 19.0. After data entry was completed, data analysis was undertaken by a senior nurse scientist in the Center. It should be noted that no construct validity analyses have been undertaken using this Chinese version of the RPPE.

TABLE 13.5: Population Size by Chinese Setting

SETTING	FREQUENCY	PERCENT
Dong Yuan	133	14.1
Surgical	134	14.2
ICU/Outpatient	121	12.9
Neurology	131	13.9
Hua Shan	64	6.8
Internal Medicine	119	12.6
Geriatrics	74	7.9
Jang Su Road	74	7.9
Operating Room	49	5.2
RNs with Less than Diploma Education	42	4.5
TOTAL	941	100.0

Demographic and Work Characteristics

Almost all Chinese RN survey respondents were female (99%) and married (55%). Their ages ranged from 21 to 67 years with a mean age of 30 +/–2 years. More than 82% reported their highest level of education was a diploma, with 17% holding a bachelor's degree and less than 1% having master's or doctoral degrees. Most respondents worked full-time (99%) on wards (55%), in intensive care units (16%), in operating rooms (8%), in emergency departments (6%). or in other settings (15%). Respondents had been in the nursing profession an average of 10 +/–8 years, worked in their institution 9 +/–7 years and worked on their current unit an average of 4.5 +/–4 years.

Internal Consistency Reliability of PPE—Chinese Version

The Cronbach's alpha internal consistency reliability scores for the eight Chinese PPE subscales are reflected in Table 13.6. They indicate that five of the eight PPE subscales are quite reliable. But three subscales displayed less than adequate internal consistency. The total Chinese RPPE score, however, indicated a very high Cronbach's alpha reliability coefficient. Thus, caution should be exercised in interpreting the Chinese PPE subscales with reliabilities below the 0.70 cutoff, namely the Clinician-physician relations, Communication about patients, and the Teamwork subscales.

TABLE 13.6: Internal Consistency Reliabilities of the Chinese RPPE (N = 941)

CHINESE RPPE SUBSCALE	NUMBER OF ITEMS	CRONBACH'S ALPHA
Autonomy and leadership	5	0.79
Clinician-physician relations	2	0.62
Control over practice	5	0.79
Communication about patients	3	0.21
Teamwork	4	0.57
Conflict management	8	0.80
Internal work motivation	8	0.91
Cultural sensitivity	3	0.82
Total RPPE score		0.95

Table 13.7 displays a comparison of PPE subscale and work satisfaction means and standard deviations between the 2011 Chinese RNs and the MGH RNs. Scores for both groups appeared comparable with only small differences noted. Chinese nurses had the same scores as MGH nurses on the PPE Autonomy & leadership subscale, slightly higher scores on Teamwork and Conflict management subscales, and slightly lower scores on the remaining PPE subscales and work satisfaction scores. Both groups' scores on all scales were fairly high, with all scores falling above the mean and median for that score.

TABLE 13.7: Comparison of the 2011 MGH & Chinese Nurses' PPE Means and Standard Deviations

PPE SUBSCALE	M	SD	MGH NURSES (N = 1481) M	CHINESE NURSES (N = 941) SD
Autonomy & leadership	2.8	0.6	2.8	0.5
Clinician/physician relations	3.0	0.6	2.9	0.6
Control over practice	3.0	0.6	2.8	0.5
Communication about patients	3.0	0.5	2.7	0.4
Teamwork	2.8	0.6	2.9	0.5
Conflict management	2.7	0.4	2.9	0.4
Internal work motivation	3.4	0.4	3.1	0.5
Cultural sensitivity	3.2	0.5	3.1	0.5
Work satisfaction	3.1	0.7	3.0	0.5

Validation of the Original PPE Scale in Australian General Practice

Halcomb, Davidson, Caldwell, Salamonson, and Rolley (2010) conducted a psychometric evaluation of the PPE in Australian general practice RNs. After slightly modifying several items to reflect the environment of general practice rather than acute care, the PPE was assessed for face validity by a group of nurse researchers and individuals with expertise in general practice nursing. They believed that these modifications would not change the intent of the instrument, only adapt it to suit the different environment (Halcomb et al., 2010).

The researchers then administered the adapted PPE online to 342 general practice nurses. The resulting data were then analyzed with SPSS, version 17.0, using PCA with Varimax rotation and Kaiser normalization. The eight-component solution accounted for 71.6% of the variance. Low component loadings (< 0.30) or cross-component loadings were detected in eight items. These items were removed from the PPE scale, reducing it to 30 items. Cronbach's alpha internal consistency reliabilities were then calculated on the resulting PCA-derived subscales and compared to the original 38-item PCA.

There was little change in the Cronbach's alpha coefficient values between the two measures. The 30-item PPE had Cronbach's alpha coefficients ranging from 0.71 to 0.89 for the subscales, and 0.94 for the total score. Halcomb and colleagues (2010) concluded, in their sample, that the 30-item version of the PPE was reliable and valid for use to assess the professional practice environment of nurses working in Australian general practice.

NOTE

See the Halcomb et al., 2010 study for in-depth information about their psychometric evaluation of the PPE.

Extant Research Using the PPE or RPPE

In addition to the previously reported research, several other research reports using the PPE or RPPE have been published in recent years. Because this chapter could not do justice to the reports, no attempt will be made to summarize them. The reader is encouraged to read these reports. They are as follows:

- Logan, J. (1994). *The relationship of decentralized organizational structure to perceived aspects of professional nursing practice environment.* (Doctoral dissertation). University of Ottawa (Canada).

- Charalambous, A., Katajisto, J., Välimäki, M., Leino-Kilpi, H., & Suhonen, R. (2010). Individualized care and the professional practice environment: Nurses' perceptions. *International Nursing Review*, 57(4): 500-507.

- Hawes, K. (2009). *Nurse job stress, burnout, practice environment and maternal satisfaction in the neonatal intensive care unit.* (Doctoral dissertation). University of Rhode Island.

- Breckenridge-Sproat, S. T. (2009). *Unit-level staffing, workload, and adverse events in Army acute care hospitals: 2003-2006.* (Doctoral dissertation). University of Maryland, Baltimore.

Furthermore, more than 96 individuals or clinical sites have requested to use the PPE or RPPE scales to support investigations of their professional practice environments and/or to provide data to support their application for Magnet Recognition (Ives Erickson, 2010). Figure 13.1 provides a graphic display of these sites, internationally.

In late 2010, a study was undertaken by e-mail to survey these individuals who requested to use the PPE or RPPE. Participants were asked to complete an evaluation questionnaire and to return it via e-mail to the researcher. Participants were also asked to provide the researcher with relevant documents that could help in better understanding the organization's use of the PPE or RPPE. The study is currently in the latter stages of analysis and findings will be reported in a future publication.

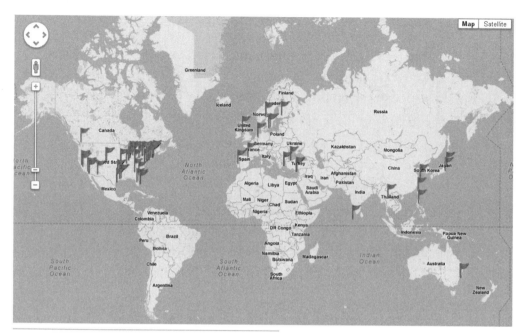

FIGURE 13.1

Location of sites using RPPE.

Summary

The PPE, RPPE, and their Chinese version counterparts continue to serve as an effective report card of the health of the professional practice environment. In addition, they are connected to a professional practice model that seeks to achieve these outcomes. This information is useful in helping nursing leadership design and/or improve the various components of an individual unit or department practice setting. Such evaluative feedback to leadership provides important information about whether or not changes have made a difference in practice.

For more than a decade, MGH patient care services leadership have used PPE and RPPE item and subscale score data in this way to provide valuable information describing effective professional practice environments. Currently,

RPPE data is linked to new initiatives, and changes in practice serve as evidence to support and/or refute leadership response to professional staff concerns.

Unit or department identifiers are available and associated with respondent data. RPPE mean scores can also be used at the unit or department level. However, we must keep in mind that moving from the individual to the unit or department level changes the unit of analysis, making the sample size much smaller, depending on the number of units or departments in the study.

For Magnet-recognized organizations or for organizations seeking Magnet recognition, the RPPE scale is an effective tool to measure baseline and ongoing reports of clinicians' impressions of their professional practice model, which are associated with the five model elements of Magnet recognition: namely, transformational leadership; structural empowerment; exemplary professional practice; new knowledge, innovations, and improvements; and empirical outcomes (American Nurses Credentialing Center [ANCC], 2008). Through annual administration of the RPPE, a greater understanding of organizational concepts that enhance clinical practice can be achieved.

The findings cited in this chapter indicate that the multidimensional PPE and RPPE are psychometrically sound measures of eight components of the professional practice environment in both acute and general practice settings. Both scales also demonstrate substantive coherence and application at both the individual and one or more organizational levels of analysis. As Ives Erickson so aptly stated:

> The increased complexity in health care delivery systems requires changes in the nursing work environment. Identifying approaches for accommodating the increased complexity is a key step in improving the quality of patient care as well as in retaining nurses in the workforce. Dysfunctional work environments have been demonstrated to be a significant contributor to dissatisfaction and turnover. Any issue that contributes to nurse dissatisfaction is particularly problematic at a time when a shortage in the supply of nurses makes retention so important. (Ives Erickson, 2010)

References

Aiken, L., Havens, D., & Sloane, D. (2000). The Magnet nursing services recognition program: A comparison of two groups of Magnet hospitals. *American Journal of Nursing, 100*(3), 26-36.

Aiken, L. H., & Patrician, P. A. (2000). Measuring organizational traits of hospitals: The Revised Nursing Work Index. *Nursing Research, 49*(3), 146-153.

Aiken, L. H., Sochalski, J., & Lake, E. T. (1997). Studying outcomes of organizational change in health services. *Medical Care, 35*(11), Supplement, NS6-NS18.

American Nurses Credentialing Center (ANCC). (2008). Magnet Recognition Program: *Application manual.* Silver Spring, MD: American Nurses Credentialing Center.

Baggs, J. G., Ryan, S. A., Phelps, C. E., Richeson, J. F., & Johnson, J. E. (1992). The association between interdisciplinary collaboration and patient outcomes in a medical intensive unit. *Heart and Lung, 21*(1), 18-24.

Bracken, B. A., & Barona, A. (1991). State of the art procedures for translating, validating and using psychoeducational tests in cross-cultural assessment. *School Psychology International, 12*(1-2), 118-119.

Buchanan, T., Ali, T., Heffernan, T. M., Ling, J., Parrott, A. C., Rodgers, J., & Scholey, A. B. (2005). Nonequivalence of on-line and paper-and-pencil psychological tests: The case of the Prospective Memory questionnaire. *Behavioral Research Methods, 37*(1), 148-154.

Chang, C. (2009). *Development and evaluation of psychometric properties of the Chinese Version of the professional practice environment scale in Taiwan* (Doctoral dissertation). Boston College, Chestnut Hill, MA.

Comrey, A. L. (1988). Factor-analytic methods of scale development in personality and clinical psychology. *Journal of Consulting & Clinical Psychology, 56*(5), 754-761.

The Cross Cultural Health Care Program. (2010). *Introduction to cultural competence.* Retrieved from http://www.xculture.org

Cudeck, R., & Browne, M. W. (1983). Cross-validation of covariance structures. *Multivariate Behavioral Research, 18*(2), 147-167.

Hackman, J., & Oldham, G. (1976). Motivation through the design of work: Test of a theory. *Organizational Behavior and Human Performance, 16*(2), 250-279.

Hackman, J., & Oldham, G. (1980). *Work redesign.* Reading, MA: Addison-Wesley.

Halcomb, E. J., Davidson, P. M., Caldwell, B., Salamonson, Y., & Rolley, J. X. (2010). Validation of the Professional Practice Environment Scale in Australia general practice. *Journal of Nursing Scholarship, 42*(2), 207-213.

Institute of Medicine (IOM). (2001). *Crossing the quality chasm: A new health system for the 21st century.* Washington, DC: National Academy Press.

Ives Erickson, J. (2000). Keeping in touch with staff perceptions of the professional practice environment. *Caring Headlines, 2.*

Ives Erickson, J. (2010). *Nurses' perception of the professional practice environment across health care settings.* Boston, MA: MGH Institute of the Health Care Professionals. DNP Capstone Project.

Ives Erickson, J., Duffy, M. E., Gibbons, M. P., Fitzmaurice, J., Ditomassi, M., & Jones D. (2004). Development and psychometric evaluation of the Professional Practice Environment (PPE) Scale. *Journal of Nursing Scholarship, 36*(3), 279-285.

Ives Erickson, J., & Ditomassi, M. (2011). Professional Practice Model: Strategies for translating models into practice. *Nursing Clinics of North America, 46*(1), 35-44.

Ives Erickson, J., Duffy, M. E., Ditomassi, M., & Jones, D. (2009). Psychometric evaluation of the Revised Professional Practice Environment (RPPE) scale. *Journal of Nursing Administration, 39*(5), 236-243.

Kramer, M., & Hafner, L. P. (1989). Shared values: Impact on nurse job satisfaction and perceived productivity. *Nursing Research, 38*(3), 172-177.

Lake, E. T. (2002). Development of the Practice Environment Scale of the Nursing Work Index. *Research in Nursing and Health, 25*(3), 176-188.

Lake, E. T. (2007). The nursing practice environment: Measurement and evidence. *Medical Care Research Review, 64*(104), 1048-1228.

Li, F., Harmer, P., Duncan, T. E., Duncan, S. C., Acock, A., & Yamamoto, T. (1998). Confirmatory factor analyses of the Task and Ego Orientation in Sports Questionnaire with cross-validation. *Research Quarterly in Exercise Sports, 69*(3), 276-283.

Marin, G., & Marin, B. V. (1991). *Research with Hispanic populations*. Newbury Park, CA: Sage.

McClure, M., Poulin, M., Sovie, M. D., & Wandelt, M. A. (1983). *Magnet hospitals: Attraction and retention of professional nurses*. Kansas City, MO: American Nurses Association.

Shortell, S. M., Rousseau, D. M., Gillies, R. R., Devers, K. J., & Simons, T. L. (1991). Organizational assessment in intensive care units (ICUs): Construct development, reliability and validity of the ICU nurse-physician questionnaire. *Medical Care, 29*(8), 709-723.

Tabachnick, B. G., & Fidell, L. S. (2007). *Using multivariate statistics* (5th ed.). New York, NY: Harper Collins College Publishers.

Warshawsky, N., & Havens, D. (2011). Global use of the Practice Environment Scale of the Nursing Work Index. *Nursing Research, 60*(1), 17-31.

Zimmerman, J. E., Shortell, S. M., Rousseau, D. M., Duffy, J., Gillies, R. R., Knaus, W. A., ... Draper, E. A. (1993). Improving intensive care: Observations based on organizational case studies in nine intensive care units. *Critical Care Medicine, 21*(10), 1443-1551.

Chapter 14

International Nursing Leadership: Impact at the Bedside

Elizabeth J. Brown, RN, MSN, MBA
Kathleen B. Scoble, EdD, RN

Practice settings worldwide are achieving advancements in nursing leadership capacity through multiple strategies and channels that leverage international best practice and customize to the local environment.

–Elizabeth Brown and Kathleen Scoble

Introduction

In this chapter, we consider nursing regulation, nursing education, and the practice environment as three broad structures in international nursing where nursing leadership converges to impact care at the bedside. Though we recognize other critical forces are in play, these particular structures are in various stages of development across global settings and provide the context for selected case studies illustrating the potential in advancing international nursing leadership and collaboration. The summaries of international nursing regulation, education, and practice environments we include here are brief but poignant and are provided for the purpose of triggering continued thinking, conversation, and action towards a new vision for global nursing. We have worked in international nursing for more than a decade, and our collective experience and insights will be evident in the discussions.

Nursing Leadership at the Global Level

"While change and chaos whirl about us, one thing agreed upon across borders and nations is the need for skilled leaders, adept at leading increasingly diverse teams in uncertain times and situations," said Judith Oulton, Chief Executive Officer, International Council of Nurses (ICN) (Shaw, 2007, p. ix).

Nursing leadership has the capacity and potential to impact health care systems and the practice setting on a global level. Current and future challenges in health care and within professional nursing are demanding that nurses internationally develop the needed leadership skills to facilitate professional accountability, expand educational innovation to influence future generations of nurses, and strengthen workforce and practice environments to improve patient care. In the face of multiple and complex challenges, nurse leaders from around the world are being called upon to lead and manage effectively, influence the changes, build the connections, and drive the improvements in and across systems to support care at the bedside, in the home, and in the community.

The challenges that confront global nurse leaders are immense. Nursing regulatory frameworks continue to impact nursing's scope of practice, accountability, and licensing standards. Nurse leaders face a number of challenges today, and this is only the short list:

- Multiple pathways for education

- Staggering shortages of nurses and other health professionals

- Migration of nurses across borders

- Work environments fraught with issues of pay, turnover, physician relationships, and limited advancement opportunities

- Gaps in expertise to advance the nursing evidence base

- Demographic and disease profiles that increase demand and complexity of health services

- Pressures associated with cost reduction (Mattison, 2007; Nichols, Davis & Richardson, 2011; Zittel et al., 2011)

Though not all countries are facing all of these issues, and unique conditions within countries and regions are influencing nursing's development, we still find many commonalties to understand and learn from (Dickenson-Hazard, 2004). Findings from the Sigma Theta Tau International (STTI) Arista conferences for envisioning nursing's preferred future identified common priority areas to address: (a) environments in which nurses practice; (b) nursing leadership; (c) essential nursing knowledge for all; (d) attention on settings in which nurses work; (e) conditions under which the profession operates; (f) the influence of nurses; and (g) the ways nurses learn (Dickenson-Hazard, 2004). To achieve sustainable impact in each of these areas requires nursing leadership at the global, regional, national, and local level. This challenge is not a unique one for nurse leaders internationally striving to elevate the profession. Dileep Kumar, President of the Indian Nursing Council, stated in a national health commission report:

> There are an inadequate number of nurse and midwife leaders at the national and state levels for nursing practice, research, education, management, planning, and policy development. Although the nurse is a member of the health team, she/he is never asked to represent the profession in planning and policy formulation for nursing services, education, etc. ... (Kumar, 2005, pg. 177).

Not only are local solutions required to advance nursing leadership, but also given the shared challenges among all nurse leaders, we see the potential for international collaboration among nurses around the world. Achieving this goal would enable development of best practice and innovative solutions to areas of great importance that impact nursing's future worldwide.

Nursing Regulation: International Leadership and Professional Self-Governance

The regulation of nursing around the world plays a pivotal role in high-quality nursing practice and patient-centric care. Professional nursing regulation is a central component in achieving health and well-being across communities and in assuring the consistent practice of the nursing profession (ICN, 2009). Creating regulatory and professional standard compliance mechanisms is one of the strategic action areas for achieving nursing's preferred future and promoting healthy communities worldwide (Dickinson-Hazard, 2004). The term *regulation* encompasses numerous processes, legitimate and appropriate, where order, consistency, identity, and control are brought to the nursing profession. The scope of nursing practice, standards of nursing education, ethical and competent dimensions of practice, and systems of accountability are defined and established through regulatory means.

Furthermore, the language of regulation encompasses credentialing processes, including registration, licensure, qualification, accreditation, certification, and endorsement (ICN, 1997). Thus, the potential and significance of nursing regulation in impacting care at the bedside cannot be minimized. Yet, worldwide, the regulation of nurses is highly diverse and varies considerably in scope and complexity (Nichols, Davis & Richardson, 2011). Many countries have had statutory nursing regulation to ensure a safe and competent nursing workforce for years. However, many other countries lack nursing regulations, rules, or other governmental, regulatory mechanisms (Nichols, Davis & Richardson, 2011). In addition, other countries provide for nursing regulation but for various reasons lack the mechanisms to establish a legal framework for nursing as an autonomous regulated profession (ICN, 2009).

Though these examples provide a broad summary of the status of nursing regulation globally, the discussions, opinions, and perceptions around issues of development and advancement of nurse regulation worldwide has been ongoing for decades. The ICN has long been recognized as a global advocate for nursing and health care and for the pivotal role it plays in promoting regulatory systems that engender strength, cohesion, and integrity within the nursing profession and its members (ICN, 1997). The activities and accomplishments of the ICN in promoting the status and advancement of nurse regulation is extensive, expansive, and best reviewed directly from relevant ICN resources (ICN, 2011b). However, as far back as 1995, ICN expressed its strong commitment to regulation as a "work in progress—always active, always up-to-date, always developing..." (ICN, 1997).

When we consider the progress and ever-developing status of international nursing regulation, a consistent and important theme centers on the responsibility of the profession to lead efforts in advancing professional governance. It could be argued that professional governance is the point at which nursing regulation begins. The ICN asserted in its established principles for developing effective professional regulation that:

> regulatory systems should recognize and properly incorporate the legitimate roles and responsibilities of interested parties—public, profession, government, employers, other professions—in aspects of standard setting and administration. (ICN, 1997, p. 23)

Commenting on the ICN principle of "multiple interest and responsibilities" in its parallel work in nursing regulation, the World Health Organization (WHO) was both direct and compelling by asserting:

> Professional self-regulation must be the responsibility of the profession concerned, both of its individual members and collectively.... It is for the profession to provide... the standards by which it will be measured and against which its members will be held accountable. Such standards should include those for education, conduct, service requirements, knowledge and skills and practice advances. (2002, p. 14)

Furthermore, the WHO's concluding statement strongly emphasized the profession assume leadership for self-regulation: "It is not for nursing to passively receive these standards as a result of decisions made on its behalf by others" (2002, p.14).

Organized and structured professional nursing organizations, associations, and councils are vehicles for self-regulation, providing a national professional voice for nurses and linkages for the concepts and processes of nursing regulation. In its conception, the Jordanian Nursing Council linked the relationship of nursing regulation to nursing care and professional self-regulation. Newly formed in 2002, the Jordanian Nursing Council recognized the need for implementing a national strategy for the development of nurses to improve nursing performance. Described as its "governing role," the Jordanian Nursing Council's national strategy involves developing regulation on standards of education, practice, specialization in nursing, and continuing education (Shuriquie, While & Fitzpatrick, 2007). The following case study describes how nurse leaders and key stakeholders in the United Arab Emirates developed the nursing and midwifery regulatory infrastructure to advance the nursing profession and patient care.

CASE STUDY: UNITED ARAB EMIRATES NURSING AND MIDWIFERY COUNCIL ESTABLISHED TO UNIFY STANDARDS FOR PRACTICE, EDUCATION, AND LICENSURE

Background on Nursing in the United Arab Emirates

The United Arab Emirates (UAE) is located in the southeast of the Arabian Peninsula in Western Asia on the Persian Gulf, bordering Oman and Saudi Arabia. It is a federation of seven independent city-states, or emirates: Abu Dhabi (the capital), Dubai, Sharjah, Umm al-Qaiwain, Fujairah, Ajman, and Ras al-Khaimah. Though this is a small country (about the size of the state of Maine), it has experienced tremendous growth over the past three decades. This growth has occurred among many changes, needs, and innovations that have increased demand for health care services and health care professionals.

The UAE has ambitious plans to build top-quality health care systems and services. Expert nursing and midwifery is essential to the realization of this vision. The UAE has urgency to establish an infrastructure that will promote the expansion of the nursing profession. Within the UAE the nurse-per-population ratio is relatively low; in fact the UAE's nurse density ratio is approximately half that found in the United Kingdom and in the United States.

Similar trends can also be used to describe midwifery density. UAE nursing and midwifery reflect a compilation of professionals from various backgrounds and countries with a wide range of qualifications. Emiratis are under-represented in the workforce, with only 3% of all nurses and midwives from its own country (UAE, Ministry of Health, 2009). Federal models do not yet exist to support the essential elements of the human capital plan for health outlined by the WHO.

It is widely believed that the overall health of a population is closely linked to the public's access to high-quality nursing and midwifery care. Nurses and midwives provide health promotion and prevention services, increasingly important in this era of chronic and communicable disease proliferation, and they are the largest group of health care providers in acute care settings.

Without well-prepared nurses and midwives, hospital quality and patient outcomes might suffer. Lacking expert caring professionals, individuals might have difficulty returning to their normal daily activities, causing productivity declines. Taken one by one, the cost of inadequate nursing and midwifery for individuals and families can be burdensome. Taking a national view of the UAE, an inadequate nursing and midwifery profession places the health of the entire population at risk, imposing high costs on national budgets for health care and lost productivity.

Over the last decade the nurse leaders of the UAE and the region have been collaborating to advance nursing and midwifery and to secure the profession's status as an essential component of the health care industry sector. Advocating for this position required vision, strategic thinking, positioning, stakeholder engagement, and, most importantly, persistence.

In 1993 the Federal Department of Nursing at the Ministry of Health assumed a leadership role in developing the nursing profession in the UAE. The department was instrumental in initiating and developing meaningful bases for nursing regulation, clinical practice, nursing human resources management, and continuing education.

Since 1996, the department worked diligently to support the development of a Nursing Practice Act (1996 draft). The department has managed to include the importance of nursing and midwifery professional regulations on the agenda of national, regional, and international forums and meetings, including the Cooperation Council of the Arab States of the Gulf Health Ministers' meetings.

This success has been influenced by the strong international collaborations with the World Health Organization (WHO) and nurse colleagues from the region. The first milestone for establishing a nursing and midwifery structure in the UAE was realized with the launching of the Emirates Nursing Association (ENA). The ENA, designed to be the professional organization representing nurses and midwives in the UAE, has made remarkable progress in creating a forum for nursing and midwifery issues and expanding the availability of continuing professional development programs. To supplement the work of the ENA, a plan was established to develop a nation-wide regulatory structure for nursing and midwifery. By 2008 the department and ENA began advocating for such a structure.

Developing a Nursing Regulatory Structure

With this national profile and the urgent demand for excellent nursing and midwifery, the nursing stakeholders formed a multi-disciplinary taskforce to study the situation and make recommendations for the UAE council structure. The work was supported by strong international collaborations with WHO and other global nursing councils. In March 2009 His Highness Sheikh Mohammed Bin Rashid Al Maktoum issued a cabinet decree establishing the UAE Nursing and Midwifery Council (NMC). The decision to establish the council reflects the government's dedication to further improve health care by investing in the unification of high-quality standards for nursing and midwifery.

The council's mandate is to "regulate and advance the nursing and midwifery professions and service and to promote the health and safety of the public based on the highest standards." The council has addressed this by unifying standards for nursing and midwifery with the ultimate goal of protecting the health of the public with consistently high-quality nursing and midwifery services. The council board consists of individuals who represent a broad range of key constituents, including the Ministries of Health, of Higher Education and Scientific Research, and of Education; UAE Nursing Colleges and Institutes; the ENA; Emirates Medical Association; Armed Forces Medical Corps; several health authorities; and representatives of the private health care sector. Her Royal Highness Princess Haya Bint Al Hussein, council president, has been a key driving force for the establishment of the council. Her commitment to improving access to high-quality health care across the UAE is expressed through her encouragement of the council and its members to identify sustainable solutions toward upgrading nursing and midwifery care by stating, "Our mission is to protect and promote the health of the people of the UAE by unifying standards for nursing and midwifery practice, education, and licensure."

Advancing the Mission of the Nursing and Midwifery Council

The council has established priorities and activities; set standards for practice, registration, licensure, and education; and prioritized the national nursing and midwifery research agenda. The council's work is organized by standing committees and task forces. Together, they address priorities identified in Table 14.1.

TABLE 14.1: UAE Council's Priorities for Nursing Policies and Standards

COUNCIL	POLICIES AND STANDARDS
Practice	Develops and issues unified scope of practice statements and standards for registered nurses, midwives, specialists, and advanced practice nurses, as well as for practical nurses and practical midwives. Scope of practice statements set the foundation for practice, education, and regulation of nursing and midwifery in the UAE to systematically advance the nursing profession across the country (UAE). Competence and specialization are key elements of the nursing and midwifery professional structure in the UAE, and through the council new roles in specialization are being coordinated.
Registration and Licensure	Develops and issues standards for registration and licensure for nurses, midwives, nurse specialists, and advanced practice nurses, as well as practical nurses and practical midwives. The aim is to have all nurses and midwives meet common standards across the UAE, replacing a currently fragmented model.
Nursing and Midwifery Education	Develops and issues a national plan for nursing and midwifery education to prioritize the investments and focus of nursing and midwifery programs, including standards that will apply to each program offered in the UAE. Working with the Ministry of Higher Education and Research, the council will assume program accreditation responsibilities to assure program integrity.

continues

TABLE 14.1: *continued*

COUNCIL	POLICIES AND STANDARDS
Nursing and Midwifery Emiratization	Places top priority on increasing the number of Emirati women and men practicing in and leading the professions. Through collaborative initiatives the council engages in community outreach, education, and workplace efforts to promote the selection of nursing and midwifery as career options and to support Emiratis to enhance retention.
Nursing and Midwifery Research	Established the UAE NMC Research Center for the purposes of building national capacity in research through research funding and skill building.

The council recognizes stakeholder engagement as key to the success of their work. The scientific committees include representation from all sectors, totaling more than 125 individuals actively engaged in designing and overseeing standards. The challenge is to embrace the many cultures that comprise the nursing and midwifery workforce in the UAE while considering the national context and needs of the UAE, make decisions that will benefit all organizations, and promote the health of the public. To accomplish this, standards are set in short-, mid-, and long-term timeframes for the ongoing advancement of the profession.

A key decision of the council is to establish entry level at the baccalaureate level. As a result all UAE nursing programs will begin with the baccalaureate preparation. New programs in specialization and advanced practice are being developed to address the burgeoning need for nursing expertise and leadership.

As an advocacy body, the council is working with government and private sectors to secure resources for the expansion of educational programs. The council intends to fulfill the role of establishing consistently high standards for practice, education, and licensure across the UAE and to operationalize accreditation structures to secure a permanent and lasting impact for the future.

[The authors acknowledge the leadership and contributions of Fatima Al Rifai, PhD, RN, UAE NMC Secretary, and Lauren Arnold, PhD, RN, nurse consultant, in the development of the UAE NMC and in the writing this case study.]

International Nursing Education: Towards a New Vision

Foundational to quality nursing practice is education. Internationally, achieving nursing education programs that prepare practice-ready nurses both now and for the future is a goal clearly influenced by regulatory and other forces. Though the landscape of international nursing education is fraught with internal and external issues, inspiring examples of pioneering innovations advance and transform nursing education to ensure global professionalism evidenced by quality care outcomes at the bedside and in specialty practice. We first provide a brief review of the challenges countries face in providing quality nursing education. The discussion to follow will highlight important concepts in the complex area of global nursing education. Advancements in higher education associated with entry into practice, development of global standards for nursing education, competency based and interprofessional education are presented as credible strategies needed to transform nursing education and continuing education. Role specialization and specialty practice to advance health care provide a context for the selected international nursing education case studies.

The ICN and the WHO Eastern Mediterranean Regional Office (2009) described the multiple and complex issues and challenges involved in closing a knowledge gap and achieving quality education of nurses within and across countries. Poorly funded nursing education programs, insufficient patient care equipment, growing staffing problems in facilities coping with an ever-increasing workload, and faster throughput of patients with higher levels of acuity and dependence are identified as factors limiting the capacity in care settings to meet educational needs of students. These factors are coupled with unprepared and insufficient numbers of faculty, inflexible nursing educational systems, and curricula broadly characterized as poorly designed and overloaded. Additionally, nursing education requirements around the world are very diverse and encompass preparation for entry into practice that includes multiple types and sizes of diploma and university-level programs and a wide diversity within these programs (Nichols et al., 2011).

Movement towards baccalaureate nursing education has a long history internationally. For example, in the Middle East and North Africa, higher education in nursing began in 1955 when the first higher institute of nursing in the region was established in the Faculty of Medicine of the Egyptian University of Alexandria (Frenk et al., 2010). The Philippines moved to baccalaureate entry into the profession in the mid-1980s (Nichols et al., 2011). In 1997, Aga Khan University in Karachi, Pakistan, introduced the first, generic Bachelor of Science in Nursing (BSN) program in Pakistan to provide generalist education for nursing at the university level (Upvall, Rehmatullah, Hashwani, Khan, Husain & Jan, 1999). In 2006, the Pakistan Nursing Council established a new, national generic nursing curriculum leading to a BSN for the country (Dias, Ajani & Mithani, 2010). Though these examples provide a few cases of international nursing education, they also illustrate the long-reaching history and movement of advancing higher education in nursing. Nichols et al (2011) report that in most cases, the rise of baccalaureate nursing programs represents a focused, often mandated policy agenda—without the complex history and challenges that has framed baccalaureate education in the United States (p. 568).

Historically, the development of global standards for nursing education has been identified as a goal for advancing nursing education and practice worldwide. Achieving global standards for nursing education is a vision of many nursing professionals and has been promoted by the ICN for over a century (Nichols et al., 2011). Proposed action advanced by the World Health Assembly in 2001 included the development of global standards for the initial education of nurses. This was followed in 2006 by the work of the WHO Task Force on Global Standards in Nursing and Midwifery Education and later in 2009 by the *Nursing and Midwifery Human Resource for Health: Global Standards for the Initial Education of Professional Nurses and Midwives* (WHO, 2009).

The goal of global standards is to establish educational criteria and ensure outcomes that (1) are based on evidence and competency; (2) promote the progressive nature of education and lifelong learning; and (3) ensure the employment of practitioners who are competent and who promote positive health outcomes in the populations they serve (WHO, 2009). The landmark *Lancet* report on transforming the education of health professionals to strengthen health systems in an interdependent world strongly urged that a new professionalism would emerge from a) using competencies based on objective criterion for the classification of health professionals and b) adopting a competency-based curricula to empower health professional schools with a curricula "responsive to rapidly changing needs rather than being dominated by static coursework" (Frenk et al., 2010, p. 1951).

The instructional reforms proposed in the 2011 *Lancet* report (Frenk et al., 2010) included the promotion of interprofessional and transprofessional education designed to break down professional silos and enhance collaborative and non-hierarchical relationships in effective teams. In proposing a framework for action on interprofessional education and collaborative practice, the WHO (2010) viewed both elements as playing a significant role in mitigating the many challenges faced by health systems around the world (p. 11). Collaborative interdisciplinary teams are believed to deliver better patient outcomes. For this to happen in the practice setting, health professional students must learn together in the academic setting (WHO, 2010). The advancement of baccalaureate nursing education, global standards for nursing education, and an approach to interprofessional education illustrated in the following case study provide a visionary college of nursing in India.

CASE STUDY: INDIA—FOCUSING ON THE FUTURE WITH A COMPETENCY-BASED BACHELOR OF SCIENCE IN NURSING CURRICULUM

India faces a profound shortage of nurses. The reported nurse-to-population ratio in India is 0.80 per 1,000. As a result less than one nurse is available per a population of 1,000 in the country (Gill, 2011; WHO, 2006). This number represents a staggering statistic, especially when you consider that India is described as "home to over one billion people, making it the second most populous country in the world" (Abraham, 2007, p. 9).

Among the many reasons cited as contributing to the nursing shortage in India are a) the disparities in health status driving increased need, particularly in states experiencing the lowest in health status; b) challenging working conditions, leading to migration of nurses from India; and c) low professional and educational opportunities (Gill, 2011). Within the government sector, these challenges are viewed as bringing a renewed opportunity to improve nursing education and its role in government health service delivery. A policy initiated in 2009 called The Development of Nursing Services is designed to significantly augment the numbers of qualified nurses in the government system through expanding numbers of nursing education and training institutes (Raha, Berman & Bhatnagar, 2009).

In a parallel situation, the country is placing a strong emphasis on improving and strengthening nursing education programs throughout India (Abraham, 2007; Gill, 2011; Raha et al., 2009). The linkage between quality nursing and health outcomes supports that nursing education is an essential element when tackling nursing workforce challenges. As reported, India is among those countries phasing out their non-baccalaureate nursing programs in a movement for higher education for nursing (Nichols et al., 2011). However, the significant gap in the number of nurses in India and the international trend to promote baccalaureate education for nurses suggests a significant need for an increased number of baccalaureate nursing programs throughout the country to improve care outcomes.

A group in northern India committed to expanding higher education in health sciences viewed the current situation in nursing as an opportunity to make significant progress to enhance national health care goals. They sought to accomplish this goal by preparing sufficient numbers of professional nurses—preparing them to deliver patient care in all settings and growing the ranks of qualified faculty, leaders, and researchers to influence the changes necessary to broadly impact health care and education in India.

To this end, a collaboration with Partners Harvard Medical International (PHMI), within the Partners Healthcare System, Boston, Massachusetts, began in 2010 to develop a College of Nursing with a visionary Bachelor of Science in Nursing (BSc.N) curriculum in India, followed by a College of Medicine and a College of Health Professionals. Planned as the first of these colleges to open, the College of Nursing was designed to pave the way for the future by implementing a contemporary curriculum and an interprofessional education framework. Within this context, the expected outcome for nursing graduates is that they will be prepared to practice as a generalist nurse in interprofessional teams across acute, chronic, and community health settings.

Core Health Professional and Nursing Competencies

The BSc.N curriculum integrates competency-based education, internationally recognized core competencies for health professionals, nursing-specific competencies, and the India Nursing Council (INC) regulatory standards and objectives for baccalaureate nursing curricula. The core competencies established for the BSc.N graduate nurse for inclusion in this curriculum are as follows:

- *Nursing knowledge*
- *Patient-centered care*
- *Care delivery across the continuum*
- *Professionalism*
- *Communication*
- *Teamwork and collaboration*
- *Leadership*
- *Technology and informatics*
- *Systems-based practice*
- *Quality improvement and safety*
- *Evidence-based practice*
- *Population health*
- *Professional scholarship*

The competencies were derived from the group's unique perspective on desired competencies for graduates and a broad range of nationally recognized guidelines and standards including:

- *The Essentials of Baccalaureate of Education for Professional Nursing Practice (American Association of Colleges of Nursing, 2008)*
- *The Institute of Medicine's Core Competencies for Health Professionals (IOM, 2003)*
- *The Bologna Accords (Davies, 2008; Zabalegui et al., 2006)*
- *The ICN Framework of Competencies for the Generalist Nurse (Alexander & Rinaman, 2003)*

- *The Competency Outcomes and Performance Assessment (COPA) Model (Lenburg, 1999)*
- *The National League for Nursing (NLN) Educational Competencies for Graduates of Associate Degree Nursing Programs (NLN, 2000)*
- *The Core Competencies for Interprofessional Collaborative Practice (Interprofessional Educational Collaborative Expert Panel, 2011)*
- *The Accreditation Council for Graduate Medical Education Core Competencies (Stewart, 2001)*

Providing a synthesis of these competencies and key resources was Massachusetts Department of Higher Education Nurse of the Future Core Competencies (2010).

Competency-Based Curriculum Development

Integration of the INC-based curricula standards with the competency set listed in the previous section helps to ensure that nursing graduates will acquire the essential knowledge, skills, and attitudes needed to achieve effective practice across settings. Each competency is levelled across the four years (level year 1 through 4) of the BSN curriculum, along with relevant course description and specific learning objectives. All courses in the curriculum meet INC standards, including course content, objectives, and prescribed hours, with additional learning objectives for each competency as appropriate to the course.

Global Nursing *provides an example of one course in Level 4 of the curriculum. Addressing the recommendation by nursing leaders for integration of global nursing into all nursing curricula (Nichols et al, 2011), this new course to the INC standard curriculum provides an innovative platform for the INC-required "research project." See Table 14.2.*

TABLE 14.2: Course Description: Global Health Nursing

This course is designed to provide students an overview of global health problems facing the world today to prepare them with knowledge to navigate the world of international health and provide a platform for the student research project. The course focuses on the global burden of disease, pattern of disease variations between and within countries, and cross-cutting issues such as poverty, environmental degradation, and the impact of globalization on health. Specific global health topics covered include maternal and child health; gender and violence; nutrition; water and sanitation; pandemics such as HIV, TB, avian flu, and malaria; as well as non-communicable diseases such as smoking, cancer, and mental health. The course will also introduce the student to the key players in global health and critical issues in global health governance that impact the implementation of international programs. Students will continue in their development of Level 4 competencies in nursing knowledge, care across the continuum, population health, professionalism, teamwork and collaboration, communication, quality improvement, evidence-based practice, systems-based practice leadership, and informatics and technology.

Research Project. In this course, the student will participate in a group to identify a research problem and conduct a research project (as specified by the INC standard BSc.N curriculum). Students will use global health issues as a research focus, apply the basic concepts of research, the research process, and statistics learned in Level 3 while conducting/participating in a selected research or quality improvement study.

Interprofessional Curriculum and Teaching

The nursing curriculum integrates a framework for interprofessional education (IPE) and learning opportunities where student nurses learn with other health professional students in selected courses within the integrated IPE Curriculum Plan, collaboratively developed by a team of nurses, physicians, and health professionals. The learning activities within the designated IPE courses are both competency-based and innovative for nursing education in India. The IPE simulation lab courses provide an excellent opportunity for interprofessional education and are included in each level of the curriculum. Each of these courses emphasizes the competency of teamwork and collaboration and uses a designated number of the INC clinical hours in a different and unique learning experience while meeting the course objectives. Participating with medical students and physician assistants allows students the opportunity to develop sophisticated communication and problem-solving skills. As an example, the course description for the first simulation lab in the nursing curriculum is provided in Table 14.3.

TABLE 14.3: Course Description: Simulation Laboratory I for Health Professionals: Introduction to Patient Problems

The simulation laboratory contains a total of 60 hours of lab for the first level nursing students with 3-4 hour labs/weekly for the 18 weeks of the semester. *Simulation Lab hours are a component of Nursing Foundations I Clinical/Lab Hours (Year 1, Semester 1) and Nursing Foundations II (Year 1, Semester 2). Medical and allied health students will be scheduled for this lab course in Year 1, Semester 2 of respective curriculums.*

Description: This interdisciplinary simulation lab course is designed to introduce the first-year health professional student to basic concepts of patient care; and to develop beginning (Level 1) competencies in nursing knowledge, teamwork and collaboration, patient-centered care, population health, communication, quality improvement, safety, and professionalism. The course uses *active learning* through simulation and *problem-based learning* methods designed to engage students from multiple health professions and promote the development of teamwork and collaboration. *Active learning* focuses on the student's individual responsibility to engage in learning new knowledge, acquisition and enhancement of skills, self-assessment in achieving competency, and the pursuit of higher levels of competency. *Problem-based learning* challenges students to learn through engagement in a real patient-care problems, which place students in an active professional role to develop both problem-solving strategies and discipline-specific knowledge bases and skills.

The IPE elements of the nursing curriculum will continue to develop as each new health professional program is implemented. Future faculty of each health professional program will collaborate on opportunities for IPE courses and learning across their curricula, which might include such courses as sociology, psychology, population health and epidemiology, health care ethics, leadership and management in health care, and research and statistics.

Innovative Teaching and Learning Methods

The nursing faculty of this future nursing college will use the established competency objectives to plan innovative learning experiences and assessment methods for evaluating the student's competency, in addition to the INC-required exams. The teaching and learning methods planned are contemporary and provide faculty with options for new ways of teaching and student learning.

Traditional methods such as lecture, large-group discussion, and demonstration will be used. Additionally, innovative methodologies have been incorporated into each course including:

- **Active and experiential teaching and learning:** Small-group learning using problem-based tutorials, case studies, and panel discussions; simulation in the skills lab, with role-playing and peer coaching; and observations and supervised clinical learning in patient care and community settings

- **Problem-based learning:** Use of real patient-care scenarios, teamwork on patient cases, and interprofessional collaboration

- **Discovery-based learning:** Use of technology to access online data and resources and web-based interactive technology

- **Self-directed learning:** Reflective papers, reflective discussion, and journaling

Table 14.4 provides an example of a teaching and learning plan for quality, patient safety, and evidence-based practice competencies focused on fall prevention.

TABLE 14.4: Fall Prevention: Competency-Based Teaching and Learning Plan

TEACHING METHOD	LEARNING ACTIVITIES
Student assignment	Research the best evidence in risk assessment and intervention for preventing and reducing patient falls in hospitals and develop plans around prevention, measurement, and quality improvement.
Skills lab	Students use role-playing exercises to demonstrate how to assist the patient and family to prevent falls and how to provide education on fall prevention.
Clinical setting	Students identify patients at high risk of fall and work together to lead a small-group discussion with clinical staff on hospital incidence of falls, best practice to reduce falls, and ways the hospital can measure fall rates.

continues

TABLE 14.4: *continued*

TEACHING METHOD	LEARNING ACTIVITIES
IPE seminar	Students develop a case study around the high risk for falls and present it for discussion with RNs and other clinical staff.

This case study as discussed provides an exemplar for the future and points to suggest how international collaboration will impact the development of a contemporary BSc.N. curriculum that focuses on integrating international competency standards for nursing and health professionals within an interprofessional education framework. It is with great enthusiasm that the international team continues its collaboration on evolving this visionary nursing program as it awaits all required regulatory approvals.

[The authors acknowledge the expertise of the Boston- and India-based collaborative interdisciplinary team members in designing this work, particularly PHMI staff members Tom Aretz, MD, and Elizabeth O'Connor; and faculty within the Partners Healthcare System, specifically the Provost, Alex Johnson, PhD, CCC-SLP, and the Dean of Nursing, Laurie Lauzon Clabo, PhD, RN, from the Massachusetts General Hospital Institute of Health Professions.]

Nursing Support for International Collaboration

The global nursing discipline contains strong support for international collaboration in nursing education. Sigma Theta Tau International (STTI), nursing's international honor society, is working to create a global community of nurses who lead in using knowledge, scholarship, service, and learning to improve the health of the world's people. Among STTI's many initiatives and accomplishments is the International Academic Nursing Alliance (IANA), a free, global, electronic community allowing nurse educators and clinicians to form alliances to advance scholarship, collaboration, exchanges, and the dissemination of nursing knowledge (Huston & Percival, 2009). Through this mechanism, nurses throughout the world are being called upon to share and learn from each other to further the development of nursing knowledge and to refine nursing practice (Sochan, 2008).

Continuing Education and International Learning

Continuing education for international nurses to support role development and specialty nursing practice following entry into practice provides numerous opportunities for international collaboration. Given the many complexities of the changing work environments, rapid advances in science and technology, and the expanding body of knowledge, organizations and countries worldwide have increased interest and investment in lifelong learning approaches to support nurses to advance in their role development and to specialize in roles much needed within their hospitals and practice environments.

The ICN (2011a) efforts continue to support positive practice environments for health professionals and have identified key factors in the workplace to strengthen and support nursing and in turn create a positive impact on patient outcomes and organizational cost-effectiveness. One of the factors constituting positive practice environments is the organization's support of opportunities for professional training, development, and career advancement. The following case study provides an exemplar for international collaboration in the continuing education of nurses.

CASE STUDY: THE INSTITUTE FOR NURSING HEALTHCARE LEADERSHIP (INHL)—INTERNATIONAL NURSING STUDIES PROGRAM

In its 12-year history, the INHL International Nursing Studies Program (Boston, Massachusetts) provides a remarkable example of advancing the education, role development, and role specialization of nurses from around the world. The international studies program represents INHL's key interest in impacting global nursing through continuing education and providing opportunities to learn from international nurse visitors.

Intensive, short-term study programs *have provided small groups of nurses— from a single or multiple countries—a topic-focused program with both didactic courses, group consultation with expert nurses, and tours of Harvard-affiliated hospitals.* Clinical observation study programs *have created an individually designed clinical observation within selected Harvard-affiliated care settings with three key features:*

1. *A specific specialty area of clinical practice*

2. *A leadership focus within the roles of clinical nurse, nurse manager, or nurse educator*

3. *A professional project*

The professional project requirement was designed to assist nurses in applying new knowledge gained through this learning experience to benefit nursing and patient care within the home hospital or practice environment. On application, nurses were asked to identify how the requested clinical observation would assist the applicant in accomplishing a professional goal or project. During the program, visiting nurses were guided by their appointed nurse preceptors from the clinical observation sites and INHL staff to develop a project description with an expected outcomes implementation plan and evaluation methods.

From 1999–2011 the INHL provided over 130 uniquely designed international nursing programs for approximately 195 international nurses from 16 countries throughout Asia, Europe, North America, and the Middle East. Among these were 11 different study groups of 4–15 nurses each who were typically provided with a five-day course focused on their defined learning objectives.

For example, in 2001, the University of Gronigen of the Netherlands sponsored a group of four nurse leaders in two study groups session (Boston-based and satellite teleconference) on developing and maintaining a professional nursing practice environment. A group from University Hospital Birmingham, United Kingdom, sponsored a nursing leadership group involved in the planning of a new critical-care unit to learn about the relationship of facility design and models of care delivery in this specialized care environment. In 2006, the Korean Hospital Nurses Association sponsored six nursing leaders in a study group focused on nursing leadership and management. Also in 2006, the China Nursing Academy sponsored nine hospital and college of nursing leaders from throughout China for a seven-day program, Strengthening Nursing in China for the 21st Century: Merging Nursing Education and Clinical Practice.

Clinical observation programs within INHL clinical observation programs proved to be highly sought after by international nurses from around the world. Over 80% (106) of the INHL international studies programs were short-term, clinical observation. In these programs, each nurse received a guided and focused observation experience in a range of two to four different settings with their area of specialty throughout the Harvard-affiliated organizations. The impressive number of international nurses who increased their knowledge and practice through these observational experiences span care settings and specialties across the continuum of inpatient, ambulatory, rehabilitative, and home care. A few notable examples are provided from Korea and Singapore, which together represented the countries who sponsored the highest numbers of nurses.

Clinical Observation Exemplar

Over a decade beginning in 2000, Asan Medical Center in Seoul, South Korea, sponsored a total of 35 nurses in 32 different clinical observation programs for numerous specialty nursing practice areas of focus, with a dominant focus in endocrinology, neonatology, pediatrics, oncology (pediatric and adult), and critical-care nursing. Over the same decade, six different hospitals and a university in Singapore sponsored a total of 40 nurses in individual clinical observation programs also focused on advancement of specialty nursing practice. More than one third of the Singapore nursing programs focused on the role and practice of nurses within the perioperative setting, including pre-surgery, the operating room, and post-care (PACU).

Many projects planned by these nurses during their clinical observation experiences initiated advancements in specialty practice and role development in their home hospitals. For example, nurses from Asan Medical Center in their experience over the different years and programs initiated the development of roles for diabetic nurse educators and specialized clinical roles in neonatal and critical-care nursing. Nurses from Acibadem Health Care Group in Istanbul, Turkey, developed roles for the oncology nurse clinician and nurse educator. Between 2006 and 2007, 14 nurses from Thailand collectively focused on developing competencies and educational structures in oncology and neuroscience nursing, improving safety and efficiency in the peri-operative area, piloting new roles in case management to improve continuity of care across settings, and developing a professional practice model. The nursing services in the hospitals in Turkey, South Korea, and Thailand all hosted local nursing conferences in which Boston-based nurses participated.

The excellent work of the INHL in developing and implementing these programs was accomplished through strong collaboration across the Harvard-affiliated nursing services. Together, the opportunities inherent in international collaboration for continued education and role development were demonstrated.

[Joyce C. Clifford, PhD, RN, FAAN, established the INHL in 1999 after serving for more than 25 years as Senior Vice President and Nurse-in-Chief at Beth Israel Deaconess Medical Center in Boston, Massachusetts. The INHL provided the Harvard-affiliated nursing community with a common platform for cross-institutional collaboration as the Consortium of Harvard-affiliated Nursing Services while serving its mission to increase nursing's participation in health service leadership through interprofessional collaboration, leadership development, and scholarly work. The INHL Consortium included Beth Israel Deaconess Medical Center, Brigham and Women's Hospital, Cambridge Health Alliance, Boston Children's Hospital, Dana-Farber Cancer Institute, the Massachusetts General Hospital, and the Spaulding Rehabilitation Hospital. Under the internationally renowned leadership of Dr. Clifford (President and CEO, 1999–2011) and the Chief Nursing Officers of the hospitals, the members of the INHL Consortium served as key advisors in shaping the direction, priorities, and programs of the INHL. With the untimely passing of Dr. Clifford in October, 2011, the Institute for Nursing Healthcare Leadership discontinued operations effective March, 2012. The international collaborative efforts continue in and across each of the member hospitals. The authors acknowledge the expertise of the nurses in these hospitals for their key role in these collaborations and the program manager, Karen Poznick, for her dedication.]

International Leadership and the Practice Environment

Nursing leadership is critical to supporting the improvements in the practice environment across all settings, whether in a rural health clinic in India, a new oncology center in Turkey, or a tertiary academic medical center in the United States. Through their impactful role, nurse leaders are a key connector between the practice setting and the health care system at large. Their efforts are essential to driving a quality and safety agenda throughout organizational and health care systems. Surakka (2008) reviewed the evolving role of nurse managers internationally and found that globally the nurse leader role has more similarities than differences.

To be effective in their role, nurse leaders must have the capacity to lead and manage. Globally, the development of nurse leader capacity is in an evolving state. Within this discussion of international nursing leadership in the practice setting, we present a brief yet relevant examination of expectations for nurse leaders, which converge with many challenges confronting their development, and strategies for nursing leadership advancement. We provide a case study to reflect one health care system that strategically built a nursing leadership development program as a foundation for improving care across the system and a launching point to develop the multilevel infrastructure to improve quality, education, and practice. The Magnet Recognition Program (American Nurses Credentialing Center [ANCC], 2008) acknowledges that one of the driving forces in achieving professional nursing practice excellence and superior patient outcomes is the significant role that nursing leadership plays at the executive level and throughout each practice setting. Sherman and Pross (2010) discussed the connection between nurse leaders and sustaining a healthy work environment, noting "the presence of expert, competent, credible, visible leadership" to a healthy work environment.

As the focus on healthy work environments gains more attention nationally, it is growing internationally. In a study of work environments in nine countries, findings revealed that despite differences in cultures and health care systems in virtually all of these countries, hospitals with consistently better work environments had lower burnout, had lower likelihood of having nurses who were dissatisfied with their jobs and thought the quality of care on their unit was only fair, and had a higher likelihood of having nurses report that their patients were ready for discharge (Aiken et al., 2011). Among the recommendations for health leaders and policymakers that came out of that study was to safeguard the nurse workforce and improve quality and safety of care, improve staffing, enhance better nurse and physician relations, increase the involvement of nurses in hospital decisions, and improve managerial support for direct care providers at the bedside (Aiken et al., 2011).

Nurse leaders—with titles such as matron, nurse director, chief nurse, nurse supervisor, nurse manager, charge nurse, clinical nurse manager, ward sister, and others in nursing leadership roles internationally—are often referred to as the link between the frontline care givers and the rest of the hospital or health care system. They are pivotal in linking the overall vision and strategy with the clinical practice at the unit level (Sherman, Eggenberger, Bishop & Karden, 2007, p. 93).

Thus, the importance of managing and connecting the macro and micro systems is essential in a nurse leader's role. This connector, or linking aspect, goes beyond communication and sharing information and requires building relationships, messaging effectively, assisting staff in understanding the relationship between goals and work, and considering impact of decisions on micro or macro system (Sherman et al., 2007). These skills and abilities are crucial for effective nursing management.

In a survey of nurse leaders in public and private health care settings within South Africa, findings indicated that "controlling," "people management," and "self-management" were considered the most valuable skills for effective and efficient nursing management. People management skills included being able to motivate employees, work with others from diverse backgrounds, be a team player, delegate and share knowledge, and resolve conflicts (Pillay, 2010, p. 550).

Nurse Leaders Advancing Quality and Safety

Recognizing international nurse leaders' contributions to driving the quality and safety agenda is increasingly needed. In the United States, effective nursing leadership is often tied to the national patient safety agenda (Wendler, Olson-Siticki & Prater, 2009), and increasingly this connection is expected globally. A recent example is provided in the 2010 seminal report, *Front Line Care: The Future of Nursing and Midwifery in England* by the Prime Minister's Commission on the Future of Nursing and Midwifery in England (2010), which highlights the robust benefits of effective nurse leaders and improved outcomes of nurse-led units (p. 84). In its recommendation for strengthening the role of the ward sister, the commission stated, "...to drive quality and safety and provide visible, authoritative leadership and reassurance for service users and staff, immediate steps must be taken to strengthen the linchpin role of the ward sister, charge nurse, and equivalent team leader in midwifery and community setting" (p. 7).

As the development of hospital accreditation matures worldwide, the expectation for nurse managers to successfully lead this process grows. Though developed nations have a long track record of accrediting bodies assessing structures, processes, and outcomes of care across practice settings, it is only over the past two decades that we have seen a more purposeful movement for accreditation of health care facilities in developing countries. In 2001 the International Society for Quality in Health Care (ISQua) developed a toolkit for accreditation internationally for the World Bank. At that time the clear and rapid growth worldwide of hospital accreditation was noted, expanding from one country in 1951 (United States) to more than 30 countries in 2001 (Shaw, 2001). Since then more countries have developed an accreditation program. For example, in India the National Accreditation Board for Hospitals and Healthcare Providers (NABH) was developed by the Quality Council of India in approximately 2005.

Though more industrialized nations have been collecting and analyzing data related to quality in hospitals for many decades, only recently have developing nations begun to understand the scope of adverse events in health care settings and the need to develop strategies to enhance care and improve safety. For nurse leaders to actively engage in this critical work, they must have access to relevant data and be competent in interpreting, synthesizing, and presenting data to various stakeholders. In addition nurse leaders are expected to prepare their staff to actively engage in organization-wide quality improvement efforts and strengthen their influence and participation in improvement efforts (Albanese et al., 2010). Whether it is facilitating unit-based teams to improve patient safety with targeted improvement projects, partnering with physicians to review outcomes of care, or leading an accreditation effort, nurse leaders internationally are being called upon to develop new quantitative and qualitative skill sets to enhance the role they play as leaders in quality and safety advances.

Developing Global Nurse Leaders

A wide range of leadership and management skills and behaviors is critical to assuring safe, efficient, patient-centered care. Critical considerations must also be given to the nurse manager's role development and their capacity to serve as leadership mentors to develop others. Given the shortages of current leaders and potentially inadequate human, technical, and financial resources, the question heard repeatedly in international forums and discussions is "how?" Speaking on leadership in a global world, Dr. Karen Morin (2011), then President of STTI, highlighted the acute need to develop global leaders (in nursing) and that in meeting with nurses around the world she is asked over and over, "How do we help prepare our leaders?" (Morin, 2011).

Although the need for leadership and management preparation is acknowledged, the advancement or promotion of nurses into management roles without preparation is a common scenario around the world. It is not unusual for the expert clinician to become a management novice by being placed into a nursing leadership role with little development. This topic was explored in New Zealand with findings that suggested when nurses were advanced to management roles without adequate preparation they encountered role ambiguity, role overload, and an awareness of deficits in managerial skills expected (McCallin & Frankson, 2010). Several strategies for a progressive investment in leadership development have been proposed as having a positive benefit to both the nurse and the organization, including a robust succession planning process to identify future nurse leaders; requiring postgraduate management education prior to taking a position; and ongoing, accessible leadership support through in-house organizational management training and mentorship (McCallin & Frankson, 2010).

Access to postgraduate and continuing professional development opportunities is often challenging for nurse leaders internationally. Though more programs exist, variations in achieving success in competently leading and managing complex health environments globally do exist. When describing the evolution of nursing roles in South Africa, Pillay (2010) underscores the importance of defining a competency model for nurse managers to both strengthen practice and provide a framework for development and learning. In moving from a stereotypical "autocratic matron" to a pivotal position in and across health care settings, nurse managers in South Africa are now required to combine leadership, entrepreneurial, and administrative skills (Pillay, 2010, p. 545). Data from a recent survey reported that South African nurses in management roles in both public and private health care settings noted that a successful nurse manager was one who could integrate a nursing background with management. An overwhelming majority of survey respondents further stated that training was needed to understand management principles and for mentoring and coaching (Pillay, 2010).

The question many struggle with is how to effectively approach "further training," recognizing that straight didactic courses and "sink or swim" on-the-job training either miss the mark in achieving managerial role development or cause incredible anxiety. Building system-wide nursing leadership capacity through the development of an evidence-based leadership program should be aligned with, and customized to, contemporary and unique nurse manager needs (Fennimore & Wolf, 2010). Many established models are available through international nursing organizations. Though not an exhaustive list, a selection of resources includes competency models from the American Association of Critical-Care Nurses in collaboration with the Association of Operating Room Nurses, the American Organization of Nurse Executives, and National Center for Healthcare Leadership.

Leadership Development Programs

The methods deployed for leadership development programs are as critical as the competencies identified; they must go hand in hand. Combining the leadership program with experiential learning and projects contributes to advancing strategic goals, changing behavior, and achieving desired outcomes. The power of experiential learning was described as a critical success factor in nurse manager development at the Brigham and Women's Hospital in Boston. This nurse manager development program used competency models as a framework for measuring outcomes of the role and included in orientation and continuing education programs. In addition the organization noted the significance of experiential learning with the use of reflection and narratives as critical for mastering complex leadership challenges (Cathcart, Greenspan & Quin, 2010).

Another project found a theoretical empowerment framework with practical leadership projects and practice issues to be a successful approach for a year-long Nursing Leadership Institute Program in Canada, resulting in positive, sustainable outcomes for nurse leaders and their staff (MacPhee, Skelton-Green, Bouthillette & Suryaprakash, 2011). Empowerment, or a lack of empowerment, is a key theme heard in nursing leadership development globally, and, therefore, approaches that build nurse leader empowerment need to be considered for broader international application.

Practice settings worldwide are achieving advancements in nursing leadership capacity through multiple strategies and channels that leverage international best practice and customize to the local environment. Yet clearly no one solution or strategy fits all, especially considering the local context such as culture, opportunities, challenges, and resources. Many groups have found great benefit in international collaborations as evidenced by the STTI Leadership Institute and the ICN Global Nursing Leadership Institutes. Though perhaps less published, many examples of successful international collaborations exist across nursing professional organizations, schools of nursing, and practice settings that speak to nursing's collective inspiration to advance the professional globally, one nurse at a time.

International Exemplar of a Leadership Development Program

A successful international collaboration model to advance a nursing leadership development agenda, articulating shared strategies and developmental goals is a "twinning model" as described between the Haushan Hospital (HH) in China and the Massachusetts General Hospital (MGH) in the United States. The twinning relationship fostered the implementation of mutual goals to advance leadership, knowledge-based practice, and a culture of quality and safety within a framework, or pillars, of practice, education, and research (Jiang, Ives

Erickson, Ditomassi & Adams, 2012). Twinning partnerships, with targeted leadership coach interventions and educational experiences, were able to identify, implement, and measure improvement initiatives across these pillars. While the teams reported quantitative improvement outcomes with selected initiatives including implementation in fall prevention measures, the qualitative results from narrative reflections from the "paired twins" offer important insights, such as this one from a MGH nursing director:

> This was an invaluable experience for the nurse leader. The twinning experience creates an ongoing relationship providing a wonderful opportunity to exchange knowledge, learn more about cultural influences and explore new ideas to ensure that our practice is always evolving and reflective of our patients and families. The twinning partnership enabled me to identify and develop contacts and networks for my HH twin, and that relationship certainly improved my professional perspective...while we think that we are so different...we easily identified many similarities about our expectations for nursing practice now and in the future.... (Jiang et al., 2012, p. 120)

As hospital and nursing school missions expand to include a global community and nurse leaders internationally develop "global competence," the opportunities for collaboration will continue to expand. Examples of successful international collaborations to advance nursing leadership capacity will only continue to increase and show tangible impact. The following case study is only one example illustrating the need for international nursing leadership development and the benefits of collaboration across disciplines and across countries.

CASE STUDY: NURSING LEADERSHIP DEVELOPMENT IN INDIA—A COLLABORATIVE MODEL TO BUILD CAPACITY AND SUSTAINABILITY

India has an acute shortage of nurses and nurse leaders. As the demand for more nurses increases, shortages are intensified as nurses migrate either domestically from rural to urban, or between private and public systems. Movement internationally has also occurred as India has become a source country for many emerging and developed economies.

The case study to follow describes a collaborative initiative between Wockhardt Hospital System (WHL), India, and Partners Harvard Medical International (PHMI), within the Partners Healthcare System, Boston, Massachusetts. Though WHL is headquartered in Mumbai, India, it is expanding health care delivery geographically and with new clinical programs. The hospital system's administrative, physician, and nursing leadership agreed that the areas of great challenge across care settings included a shortage of nurses and nurse leaders, a gap in leadership expertise of current and future leaders, and needed educational resources to close that gap.

Nursing colleagues in India and Boston strategized together to identify outcome-based, sustainable local solutions leveraging evidence and expertise brought from both teams. The strategic decision was made to pilot an innovative nursing leadership development program in 2007. A project team was formed with India and Boston colleagues, representing nursing, human resources/organizational development, quality management, and project management. The mindful partnering was not only critical to building knowledge across domain experts, but also to setting up the train-the-trainer component for success.

Project Scope

The project scope began as a 12–18 month Nursing Leadership Program (NLP) to include between 25–30 nurse leaders across the hospital system that would develop their leadership capacity through an integrative approach of leadership content in structured sessions applied to unit-based issues in a learning community. The goals were for nurse leaders to increase leadership/management capacity in their current role, prepare leaders to assume new positions and enhance purposeful succession planning, and jointly increase the training and education capabilities of a core group of local faculty to participate and eventually manage the nursing leadership program in the long term.

Baseline Assessment

A baseline assessment data used to drive program development revealed several issues. Nurse turnover was significant across the system, reaching a high of 35% in some institutions. Internal and external push for quality improvement, patient safety, and hospital accreditation requiring substantial involvement, confidence, and skill development of the nursing leadership team had increased. The highest percent of training costs was geared towards orienting new nurses, while very limited resources and expertise were geared for developing nurse managers and leaders. Hospital leadership recognized that a higher level of functioning of "sisters in charge" was required beyond task development, such as "managing the stores" (managing inventory), to leadership skills, such as managing performance in an increasingly complex environment. In terms of satisfaction with nurse leadership, the organizations had an overwhelming interest for professional development opportunities.

Response to the Assessment

Three key strategies resulted from analyzing the assessment findings. They included:

1. *Developing a strategic, visible goal, with system-wide support to leverage the role of nurse manager as critical to impacting nurse retention and driving strategic goals, quality improvement, and unit performance.*

2. *Designing a customized and comprehensive nursing leadership development program using evidence-based leadership competencies and action learning as a collaborative initiative between nursing, human resources, and quality expertise.*

3. *Harnessing external expertise judiciously for design, models, and train-the-trainer solutions to build internal capacity and program sustainability and to increase the likelihood of exposing the best practice against local realities.*

The start-up phase for a key strategic program such as this one is critical, especially across cultures, in order to understand the appropriate baseline data, clearly align expectations and expected outcomes, and plan program parameters to help ensure success in the program planning and implementation phases.

Core Program Elements

The goals of this nursing leadership program were mutually supporting a program geared towards developing a cohort of leaders and building sustainability for the WHL team to implement this program independently without international collaboration. The team worked diligently to be explicit in describing core program elements and in designing, implementing, and refining the program. Some of these elements are found in Table 14.5.

TABLE 14.5: International Leadership Program Core Elements

Sponsorship	Multidisciplinary executive sponsors that participated in program design, teaching, and project report-outs.
Competency based	Creation of localized, evidence-based competency model; starting point evidence-based model drawn from the Beth Israel Deaconess Medical Center Competency (BIDMC) Model created for their nurse leadership development program, Strategies for Accelerating Growth and Excellence (SAGE). Model then customized to local situation through research, surveys, focus groups and interviews, self-assessments, evaluation feedback, and stakeholder input.
Curriculum Design	A highly experiential curriculum grounded in theory: • *Maximize action, experiential learning that is project based:* Nurse leaders focused on improving care on their units and tied to practical organizational goals; nurses brought forward real cases they were dealing with in quality and patient safety. • *Experiential anchor:* Challenge-Assess-Support Leadership Development Model from the Center for Creative Leadership (McCauley, 2004) to foster realistic development through honest assessment, system support, and stretch assignments. • *Grounded in management/leadership theory:* Utilized theory, frameworks, and models to drive home competency and connection to practice, experiences, and learning. For example, Myers-Briggs Type Indicator (MBTI) in modules on Managing Self and Leading Teams; John Kotter's work on tasks of management versus task of leadership.

Teaching	Critical need for continual reinforcement of transition from "training" to "development" given the cultural context of India.
	• *Link to frameworks:* Utilize framework of novice to expert for evolution of development to move beyond current lens of "weakness" and provide a framework for assessing knowledge, skills, behaviors, and attitudes outlined in competency model.
	• *Interdisciplinary approach:* Expectation to lead interdisciplinary projects and use interdisciplinary faculty.
	• *Highly interactive:* Use of cases that were formally written, such as Harvard Business School and Massachusetts Institute of Technology Sloan School of Business and cases that were local scenarios; teaching style more facilitative than didactic with break-outs, role-plays, participant presentations, exercises, etc. Ice-breakers were noted to be highly effective in nursing context to build cross-departmental rapport and sense of confidence and engagement; micro teaching, small group teaching.
Measurement	Data measurement component: Team and individual, organically built, unit-based dashboards to measure and track nursing sensitive indicators for both project evaluation and measure of unit performance. This local, nurse-driven framework eventually migrated to hospital-wide quality dashboards.

continues

TABLE 14.5: *continued*

Evaluation	Focused efforts to develop more robust concept of evaluation:

- *Sustainability* on many levels: 1) unit-based: nurse managers had to foster/delegate "second in command" to leave unit for program elements, very big cultural change to relinquish control; 2) expectation to develop other staff to assume leadership positions; 3) expectation to be coach or mentor for next group of program participants; 4) expectation of select faculty to gain skill set as facilitators and educators of content through train-the-trainer modules.

- *Impact:* The team used the Donald Kirkpatrick Model (Kirkpatrick, 1996) for evaluation, which considers four levels of impact:

  - *Reaction:* How did participants feel about the program?

  - *Knowledge:* Did learning occur? Was content applicable to daily job?

  - *Change in behavior:* Was there any change in behavior? Did they implement what they learned?

  - *Measurable impact:* Was there any measurable results from this program? Did the organization benefit?

- *Feedback:* Reflection was threaded throughout the program to capture ongoing feedback, not only in each module with debriefs, but also through exercises, self-assessments, discussions with mentors, journaling, case write-ups, and presentation of individual projects.

Outcomes Metrics

Though this project was not designed explicitly to measure pre and post metrics that were attributable solely to this program, the sponsors, nursing leadership, faculty, and nursing participants believe many elements of success were associated with this initiative, such as:

- *Successful national and international hospital accreditation in multiple sites*

- *Increased staff retention and patient satisfaction (called customer delight)*

- *Improved nursing-sensitive indicators based on data from pre and post unit-based projects, particularly improved pain management, decreased ventilator-associated pneumonia, decreased falls, and decreased thrombophlebitis*

- *Increased hand hygiene and more appropriate use of gloves*

- *Improved efficiency, decreased discharge times across many units*

- *Team of faculty trained as train-the-trainer to deliver curriculum throughout system*

- *Improved succession planning structures in place and development of future leaders*

- *Abstracts accepted and presented in two international quality and safety forums*

The sponsors and the key stakeholders noted that both quantitative and qualitative milestones were reached and that program goals focused on developing a cohort of nurse leaders, building sustainability through a new team of trainers, and improving organization- and unit-based projects were met.

Program Insights

Beyond the actual evaluation and outcome metrics, key qualitative insights gained included:

1. *The hidden curriculum is an important consideration. These sessions provided opportunities for nurses who surprisingly never met or engaged to meet and learn from each other in areas outside the actual content.*

2. *Twelve-month timeframe is realistic—current discussion centers on the question, "Within the 12 months are 3 or 4 one-week intensive sessions more efficient/effective?"*

3. *Utilizing a multidiscipline program team to maximize expertise, for example, nursing, human resources, quality, and global health care, was highly effective and provided learning and respect across faculty.*

4. *Location is important: Being off-site makes a significant difference.*

5. *Multiple data points in assessment beyond self-assessment are valuable, but 360 assessment needs to be thoughtfully used, culturally appropriate, and debriefed thoroughly.*

6. *Create more opportunities for the chief nurse and other executives to teach and to participate along the way.*

7. *Utilize variety of cases: One size does not fit all nurse leader groups.*

8. *Knowing the culture and recognizing language issues are critical.*

9. *Build in formal mentorship.*

10. *Branding of the program was surprisingly effective: Everyone, from hospital CEO to staff nurses, consistently spoke of the NLP (nursing leadership program) and the TTT (train-the-trainer).*

11. *Recognition and celebration is critical: Each graduation ceremony not only had recognition of participant's accomplishments, but also exemplified team-based recognition through cultural celebratory elements of song, dance, dress, and awards.*

Creating many avenues for formal and informal evaluation and reflection among and across the international team members and participants allowed for the identification of subtle elements that perhaps were not intentionally planned yet had real impact and became core elements of the next generation of the program.

Moving Forward

The program is now implemented and delivered by Indian faculty with remote phone and e-mail consultation as needed. Over 100 nurse leaders have participated, and the local faculty base is growing. Work on Phase 2 has begun with a focus on developing a shared governance council structure for a multilevel infrastructure for quality, education, and practice.

[The authors would like to acknowledge the leadership of Susanna Chourochen, RN, and Elizabeth Joseph, RN, MS, and their team in India, and the expertise, time, and cultural competence of Patricia Folcarelli, PhD, RN, and Joanne Ayoub as PHMI core faculty to this program, and their institution's (the Beth Israel Deaconess Medical Center) departments of nursing, quality, and human resources in contributing to this collaboration.]

Summary

Capable and confident nursing leadership is the converging point for opportunity and change in the areas of nursing regulation, education, and practice settings and is necessary at all levels—global, regional, national, and local. Over many years and interactions with nurse leaders globally, we have developed a strong appreciation for the unique and common challenges that nursing leaders encounter in their roles and their ability to lead and manage effectively. Nurse leaders provided the critical link between caregivers at the bedside and their unique hospitals and health systems and the community and policy structures.

Yet, nursing leadership participation at the highest levels of a system or organization varies considerably across countries, hindering the full potential to influence and impact change. Many nurse leaders internationally reveal that they often feel they are working in isolation, whether in a professional organization, academic department, or their practice settings. They report it challenging to connect with the people and systems that would foster their ability to truly fill that critical link and operationalize their roles. More often, nurse leaders describe their lack of preparation and development as leaders and managers to be effective in their challenging roles. We have presented four case studies where nurse leaders globally are making a difference in advancing the regulatory structures, educational frameworks, and practice settings. Each of these endeavors emanated from a common global vision of advancing the nursing profession and nursing leadership, improving outcomes of care, and furthering bilateral transfer of knowledge among global nursing colleagues.

When considering the many comprehensive global changes that are needed for continued advancement of international nursing leadership and practice reviewed in this chapter, we, like other international colleagues, might see the changes needed as a daunting challenge. Thus, what is or can be our role in international nursing? In a framework of collaboration and partnering, nurses can serve as catalysts for enhancing and advancing nursing worldwide. Numerous ways to connect or partner in sharing and exchanging expertise exist through roles such as consultant, educator, researcher, or clinician—at home or abroad.

Nursing education is one critical area essential to the development and promotion of global competence. Integrating global nursing into nursing curricula promotes the recognition of a workforce that is globally competent with current international and national knowledge that can be applied to patient care and nursing practice. Participating with international colleagues in the development of higher education models that efficiently advance nurses from baccalaureate to graduate and doctoral preparation is critical to streamline and innovate within their nursing education pathways. As all of nursing is advancing competency-based curricula and interprofessional education frameworks, international collaboration provides rich opportunity to learn from each other as experiences and expertise are shared. Many colleges and universities have long histories of partnerships for faculty and student exchanges and fellowships, which, among many advantages, provide opportunity to connect with and build a global nursing community for both national and international students and faculty.

Within practice settings globally exists a great opportunity for collaboration between organizations and nurses who have a shared vision and goals for strengthening leadership and practice. Partnering and twinning models, observations studies, visiting nurse consultants, collaborative conferences, and online and videoconferencing sharing of resources are just a few ways that nursing services globally can collaborate to learn from each other. Individual nurses also have many ways to embrace a role in international nursing. The INHL case study describing clinical observation programs illuminated the important role of numerous individual nurses who served as preceptors for international nurses to share their knowledge and clinical expertise.

The ICN and STTI are two organizations that provide avenues for mentorships, often drawing upon online communities and networks comprising nurse clinicians, researchers, and leaders from around the world to disseminate best practices and address challenges facing nursing. Publicizing collaborative international initiatives and outcomes, whether through organizational websites and publications, presentations in various multiple local and international forums, and publishing in international journals, provide valuable connections and increase awareness for nurses around the world to learn and use global knowledge to translate into local solutions.

As we consider our role in international nursing leadership development in this age of globalization, we need to find areas of common purpose and just begin. As Florence Nightingale noted, "[N]ever lose an opportunity of urging a practical beginning, however small, for it is wonderful how often in such matters the mustard-seed germinates and roots itself" (Cook, 1914, p. 406).

References

Abraham, E. J. (2007). Pulse on health and nursing in India. *Nursing and Health Sciences*, 9(2), 79–81.

Aiken, L. H., Sloane, D. M., Clarke, S., Poghosyan, L., Cho, E., You, L., … Aungsuroch, Y. (2011). Importance of work environments on hospital outcomes in nine countries. *International Journal for Quality in Health Care*, 23(4), 357-364.

Albanese, M. P., Evans, D. A., Schantz, C. A., Bowen, M., Disbot, M., Moffa, J., … Polomano, R. C. (2010). Engaging clinical nurses in quality and performance improvement activities. *Nursing Administration Quarterly*, 34(3), 226-245.

Alexander, M., & Runciman, P. (2003). International Council of Nurses (ICN) framework of competencies for the generalist nurse. Geneva, Switzerland: International Council of Nurses.

American Association of Colleges of Nursing (AACN). (2008). *The essentials of baccalaureate education for professional nursing practice* (2nd ed.). Washington, DC: Author.

American Nurses Credentialing Center (ANCC). (2008). *Application manual: Magnet Recognition Program*. Silver Spring, MD: Author.

Cathcart, E., Greenspan, M., & Quin, M. (2010). The making of a nurse manager: The role of experiential learning in leadership development. *Journal of Nursing Management*, 18(4), 440-447.

Cook, E. (1914). *The life of Florence Nightingale, Volume II*. London, UK: MacMillan.

Davies, R. (2008). The Bologna process: The quiet revolution in nursing higher education. *Nurse Education Today*, 28(8), 935-942.

Dias, J. M., Ajani, K., & Mithani, Y. (2010). Conceptualization and operationalization of a baccalaureate nursing curriculum in Pakistan: Challenges, hurdles, and lessons learnt. *Procedia - Social and Behavioral Sciences*, 2(2), 2335-2337.

Dickinson-Hazard, N. (2004). Global health issues and challenges. *Journal of Nursing Scholarship*, *36*(1), 6-10.

Fennimore, L., & Wolf, G. (2011). Nurse manager leadership development: Leveraging the evidence and system-level support. *Journal of Nursing Administration*, *41*(5), 204-210.

Frenk, J., Chen, L., Bhutta, Z. A., Cohen, J., Crisp, N., Evans, T., ... Zurayk, H. (2010). Health professionals for a new century: Transforming education to strengthen health systems in an interdependent world. *The Lancet, 376* (9756), 1923-1958.

Gill, R. (2011). Nursing shortage in India with special reference to international migration of nurses. *Social Medicine*, *6*(1), 52-59.

Huston, C. J., & Percival, E. (2009). The international academic nursing alliance: A resource for global nursing knowledge exchange. *Nursing Education Perspectives*. Retrieved from http://findarticles.com/p/articles/mi_hb3317/is_3_30/ai_n32099460/

Institute of Medicine. (2003). *Health professions education: A bridge to quality*. Washington, DC: National Academies Press.

International Council of Nurses (ICN). (1997). *ICN on regulation: Towards 21st century models*. Geneva, Switzerland: Author. Retrieved from http://www.icn.ch/images/stories/documents/pillars/regulation/on-regulation_complete_english.pdf

International Council of Nurses (ICN). (2009). *Regulation 2020: Exploration of the present: Vision for the future*. Geneva, Switzerland: Author.

International Council of Nurses (ICN) and World Health Organization (WHO), Regional Office for the Eastern Mediterranean (2009). *Reducing the gap and improving the interface between education and service: A framework for analysis and solution generation. ICN Regulation Series*. Geneva, Switzerland: Author. Retrieved from http://www.icn.ch/images/stories/documents/publications/free_publications/reducing_the_rap.pdf

International Council of Nurses (ICN). (2011a) *Positive practice environments for health professionals. Key characteristics*. Retrieved from http://www.ppecampaign.org/content/key-characteristics

International Council of Nurses (ICN). (2011b). *Regulation*. Retrieved from http://www.icn.ch/pillarsprograms/regulation/

Interprofessional Education Collaborative Expert Panel. (2011). *Core competencies for interprofessional collaborative practice: Report of an expert panel*. Washington, DC: Interprofessional Education Collaborative.

Jiang, H., Ives Erickson, J., Ditomassi, M., & Adams, J. (2012). Promoting a culture of international professional practice for nursing through a twinning relationship. *Journal of Nursing Administration, 42*(2), 117-122.

Kirkpatrick, D. (1996). Great ideas revisited. *Training & Development*, *50*(1), 54-59.

Kumar, D. (2005). *Nursing for the delivery of essential health interventions*. Retrieved from http://www.whoindia.org/LinkFiles/Commision_on_Macroeconomic_and_Health_Nursing_for_the_delivery_of_essential_health_interventions.pdf

Lenburg, C. (1999). The framework, concepts, and methods of the Competency Outcomes and Performance (COPA) Model. *Online Journal of Issues in Nursing, 4*(2). American Nurses Association.

MacPhee, M., Skelton-Green, J., Bouthillette, F., & Suryaprakash, N. (2012). An empowerment framework for nursing leadership development: Supporting evidence. *Journal of Advanced Nursing*, *68*(1), 159-169.

Massachusetts Department of Higher Education (2010). *Nurse of the future core competencies.* Retrieved from www.mass.edu/nursing

Mattson, J. (Ed.) (2007). RNL WORLD PULSE: Global leadership challenges of nurses: Perspectives from members of RNL's International Advisory Board. *Reflections on Nursing Leadership, 33*(2). Retrieved from http://www.reflectionsonnursingleadership.org/Pages/Vol33_2_Mattson_World_Pulse.aspx

McCallin, A., & Frankson, C. (2010). The role of the charge nurse: A descriptive exploratory study. *Journal of Nursing Management, 18*(3), 319-325.

McCauley, C. D., Van, V. E., and Center for Creative Leadership. (2004). *The Center for Creative Leadership handbook of leadership development.* San Francisco, CA: Jossey-Bass.

Morin, K. (2011, November 15). *Lessons Learned: Leadership in a global world.* Presentation, Connell School of Nursing, Boston College. Retrieved from http://frontrow.bc.edu/program/morin/

National League for Nursing Council of Associate Degree Nursing Competencies Task Force. (2000). *Educational competencies for graduates of associate degree nursing programs.* New York, NY: Author.

Nichols, B. L., Davis, C. R., & Richardson, D. R. (2011). Appendix J: International models of nursing. In Institute of Medicine, *The future of nursing: Leading change, advancing health.* Washington, DC: The National Academies Press.

Pillay, R. (2010). Towards a competency-based framework for nursing management education. *International Journal of Nursing Practice, 16*(6), 454-554.

The Prime Minister's Commission on the Future of Nursing and Midwifery in England. (2010). *Front line care: The future of nursing and midwifery in England. Report of the Prime Minister's Commission on the Future of Nursing and Midwifery in England.* Retrieved from http://webarchive.nationalarchives.gov.uk/20100331110400/http:/cnm.independent.gov.uk/

Quality and Safety Education for Nursing. (2007). *Quality and safety competencies.* Retrieved from http://www.qsen.org/competencies.php

Raha, S., Berman, P., & Bhatnagar, A. (2009). Some priority challenges of the nursing sector in India. *India Health Beat, 1*(5). Retrieved from http://www.hrhindia.org/assets/images/HRH%20Policy%20Note5.pdf

Shaw, C. D. (2001). *Toolkit for accreditation programmes: Some issues in the design and redesign of external assessment and improvement systems.* International Society for Quality in Healthcare (ISQua). Dublin, Ireland: Author. Retrieved from http://siteresources.worldbank.org/HEALTHNUTRITIONANDPOPULATION/Resources/AccreditationToolkit.pdf

Shaw, S. (2007). *International Council of Nurses: Nursing Leadership.* Oxford, UK: Blackwell Publishing.

Sherman, R. O., Eggenberger, T., Bishop, M., & Karden, R. (2007). Development of a leadership competency model. *Journal of Nursing Administration, 37*(2), 85-94.

Sherman, R., & Pross, E. (2010). Growing future nurse leaders to build and sustain healthy work environments at the unit level. *The Online Journal of Issues in Nursing, 15*(1).

Shuriquie, M., While, A., & Fitzpatrick, J. (2007). The development of role adequacy for professional nurses in Jordan. *International Nursing Review, 54*(2), 144-150.

Sochan, A. (2008). Relationship building through the development of international nursing curricula: A literature review. *International Nursing Review, 55*(2), 192-204.

Stewart, M. G. (2001). *Accreditation council for graduate medical education core competencies.* Retrieved from http://www.acgme.org/acwebsite/RRC_280/280_corecomp.asp

Surakka, T. (2008). The nurse manager's work in the hospital environment during the 1990s and 2000s: Responsibility, accountability and expertise in nursing leadership. *Journal of Nursing Management, 16*(5), 525-534.

United Arab Emirates, Ministry of Health. (2009). Ministry of Health Statistics, 2009. (Unpublished data).

Upvall, M. J., Rehmatullah, S., Hashwani, S., Khan, S., Husain, P., & Jan, R. (1999). The implementation of a bachelor's of science in nursing education in Pakistan. *Nursing and Health Sciences, 1*(4), 221-228.

Wendler, M. C., Olson-Siticki, K., & Prater, M. (2009). Succession planning for RN's: Implementing a nurse management internship. *Journal of Nursing Administration, 39*(7/8), 326-333.

World Health Organization (WHO). (2006). *World health statistics.* Geneva, Switzerland: Author.

World Health Organization (WHO). (2009). *Nursing and midwifery human resources for health: Global standards for the initial education of professional nurses and midwives.* Geneva, Switzerland: Author.

World Health Organization (WHO). (2010). *Framework for action on interprofessional education & collaborative practice.* Geneva, Switzerland: Author.

World Health Organization (WHO). Regional Office for the Eastern Mediterranean: WHO Regional Office for Europe (2002). *Nursing and midwifery: A guide to professional regulation.* WHO EMRO Technical Publication Series: 27. Cairo: WHO Regional Office for the Eastern Mediterranean.

Zabalegui, A., Macia, L., Marquez, J., Ricoma, R., Nuin, C., Mariscal, I., ... Moncho, J. (2006). Changes in nursing education in the European Union. *Journal of Nursing Scholarship, 38*(2), 114-118.

Zittel, B., Ezzeddine, S. H., Makatjane, M., Graham, I., Luangamornlert, S., & Pemo, T. (2011). Divergence and convergence in nursing and health care among six countries participating in ICN's 2010 Global Nursing Leadership Institute. *International Nursing Review, 59*(1), 48-54.

Chapter 15
Concluding Thoughts

Jeanette Ives Erickson, RN, DNP, FAAN
Dorothy A. Jones, EdD, RN, FAAN
Marianne Ditomassi, RN, DNP, MBA

> *Life and nursing are products of all conditions, events, and actions*
> *of yesterday. Life and nursing tomorrow will relate to today.*
>
> (Johnson, 1965, p. 38)

Core to developing and sustaining a high-quality, affordable care delivery environment is aligning the mission and values of the organization with a long-term strategic plan. The strategy must include implementation of a professional practice model (PPM) that interconnects a strong practice environment with optimal patient care and motivates clinicians and support staff to do their best. A PPM can, and should, unify care delivery; advance opportunities to accelerate interdisciplinary contributions to organizational and patient outcomes; and enhance nursing presence at the bedside and in all health settings where care is being delivered.

As changes in health care reform are driving and influencing care redesign, providers must respond to accelerated change while integrating improvements in the treatment and management of illness. In addition, providers must extend care connections to transition with the patient and families following discharge from the acute and non-acute settings while attending to risk reduction and health promotion. Throughout these challenges, nurses emerge as key care providers responsible for ensuring that all aspects of care are timely, effective, and efficient (Institute of Medicine [IOM], 2001).

At the Massachusetts General Hospital (MGH), the PPM implemented and revised over the past 16 years has effectively guided the redesign of care, fostered creative innovations, and enhanced nurses' ability "to practice to the full scope of their knowledge and competence" (IOM, 2010). The outcome and sustainability of this PPM continues to be realized in evidence that reflects improved systems outcomes and increased patient, family, and staff satisfaction. Careful attention by the chief nurse and nursing leaders across the MGH continues to shepherd the advancement of a practice environment that fosters high-quality, affordable care. This transformational leadership enables nurses to realize attributes such as professional autonomy, control over practice, and teamwork, which enhances every discipline's accountability and responsibility while realizing a practice environment of care dedicated to "excellence every day." By being intentionally present to patient and families across the health care experience, nurses come to know the patient and work to coordinate care and promote continuity across health care settings.

Moving Professional Practice Forward

A PPM creates the structure to advance disciplines and improve care. To sustain the professional practice environment that supports the PPM requires knowledge and a culture of inquiry. The development, use, and continued refinement of knowledge enables the clinician to bring the best of the discipline forward to advance care. The discussion to follow addresses the concept of knowledge as well as a focus on using knowledge to enhance practice, uncovering knowledge within the nurse-patient relationship, and translating knowledge into the professional practice environment.

Knowledge

Knowledge is integral to the advancement of effective patient care. Creating and sustaining a practice environment that assures patients the opportunity to experience quality care is not only linked to organizational mission, visionary leadership, and the resulting PPM, but also to the continuous assurance that nurses are competent to care for the highly complex patients they serve. Advancing professional practice is contingent upon support and resources to deliver the best care possible and a commitment by each discipline to integrate advances in knowledge and competencies into promoting care that is responsive and proactive. Establishing partnerships with other disciplines and academic settings outside of the hospital can lead to the development of new knowledge and enhance collaboration among health providers in pursuit of offering patients and their families the best in health care possible.

Using Knowledge for Practice

Knowledge for practice addresses the integration of disciplinary knowledge into practice that helps to inform organizational, nursing, and practice goals. The inclusion of critical thinking and decision-making into the process of caregiving provides disciplinary visibility; creates the data needed to communicate care; and designs, with the patient, a plan of care that is responsive to the patient/family situation. The generation of nursing diagnoses, responsive interventions, and measures to evaluate evidence informs and reforms the practice environment, impacts care outcomes, and influences knowledge development.

Documenting data within the patient's electronic health record (EHR) is an effective strategy to share how knowledge (evidence) is communicated within and across disciplines about the patient and articulates the contributions of the disciplines on patient outcomes. The communication of the patient experience through documentation can help to cost out care and guide the care needed and resources necessary to impact outcome indicators such as length of stay (LOS). In addition, understanding the patient experiences, including lifestyle and responses to illness, can provide narrative evidence of the patient's perception of health and expectations around recovery. Transformations in teaching and patient/family learning, along with the use of new technology care, can be used to give the patient the knowledge needed to sustain care at home, promoting comfort and contributing to decreased hospitalizations. Innovation around the use of follow-up phone calls can address post-discharge issues and affect care transitions and influence recovery.

Uncovering New Knowledge

The nurse-patient relationship is an essential element to advancing care at the bedside. Through the experience the clinician uses knowledge to uncover the patient's story and in so doing uncovers new information and the meaning of health and illness. Organizational support, adequate resources, and sustained commitment by nursing leadership to knowing patients will increase the knowledge nurses need to understand patients' experiences and the impact of illness on their lifestyle. Using a standardized assessment framework that uncovers what is meaningful to patients, guides care, and incorporates the individual into goal setting and recovery is vital. Assessing the degree to which the patients feel known by the provider enables organizations to identify and evaluate outcomes and increase patient/family satisfaction with care. Empowering patients and staff to knowingly participate in change (Barrett, 2003) fosters patients' and families' active roles in care teaching and learning and encourages professional growth and development.

Knowing patients allows nurses to journey with patients and uses professional knowledge to facilitate decision-making, promote choice, and actualize change and personal transformation. Embedded in the nurse-patient relationship is respect for the dignity of patients and families in all aspects of care. Implementation of creative practice innovations such as hourly rounding, ethics rounds, and conflict management skill-building can reduce risks, promote a culture of safety, and foster adherence to the patient's plan of care.

Translating Knowledge and the Professional Practice Environment

A professional practice environment (PPE) provides a framework within which multiple dimensions of quality patient care can be realized. To accomplish this, leaders within the practice setting use systems as well as disciplinary knowledge to develop, implement, and evaluate the environment of care. Translating knowledge into the practice environment actualizes professional expectations across disciplines and provides the needed resources to help realize full implementation of knowledge in the care settings. Continued evaluation of the effectiveness of a PPM (Ives Erickson et al., 2009) is required to monitor the implementation of innovations in practice, to obtain needed evidence to support the continuation of a practice change, or to introduce new innovations to respond to challenges within the environment of care. This is leadership at the bedside at its finest and offers an opportunity for long-term impact on sustaining the changes needed to prevent illness and promote health over time.

Professional Development

Support, leadership, and mentoring help actualize the potential of multiple providers within a PPE. Through continued education, mentoring, and support provided by administration and organizational leaders, staff are motivated to actively participate in a learning environment. The realization that knowledge, like change, is a continuing and evolving process can be an important guide for leaders to ensure the continued development of nurses at the bedside. Learning opportunities experienced through programs such as nurse residency programs and simulation can enhance the transition of the novice nurse into the complex practice environment and bring new knowledge to the more experienced clinician. The ability of leaders to come to know their staff and provide the personal and programmatic leadership that advances their professional scholarship can not only foster professional growth and leadership but also ultimately translate to the bedside to improve patient care based upon advanced knowledge and expertise of all providers.

Evaluation of the PPE

Evaluating the effectiveness of the PPE is an ongoing process. Developing a plan to evaluate nurses' satisfaction with the care setting can enhance the care delivery setting and optimize nurse, patient, and family outcomes. Achieving professional distinction through external evaluation such as the American Nurses Credentialing Center's Magnet Recognition Program gives public, as well as professional, testimony to nursing care excellence. Continued evaluation of the PPE from multiple dimensions is a critical measure of nursing excellence and quality care at the bedside that can be benchmarked over time to acknowledge success, make needed course corrections, and sustain positive changes.

Being Responsive: Future Directions in Health Care

Freire is quoted as saying, "It is necessary that we should always be expecting that a new knowledge will arise transcending another that, in being new, would become new" (1980, p. 32). Therefore, it can be anticipated that the work on health care reform will change and evolve at the local, state, and global levels. All nurses, especially those providing direct care at the bedside or in the community, need to remain at the forefront of new knowledge. Programmatic initiatives within practice environments (e.g., residency programs, new technology, innovative care strategies, and practice delivery model redesign) will bring new knowledge to the nurse, enhance personal development, and improve care outcomes. Creative teaching and learning strategies, along with continued academic advancement, can accelerate information sharing, optimize patient care, and enhance nurse satisfaction.

Partnerships between academic and practice settings are essential to assure the best preparation of students and clinicians practicing within a dynamic and changing health care environment. In addition, new partnerships between community and large medical centers can foster cooperation, advance the development and translation of knowledge through research and evidence-based practices, and foster inquiry. Clinical practice environments that promote the development of knowledge are laboratories for discovery where new questions are generated and answers to existing challenges and creative innovation are proposed and tested. This is reinforced through the words of Rogers, "We cannot begin to deal with question about whether, or how well, a problem has been solved until that new knowledge is evaluated in the situation from which the problem was derived" (2007, p. 115).

Nurse leaders at all levels in the organization have a significant role in health care reform. The seminal IOM *Future of Nursing* report cites that

> With more than three million members, the nursing profession is the largest segment of the nation's healthcare workforce. Working on the frontlines of patient care, nurses can play a vital role in helping realize the objective set forth in the 2010 Affordable Care Act, legislation that represents the broadest health care overhaul since late 1965 and the creation of the Medicare and Medicaid program. (2010)

The report also underscores that not only should nurses practice at the full extent of their education and training, but also they should be full partners, with physicians and other health care professionals, in redesigning health care in the United States. Nurses must heed this "call to action" and view health care reform and redesign as a strategic window to innovatively design, pilot, and implement new care delivery models that promote patient and family-focused relationship-based care.

Lastly, one of the most influential leadership roles nurses can play is as a leader in the international health care community. As nurses, we must seize the opportunity to enter into closer relationships with one another on a worldwide scale and share our expertise as educators, mentors, and innovators to promote access to health care for at-risk populations. The establishment of twinning relationships with health care organizations throughout the world is a high-leverage way to collaborate with clinicians globally in the provision of health care services. Roy eloquently captures the importance of the mental model change that is necessary to advance the care delivery agenda, "The paradigm shift that is needed is inevitable as the intertwining of our natural world and health has become increasingly evident" (2007, p. 321).

References

Barrett, E. A. M. (2003). Update on a measure of power as knowing participation in change. In O. L. Strickland & C. DiIorio (Eds.), *Measurement of nursing outcomes: Focus on patient/client outcomes, Vol. 4* (pp. 21-39). New York, NY: Springer.

Freire, P. (1980). *Pedagogy of the oppressed.* New York, NY: Continuum.

Institute of Medicine (IOM). (2001). *Crossing the quality chasm: A new health system for the 21st century.* Washington, DC: National Academies Press.

Institute of Medicine (IOM). (2010). *The future of nursing: Leading change, advancing health.* Washington, DC: National Academies Press.

Ives Erickson, J., Duffy, M. E., Ditomassi, M., & Jones, D. (2009). Psychometric evaluation of the revised professional practice environment (RPPE) scale. *Journal of Nursing Administration, 39*(5), 236-243.

Johnson, D. E. (1965). Today's action will determine tomorrow's nursing. *Nursing Outlook, 12,* 38.

Rogers, B. (2007). Knowledge as problem solving. In C. Roy & D. A. Jones (Eds.), *Nursing knowledge development and clinical practice* (p. 115). New York, NY: Springer Publishing.

Roy, C. (2007). Global application of the cosmic imperative for nursing knowledge development. In C. Roy & D. A. Jones (Eds.), *Nursing knowledge development and clinical practice* (p. 321). New York, NY: Springer Publishing.

Index

B

Find more learning and education resources from STTI

Reflective Practice: Transforming Education and Improving Outcomes

In this breakthrough book, the authors share their framework and provide a rich resource for nurse educators in academic and clinical settings, nurses interested in developing leadership capacity, and nurses seeking to advance their professional development.

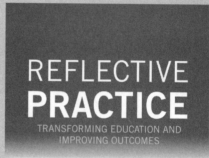

Reflective Practice
ISBN-13: 9781935476795

To order, visit www.nursingknowledge.org. Discounts are available for institutional purchases. Call 888.NKI.4YOU for details.

www.nursingknowledge.org